Tom Cand

# Tom Candiotti

*A Life of Knuckleballs*

K. P. Wee

McFarland & Company, Inc., Publishers
*Jefferson, North Carolina*

ISBN 978-0-7864-9425-5 (softcover : acid free paper) ∞
ISBN 978-1-4766-1559-2 (ebook)

LIBRARY OF CONGRESS CATALOGUING DATA ARE AVAILABLE

BRITISH LIBRARY CATALOGUING DATA ARE AVAILABLE

On the cover: Tom Candiotti in his stint with the Cleveland Indians
(National Baseball Hall of Fame Library, Cooperstown, New York)

Printed in the United States of America

*McFarland & Company, Inc., Publishers
Box 611, Jefferson, North Carolina 28640
www.mcfarlandpub.com*

To Rick Ambrozic and Rick Jessup,
for your words of encouragement
and for believing in me.

# Table of Contents

# *Preface*

Dodger Stadium, Los Angeles. On August 25, 1993, knuckleballer Tom Candiotti had a bat in his hand in the bottom of the eighth, ready to move onto the on-deck circle against the Pittsburgh Pirates. Lenny Harris was on first base with nobody out. If Jody Reed, the hitter at the plate, could get on base, then Candiotti could step up, get that bunt down, and move both runners over to bring up the top of the order. Surely Brett Butler, the leadoff man, could at least drive Harris in. But manager Tommy Lasorda had already ordered Reed to bunt, and had signaled for Dave Hansen to pinch-hit for Candiotti. The crowd of 33,914, realizing Candiotti was going to be pulled from the game because he was due up third in the batting order, had already given him a huge standing ovation as he walked off the field after working a scoreless top half of the eighth.

Candiotti certainly deserved the ovation. After giving up a first-inning run, the Dodger knuckleballer had retired 21 of the next 24 Pirates—including the last 13. His pitching line was 8 IP, 4 H, 1 R, 1 BB, 7 SO. It was his eighth consecutive start where he'd pitched at least seven full innings while allowing two runs or fewer, a month-long dominance that had begun on July 18. Candiotti, according to Baseball-Reference.com, would be one of only five pitchers in the 1990s to have a stretch of eight straight such starts—a short list which also included Roger Clemens, Randy Johnson, and Pedro Martinez—and the fourth-to-last pitcher to do so in the 20th century. (For years, Tom Seaver held the longest such streak in major league history, going 13 straight starts in 1971 with two runs or fewer allowed while pitching at least seven innings. The record, however, was broken in July 2014 by Felix Hernandez. In 2001–2013, only six pitchers had such a streak of at least eight consecutive starts.)

What Tom Candiotti didn't deserve was the fact he was trailing, 1–0, against Pittsburgh's Paul Wagner (who had a 5.23 ERA at the start of the game). His hard luck was nothing new. In his last 14 starts entering this game, Candiotti was undefeated, with a 1.65 ERA. But he'd won only five of those 14 starts, recording nine no-decisions thanks to an inept Dodger offense. And with his eight-inning effort against the Pirates on this evening, Candiotti lowered his ERA to a major league-best 2.43. Yet, his record was just 8–5 through 25 starts on the season.

For seven innings on this August night, Los Angeles was blanked by Wagner and reliever Mark Dewey, a pair of journeyman pitchers. And granted, Pittsburgh had little success against Tom Candiotti. But it wasn't just the Pirates. Since May 1, Candiotti had posted a Koufax-like 1.85 ERA in 22 starts. Candiotti, trailing, 1–0, and having just been pinch-hit for, sat on the bench hoping for a rally while wondering why his luck was *this* bad. Just an inning earlier, the Dodgers had loaded the bases with one out but couldn't score, with Dewey retiring Eric Karros and Eric Davis to end the threat. Candiotti had seen this script before. He had pitched well enough during the course of the season only to leave games trailing 1–0 or 2–0 or deadlocked 0–0. It was no different on this night.

When Jose Offerman's eighth-inning sacrifice fly tied the score—after the Dodgers had stranded 12 baserunners through the first seven innings—it gave Candiotti his 10th no-decision in the last 15 starts. The game marked the 13th time in 19 starts that he had allowed two runs or fewer while pitching at least seven innings. In all 19 outings, which spanned from May 19 to August 25, Candiotti allowed three earned runs or fewer. Alas, that amazing stretch—which also included 135.2 innings, 100 hits, 100 strikeouts, 38 walks, six homers allowed, and a 1.66 ERA—translated only to a 7–1 record. (To put things in perspective, when fellow knuckleballer Tim Wakefield held opponents to three earned runs or fewer in 19 straight starts from 1993 to 1995, he went 16–1.)

Candiotti would finish the year just 8–10, and his 1993 season has long been forgotten. The mediocre won-lost record wasn't just a one-year anomaly. From 1991 to 1993, Candiotti compiled a 2.91 ERA while striking out 6.5 batters per nine innings and allowing 7.8 hits per nine, and gave up only 37 homers in 655.1 innings. He averaged 32 starts and 218 innings along with 69 walks and 158 strikeouts for a 2.29 strikeout-to-walk ratio. His record, however, during those seasons was only 32–38. Ironically, in the eight seasons from 1986 to 1993, Candiotti's numbers were almost identical: 217 innings, 153 strikeouts, 3.38 ERA, and 71 walks.

Two years later, in 1995, Red Sox knuckleballer Tim Wakefield went 14–1 with a 1.65 ERA in his first 17 starts for Boston, going undefeated in 12 starts in one stretch. Wakefield received a lot of accolades—which, obviously, he deserved—for pitching Boston to an improbable American League East Division title. He won his Red Sox debut in Anaheim on May 27, and returned on only two days' rest to defeat Oakland, 1–0, on a night when Boston had no other starter available. Over his first 17 starts, his numbers included 131 innings pitched, 98 hits, 79 strikeouts, and a 1.65 ERA, and nobody in baseball was more valuable than Wakefield.

Oddly enough, Candiotti did most of the above in 1993 but somehow flew under the radar. That year he had a 1.53 ERA over a 17-start stretch, losing only once. He had a 15-game unbeaten streak from June 12 to August 25. He even started three games over an eight-day period. On July 4, Candiotti pitched a two-hit, no-walk shutout over seven innings as Los Angeles won, 1–0, in Montreal. Four days later, he pitched six innings of three-run ball at Shea Stadium against the Mets. He then returned on two days' rest to face the Mets again because the Dodgers had no other starter available. In September, the Dodgers even had him pitch on only one day of rest against the Houston Astros. No, Candiotti didn't go 14–1, but who could quibble with his 1.53 ERA during his 17-start stretch and 15-game undefeated streak?

In 1997, sportswriter Bob Ryan praised Wakefield in a piece for the *Boston Globe* with the following:

> Wakefield did a very silly thing two years ago. He created a monster by coming to Boston and embarking on the greatest prolonged stretch of knuckleball pitching in the history of baseball. Better than anything Hoyt Wilhelm ever did. Better than anything Wilbur Wood ever did. Better than anything Charlie Hough ever did. And it was surely better than anything Wakefield ever will do again. He went 14–1 and he personally made sure there would be no pennant race in the American League East. Few pitchers are ever that good, and no knuckleball pitcher ever has been that dominant for a two-month period.[1] The public must understand that it simply is not the essential nature of the beast. What Wakefield did by going 14–1 with a 1.65 ERA in his first 17 starts as a member of the Red Sox was inexplicable, even to him.[2]

Only three-plus years had elapsed at the time of Ryan's piece, but he didn't consider Candiotti's accomplishments. The Dodger knuckleballer's 1993 efforts were not even a footnote to the story, which suggests he was overlooked because he didn't compile a gaudy won-lost total. And 1993 wasn't the only time Candiotti had a prolonged stretch of knuckleball pitching where he logged an earned run average around 2.00. In 1991, Candiotti had a 2.01 ERA in his first 19 starts but somehow went just 9–8. In 1995, he had a 1.74 ERA over a 13-start run only to go 4–6. The numbers from those summers:

| | GS | IP | H | R | ER | BB | SO | HR | ERA | BA | (W–L) |
|---|---|---|---|---|---|---|---|---|---|---|---|
| Wakefield | 17 | 131.0 | 98 | 30 | 24 | 37 | 79 | 12 | 1.65 | .209 | (14–1) |
| Candiotti '91 | 19 | 138.2 | 114 | 40 | 31 | 34 | 109 | 7 | 2.01 | .222 | (9–8) |
| Candiotti '93 | 17 | 123.1 | 87 | 27 | 21 | 34 | 94 | 6 | 1.53 | .200 | (6–1) |
| Candiotti '95 | 13 | 93.0 | 72 | 26 | 18 | 28 | 71 | 4 | 1.74 | .213 | (4–6) |

Naturally, over time Candiotti's accomplishments are no longer remembered. When New York Mets knuckleballer R.A. Dickey began the 2012 season with an outstanding 12–1 record and 2.15 ERA in 16 starts, nobody brought up Candiotti's dominant stretches of knuckleball pitching during the 1990s as a comparison.

Fans and the media just never got it. Most of them, anyway. Tom Candiotti's mastery of the knuckleball and his excellent curveball made him one of baseball's best pitchers for more than a decade. Candiotti was a consistent winner on a bad Cleveland Indians team—going 72–65 with a 3.53 ERA from 1986 to 1991—and became just the 25th pitcher in Indians history with 70 career victories and the 16th to surpass 750 strikeouts. But after he'd retired as a player, people still took shots at him. Every time Toronto sportswriters bring up past Blue Jays teams that "choked" or acquisitions that "fizzled," Candiotti's name comes up because he went 0–1 in his two starts in Toronto's five-game loss to the Minnesota Twins in the 1991 AL Championship Series. Forgotten is the fact that without Candiotti's efforts—a 2.98 ERA over 19 regular-season starts replacing injured ace Dave Stieb—the team might not have made the postseason.

Then there's this in March 2009 from *Los Angeles Times* sportswriter Bill Plaschke, whose column begging the Dodgers to sign free agent pitcher Pedro Martinez turned somewhat into Candiotti-bashing. Plaschke praised Martinez, who in 1993 went 10–5 with a 2.61 ERA with the Dodgers as a 21-year-old (10–3 with a 2.26 ERA in relief; 0–2, 7.36 as a starter). But Plaschke, it could be argued, went further by including the veteran knuckleballer in the commentary. Wrote Plaschke, there was "a confidential opinion issued by the club's medical guru, Dr. Frank Jobe, who didn't think Martinez's small frame could withstand the prolonged rigors of pitching. The Dodgers' field personnel seemed to agree, starting Martinez only twice despite a rotation that included Kevin Gross and Tom Candiotti."[3] Plaschke was lamenting the fact the Dodgers had made a serious blunder in November 1993 by trading Martinez to Montreal for second baseman Delino DeShields, who didn't pan out in Los Angeles (batting just .241 in three seasons with the Dodgers from 1994 to 1996). But there was no way to predict Pedro Martinez, who struggled in his only two starts in 1993, would eventually become a three-time Cy Young Award-winning starting pitcher and one of the most dominant hurlers in baseball history. And suggesting that Candiotti shouldn't have been in their rotation that season?

That's a blunder for Plaschke. Candiotti *led* the Dodger staff in 1993 with 155 strikeouts and a 3.12 ERA (which was seventh-best in the NL). He ranked second in innings (213.2) while allowing the fewest number of home runs (12) amongst Dodger starters (0.51 per nine innings, lowest among LA starters). Candiotti's home ERA of 1.95 was the *best* in the majors in 1993, a season in which he also held the opposition to one earned run or none 18 times. On August 31, Candiotti had a *major league-leading* 2.43 ERA.

In 1993, Candiotti's strikeout-to-walk ratio of 2.18 was second on the team only to closer Jim Gott (3.94), just ahead of Pedro Martinez's 2.09. The Dodger knuckleballer walked only 71 batters over 213.2 innings for an average of 2.99 walks per nine innings. Dodger righthander Orel Hershiser, meanwhile, issued 72 walks over 215.2 innings for a walk rate of 3.00. Ramon Martinez, Pedro's older brother, was a different story as he had an NL-leading 104 walks in 211.2 innings—an average of 4.4 walks—while compiling a 6.19 ERA over his final seven starts. Perhaps the Dodgers should have kept Pedro Martinez and used him as a closer or set-up man in 1994, and converted him to a starter after Hershiser and Gross—free agents after that season—moved on.

Did Plaschke mean to say the Dodgers started Pedro Martinez only twice in 1993 "despite" a rotation that included *Ramon* Martinez, who walked *104* batters (with only 127 strikeouts) that season? But it seemed extreme to suggest Candiotti was unworthy of being in the Dodger rotation. Candiotti, in fact, was an underrated ace for the first half of the 1990s. From 1991 to 1993, Candiotti *led* the majors with 42 starts in which he allowed one earned run or fewer while pitching at least seven innings, just ahead of Roger Clemens (41) and Tom Glavine (38). From 1992 to 1995 (covering the length of his four-year free agent contract with the Dodgers), he logged a respectable 3.38 ERA. Candiotti went just 33–46 because he consistently received very little run support and plenty of shoddy fielding. In that same span, Ramon Martinez—generally referred to as the Dodger staff ace—was 47–37 with a 3.74 ERA and had a worse WHIP. And get this: Candiotti even averaged more strikeouts per nine innings, and walked *fewer* batters while pitching *more* innings!

The numbers, 1992–95:

|  | IP | H | BB | SO | HR | WHIP | SO/9IP |
|---|---|---|---|---|---|---|---|
| Candiotti | 760.2 | 705 | 246 | 550 | 52 | 1.250 | 6.51 |
| R. Martinez | 738.2 | 679 | 310 | 485 | 63 | 1.339 | 5.91 |

From 1991 to 1995, Candiotti was fourth in the majors with 60 starts of one earned run or none, behind only Greg Maddux (66), Glavine (64), and Clemens (61). But he simply never got much support in that span:

- In 1991, Candiotti had a 2.65 ERA while pitching for Cleveland and Toronto, but finished just 13–13.
- In 1992, Candiotti led the Dodgers' starting staff with a 3.00 ERA—allowing two runs or fewer 17 times—but finished 11–15 as Los Angeles scored just 23 runs in his 15 losses. Over his final 25 starts, his ERA was 2.74 but he went 7–14.
- In 1993, Candiotti led the Dodgers in ERA (3.12) and strikeouts, but went 8–10 with the club tallying only 16 runs in his 10 losses. During a 22-start stretch, his ERA was 1.85 but he was just 8–2 with 12 no-decisions.
- In 1995, Candiotti finished 7–14 despite a respectable 3.50 ERA for the playoff-bound Dodgers, who scored just 19 runs in his 14 losses.

Candiotti isn't recognized as one of the better pitchers in Dodger history. Dodgers reference books don't mention the knuckleballer's name prominently, even though he immediately became the staff ace when he arrived in town. In each of his first two seasons in Los Angeles, in 1992–93, Candiotti led the club in ERA. He would become the 12th pitcher in LA Dodger history to surpass 700 strikeouts and the 20th to win 50 games. In 1997, Candiotti's 3.57 ERA ranked 14th all-time in LA history for pitchers with more than 1,000 innings pitched.

Blue Jays history books also do not mention Candiotti's name. If he is referred to at all, he's talked about as one of the reasons Toronto lost the '91 ALCS to Minnesota. People have somehow forgotten that Candiotti helped the Blue Jays win the division after the team had lost ace Dave Stieb for the season after only nine starts. They have forgotten that Candiotti joined the club midseason, had no spring training to work with two catchers who had no experience handling a knuckleball, and still compiled a 2.21 ERA from June 28 to September 18. Toronto sports historians fault him for the ALCS loss, forgetting that he actually left Game Five with a 5–2 lead. They've forgotten that the bullpen faltered in Game Three, and coughed up Candiotti's three-run cushion in the final contest. Besides, the Jays were starting that series at the tough Metrodome, and managed to split the first two contests just as everyone had hoped. Candiotti wasn't the reason they then lost three straight at SkyDome. Nonetheless, his name still went down in infamy—in the eyes of Toronto fans and media—as a loser and a choke.

Candiotti was the second player ever to come back from Tommy John surgery when he reached the majors in Milwaukee in 1983. When he won his first four major league starts with a 0.84 ERA just 22 months after the surgery—helping the Brewers stay in contention in early September—he was affectionately known as "The Stopper" in Beertown. That year, he went a combined 19–8 in the majors, minors, and winter ball. He then added three playoff victories in winter ball. While with Milwaukee's Triple-A affiliate in Vancouver in 1985, Candiotti logged 150.2 innings and was a member of the first Pacific Coast League championship team in that franchise's history. Yet, there is no mention of him in Brewers history books, either.

Though Candiotti's return from Tommy John surgery did not make the news globally, it was still one of the most courageous comeback stories in baseball history. Had social media existed then, his being the second player to ever come back from reconstructive elbow surgery—at a time when recovering from it was highly unlikely—would have resulted in a movie being made out of his story. His life in the minors—he traveled through six minor league cities plus two winter ball stops from 1979 to 1985—would have been chronicled, such as the way he was sleeping on the floor at a teammate's place, in the locker room, and on the field at the ballpark, before he finally made it to the major leagues for good.

Despite throwing a knuckleball as his primary pitch, Candiotti nearly won the American League ERA title in 1991 (with Roger Clemens's 2.62 topping him by three-hundredths of a point). Candiotti never led his league in walks, and actually finished in the top 10 three times for the lowest rate of walks per nine innings. He also finished in the top four in his league a total of five times for the lowest home run rate per nine innings. Candiotti never had a high ERA over a full season other than in 1987 (4.78), 1996 (4.49), 1998 (4.84), and 1999 (7.32). From 1988 to 1997, Candiotti's ERA was 3.38 over 1,910.2 innings. He allowed fewer hits (1,827) than innings pitched, and had a 2.25 strikeout-to-walk ratio (1,274 to 565), averaging six strikeouts per nine innings.

I began following Candiotti's career in 1991 when he was with Toronto. Living in Vancouver, Canada, I was able to see many Blue Jays games on CTV/ TSN television. When he pitched for the Dodgers the following year, I saw many of his starts on superstations KTLA, WGN, and TBS. Watching many of his starts and seeing how he seemed to always receive bad run support led to my interest in his career. In 1995, I began collecting articles about Candiotti from newspaper archives such as *latimes.com* and *usatoday.com*. Twice that season, Candiotti lost, 5–0 and 3–0, to a rookie named Tyler Green (who would go just 13–21 for the rest of his career with *zero* shutouts). One day before his 38th birthday in 1995, Candiotti pitched a quality start against the Mets but lost because Mike Piazza struck out three times with the bases loaded, twice against journeyman Dave Mlicki. Eleven days before that, he'd lost, 2–1, to Mlicki despite tossing a seven-inning three-hitter with no walks and nine strikeouts. That season, even with a 3.50 ERA that was the 22nd-best in the majors, Candiotti somehow finished with a 7–14 record, as 89 big league pitchers won more games than the knuckleballer.

Of course, receiving poor run support was just one aspect of Candiotti's career. When you add in the elements like Candiotti not having a 95-mph fastball and his needing to learn a knuckler just to return to the majors, it makes his career even more remarkable. Here's a guy who was not drafted, developed arm trouble, and came back from a revolutionary surgery at a time when only one player had ever returned from it. He made $10 a day playing minor league ball in Victoria, Canada, slept in the clubhouse because he had no place to stay, and through his hard work and determination finally made it to the big leagues four years later. After a couple of brief stints with Milwaukee, Candiotti was told in 1985 he had to reinvent himself by throwing a knuckleball in Triple-A. He returned to the majors to stay in 1986, and had one of baseball's best earned run averages for a full decade (3.44 ERA from 1986 to 1995). Of his 151 career victories, 70 came in starts where he allowed one run or none. Even though he would throw the knuckleball primarily during his career, he consistently had a 2-to–1 strikeout-to-walk ratio.

In 1997, Candiotti announced on his website that he would soon release a book sharing the secrets of his knuckleball. (He might have been one of the first professional athletes to have his own website.) Alas, no book was ever released and that website disappeared soon enough. Soon after, the MLB Players Association launched *bigleaguers.com*, where fans could email their favorite players. In July of 1998, when Candiotti was 5–10 for the Athletics—and dealing with a back injury as well—I finally wrote him through *bigleaguers.com*. "Tom, sorry to hear about your bad back," I wrote. "Hope you get a win in your next start." I received a reply shortly after, with the message, "Thanks KP! I'll try my best!" In that next start, on July 10, Candiotti tossed eight shutout innings against a first-place Texas Rangers team that would go on to lead the league in hitting (.289). Then on August 5, Candiotti did even better, becoming the *only* pitcher in 1998 to toss a complete-game victory against the 114-win New York Yankees, as Oakland won 3–1.

When I was conducting research for this book, I was fortunate enough to interview Candiotti extensively as well as several of his former teammates, managers, and general managers (who are listed below in alphabetical order). When I spoke with Pat Gillick, he asked me what a guy like me from Vancouver was doing writing a book about Candiotti because there was no obvious connection between us. Well, it's simply because I wanted to finish the project that Candiotti talked about doing back in late 1990s—writing a book—but never got around to completing.

Thank you to the following individuals, for taking the time to talk to me: Bill Bryk, special assistant to the general manager and major league scout with the Arizona Diamondbacks; Fred Claire, former general manager of the Los Angeles Dodgers; Doc Edwards, former manager of the Cleveland Indians and current manager of the San Angelo Colts; Pat Gillick, senior advisor to the president/general manager with the Philadelphia Phillies; Art Howe, former manager of the Oakland Athletics; Joe Klein, executive director of the Atlantic League of Professional Baseball; Bob MacDonald, former Toronto Blue Jays pitcher; Mark Shapiro, president of the Indians; and Cory Snyder, former Indians player and current hitting coach of the Tacoma Rainiers. Thanks as well to several of Candiotti's childhood friends and neighbors— Russ Chaney, Guy S. Houston, Rocky Lucia, and Mark Mazza—for their input and anecdotes.

My thanks also go out to Candiotti's son, Brett, for the stories and photographs he shared; to Adrian Brijbassi for sharing his perspective on Candiotti's career; and to Rick Jessup, for photos he took of Candiotti at Chase Field in Phoenix. I'd like to acknowledge the photo help provided by John Horne of the National Baseball Hall of Fame Library, Robbin Barnes of the Milwaukee Brewers, and Holly Purdon of the Toronto Blue Jays. Thanks to CTV Sports' Perry Solkowski, as well, for his input on this project. In addition, vintage baseball video collectors Rick Ambrozic and Steven DeBraccio helped me locate various video records of Candiotti's games. I should thank as well Adele MacDonald from the Phillies, Marlene Lehky from the Indians, and Bridgette Glass from Rains Lucia Stern, all of whom handled my requests for various correspondences with personnel within their organizations. If not for everybody's assistance, I would never have been able to pull this project off.

Finally, thank you, Tom Candiotti.

# *Introduction*

Tom Candiotti pitched 16 seasons in the major leagues (1983–99). Near the end of his career, he ranked among the top 100 all-time in major league history in starts and strikeouts. Since then, Candiotti—nicknamed "Candy Man" or "Candy"—has been surpassed in both categories, but life is still sweet. These days, he calls the Phoenix area home and enjoys going to the ballpark every day. You see, he's still involved in the game, working as a TV and radio analyst for the Arizona Diamondbacks. "I had a good run, winning 151 games in the big leagues," Candiotti laughs. "And now, I get to watch baseball and talk about the game. Pretty amazing, when you think about it."

Candiotti's primary pitch was the knuckleball. While he can still throw it these days—as the Diamondbacks hitters found out when they all flailed miserably against his knuckleballs during batting practice recently—there is one place he can't throw the pitch that he is best known for. "After my baseball career ended, I was watching the bowling pros on TV," explains Candiotti. "I thought, 'Hey, I can do this.' These guys were throwing a curve for a strike, and I was like, 'I've done that my whole life. Why not give it a shot?' I began to practice about five hours a day for several weeks. Once I got confident in my abilities, I joined a league and eventually got my PBA card."

Candiotti actually began bowling at a young age. "My mom entered me in a junior league when I was growing up in Walnut Creek," Candiotti says. "Now, being a broadcaster, I have a lot of time to go bowling. I bring my bowling ball with me on road trips!" Candiotti was good enough that he even ended up in the Hall of Fame in 2007. Not the Baseball Hall of Fame, but the International Bowling Museum's Hall of Fame, in the celebrity wing. When baseball fans look back at his career, though, they remember Candiotti first and foremost as a knuckleballer. "But I wasn't a knuckleball pitcher

11

when I got to the big leagues," says Candiotti. "And I almost didn't make it there."

Candiotti graduated from Saint Mary's College of California in 1977 but was not a major league prospect. At the time, he didn't throw his knuckleball, a pitch he used only when messing around playing catch. His father, Caesar, had taught it to him when he was a child, but it wasn't a primary pitch he actually used in a game. Instead, Candiotti was throwing fastballs and curveballs while trying to get to the majors. The knuckler wasn't something he thought much of. He threw that pitch in high school, just for fun, but was otherwise a conventional pitcher. "Then in 1985, I began using the knuckler seriously in the minor leagues," Candiotti says. "It was kind of trial and error."

Not a hard thrower at the end of his career at St. Mary's, he wasn't drafted by any big league club. Candiotti instead had to continue his baseball aspirations in the summer of 1979 by driving from Northern California to Victoria, Canada, for an uninvited tryout with the independent Victoria Mussels of the Northwest League. The team's manager, Bill Bryk, wasn't overly impressed with his velocity but still signed him because of his impeccable control. "We're having this workout, and this guy walks onto the field and says he wants to pitch," recalls Bryk, who is now a scout with the Diamondbacks. "I gave Tom a tryout because I gave everybody a tryout. He threw in the mid-to-low 80s on the radar gun. He made the team because he threw strikes. [And] he [became] one of the best pitchers in the Northwest League."

Candiotti went 5–1 with a 2.44 ERA in 12 appearances for Victoria. The Kansas City Royals then came calling, purchasing his contract in January of 1980. He pitched that summer for their minor-league clubs in Fort Myers (Class A) and Jacksonville (Double-A), going 10–10 with a 2.63 ERA in 161 innings. However, it was not all smooth sailing. In Jacksonville, manager Gene Lamont chewed him out for throwing a knuckleball during a game—Candiotti had been throwing one sparingly—demanding that he never throw the knuckler again.

Candiotti wouldn't make it past Double-A with the Royals, and was claimed by the Milwaukee Brewers in the Rule 5 draft that December. In 1981, Candiotti pitched for Milwaukee's Double-A club in El Paso, going 7–6 with a 2.80 ERA despite a sore arm. Following the season, he underwent reconstructive elbow surgery—now known as "Tommy John surgery"—performed by Dr. Frank Jobe, a famous orthopedic surgeon.

In 1974, Dr. Jobe reconstructed Tommy John's left elbow, using a tendon from his right forearm. Since the operation, the Dodger southpaw had proceeded to post three 20-win seasons. Candiotti had his surgery performed on October 14, 1981, when Dr. Jobe used a tendon from the pitcher's right wrist

After Tom Candiotti finished his pitching career, he still remained involved in the game as a television and radio analyst. Candiotti is shown here with his two sons, Clark and Casey, in the ESPN2 broadcast booth for a Wednesday Night Baseball contest in the mid–2000s (courtesy Tom Candiotti).

to reconstruct the right elbow. Since there was no guarantee Candiotti would ever be able to come back from the surgery, he took a real estate course just in case. "If baseball didn't work out," he says, "I had my real estate license to fall back on."

At the time of Candiotti's surgery, Dr. Jobe had performed that operation only eight times. "It was really an experimental procedure back in 1981," says Candiotti. "The only guy that had come through it successfully was none other than Tommy John himself. It wasn't the best odds, but I loved baseball and it's any kid's dream to make it to the majors one day ... to say you're able to pitch in the big leagues for just one day. That's what I was shooting for. So, if the odds were one out of eight, why not go for it?"

Candiotti missed the entire 1982 season before pitching for Milwaukee's Triple-A club in 1983, the Pacific Coast League's Vancouver Canadians. In Vancouver, he went 6–4 with a 2.81 ERA that was the third-best for a starting pitcher in the PCL, which was known as a hitter's league.[1] His performance earned him a call-up with Milwaukee as a 25-year-old during the 1983 pennant race. When Candiotti stepped on the mound at Royals Stadium in the seventh inning for his first major league appearance on August 8 in front of 42,039 spectators, he became only the second player to appear in the majors following Tommy John surgery. That night, Candiotti worked 2.1 scoreless innings despite the fact that he had to face George Brett, Willie Wilson, and Hal McRae— three of the American League's toughest hitters—in his first inning of work. As the *Milwaukee Journal* noted, the trio of Brett (the two-time batting champion who had hit .390 in 1980), Wilson (1982 batting champion), and McRae (1982 RBI leader) was a "latter-day Murderers' Row."[2]

On August 17, 1983, at County Stadium, Candiotti made his first big league start and pitched Milwaukee into first place with a 5–1 complete-game victory over Boston. Candiotti did not allow a walk, and held future Hall of Famers Jim Rice and Carl Yastrzemski hitless in eight at-bats. For Candiotti, facing Yastrzemski—in what turned out to be the Red Sox legend's final season—was a big thrill. "When I grew up, one of my idols was Carl Yastrzemski," Candiotti says. "There were times when I'd pitch against him in my mom's front yard against the garage door, throwing a tennis ball against the garage door. I'd have my make-believe games, [pretending] I was Don Drysdale and I was facing Carl Yastrzemski in the World Series."

In the second inning, Candiotti looked up from the mound and there was Yastrzemski, bat up high in the air, standing in the batter's box, with 34,038 spectators watching from the stands. "I had to step off the mound for a moment," Candiotti recalls. "It was like, 'Wow, this is a flashback to my childhood right here, back to my mom's garage door. Here I am in my first major league start and I'm facing Carl Yastrzemski ... for real!'" Candiotti gathered himself, stepped back onto the mound, and retired his boyhood idol on a grounder to second base. Fast forward to the ninth, when Candiotti retired Yaz on a fly to centerfield to end the game, capping an 0-for–4 night for the future Hall of Famer.

On August 25, Candiotti twirled a 7–0 eight-hitter over California, out-pitching none other than Tommy John. Five nights later, in a 3–2 victory over Seattle, Candiotti became the last pitcher of the century to break into the majors by throwing at least seven innings while allowing one earned run or fewer in each of his first three starts—a feat unmatched for another 20 years (by Oakland's Rich Harden in 2003). "In those days, starting pitchers tried to go as long as they could," Candiotti says. "Normally, if you went seven innings and gave up two runs or fewer, you were doing a fantastic job. I was happy I was able to do that in my first month with the Brewers." On September 5, he defeated the Yankees, 3–1, holding the quartet of Willie Randolph, Ken Griffey, Dave Winfield, and Don Mattingly hitless in 14 at-bats.

Despite not having a major league fastball—and throwing a lot of off-speed pitches—Candiotti went 4–0 with a 0.84 ERA in his first four starts before finishing 4–4 due to poor run support in the season's final weeks. For the 1983 campaign overall, including his time in the minors, Candiotti made 22 starts and went 11–8 with a 2.96 ERA in his first season following his 1981 elbow ligament replacement surgery. He registered 100 strikeouts in 179.2 innings, allowing 39 walks. Following that season, Candiotti pitched in winter ball and went 8–0 for Mayagüez of the Liga de Béisbol Profesional de Puerto Rico (LBPPR). Candiotti led Mayagüez to the 1983–84 league championship and pitched in the Caribbean Series, coming within three outs of a no-hitter against Los Mochis of the Mexican Pacific League. Though he acquitted himself well in 1983, Milwaukee sent him to Triple-A to begin the next season. He was called up midseason but was limited to just 32.1 major league innings.

During his first two seasons, Candiotti threw the knuckleball only 10 percent of the time. He threw mostly 80-mph fastballs as well as curveballs and sliders. But without a major league-caliber fastball, it looked as though his career was finished. Then came the practical joke that changed everything. During spring training in 1985, Candiotti pulled a prank on catcher Bill Schroeder by throwing him knuckleballs in the bullpen, trying to nail him. Unbeknownst to Candiotti, manager George Bamberger witnessed the whole incident. Afterward, Bamberger instructed him to develop the knuckleball in Triple-A, figuring that pitch would be the only way to prolong his career. "I saw his knuckleball," Bamberger said the following year. "My advice was, 'Why don't you throw it? It might mean a new career for you.'"[3]

Candiotti spent all of 1985 developing his knuckleball in the minors. Though his numbers were mediocre—10–13 with a 3.75 ERA in 180 innings—it still proved to be an important learning experience. Candiotti had a lot of practice throwing that knuckleball in every situation, including with runners on base and in hitter-friendly counts, which was key for his confidence in using that pitch. Milwaukee, however, opted not to re-sign Candiotti at season's end.

In winter ball in 1985 with Ponce, Candiotti continued to mess around with the knuckler. He had better success there, leading the LBPPR in strikeouts. "There were games where I mostly threw knuckleballs," Candiotti recalls. His performance paid off, as the Cleveland Indians gave him a shot after seeing him throw that knuckleball in Puerto Rico, signing him in December of 1985. But he wasn't totally convinced he could succeed as a knuckleballer, admitting then that he would give the experiment a year. If it didn't work out, he would retire from the game. "If I could see I wasn't going anywhere, then I was prepared to give up baseball and go out and sell real estate," Candiotti later said.[4]

As it turned out, his real estate license wasn't needed. Cleveland signed veteran knuckleballer Phil Niekro before the 1986 season, giving Candiotti a valuable mentor. Thanks to the tutelage of Niekro and to his own hard work, Candiotti became the team's staff ace. He made the knuckleball his number one pitch and compiled a 3.57 ERA (3.45 as a starter), leading the Indians in wins (16), ERA, starts (34), innings (252.1), complete games (17), shutouts (three), and strikeouts (167). And while it normally took knuckleball pitchers a few innings before they got the feel for the pitch, Candiotti posted a 2.57 ERA during the first two innings of his 34 starts as he effectively mixed in his curveball with the knuckler. "I think you could say that year he quickly became the ace of the Cleveland pitching staff," recalls Indians general manager Joe Klein, who is currently the executive director of the Atlantic League. "He was getting us into the seventh inning, and he had a three-point-something earned run average. We knew we had a pretty good chance of winning when Candy went out there."

Thanks to the knuckleball, Candiotti soon became a top-of-the-rotation starter. In 1991 with Toronto, the Blue Jays believed that knuckler gave the club a huge advantage, and had him start the first game of the ALCS. That Game One start, according to Baseball-Reference.com, also made Candiotti only the third pitcher since 1918 to win his first four major league starts and then later start the opening game of a post-season series (joining All-Star pitchers Vic Raschi and Fernando Valenzuela).

Bill Bryk, his first manager in professional baseball, marvels at the fact that Candiotti was able to pitch 16 seasons in the majors. "Tom was smart enough to realize that he could get to the big leagues without a knuckleball but probably would've never stayed there and been as successful," reflects Bryk. "That knuckleball prolonged his career. Once he developed that pitch, he became really successful for many years in the big leagues."

# 1

## *Coming Back from Tommy John*

"Are you a prospect?" the orthopedic surgeon asked.

"Yeah," answered Tom Candiotti. "I've just come out of Double-A ball this year. The Brewers just put me on their 40-man roster, so I think that means they wanna protect me. So yeah, I'm a prospect."

"I think you need to have a reconstruction," replied the surgeon. "An ulnar collateral ligament reconstruction. If you're not a prospect, I'd recommend against the procedure."

"Well, yeah, I'm a prospect."

"Good. Because if not, I wouldn't do the surgery for you."

"How many have you done?" asked Candiotti.

"I've done eight, but there's only one guy that you've heard of, and that was Tommy John."

That conversation between Candiotti and Dr. Frank Jobe took place in 1981, after he developed elbow problems while pitching for the Double-A El Paso Diablos that season. It got so bad he had to see Dr. Jobe, a Los Angeles orthopedic surgeon specializing in sports medicine, for an examination. Candiotti was 24 years of age—a little old for a legitimate big league prospect—and did not throw hard. But if Candiotti insisted he was a prospect, the doctor wouldn't know any better. "I didn't get drafted out of college," Candiotti says. "I got a tryout with an independent team in Victoria in 1979. Two years later I was in the Brewers' organization pitching for their Double-A team. I wasn't really a prospect. I didn't have a 90-mph fastball. I was also feeling a lot of pain in my elbow. Sometimes it'd swell up so bad that it took me maybe three days to straighten my arm out. It really hurt a lot. But whenever I pitched, I did pretty well."

With El Paso in 1981, Candiotti had a team-high six complete games while finishing 7–6 with a 2.80 ERA. But with his arm trouble, he probably didn't have a shot at pitching again. Ever. His elbow was hurting too much. "Dr. Jobe told me my right arm had some problems," recalls Candiotti. "There was too much calcium built up on the medial collateral ligament. He told me I needed that surgery ... the surgery which he'd performed only eight times."

"Tom Candiotti came in many years ago," Dr. Jobe once recalled. "And I said to him, 'Are you really going to be a pitcher? Do you think you're a prospect?'"[1] Dr. Jobe would ask people coming in if being a pitcher was something they really wanted, because the procedure was going to take at least a year to recover from.[2] Of course, there was no guarantee, so who knew if they were ever going to be able to throw a baseball again?

"When I went in to see Dr. Jobe," continues Candiotti, "he was 1-for-8 at the time in terms of guys being able to come back from this reconstructive elbow surgery. That one guy was Tommy John." But in reality, Tommy John didn't even have those odds in 1974, when he permanently damaged the ulnar collateral ligament in his left arm. It was the same injury that had prematurely ended Dodger great Sandy Koufax's career in 1966.[3] Unlike Koufax, though, he had an opportunity to undergo this revolutionary surgical procedure, with Dr. Jobe informing John that his chance of returning was one in a hundred. Even then, the medical and baseball opinions of the day were unanimous: John would never be able to throw a baseball again. He was simply going to be a guinea pig for this new ligament transplant surgery.

It was a damned-if-you-do-damned-if-you-don't situation for John. If he went through with the surgery, he would likely never pitch again, as the biggest risks with the operation were nerve damage and restricted arm movement. If he didn't go through with the procedure, though, the result would be the same. "Dr. Jobe told me if I didn't have it," John once said, "I would never pitch in the major leagues again. He said I could throw batting practice to kids but that would be it. I didn't think I was done and wanted to play. I didn't know how difficult the surgery would be but said, 'Get it on.'"[4] Heck, a one-in-a-hundred chance was a better gamble than not having the surgery performed, right?

But Dr. Jobe told ESPN three decades after John's surgery that the odds for the lefthander were actually *worse* than one in a hundred. At the time, Dr. Jobe had performed the surgery only three times, and never before on a professional athlete. "He realized that the options were to go back to [his hometown of] Terra Haute, Indiana, or to have the operation, with a high risk of failure," the orthopedic surgeon said of John.[5]

On September 25, 1974, Dr. Jobe performed the surgery on John, reconstructing the southpaw's left elbow, using a tendon from his right forearm.

Though the operation took about three hours, the recovery took a lot longer. Tommy John missed the entire 1975 season before making a comeback the following year. "I had the operation in September [1974] and then pitched in a game one year and one day after surgery," John once said. "I started seven games in 28 days and knew I was okay."[6]

John was better than "okay." In the six years after the surgery, the left-hander posted three 20-win seasons and was 99–53 with a 3.06 ERA, receiving Cy Young votes for four straight years, beginning in 1977. In his second season back from the surgery in 1977, John went 20–7 with a 2.78 ERA for the Dodgers, finishing second in the NL Cy Young Award balloting. Before the surgery, he had never won 20 games in a single season or received any Cy Young votes, going 74–59 with a 3.16 ERA in the six years prior to the procedure.

But while John had made a miraculous comeback from the surgery, there was no guarantee for anyone else that followed in his footsteps. Candiotti, who never spoke with John during this time, needed to think about whether to go through with the surgery, which involved having a tendon from the wrist transplanted into the elbow. After four days of contemplating, Candiotti made his decision. "Baseball was my dream," he says. "I knew the odds were against me. I wasn't drafted. I had to get a tryout with the Victoria Mussels. I got a shot in the Milwaukee organization. They'd just put me on their 40-man roster. Now I needed this surgery if I ever wanted to have a shot at making the big leagues. I decided, 'No, I'm not giving up.' I mean, what if I could become the second guy after Tommy John to come back from that surgery?"

Dr. Jobe performed the procedure—then called the "ulnar collateral ligament reconstruction" but today known simply as "Tommy John" surgery—on Candiotti at Centinela Hospital in Los Angeles on October 14. "It was the exact same operation as the one Tommy John had," says Candiotti. Dr. Jobe scraped the calcium off the medial collateral ligament and used a tendon from Candiotti's right wrist to reconstruct the right elbow.

While there was no guarantee that Candiotti would ever come back from the surgery then, the procedure is so commonplace today that Dr. Jobe and Dr. James Andrews—another renowned orthopedic surgeon—estimate there is a 95 percent chance patients will recover from Tommy John surgery and pitch as well as—or maybe even better than—before.[7] "Now, this surgery is one of the most frequently performed medical procedures for baseball players," Candiotti says. "Guys that have had the surgery done tell me they get back on the mound after a year but they don't really get to 100 percent for maybe a year-and-a-half or two years after. In my case, it took me about two full years to feel like I was at full strength and really be able to throw my curveball."

Candiotti understood the long odds. Out of the eight prior procedures, only Tommy John was able to pitch again. Nobody had ever heard from the other seven guys. There was never a guarantee Candiotti could even be able to pick up a baseball and throw, much less make it to the major leagues. "The Tommy John surgery," says former *Toronto Star* journalist Adrian Brijbassi, "was very controversial in 1981. You didn't know if guys were going to come back. At that time, nobody knew much about the surgery. Not the trainers. Not the players. Only Tommy John himself knew about the recovery process."

Pat Tabler, who played 12 seasons in the majors, from 1981 to 1992, also recalls those days when the surgery was virtually unknown. "I remember when that first happened," Tabler, now a television analyst for the Blue Jays, once said, "I believe [Tommy John] was in a cast for like a year. They said, 'It's a radical new way of saving pitchers' arms.' And I didn't fully understand it till I got a little bit older. And then when I understood what happened, I mean, it is a miracle what they came up with. Taking a tendon from your wrist or your leg and putting it in that ligament in your elbow."[8]

For Candiotti, the hardest part after the surgery was the lack of data about what he needed to do to recover from it. What did he need to do? How would he deal with the pain? "There was still a lot of guesswork in that operation, unlike today," Candiotti says. "At the time, everyone figured my career was over. It was like, 'This guy can't possibly recover from this surgery.... Is this guy nuts for going through with the surgery?' There was a lot of uncertainty with the operation, and I really didn't know what to do to recover from it."

Broadcaster Buck Martinez, a former big league player and manager, spoke with Tommy John years ago about his recovery process. According to Martinez, the southpaw had to take it step by step. "[John] had a phenomenal career after the surgery," Martinez once said. "And I talked to Tommy about his rehab and I said, 'What did you do once you got the cast off?' He said, 'I started playing catch.' And he actually played catch with his wife 15 feet at a time and they'd start 15 feet just playing catch. But he built up [his arm strength] until he got on the mound."[9]

Candiotti, meanwhile, did a lot of finger and hand exercises. For him, it was a lengthy recovery process before he could develop the finger pressure to hold a ball again. "I remember [Dr. Jobe] giving me the hand grippers, rubber bands to put between my fingers and thumb, the little tendon things in my hand," says Candiotti. "I had to see Dr. Jobe every six weeks or so, and I had to let it heal, and do little things. I must have done 10 million hand grippers, these things that you just squeezed. I must have done that all day long, every single day, to the point where I could start throwing again."

By May 1982, Candiotti could still barely toss a ball. The first time he could throw, he threw it about three feet against the wall—which was nothing considering the distance from the mound to home plate is 60 feet. One year after the operation, he still couldn't throw. By November 1982, however, his arm finally started to respond, and Milwaukee assigned him to its Double-A club in El Paso for rehab. "Because of the surgery, nobody had any expectations of me ever coming back," Candiotti continues. "I missed the 1982 season and was able to pitch in Double-A and Triple-A in '83. Later that '83 season, I got called up to the big leagues, and then pitched winter baseball. I ended up having pretty good numbers. So not only was I able to come back, I did pretty well too."

Candiotti would enjoy a 16-year major league career, winning 151 games and recording nine 200-inning seasons. He started 410 games and struck out 1,735 batters. The one number that amazes Candiotti the most, though, is 200,000. He figures he threw that many pitches after the surgery, subjecting Dr. Jobe's work to a lot of wear and tear over the years. "I probably threw at least 12,000 pitches per season, and that includes warm-up pitches on game days and two days of throwing between starts," explains Candiotti.

It could have been even more had he been a few years younger at the time of the surgery, says former Indians general manager Joe Klein. "When we signed Tom in Cleveland in the winter of 1985, he was a 28-year-old," explains Klein. "I wish he'd been 18 when we first signed him, because this guy could pitch. We could be talking about a guy who would've won a lot more games in the big leagues. He was in the minor leagues developing the knuckleball in 1985, and boy, he could really throw that pitch. He wasn't just a knuckleball pitcher, though. As we found out later when we saw him in Cleveland, he had an excellent curveball and he threw a good fastball once in a while and got a lot of guys out. Candy really knew how to pitch."

Still, mention the name Tom Candiotti today, and people think about a knuckleballer. Nobody realizes he was the second person to ever come back from Tommy John surgery to get to the majors—or the fact that Candiotti was the first minor league player ever to have the procedure and then make it to the major leagues afterward. "I never knew that about Candiotti," says Brijbassi, a lifelong baseball fan who covered the sport in the 1990s and early 2000s as a journalist. "And honestly, I don't think anybody knows."

Candiotti shrugs. Every year, articles are written about the surgery whenever a big league pitcher undergoes the procedure or comes back from it. None of those articles ever bring up Candiotti's name, even though they do mention Tommy John and a host of those who have survived the operation. "Everyone knows Tommy John himself was the first," says Brijbassi. "But when you think of others who've come back, you probably think of the All-Stars, like Chris

Carpenter, A.J. Burnett, Tim Hudson, John Smoltz, Mariano Rivera ... Tom Candiotti? Well, he's the guy that threw a knuckleball."

But those who played with or managed Candiotti know he did not always throw the knuckler, even if they don't know he is the answer to the Tommy John trivia question. "As a senior at St. Mary's College, Tom was still a fastball pitcher," says Guy S. Houston, the politician from California who was a teammate of his in college. "It wasn't till later on in his pro career that he started to [throw] the knuckleball. He was a great pitcher at St. Mary's, and he threw hard back then."

"Tom was not a knuckleball pitcher when he first got to the big leagues," says former Los Angeles Dodger general manager Fred Claire. "He made it to the big leagues as a regular pitcher and then had to develop the knuckleball to stay there. But Tom, really, was a quality pitcher for a very long time. You look at his career. There really aren't a lot of guys that pitched 16 years and won over 150 games. He certainly should be remembered for his accomplishments in the game of baseball." Dr. Jobe remembers. Candiotti makes sure of it. As Dr. Jobe once said, referring to the conversation the two had the first time Candiotti visited his office: "And he said to me, 'Yes, I'm a prospect.' So every year since then, I've gotten a Christmas card from him, and every year it says: 'To Dr. Jobe, I'll always be your prospect.'"[10]

Candiotti and Dr. Jobe, now a special advisor to the Dodgers, didn't see each other again for a decade until the "prospect" was about to sign with Los Angeles as a free agent in December of 1991. "Dr. Jobe, who was the team doctor, got to give me a physical on my arm before the Dodgers could sign me," says Candiotti. "I hadn't seen him for years, and he looked at me and had a big smile on his face. He goes, 'This elbow's still nice and tight.' When I was with the Dodgers for six years, I saw Dr. Jobe almost every day down there. And, oh yeah, we'd trade Christmas cards all the time. Dr. Jobe would call me, 'My prospect,' because that was our little joke. If I wasn't a prospect, he'd never have done that operation. He'd always call me a prospect."

But it's no joke that Candiotti had a successful career after the surgery. His 151 post-surgery victories, at the time of his retirement in 1999, was second all-time behind Tommy John, who had 164 wins after the surgery bearing his name. (On June 17, 2000, Tommy John-comeback pitcher David Wells surpassed Candiotti by registering win number 152 in his 459th appearance, with all of his major league victories coming after he had the surgery. Wells would finish his career with 239 wins.) As Joe Klein says, though, Candiotti could have had more than 151 victories had he gotten an early start. "Too bad Candy wasn't 18 years old when we got him in Cleveland. Candy really knew how to pitch and he was very successful in the big leagues."

If Candiotti had not been able to pitch after the surgery, he might have gotten into real estate since he had a business degree. That would have been a lot less fun than some of the odd jobs he did as a youngster in California, such as picking apricots. He certainly made more money doing that job than he did in his first summer playing professional baseball. "When I played for the Victoria Mussels, I didn't have any money," he recalls. "It was a big night when I was able to afford a loaf of bread and some bologna!"

No money? How about using some magic, some mystical powers to create more? Bill Bryk, Candiotti's first manager in professional baseball, sheds some light on this. Bryk is convinced Candiotti would have done just fine in life as a magician. Or a fortune teller. Bryk recalls stories of how his pitcher performed magic tricks for his Victoria Mussels teammates in 1979. "He'd predict scores of other games around the league, and we'd all fall for it. I still don't know how he did it. I thought he was a psychic or something. He'd do all sorts of crazy stuff like that."

David Wells, a big league pitcher from 1987 to 2007, wrote as a footnote in his 2003 autobiography that Candiotti was "the best jokester in all of baseball." While Wells didn't elaborate with any examples, Candiotti laughs when he thinks back to the jokes the two pulled off together. "Stink bombs," the knuckleballer says. "We did that all the time in Toronto [in 1991], everywhere we went! A lot of those stink bomb jokes I played was with David Wells. I'd always have some stink bombs that I'd get from the novelty stores."

One time they were going to grab a bite at McDonald's in a mall. "But there were about seven lines of about 10 or 15 people deep," continues Candiotti. "David was like, 'Man, we're never gonna get something to eat.' I go, 'Hey, watch this.' I had one of those little stink bombs in my hand, and David goes all the way to the back of the store, to the end of the lines. I walked up to the front like I was looking at the menu, and I dropped the stink bomb and squished it with my foot. And then I just walked away. So David and I were standing at the back, and then suddenly the place was stinking up so bad. I think the bomb was made of sulfur, but it was just such a bad smell. Next thing you know, everyone was looking at everyone else, and it got so bad people started leaving the lines. Soon enough, everyone vacated, so David and I just walked up and ordered!

"We did that again in a restaurant in Baltimore on our way out. It was a little neighborhood in Baltimore called Little Italy. There was a restaurant there that we had gone to. It was a little restaurant where there wasn't a lot of ventilation. So, as we were leaving, we dropped one, broke it, and walked outside. The next thing you know, about five minutes later, there must have been 30 people coming out of that restaurant, waving their hands! We were watching from across the street just laughing our butts off!

"But the funniest one ever happened during a game. Candy Maldonado, an outfielder with the Blue Jays, was the hitter. David Wells and I were sitting on the bench. Neither one of us was pitching that day. Maldonado happened to hit a home run. But before that, I'd given one of the clubhouse kids a stink bomb. When Maldonado hit the home run, the kid ran up to the plate, as he normally did, to get the bat. And the kid put the stink bomb on home plate. These stink bombs only looked like the size of your pinkie; they're just these little plastic-coated things, like a little plastic vial.

"Then the clubhouse kid smashed it on home plate as he picked up Maldonado's bat! Maldonado ran around the bases and as he crossed home plate, the kid gave him a high five and then ran back to the dugout. As everyone was high-fiving Maldonado in the dugout, David and I were dying laughing. Now the umpire and the catcher were looking at each other, waving their hands, going, 'Gosh, what the heck is this smell?' So finally [the umpire] brought out a whisk broom brush and started cleaning off home plate—and he could see this little broken plastic there! He then started looking around like, 'What the hell happened here? How did a broken glass get on the plate?' He couldn't figure it out. We were laughing so hard at that. I call this one my ultimate stink bomb!"

Candiotti probably would not have had a bad life without baseball. He could have been a real estate agent, selling houses to young couples in California. Perhaps a magician to entertain kids. A psychic to entertain adults. A clown, too, with those stink bombs in his pockets? Still, nothing was sweeter for Candiotti than getting to the major leagues. After he made it, he became somewhat of a magician for friends and family. Magically, his relatives had big-screen TVs and his old baseball team at St. Mary's College got spikes. "I bought a garage door for my mom to pay her back for all the dents I made in her garage door at home throwing balls against it!" says Candiotti. "I got things for family and my college baseball team. When guys get to the big leagues, they do stuff for everybody. It's great to be able to do things like that for everybody you knew, to help make a difference in their lives."

Tom Candiotti loves baseball trivia. When Candiotti was a little kid, he read up on all kinds of trivia about the sport to learn about its history. Little did he know that he would be a part of baseball trivia all of those years later. "Here's one," Candiotti says. "Who was the second guy to pitch again after having Tommy John surgery?" He asks that question every chance he gets—and nobody comes up with the correct answer. Then, Candiotti would announce: "I'm the answer." This trivia question can't be found in a baseball almanac or encyclopedia, but the answer is Tom Candiotti. "You'll need to go back to the newspapers from 1983 to be able to find that one," laughs Candiotti. "Not many people know it, but you can look it up."

Sometimes, though, the record books might be inaccurate. With the Blue Jays in 1991, Candiotti tied the club record for most strikeouts in a single game (12) on August 8. The mark has since been eclipsed, so his name is not in the books for that feat. But Candiotti's name is still erroneously listed on the bluejays.com website on the single game records page as well as in the team's media guide. It lists him tied with four other pitchers for issuing the most walks in one game in club history, with nine free passes, and states that he did it on August 8. In reality, he walked only three—with the 12 strikeouts—that night against Detroit.[11] The most walks Candiotti issued in a Toronto uniform was five, nowhere close to the club record. "But that would be an obscure record," Candiotti says. "The Tommy John surgery ... that's big, right?"

Baseball is a sport where everybody knows the important milestone numbers; 56, 61, .406, 511, 714, and 755 all mean something to hard-core fans. We remember the names of the players who set records. We remember the guys who were the first to accomplish something significant in the game. Somehow, we have forgotten that Candiotti was the second guy to ever come back from Tommy John surgery. Fans of today's generation can name nearly every pitcher who has had the procedure done within the past two decades. Of course, every die-hard fan old enough knows about Tommy John the pitcher. But there's probably a 99.9 percent chance nobody knows Candiotti was number two on the list.

The current decade has been no different when it comes to Tommy John surgery making headlines. The 2010 season, for example, saw one All-Star caliber pitcher after another returning from the operation successfully to lead his team into the postseason, including the two Comeback Players of the Year—Minnesota's Francisco Liriano (AL) and Atlanta's Tim Hudson (NL). Cincinnati's Edinson Volquez, another Tommy John "graduate," compiled a 1.95 ERA in September of 2010 and was the Reds' Game One starter in the NL Division Series. Nine pitchers who underwent Tommy John surgery were selected for that year's All-Star Game.[12] In 2012, it was the White Sox's Phil Humber, who'd had the surgery seven years earlier, tossing a perfect game in Seattle.

The biggest name recently to be associated with Tommy John surgery was Washington Nationals rookie phenom Stephen Strasburg in 2010. The first pick of the 2009 major league draft, Strasburg was called the "most hyped pick in draft history" and the "most hyped and closely watched pitching prospect in the history of baseball" by the media.[13] Unfortunately, in 2010, the righthander had to undergo the operation due to a torn ulnar collateral ligament. As Candiotti noted in September that year, Strasburg's career isn't finished. "Everybody hopes Strasburg will be the next Nolan Ryan, and people were flocking out to see him," Candiotti said. "He's very important to the

Nationals' organization. And then boom, his arm's done. But luckily nowadays, you can come back from it. It's not if you come back, but when."

Today, hundreds of journalists and bloggers write about the miracle of Tommy John. But the name of one Tommy John "graduate" is always omitted. "I can't believe they left me off this list," a surprised Candiotti said recently after being shown an article on the procedure that listed many of the prominent pitchers, past and present, who underwent the surgery. His name wasn't mentioned. Candiotti's name isn't listed on the Tommy John surgery page on Wikipedia, either. Adrian Brijbassi, a former *Toronto Star* journalist who covered baseball for several years, thinks he knows the reason. "It's probably because he threw the knuckleball," admits Brijbassi. "It's just the perception of a guy who didn't throw hard, who tricked the ball past hitters. So, that's probably it."

But when Tom Candiotti made his major league debut in 1983, he was not known as a knuckleballer. Not really as the guy who'd had Tommy John surgery, either. He was simply known as "The Stopper."

# 2

## *The Stopper in Milwaukee*

Outfielder Pete Gray, best known for playing one season in the majors despite having just his left arm, saw action in 77 games for the St. Louis Browns in 1945. He batted .218 in a year that saw the Browns remain in the pennant race entering September. St. Louis got as close as three-and-a-half games behind first-place Detroit on September 3, only to fade down the stretch and finish third in the American League with an 81–70 record. Unfortunately, Gray arrived in town one year too late and missed out on playing in the World Series, which the Browns had reached the year before when they lost in six games to the Cardinals.

Pete Gray's story was not unique. For many players throughout baseball history, that was the sad tale. Get to a team one year too late, just after it had gone to the World Series. And never play for a world championship in their careers.

That was Tom Candiotti's fate on the 1983 Milwaukee Brewers. "I never made it to the World Series," Candiotti reflects. "The Brewers had just gotten there the year before my rookie year. I played for a very good Toronto team later in my career, and with the Dodgers we were in the playoffs twice. But I never got to a World Series. For a while in my rookie year, though, we were right in the thick of things in Milwaukee."

The 1982 Brewers, under manager Harvey Kuenn, had fallen to the Cardinals in seven games in the World Series. Those Brewers, known as "Harvey's Wallbangers" for their hard-hitting lineup, won a major league-best 95 games while averaging five-and-a-half runs per game and bashed 30 more home runs than any other team in baseball. With a lineup that included Gorman Thomas, Cecil Cooper, Robin Yount, Ben Oglivie, Paul Molitor, and Jim Gantner, Milwaukee led the majors in homers (216) and runs (891) while finishing second in batting (.279).

Milwaukee might have been known for its offense, but the pitching staff

27

wasn't too shabby either, compiling the AL's sixth-best ERA (3.98). Pete Vuck-ovich, the staff ace, won the 1982 AL Cy Young Award after going 18–6 with a 3.34 ERA. Closer Rollie Fingers—the winner of the 1981 AL MVP and Cy Young awards—saved 29 games and won five others in 1982. Veteran right-hander Don Sutton, acquired from Houston on August 30, was 4–1 with a 3.29 ERA for the Brewers, going undefeated in his final six starts. Mike Cald-well led the club in starts (34), complete games (12), and innings (258), while going 17–13. Bob McClure (12–7), Jim Slaton (10–6), and Moose Haas (11–8) each won at least 10 games.

In 1982, nobody even knew who Tom Candiotti was. He was in the Brew-ers' organization but had missed the entire season recovering from the recon-structive elbow surgery performed by Dr. Frank Jobe in 1981. But by August of 1983, every baseball-mad Milwaukeean got to know just who Candiotti was—even though he began the season with the Double-A El Paso Diablos on a rehab assignment and wasn't even invited to big league camp in the spring. "Nobody really knew how far along I was with my recovery from Tommy John surgery or even if I'd be able to regain full strength in my arm," recalls Can-diotti. "Nobody was sure that I'd even be pitching again. If I was able to throw the ball and pitch a few games, that would've exceeded everyone's expecta-tions."

Candiotti appeared in seven games—all in relief—for the Diablos before a roster spot opened on the Triple-A Vancou-ver Canadians of the Pacific Coast League on May 2, when

In 1982, nobody even knew who Tom Candiotti was, as he sat out the entire season recovering from Tommy John surgery. One year later, though, Can-diotti made his major league debut and became known in Milwaukee as "The Stopper" and the best fifth starter in baseball, as his pitching kept the Brewers in the American League East pennant race as late as the first week of September (courtesy Milwaukee Brewers).

Canadians pitcher Chuck Porter was called up to Milwaukee. Candiotti, 1–0 with two saves and a 2.92 ERA in El Paso, was transferred to Vancouver to fill Porter's spot. For Candiotti, the key was the fact his arm was responding. "When I was pitching for El Paso," he recalls, "I had no pain at all in my arm. There was no swelling or anything like that. Then I got sent up to Vancouver and pitched as a starter. I did really well there, and again I didn't feel any pain. I threw a couple of shutouts in Triple-A, and it was really a good year for me."

Candiotti's 12-week stint in Vancouver included five complete games in 15 appearances, two shutouts, 99.1 innings, 87 hits, 61 strikeouts, only 16 walks, six home runs allowed, and a 6–4 record. His 2.81 ERA was the third-best for a starting pitcher in the PCL, which was a notorious hitter's league. It might be easy to discount his Triple-A numbers since the success was coming against minor league hitting. But ask those who pitched in the PCL and they would tell you a different story. Jose DeLeon, who pitched in that league during the 1982–83 seasons before earning a call-up to Pittsburgh in July 1983, offered some perspective that summer. "[Pitching] in the Pacific Coast League really helps you when you come to the majors," DeLeon told the *Philadelphia Inquirer*. "Down there, every park is a hitter's park, and you have to learn to pitch every hitter very carefully, to give thought to every pitch you make. And that has to help up here."[1]

Candiotti had not been invited to the Brewers' major league camp during the spring. He had the Tommy John surgery in October of 1981. He still could not throw a baseball a full year after that operation. It was unprecedented that a pennant-winning team like Milwaukee would give a roster spot to a pitcher with a surgically repaired elbow such as Candiotti, but the Brewers were desperate for pitching help.

During spring training, the Brewers were already facing the reality that they would be without closer Rollie Fingers, who'd miss the entire '83 campaign. Fingers had pitched most of 1982 in pain and had been forced to miss the postseason, having been sidelined since September 2. The club was then dealt a double whammy when news of Pete Vuckovich's shoulder problems surfaced in the spring. It was discovered that he had torn his rotator cuff and would miss the first five months of the '83 season. Don Sutton, meanwhile, was healthy and pitching well—at least before the All-Star break. On July 14, Sutton was 7–5 with a 3.41 ERA after defeating Minnesota, just three weeks after becoming the eighth man in major league history to reach 3,000 strikeouts. But he would then proceed to go 0–8 with a 5.45 ERA in 11 starts from July 19 to September 14. Suddenly, not only were the Brewers without their Cy Young-winning starter and Cy Young-winning MVP closer, they were also unable to rely on their slumping hired gun.

Miraculously, Milwaukee was still in contention despite the woes on the pitching staff and despite the Brewers not bashing homers the way they had in '82. As the *Washington Post*'s Thomas Boswell noted, the 1983 Brewers were "more likely to hit-and-run or bunt or slice a double down the line" or manufacture runs than they were to "bludgeon you with bleacher blasts."[2] After falling a season-high eight games behind and into last place on June 22, the Brewers somehow turned things around within the next month, going on a 22–6 run to make up a half-dozen games in the AL East standings. By July 25, they were only two games out of first, behind three teams tied for the top spot (Detroit, Toronto, and Baltimore) and fourth-place New York (which was one game back).

But just as Milwaukee had gotten back into the AL East race, Don Sutton was slumping. On August 4, the veteran righthander lost his third straight decision, 6–2 to Kansas City, and the fourth-place Brewers fell three-and-a-half games behind the division-leading Orioles. Milwaukee needed another pitcher, and on August 6, called up Tom Candiotti from Triple-A Vancouver to take the major league roster spot of seldom-used DH Don Money, who was placed on the disabled list with tendinitis in his right elbow.

When Bruce Manno, the Brewers' minor league director, phoned him with the news, Candiotti was ecstatic. "It was a dream come true," he recalls. "When you're a kid, that's what you dream about, becoming a major league baseball player one day. And all of that hard work, the running, the weight-lifting, the aggravation, everything, seemed to pay off. That phone call was a flashback to your whole life. The times you were in Little League to high school to college. All of the games, innings, strikeouts ... and boom, you've made it. I wasn't even on the Brewers' 40-man roster, but I'd made it to the big leagues. In that one year in 1983, I went from Double-A to Triple-A, and suddenly, I was in Milwaukee. It was like, 'Hey, I did it.' What a big moment that was."

The first person Candiotti phoned to share the news was his mother. "My mom never missed one game ever," he says. "Every high school game, every summer league game, every college game, she was there. [I thought back to] all of the sacrifices my mom made to get me to games on time, pick me up, and all that stuff. Then, wow, all of a sudden, you've made it to the big leagues." During that conversation with his mother, Candiotti remembered the times he and the kids in the neighborhood abused her wooden garage door. "We used to play this game called 'strikeout' against my mom's garage door," Candiotti continues. "We were only allowed to use tennis balls. Kids would come over and we'd have two-on-two or three-on-three baseball. I was the pitcher, and I'd pitch against my mom's garage door. Back then, garage doors were made of wood and had a little handle to pull it up. The handle was home plate for me.

I tried to hit it as many times as I could with that tennis ball—and so there were many holes on that garage door, broken boards, the whole bit. So, one of the first things that I bought my mom when I got to the big leagues was a brand new garage door."

On August 8, Candiotti became the second player ever to have had Dr. Jobe's reconstructive elbow surgery and then go on to appear in a major league game. With Milwaukee leading, 8–3, in the seventh inning in the second game of a doubleheader in Kansas City, he was brought in to pitch with two runners aboard and one out. "The first time I ever came into a game in the big leagues was at Royals Stadium," Candiotti recalls. "Bob McClure started the game, and I came on in relief. Ted Simmons was the catcher. I remember standing on the mound and having a conversation with Simmons, right after [manager] Harvey Kuenn handed me the baseball."

As Kuenn gave Candiotti the ball, Simmons asked, "What do you throw?" Since the rookie call-up had never been to the Brewers' major league camp, the veteran catcher hadn't seen him pitch. Candiotti responded, "Well, I throw a fastball, curveball, slider, and every once in a while, I throw a knuckleball."

"All right," said Simmons. "Just show me what you've got."

After Simmons and Kuenn left the mound, Candiotti proceeded to throw eight warm-up pitches. He threw two fastballs, two curveballs, two sliders, and finished off with two knuckleballs. Candiotti was now ready to throw his first major league pitch, but couldn't believe the sign from Simmons.

"U.L. Washington was the first batter to face me," Candiotti recalls. "And Simmons called a knuckleball on my first pitch in the big leagues! I was thinking, 'Man, I can't shake him off! This is my first major league game!' Ted Simmons must have known something that I didn't even know. The knuckleball was a pitch that was kind of a fun, jerk-around pitch for me. But that was the first pitch that Simmons called, so he knew something that nobody else knew at the time—including myself. At that point, I was a control pitcher with a decent curveball. My stuff was decent, and it took me all the way to the big leagues. But Ted Simmons called a knuckleball on my first pitch!"

Candiotti walked Washington on five pitches before George Brett delivered a pinch-hit, two-run single to cut the deficit to 8–5. Candiotti, however, struck out Willie Wilson looking and retired Hal McRae on a deep fly to left to end the inning. He went on to pitch 2.1 innings and did not allow a run (with the two runs driven in on Brett's single charged to McClure). The following day, also against Kansas City, Candiotti entered the game with two outs in the seventh inning and retired all four batters he faced, getting three groundball outs.

In Candiotti's first major league start, on August 17, 1983, he pitched a complete-game victory against the Boston Red Sox to put the Brewers in first place by a half-game over the Baltimore Orioles. Candiotti would go on to win his first four big league starts with a 0.84 earned run average. He would also pitch at least seven innings in each of his first three starts while allowing one earned run or none, the last major league pitcher in the twentieth century to accomplish that feat (courtesy Milwaukee Brewers).

Harvey Kuenn, impressed with those two mop-up outings, decided to give Candiotti his first major league start on August 16 with Milwaukee in the midst of a tight pennant race. The Brewers had a doubleheader that day against Boston at County Stadium, and the rookie would start the second game. Kuenn decided to bypass righthander Don Sutton, whose turn in the rotation had already been skipped once because of his recent struggles. "We just want to give him a couple more days' rest," said Kuenn of Sutton. "He hasn't been throwing at all. He'll probably throw tomorrow or the next day."[3] Responded Sutton, who had missed a start for only the sixth time in 18 years, "McClure won eight in a row at one point. Chuck Porter's 5–1 since the All-Star break. If I'd done my job, where would we be?"[4]

Still, Milwaukee found itself tied for first place in the AL East after a 14-inning, 4–3 victory in the first game of the doubleheader. Alas, the second game was postponed after a 90-minute rain delay, meaning Candiotti—who had already sat through the four-hour marathon in the opener—would have to wait another day to make his first start. But he didn't seem too bothered about it. "There's not much you can do when it rains," Candiotti noted afterward.

The rained-out game was rescheduled as part of a doubleheader the following day, on August 17. Kuenn would not take the start away from the rookie, naming him the starter in the nightcap. Candiotti would not disappoint. Relying mostly on a sinker and tailing fastball, Candiotti defeated Boston 5–1 on a seven-hitter after Milwaukee had won the first game in 10 innings. His first major league victory in his first start put the Brewers back atop the division by themselves, capping an amazing eight-week run in which Milwaukee went from worst to first.

"I went nine innings and beat the Red Sox," recalls Candiotti. "My first start in the big leagues put us in first place. I couldn't believe it. I didn't even think I'd get called up that year. But once the game started, I knew if I threw my four pitches over the plate and mixed them up, the hitters wouldn't know what pitch was coming next. There were moments when I had to step off the mound to gather myself, but most of the night I was focused on trying to use all my pitches and go as many innings as I could."

Candiotti, whose fastest pitches were clocked in the 80s, recorded no walks and a strikeout. "Candiotti was outstanding," said Kuenn. "All we were hoping for was five good innings out of him. He did a lot better than that."[5] For Brewer pitching coach Pat Dobson, the most impressive part about Candiotti's pitching was his control. "Usually a kid will get nervous in that situation and walk a lot of people," Dobson noted, "but he didn't get close to walking anyone."[6] Kuenn, meanwhile, had nothing but praise for the rookie. "He knows how to pitch," the manager added. "He's in and out, up and down and stays ahead of the hitters. He's got a good sinker, a good change and throws an occasional knuckleball."[7]

Milwaukee and Baltimore had entered the day tied atop the AL East. But since the Brewers played twice—and got the sweep thanks to Candiotti's effort in the nightcap—they moved into sole possession of first place when the night ended, a half-game ahead of the Orioles. After Milwaukee then won four of its next six games to maintain its half-game lead, Candiotti was given his second major league start on August 25 at County Stadium against Tommy John and California. Naturally, it was a big deal for Candiotti. "Tommy John became an idol because he'd gone through that whole operation [with Dr. Jobe] the first time," admits Candiotti. "It was just an honor to pitch in the same game as Tommy John, the first guy to come back from the surgery. Tommy had a lot of success after that, and he won a lot of games.... The way Tommy never gave up, went through with the operation, and all the success after that, I mean, what a great story."

Candiotti, though, was the story against California. In a game that featured 11 All-Stars, including John, it was the Brewers' rookie who shined. Reggie Jackson and Rod Carew, two future Hall of Famers for the Angels, went hitless in five at-bats against Candiotti. John, their 246-game winner, allowed seven runs and 13 hits. Candiotti, meanwhile, threw a complete-game eighthitter with only two walks, leading Milwaukee to a 7–0 victory on an afternoon where the Brewers broke their single-season attendance record. With a crowd of 32,951 on hand, Milwaukee pushed its season total to 1,992,055, surpassing the club record of 1,978,896. The shutout gave the Brewers their ninth win in 11 games and kept them in first place in the AL East. "While the Brewers were giving John a rare shelling," noted the *Milwaukee Journal* the following day, "Candiotti was breezing through the Angels' dangerous lineup with the poise of a veteran."[8]

Kuenn originally wanted to pull Candiotti in the middle innings so that Pete Vuckovich could make his season debut and work at least one inning in relief. But as Dobson said, "He just kept putting those zeroes up there." The Brewers' pitching coach, impressed with Candiotti's location on his fastball and the way he was changing speeds on his breaking pitches, added: "You don't hope he gives up a run. But you can't take a shutout from the kid."[9] Kuenn echoed Dobson's sentiments, admitting he just couldn't pull Candiotti. "Because he had a shutout going, I didn't want to take Tommy out," Kuenn said. "If he'd given up a run, I'd have brought Vuke in in the ninth."[10] The skipper also marveled at the fact Candiotti simply knew how to pitch. "He gets behind a hitter," Kuenn added, "[but] it doesn't bother him. He comes right back and throws a strike—with all of his pitches."[11]

Candiotti still smiles about that matchup against Tommy John, whom he had never met before that game. Recalls Candiotti: "I'll never forget this. In my second major league start, I faced Tommy John and the Angels, and the Milwaukee newspapers were calling it the 'Battle of the Reconstructed Arms.' [More accurately, they called it the 'Battle of the Bionic Arms.'] The cool thing was Tommy talked to me the next day for almost an hour about my rehab. He told me what I had ahead of me with this injury, how to stay strong with the injury, all the stuff that he'd gone through, his peaks and valleys and everything. It was awesome. I'll never forget that day."

Milwaukee was still in contention entering September even with the struggles of Don Sutton, who went two months without a victory. Sutton finally snapped his 0–8 skid on September 21 but would win only one of his final 13 starts. Reigning Cy Young winner Pete Vuckovich, meanwhile, would not make a difference after making his long-awaited season debut on August 31. Vuckovich would last only 14.2 innings in three starts, going 0–2 with a 4.91 ERA. As *Washington Post* writer Thomas Boswell noted in late August, "The core of the Brewers' suspect rotation—Sutton, Mike Caldwell and Bob McClure—has a combined 25–26 record and an ERA over 4.40. When you have to give 27 starts in the pennant race to Chuck Porter, Tom Candiotti, Bob Gibson, Jerry Augustine and Rick Waits, you're in line for baseball sympathy."[12]

The veterans Augustine (2–2, 7.71 ERA as a starter) and Waits (0–1, 7.15 ERA) had struggled, but the rookies were getting it done as late as August 25. Including Candiotti's shutout against the Angels, Milwaukee had four rookies who had combined for a 19–10 record and 10 saves, led by reliever Tom Tellmann (9–3, eight saves), Porter (6–5), and Gibson (2–2, two saves). As it turned out, after Candiotti's shutout against California, the Brewers would not win another game in which Tellmann, Porter, and Gibson appeared until the final three days of the season. Tellmann would pitch well down the stretch (2.31 ERA) but the Brewers would go 0–9 in his final nine appearances. They would be 0–4 in Gibson's outings—he was 0–2—until he defeated Detroit 6–2 on September 30. Porter, meanwhile, would be 0–4 with a 7.16 ERA— with Milwaukee losing all six of his starts—before beating the Tigers, 7–4, in the season finale on October 2.

But on August 25, things looked great for the Brewers, who were in first place. Candiotti was 2–0 with a 0.42 ERA, with two complete-game victories in two starts. Pennant fever in Wisconsin was probably at an all-time high, with the Brewers vying for their second straight pennant. As the *Milwaukee Journal*'s Jim Cohen put it, this was, perhaps, their year: "Suddenly some guy by the name of Candiotti is pitching like [Hall of Famer Sandy] Koufax, and now Vuckovich seems ready to help out. Are the Brewers a team of destiny, or does it just appear that way?"[13]

It was all a mirage. On August 26, Milwaukee lost 4–3 in Oakland and fell out of first place for good. The Brewers then lost three of four to drop to two-and-a-half games back, before Candiotti got his third major league start on August 30. Pitching one night before his 26th birthday, he defeated Seattle 3–2 with a mix of curveballs and off-speed pitches, allowing five hits over 7.1 innings. Even the person clocking Candiotti's pitches was frustrated at his slow stuff. Lamented Mariners manager Del Crandall: "Does he have a fastball? I don't know, but when I looked over at the guy measuring Candiotti with the speed gun, he kept hitting it to make sure it was working.... He's not a hard thrower, but he gets that curve over consistently. He mixes up his spots and changes speeds. That's what you call pitching."[14] Brewers skipper Harvey Kuenn added of Candiotti, "He's something else, isn't he? He has some kind of poise out there."[15]

The victory kept Milwaukee two-and-a-half games behind first-place Baltimore, but the Brewers again faltered when Candiotti was not pitching. They lost three of the next four, and found themselves five games out—having fallen to fourth place—by the time Candiotti pitched again on September 5. It was their first home game since he blanked California 11 days earlier. With the Yankees in town, a Labor Day crowd of 31,115 showed up at County Stadium, allowing Milwaukee to surpass the 2,000,000 mark in single-season attendance for the first time in franchise history.[16] Candiotti wouldn't disappoint the crowd, taking a three-hit shutout into the seventh in a 3–1 win to knock the Yankees out of second place in the AL East. That victory also pushed Milwaukee back into second, ahead of both New York and Detroit, prompting talk that Candiotti was a "stopper," having twice won after Brewers defeats.

Candiotti, 4–0 in four major league starts, was the best fifth starter among the AL East contenders, a commodity nobody else in the division seemed to have down the stretch. To wit, Matt Keough was 2–4 with a 5.44 ERA at that point as the Yankees' fifth starter, Larry Pashnick was 0–3 with a 5.35 ERA in that role for Detroit, and Doyle Alexander was 2–6 with a 4.60 ERA for Toronto while losing six consecutive decisions in one stretch. Candiotti had allowed only eight walks and three earned runs in his 35.2 innings (for a 0.76 ERA), as the Brewers were only four games behind Baltimore. "The way he has pitched in the pennant race is amazing," Kuenn said. "He has shown a great amount of composure for a young kid."[17]

Today, Candiotti is known first and foremost as a knuckleballer. In 1983, though, he was "The Stopper" and "pitching like Koufax." He was known as the best fifth starter in baseball. "They were calling me 'The Stopper.' That was really something," Candiotti recalls. "My first start in the major leagues put us in first place. In my second start, I faced Tommy John and got a shutout. It was just a great start to a great career. But what makes me most proud was that I wasn't a knuckleball pitcher when I got to the majors—I threw maybe five or six knucklers in my first big league start and got pop-ups on a couple of them. Sure, to keep myself in the majors, I had to throw the knuckleball a few years later. But it was big for me, to make it to the big leagues as a regular pitcher."

Bill Brophy of the *Wisconsin State Journal* summed up Candiotti's performance best following the win over the Yankees. "It was the start of the stretch drive and the Brewers were coming off their worst slump in three months. In spring training, you would have thought it would be a spot for a guy like Pete Vuckovich or Don Sutton or Moose Haas to pitch, but never a rookie who started the year in El Paso," Brophy wrote. "However, just as he has each of the six times he has been handed the ball, Tom Candiotti, Milwaukee's man with the bionic arm, coolly walked to the mound, dazzled hitters with a fastball that couldn't break a bat and pitched the Brewers to a 3–1 Labor Day victory over the New York Yankees at County Stadium."[18]

The big names were not there for Milwaukee. Vuckovich was hurt, and Sutton would be 1–8 with a 5.15 ERA down the stretch. The two veterans had exactly zero victories from July 15 to September 20, nearly the entire second half. Haas, who finished 13–3 in 1983, would sit out the final five weeks of the season because of a tired arm (which was later diagnosed as a strained bicep muscle). Bob McClure, another starter, would pitch only twice from mid–August on, lasting a total of 1.1 innings, before being shut down because of arm problems. Milwaukee was, essentially, still relevant in early September even though its best starter was an undrafted non-prospect with a surgically repaired elbow pitching in his first month in the majors.

For that one month, even some of baseball's all-time greats could not hit Candiotti. Against Boston, New York, and California, he held future Hall of Famers Jim Rice, Carl Yastrzemski, Dave Winfield, Reggie Jackson, and Rod Carew hitless in 15 at-bats. Candiotti's best fastballs were clocked in the low 80s, but he relied on pin-point control and a variety of off-speed pitches to keep hitters off balance in getting it done. "I threw sinking fastballs, cutters, and curveballs," Candiotti says. "I got hitters out with slow breaking balls. It was about having command of my pitches and being able to mix them up. You hear coaches and hitters saying, 'This guy's doing it without much of a fastball.' But I was determined to make it to the big leagues, and I made it."

Unfortunately, Milwaukee would collapse badly, losing 12 of 13 to fall 14 games out by September 19. The Brewers finished with an 87–75 record that placed them in fifth, and manager Harvey Kuenn was fired at season's end. Candiotti, meanwhile, concluded the year with a 4–4 record (and a 3.23 ERA), receiving a total of three runs of support in three of his losses. "In '83, there were high expectations [for the Brewers], but they had some injuries," recalls Candiotti. "Pete Vuckovich was hurt. Rollie Fingers wasn't there. Robin Yount had a bad back during the second half of that season. Late in the year, they just stopped hitting and really fell out of it."

Following the 1983 season, Candiotti pitched winter ball in Puerto Rico for the Mayagüez Indians and compiled an 8–0 record, finishing just two wins shy of league leader Rick Mahler. Candiotti's efforts led Mayagüez to the Puerto Rican League regular-season title and the playoff championship. "I threw really well," Candiotti recalls. "I threw a lot of fastballs. There were also a couple of games where I threw mostly knuckleballs. I threw a bit of everything, whatever I could, to get outs."

Candiotti defeated the Ponce Lions twice in the Puerto Rican League finals, helping Mayagüez advance to the Caribbean Series, the championship tournament consisting of the league winners from the Latin American winter leagues of the Dominican Republic, Mexico, Puerto Rico, and Venezuela. Then in the Caribbean Series, Candiotti came within three outs of a no-hitter in his last start against the Los Mochis Sugarcane Growers, champions of the Mexican Pacific League, before finishing with a three-hitter. It was Mayagüez's only win in the Caribbean Series. "The first guy up in the ninth was really hanging over the plate," Candiotti said then. "I threw him a changeup outside, and he pulled it foul. I thought, 'I'm going to have to move him off the plate.' I came inside and hit him on the helmet. The next guy got a hit-and-run single. We were ahead, 14–0, and I don't know what they were hit-and-running for."[19]

Candiotti's Mayagüez teammates, meanwhile, were mad at their own rightfielder for not catching the ball. "Ron LeFlore was a late addition to our team," Candiotti recalls today. "He'd been a good player for the Tigers early in his career but was nearing the end at the time. Ron was playing right field in that game. The ball was hit out there and it was very catchable." LeFlore, however, let the ball drop for a single, ruining the no-hit bid. Though disappointed, Candiotti shrugged the incident off. "I looked out there," he recalls, "and couldn't believe it when the ball fell in. The whole team was mad at him for not giving an effort. He just stopped and let the ball drop. Oh well, it was just one of those things."

In his first year back from the Tommy John surgery, Candiotti won 19 games, combining his stints in El Paso (1–0), Vancouver (6–4), Milwaukee (4–4), and Mayagüez (8–0). He followed that up with three playoff victories in winter ball. "That year was such a magical year for me," says Candiotti. "My earned run average [with the Brewers] was 3.23. I probably should've been 6–2 instead of 4–4. I went to winter ball after that season was over, and I did well. I almost threw a no-hitter in the Caribbean Series."

As he'd soon find out, though, his efforts would not guarantee him a job in 1984.

# 3

## *The Non-Prospect*

Candiotti won his first four major league starts in 1983. Though he lost his next four starts, he still finished the season with a respectable 3.23 ERA. He pitched the Brewers to first place in his first career start and kept them in the race that first month he was called up. He was the best fifth starter in baseball. Everything pointed to him being a solid pitcher ready for the big leagues.

In that case, why wasn't he drafted? "I just didn't throw hard enough," says Candiotti matter-of-factly. "Scouts were always looking for hard throwers, guys who throw 100 mph. Even today." Tim Wakefield, a knuckleballer who made his major league debut in 1992 and is the all-time innings leader in Boston Red Sox history, agrees. "The problem is that [baseball] is so radar gun-oriented," Wakefield once said. "You might see a kid in college that knows how to pitch but doesn't throw 95 [mph] and he won't get looked at."[1]

Indians president Mark Shapiro, who worked for 10 years as a major league general manager, admits teams are eager to draft and sign hard-throwing young pitchers. He says, however, that at the end of the day, major league clubs want pitchers who have the ability to retire hitters, period. "Traditionally, yes," Shapiro says in regards to the preference of hard throwers for big league teams. "[But] I think there's more openness today if a guy can get people out, regardless of how hard they throw."

"You look for hard throwers, sure," admits Bill Bryk, an Arizona Diamondbacks scout and the first manager Candiotti had in pro ball in 1979. "When Candiotti came up to the big leagues, he wasn't a knuckleball pitcher. He did throw a knuckleball occasionally, but teams don't really go around scouting for guys that throw it." One would think that a pitcher who threw a variety of pitches, including a knuckleball for a change of pace, would be an attractive option. But not so, says Bryk. "There aren't that many guys throwing

40

the knuckleball," continues Bryk. "It's not the easiest pitch to throw. It's something you got to be patient with. A lot of guys got to the big leagues without the knuckleball, like a Candiotti, who ended up not getting drafted at all. But these guys develop the knuckler after they get to the big leagues, and the organization needs to be patient enough to stick with them."

The knuckleball is not regarded as one of baseball's conventional pitches. Since the pitch made its first appearance in the majors in the early 1900s, there have been only a handful of successful knuckleball pitchers in the entire history of the game. Knuckleballers are essentially seen as guys that don't throw hard enough, guys that resort to a trick pitch in order to salvage their careers. If these pitchers threw their best fastballs in a big league game, it would be like a batting practice session and they'd be out of the majors soon enough. To hang on to a fading career, a pitcher tries the knuckler. A very common characteristic of knuckleballers is they rarely enjoy major league success before the age of 30 but often pitch into their 40s once they have mastered the pitch. "The pitch is difficult to learn," says Bryk, "and many who experiment with it ultimately abandon the knuckleball because it's hard to control. It's hard to master that pitch."

Bryk says, however, if a pure knuckleballer comes along, then it'd be a different story. Teams would not say no to a young kid who has mastered the knuckler, but it is extremely rare to find a teenage knuckleball prodigy. "You look for hard throwers, yes, but there aren't that many knuckleball pitchers out there to begin with that come out of high school. It's not the easiest pitch to learn. Scouts look for hard throwers, including me, but they're certainly not going to walk away from a knuckleball pitcher. But the thing is, nobody can teach the knuckleball to a young kid. It's just a pitch that's not being taught."

Contrary to what Bryk says, however, there was at least one big league club that had a history of wanting nothing to do with knuckleball pitchers: the Cincinnati Reds. Bill Clark, a long-time Reds scout, once told a story about how he was not allowed to sign knuckleballers. He had signed a pitcher by the name of Randy Easley in the 1970s, noting "he had a pretty good fastball and a pretty good curveball. He was successful with the knuckleball, so he just started relying on it."[2] Cincinnati was not happy that its fastball-curveball pitcher started falling in love with the knuckler. One year later Easley was released, and the Reds told Clark not to bother with knuckleball pitchers anymore. "I haven't gone out and signed any knuckleballers [since then]," the scout said in 1993.[3] Butch Henry, who won 33 major league games from 1992 to 1999, knows about Cincinnati's reluctance to have a knuckleballer in its system. "I struck out a guy in the Texas high school all-star game at the Astrodome," the lefthander once said, recalling his youth when he threw the knuckler once in a while. "But when I signed with the Reds, I could tell right away they frowned on it. Pitching coaches hate the knuckleball."[4]

"Major league baseball is not looking for knuckleballers," Northern Illinois University's Ed Mathey, who has spent two decades as a college baseball coach, noted in 2006.[5] According to Mathey, everyone wants a hard thrower. "They are looking for guys who throw in the 90s with great command and a hard breaking ball. That's what's taught and learned down the rest of the line."[6] Knuckleballer Dennis Springer, probably best known for giving up Barry Bonds's 73rd homer in 2001, once recalled how major league teams did not really consider him to be a real pitcher. "When I was trying to find a job before [the 1999] season," Springer once said, "I called Kansas City and they said, 'Sorry, but we don't want anything to do with a knuckleballer.'"[7]

Candiotti agrees with Bryk's last statement about how no one teaches the knuckleball. "Maybe I should've been more serious learning and throwing the knuckler as a kid," he laughs. "I did throw it as a mess-around pitch. In fact, lots of kids do. But nobody takes it seriously. Everybody wants to throw hard because that's how you end up getting to the big leagues. That's how you end up getting drafted. It's all about the radar gun. Unfortunately, in my case, I just didn't throw hard enough."

Former Dodger general manager Fred Claire, though, does not think velocity necessarily equates to success. "Tom was a knuckleball pitcher," Claire says, "which puts him in a different category. No, he didn't start out as a knuckleballer, but he wasn't a player who was going to be a high draft choice based on his amateur performance. But then he won a lot of games in the big leagues. He was one of those players who developed later as an athlete—he was always a good athlete—so just because he wasn't drafted doesn't mean he wasn't a successful major league pitcher. You can look at players who had not been drafted. It's unusual for those players to have great success in their careers. It's not unprecedented, but it's not usual."

Claire acknowledges there is a difference between nondrafted players and those who do get selected in the lower rounds. According to him, the latter group of players are perhaps more likely to succeed—as a couple of Dodger greats from the 1980s and 1990s proved—which makes Candiotti's lengthy career seem all the more remarkable. "By the same token, many players who were drafted in the lower rounds go on to great success," says Claire. "Mike Piazza [selected in the 62nd round in 1988] was all but an undrafted player from the point where he was drafted. Orel Hershiser was a player who was drafted in the later rounds [in the 17th round in 1979]. General managers and baseball people realize once a career has started, no matter how it starts, the player has a chance at professional baseball. All of us realize that no one knows where the road will lead and everyone has an opportunity for success. Tom was one of those people who developed later as an athlete, so it's not unprecedented."

Knuckleballers aren't the only ones who do not throw hard. Finesse pitchers like Jamie Moyer, for example, relied on location and changing speeds to get hitters out. Those pitchers can win in the majors, but Candiotti doesn't believe scouts go out looking for them. Guys such as Moyer, whose fastest pitch is clocked in the 80s, would not be drafted today simply because scouts are always looking for pitchers who can reach triple digits on the radar gun. *Sports Illustrated* senior writer Tom Verducci perhaps said it best in 2011 when discussing why everyone seems fascinated with hard throwers. "Velocity is the eye candy of pitching," Verducci wrote, "especially with radar gun readings flashed in ballparks, on television and in online game accounts. General managers, managers and coaches all love velocity too because speed allows for a greater margin of error. The 17 hardest-throwing starting pitchers [in 2010], whose fastballs averaged at least 93 mph, combined for a 3.43 ERA and a .601 winning percentage (244–162). The 17 softest-throwing starting pitchers, who averaged 89 mph or less, had a 4.13 ERA and a .476 winning percentage (185–204)."[8]

While there is some debate about whether or not teams would draft a soft-tosser and whether or not such a player would succeed, based on the varying opinions of Shapiro, Bryk, and Claire, one thing is certain. Those who grew up around Candiotti are not surprised by his success, according to childhood friend Rocky Lucia. "One thing that's really cool about Tom," says Lucia, "is he was

In Concord, California, Tom Candiotti was known as "Tommy No-No" during his days in youth baseball. Candiotti, shown here in his Concord High School uniform in his junior year, delivered a pitch during a game against Miramonte (author's collection).

known as a very good pitcher growing up in California. He threw hard back then. He knew how to pitch. He was a student of the game. He was just a really good pitcher."

How good? "Well," continues Lucia, "everyone used to call him Tommy No-No."

Growing up in Concord, California, Candiotti played high school baseball for the Minutemen of Concord High School in the Diablo Valley Athletic League. Not only did he excel in baseball—earning Athlete of the Year honors in baseball during his senior year in 1974—he was also the second-ranked tennis player in the North Coast Section in '74. To top it off, Candiotti was an All-DVAL in 1973–74.

Candiotti started playing organized baseball as a kid. In Little League, he was a shortstop and pitcher. "I was involved in youth baseball from Little League on and did very well," Candiotti says. "As a 12-year-old in 1969, we came one game from getting to the Little League World Series. On my team I was the best pitcher and I played shortstop. We ended up losing in the tournament to Santa Clara."

But it was not because of Candiotti that they didn't make it to the Little League World Series; he was certainly the best player in Concord. So much so, he wasn't known as "Candy Man" back then but by another moniker. "In the city of Concord, if you talk to anyone who played Little League or anyone who was involved in sports," recalls Rocky Lucia, "they know about this kid called Tommy No-No. They'd call him that because Tom threw so many no-hitters in Little League." Candiotti once threw four no-hitters in a row, including two perfect games, according to Lucia. "Tom was known by many people in the Concord area as a pretty good pitcher. And a good hitter too, actually."

Mark Mazza knows. He used to live in the same neighborhood as Candiotti, and batted against him all the time when they were kids. Mazza might have thought he could clobber everything Candiotti threw, but that was not the case. "He was so much ahead of his time when he was nine, 10, 11," Mazza, now a racehorse jockey, says. "He and his catcher, Dave Barberio, played for a team called the Rockets. Both these guys were the best hitters in the league. And Tom was just leaps and bounds the best pitcher. He had a curveball, a knuckleball, a fastball ... and we're talking about a nine-year-old kid. It was so incredible."

Mazza remembers being Candiotti's toughest out in Little League because of his height. After all, bigger kids had bigger strike zones, whereas Mazza, being a shorter kid, would appear to have an advantage with a tiny strike zone. However, he simply could never hit Candiotti. "I was one of Candy Man's toughest outs ever!" Mazza recalls. "The reason is because I was so little. I was 4'3" in

Little League, bringing the smallest strike zone in the history of baseball to the plate. And Tom still struck me out. He still shut me out every time!"

That wasn't all. "Barberio would call pitches for Tom, whether it was a knuckleball or curveball or fastball," continues Mazza. "It didn't matter what pitches he called, Barberio would tell you exactly what was coming. Even though I knew what pitches I would be seeing, I still couldn't hit Tom! The rest of the guys couldn't hit him!" To which Candiotti responds, "Everyone liked Mark Mazza as a kid. But he was a lousy hitter so it didn't matter if my catcher was telling him the signs or not!"

Candiotti's athletic ability, though, was not restricted to baseball. He could play every

Not only did Candiotti play baseball in high school, he also was on the Concord tennis team. Here, Candiotti showed his backhand shot during a match (author's collection).

sport and perform at an extremely high level. "He was just a great athlete," says Lucia. "In high school, he was on the golf team, tennis team, and baseball team." Candiotti even entered a junior bowling league while he was growing up. Despite playing all kinds of sports—and being good in most of them—it was clear tennis was number one. "Tom was the number one tennis player in high school," adds Lucia. "He was THAT good. He dominated. He didn't have a baseball scholarship. He actually went to St. Mary's [College] to play tennis. He was a good baseball player in high school but a REALLY good tennis player."

Though he had some success in high school baseball, Candiotti wasn't regarded as a future major league prospect. But it was in Concord where he began experimenting with the knuckleball. Every day he'd wait for his dad Caesar to return from work so they could play catch. Caesar didn't have a baseball background—he was a statistician at a naval weapons station—but he was the one who taught Tom the knuckler. "I was around nine or 10 years old at the time," recalls Tom Candiotti. "It was during the many afternoons we threw to each other that my father taught me the knuckleball. I throw it with three fingers—unlike other knuckleball pitchers—because that was how he taught me."

The Candiottis didn't lob knuckleballs at each other; son always played catch with dad working on every pitch. "I remember him pitching for hours at a time in his driveway with his dad," says Mazza, the racehorse jockey and Candiotti's childhood friend. "We grew up about two blocks from each other. All the kids from the neighborhood would go by his house when they went on bike rides. Everyone saw how devoted Tom was to pitching. Every time he'd pitch with his dad on the driveway, with his dad's back against the garage door. His dad would teach Tom how to pitch, every day."

Like many young boys, Tom Candiotti learned about the game of baseball from stories his dad told him and from baseball cards. Caesar would tell him stories about Babe Ruth and the great legends from that era. "I became fascinated about baseball history and wanted to know everything about the game," recalls Tom Candiotti. "I even thought, 'If I ever get to the big leagues, I'll throw a knuckleball too, even if it was to just one batter.' It'd be a way to honor my dad for teaching me that pitch."

Unfortunately, Caesar Candiotti would not be able to see his son's achievements with the knuckleball. Caesar died suddenly of a heart attack during Tom's senior year of high school. "It was kind of sad because his dad passed before he became successful," Mazza laments. "Caesar never got to share that with Tom. But he meant so much to Tom." Tom Candiotti has a way of remembering Caesar through the baseball stories and the baseball cards that father passed down to son. "I used to have a great baseball card collection," Candiotti says. "When I looked at my collection, it really brought back so many great memories of my dad."

Tom Candiotti wanted to play college baseball and tennis at St. Mary's College in Morga, California, where he was double majoring in business administration and health/physical education. "I went to St. Mary's because my dad had gone there," Candiotti recalls. "It was only 30 minutes away from my mom's house. My dad had died when I was a senior in high school, and I had three younger sisters. I was kind of the man of the house, and I didn't wanna go too far away. So it was a perfect fit."

The athletic schedule, however, was not a fit for Candiotti, and he was forced to choose between tennis and baseball. "When I got to college, I worked out with the baseball team and also with the tennis coach," he says. "I was going to play tennis on the team. But I found out tennis was in the spring, the same time as baseball. When I was in high school, it was in the fall, during football season, so I played tennis. So I had to make a choice on what I wanted to play. I eventually picked baseball because it seemed like a much more glamorous sport."

Candiotti chose the right sport. The St. Mary's Gaels were a good team in Division I baseball playing against good colleges like Cal State, Stanford, USC, and Pepperdine. Candiotti became a big winner for the Gaels; he was an all-league pitcher for the team for four years, being named league co–Pitcher of the Year and earning honorable mention All-America honors in 1977. In his junior year in 1977, he led the Gaels to a 41–13 record, the best single-season mark in St. Mary's history, a record that still stands today.[9] In 1976, the team was 33–15. "We had great baseball teams at St. Mary's," Candiotti recalls. "We really had some teams that I don't even know how we didn't win the [Division I baseball championship] tournament. We didn't win our league, but we had records like 41–13. We were tremendous."

He recalls a weekend in 1977 when he won a game as a starter and then recorded a pair of saves during a doubleheader sweep the following day. "One series against Reno, I pitched the Friday game and won it, and then came in Saturday in the first game and got a two-inning save," says Candiotti. "Then in the second game of the doubleheader on Saturday, I got another two-inning save. In those days, you give me the ball, I go out and I throw as hard as I can for as long as I can. Not that I was a hard thrower or anything. I liked to move the ball around. My repertoire was fastball, curveball, slider, changeup." Pitching on back-to-back days? As Candiotti explains, that was how the schedule was set up. "Our conference games were Friday and then a doubleheader on Saturday. We'd play Pepperdine or Santa Clara and whoever was in our league, and there was always a game on Friday and then a doubleheader Saturday. I always would pitch the Friday game. You had your number one starter going Friday, and so I would pitch that game."

"I remember him dominating in college," says Lucia. "He was so dominating that they'd use him twice a week. People saw that he had big league talent in college. He always pitched well in those rivalry games, for example, against Fresno State and Pepperdine, teams like that." Unfortunately, Candiotti was used way too much. A sore arm finally caught up with him, and he was forced to sit out his senior year. He attributed his arm problems to being overused by his college coach, Miles McAfee. "Can you imagine doing that to a pitcher nowadays?" Candiotti asks rhetorically, referring to the fact teams these days often nurse their star pitchers along by having hard pitch counts and innings limits to protect their arms. "That's what that coach did to me. He didn't care. He overused me. I had to red-shirt a whole season in college because of that."

McAfee, the legendary coach at St. Mary's, would have a lengthy career in baseball. He played in the Pittsburgh Pirates' organization and would be a scout and player agent for big leaguers (including future Hall of Famers Wade

Boggs and Rickey Henderson). From 1973 to 1980, McAfee managed the Gaels, compiling a 220–185–7 career record.[10] He had six winning seasons in eight years before resigning in July 1980 as the winningest baseball coach in St. Mary's history.[11]

Candiotti, however, felt that McAfee did not focus enough on protecting his players. "It was one of those horror stories you read about, a coach just trying to do whatever he could to win," reflects Candiotti. "That's exactly what happened. The coach just abused me. I hurt my arm because of that, going out to pitch Friday and then again in both games of a doubleheader Saturday. I did that all the time that one year."

While Candiotti—like many pitchers in that era—had to endure the innings and the short rest, the landscape has dramatically changed in the 2010s because of studies done to show that clubs have to nurture their pitchers along to avoid serious injuries. In fact, nowadays teams have no excuse for overusing their pitchers, whether in college or the pros. In 2010, for instance, the Seattle Mariners skipped ace Felix Hernandez's start in the regular-season finale even though he wanted to pitch. Team management decided it was best to protect the young righthander's arm instead of letting him make one more start to improve his chances for the AL Cy Young Award. At that time, Hernandez led the majors with a 2.27 ERA and 232 strikeouts, and had a 13–12 record.

However, Hernandez had also thrown 249.2 innings, which management decided was too many. "[This] is something that he has to understand that it's in his long-term best interest, the organization's best interest," said general manager Jack Zduriencik about taking the start away from him.[12] Interim manager Daren Brown echoed the same sentiments: "You're looking at a 24-year-old kid who's the cornerstone to the rotation as long as he's in Seattle.... We're going to do what's best for Felix and what's best for the organization."[13] Hernandez sat out that last start—allowing Angels righthander Jered Weaver to surpass him in strikeouts—but still won the Cy Young.

Two years later in 2012, the big story throughout the summer was whether or not the Washington Nationals would shut 23-year-old Stephen Strasburg down early even if they were contending for a division championship. With Strasburg coming off Tommy John surgery, the Nationals eventually capped him at 159.1 innings on September 8 so that he wouldn't overstretch his arm even with the club vying for Washington's first taste of post-season baseball since 1933.

In Candiotti's day, there was no such thing as an innings limits. Good pitchers threw as much as possible and as many innings as they could. Matt Keough, who pitched for Oakland from 1977 to 1983, recalled a time when starters were workhorses and tried to complete every game, an era when bullpens still didn't play a big role in baseball. "People ask me why I let anyone pitch you nine innings every time out and I told them I wanted to stay in the big leagues and I wanted to get paid," Keough once said. "Bullpens were different back then and I didn't want to hand the ball over to someone who I felt wasn't going to do as good a job as me."[14]

Pitching a lot of innings was still the norm in 1980, as Keough wasn't even in the top 10 in the AL despite logging 250 innings that season. He went the distance 20 times out of his 32 starts—including a 14-inning effort in Toronto on May 17—but didn't lead the league in complete games, as Athletics teammates Rick Langford (28) and Mike Norris (24) finished first and second, respectively. "The object of the game back then," Candiotti says, "was to win. You pitched as many innings as you could to help the team win."

Win Candiotti did whenever McAfee called upon him. In 1977, Candiotti went 13–3 with a 1.53 ERA and five saves.[15] However, there was a steep price to pay for the workload. "Unfortunately, I had a coach that was more worried about his own record than really taking care of the players," laments Candiotti. "How do you send a pitcher out to pitch on Friday and then again in both games of a doubleheader Saturday? And he did that multiple times. Eventually, I did need that Tommy John surgery to fix my arm."

The arm problem did not stop Candiotti from amassing a 37–13 career mark at St. Mary's with a 2.51 ERA by the time he graduated in 1979. "For a few years, he carried the team there," Lucia says. "He just flat-out knew how to pitch. But they used him too much, and that was when he injured his arm, and he had to red-shirt his senior year. He dominated but when he came up with that arm injury, he lost his fastball." By the end of his four years there, Candiotti had set the Gaels' career record for strikeouts with 280.[16] He also set St. Mary's career marks in innings (413.1), wins (37), ERA (2.51), shutouts (eight), complete games (30), and winning percentage (.740).

That wasn't all. Candiotti, who was elected to the St. Mary's Hall of Fame in 1989, set the school's single-season records in wins (13), ERA (1.53), shutouts (four), and winning percentage (.834). His 37 career victories ranked third all-time in the West Coast Conference, while his innings pitched total placed him sixth.[17] "I couldn't throw hard anymore, so I started winning games by really mixing all my pitches," Candiotti explains. "That's probably when I really learned how to pitch, what pitches to throw to certain hitters to get out of certain situations."

But after the arm injury, Lucia says, Candiotti was not the same pitcher. He didn't impress scouts on the radar gun and wasn't regarded as a major league prospect. "He had a decent season in his fifth year, but not a great season," Lucia continues. "He ended up not getting drafted." Not that scouts weren't showing up at St. Mary's games; they were all watching outfielders Von Hayes and Mike Young, a pair of great hitters regarded as good athletes. Hayes ended up being selected by Cleveland that year in 1979, while Young was drafted by Baltimore in the secondary phase of the January 1980 draft.

As for Candiotti, pro scouts told him he just didn't throw hard enough to merit a professional contract. He ended up not getting drafted. "In my case, it was just the matter of the scouts not liking what they saw with me," Candiotti says. "Scouts just don't go after pitchers with 85-mph fastballs. I could pitch, but scouts were saying, 'Well, he's just another guy. He's just another pitcher who doesn't throw hard.'"

There was another reason scouts stayed away. "Miles McAfee told all the scouts—and I didn't find this out until later—not to draft me," says Candiotti. "He told them, 'This guy's not going to sign. He's going to continue his education.' So all the scouts stayed away my junior year when I won 13 games. It was selfish on his part because he didn't want me to leave the program and I ended up hurting my arm anyway. So, really, there were a couple of things working against me on that. I think the scouts knew that I didn't throw hard and I ended up hurting my arm. They were staying away from me, but I think someone still would've taken a chance on me. I was a winner, my record was 13–3 that year, [and] I had all of the pitching records at St. Mary's. But when the coach tells the scouts, 'He's not gonna sign, so don't bother drafting him,' well, I went undrafted."

Since Candiotti wasn't drafted by any team in 1979, he was prepared to find work with his business degree, perhaps get into real estate. Regardless, he had graduated recently and wanted to take his time to figure out what to do career-wise. Baseball was not in the cards for him. After he was forced to redshirt a season in college, he came back but really couldn't throw. He couldn't even hit the 80-mph mark on the radar gun.

"All of a sudden," Candiotti recalls, "I was playing summer ball—semipro baseball—and I started feeling good. I was getting all the strength back. Suddenly I could throw the ball 88 miles an hour again, whereas I was throwing only in the 70s. To this day, I don't know what happened. I could throw the ball 75 miles an hour, and then all of a sudden, something happened. Next thing I knew, I was throwing like I used to—86, 87, 88 miles an hour—which wasn't hard, but it was 13 miles harder than what I was throwing."

Candiotti figured he had two months of summer vacation before trying to look for work. That summer, a friend asked him to go on a road trip for a baseball tryout. Hey, why not? After all, his arm had suddenly felt okay. Why not give it one last shot? "My buddy was going up to try out for the Victoria Mussels," Candiotti recalls. The Mussels, an independent team in the Class A

Northwest League with no major league affiliation, were looking for players, according to the buddy.

Continues Candiotti: "My buddy asked me to come with him. He said, 'Hey, wanna try out for the team?' I said, 'Try out? Sure!' I'd just graduated from college. With my degree, I thought I'd probably work in business. But I was only 21 years old at the time, and I had a few months to just mess around before I got into the workplace. I went along, thinking that the drive from California to [Victoria, British Columbia], where the tryout was taking place, was going to be nice, if nothing else. I just had a bag and a fishing pole and that was it. So I go with my buddy, and the guy gives me a tryout. The guy goes, 'Hell, yeah. I'll give you the ball.' I went out there on the mound and showed him what I had."

"The guy" was Mussels manager Bill Bryk, who was impressed enough with Candiotti that he signed him. But the friend had no such luck. "So, [Bryk] signs me and not my buddy," says Candiotti. "That's how I got to pro ball. I did well for him. I won five games with a good ERA. We were in the pennant race and I did well for him." Bryk, now a scout with the Arizona Diamondbacks, echoes that fact. "Tom did a really good job for us," says the former Mussels skipper. "We were going for the North Division pennant on the last day of the season. We split a doubleheader with the Mets [affiliate in Grays Harbor] but we lost the division by two percentage points [to the Walla Walla Padres] and didn't go to the playoffs."

With a 41–31 record and a .569 winning percentage, the Mussels fell just short of the Padres, who won the pennant at 40–30 and .571. "But Tom," says Bryk, "was one of the best pitchers in the league." The numbers support that claim. Candiotti went 5–1 with a save and a 2.44 ERA in 12 appearances, including nine starts. He struck out 66 batters over 70 innings, allowing 63 hits and only 16 walks.

While Candiotti wasn't impressive on the radar gun, Bryk was convinced he could be an effective pitcher. "I signed Tom because his stuff was good," Bryk recalls. "It wasn't overwhelming but it was quality stuff, average major league stuff. He probably threw 86–90 mph with average breaking stuff and a good change. I thought he could get to the big leagues with those pitches." If there was one thing Bryk loved about Candiotti, it was his ability to pitch out of trouble. "Tom was a guy that had what I call 'moxie.' He really had a feel for what he was doing, he knew his strengths and weaknesses, and he knew how to get people out," adds the former Mussels manager. "He really pitched above his stuff. He really knew how to pitch and was very poised and confident on the mound. The more I saw him during the year, I thought, 'Man, this guy can really pitch. He's going to move up.' And as it turned out, he continued to get better every year. He was able to get to the big leagues a few years later before he developed his knuckleball."

The more Bryk saw him that year, the more the skipper was convinced that Candiotti had other talents. "He'd do magic tricks," Bryk says. "I still don't know how he did it." Victoria was trying to catch the Walla Walla Padres down the stretch, and Candiotti would have one of the clubhouse kids secretly tell him the scores of the Padres' games. Says Candiotti, "What I would do was—and it was a trick that no one could get—draw the score on my forearm with soap. You couldn't see it." He would then have teammates gather around him and burn a piece of paper together to create ashes, which they'd rub on his arm. Magically, the score of the Padres' game would come out. "Bill Bryk could never figure it out," laughs Candiotti. "He used to go crazy!"

While Candiotti did just fine on the mound in Victoria, he struggled with living conditions. Bread and luncheon meat were all he could afford for food. If he wanted a proper meal, he had to resort to more creative and sneaky methods. "I was probably the king of dine-and-dash," he jokes. "But that was the only way I could eat. I didn't have any money when I was there." As Candiotti recalls, he lived in the clubhouse initially and made $400 Canadian a month. "That was like $320 American at the time," he says. "That was all the money I had, and I had no place to stay. So I actually lost money playing for that team in Victoria. For a week, I stayed in the locker room. After that, I stayed with a buddy. I slept on the floor at his place. I didn't have any money. I didn't have a car or anything. There were even a couple of times when I slept on the field in my sleeping bag. It was that bad."

Candiotti's living arrangement wasn't unique, according to Bill Bryk. Minor leaguers playing independent league baseball often had nowhere to stay. The players either weren't drafted, like Candiotti, or they'd been released. Many of them were good college players who were unwanted by major league teams and simply wanted a chance to play pro ball. "A lot of the guys on the club didn't make much money and it was very expensive to live in Victoria," says Bryk. "They did what they had to do to get by. Tom probably wasn't the only one living in the clubhouse."

Candiotti's story turned out to be different from the other Mussels players. He became the only member of that 1979 squad to reach the majors. "Nothing came easy for me," Candiotti says. "This became why I wanted to make it to the big leagues. It was because I really had to pay the price. I wasn't drafted. I had to go earn a tryout with Victoria. I wasn't handed a big contract after coming out of college. I look back at my career now, and this is one of the things I'm most proud of: the determination and the drive to succeed, and to follow my dream. More than anything else, this is it. Forget the numbers.

Forget the wins. Forget the ERA. It's how I challenged myself and made it. It wasn't easy. I was just driven. It was like, 'I could make it and nobody was going to tell me I couldn't.' And they tried. They tried along the way. They said I couldn't do it, but I wouldn't listen to them."

One of the culprits who felt Candiotti couldn't do it was the Kansas City Royals' organization, which purchased his contract for $2,000 from Victoria. Candiotti was in the Royals' minor league system for only one season, in 1980, appearing in 24 games for Class A Fort Myers and Double-A Jacksonville. He never pitched for Kansas City, but remembers an incident while he was with Jacksonville pitching against Montgomery. "Gene Lamont was the manager," Candiotti recalls. "Glenn Wilson came up and hit a ball hard in his first at-bat and there was a guy after him, a lefty. I think his name might've been Cochrane. I threw a couple of knuckleballs to the lefty and struck him out."[18]

Thinking that he'd had some success with the knuckler, he wanted to try the pitch again later that same game. The next time Wilson was up, Candiotti threw him a knuckleball. After all, Wilson had smoked the ball in his first at-bat and Candiotti wanted to give him a different look. Wilson, however, managed to hit a blooper that fell in between the leftfielder and centerfielder. Lamont, who was watching from the dugout, was furious. When Candiotti returned to the dugout after the inning, Lamont asked what that pitch was. "It was a knuckleball," he responded, which made the skipper even more furious. Screamed Lamont, "I don't ever, ever want to see you throw a knuckleball ever again!"

"But I do throw it once in a while," Candiotti protested. "I've always done it. I even threw it in Fort Myers in A ball!" Lamont, though, wasn't buying it. "You've got too good stuff," the manager yelled, "to be throwing a knuckleball!" Candiotti didn't win that argument. "So," he says today with a laugh, "I wasn't allowed to use the knuckler anymore that year."

Ironically, in the 1970s the Royals' organization had experimented with knuckleballers in the minor leagues but saw no results. According to Lou Gorman, a farm director with Kansas City at the time, the Royals had their 20 worst pitching prospects try to develop the pitch but "not one of them made it.... There just were no good teachers out there."[19] And then in 1980, Candiotti wasn't allowed to throw a knuckleball for the Royals' Double-A team.

As Candiotti admits, the lack of good pitching coaches to teach the knuckleball makes it difficult for pitchers to learn it. It also frustrates managers when they don't understand the pitch. "You never can really control the knuckler like you can with other pitches," Candiotti explains. "The key, though, is to aim for the catcher's mask, take the spin off the ball, and usually the ball will dive down to the left or right. You make the ball come out of your hand taking the spin off of the ball. The resistance of the air will handle the movement. I couldn't control if it was a strike or if they hit it. When you strike out a guy with a knuckleball, you look great throwing it. But if it goes for a double, then the manager wants you to stop throwing it."

Candiotti made 17 starts with Jacksonville, completing eight and throwing two shutouts. His 2.77 ERA, among pitchers with at least 100 innings, ranked seventh-best in the Southern League. For the 1980 season, combining his efforts in Fort Myers and Jacksonville, Candiotti went 10–10 with a 2.63 ERA and 11 complete games. He also messed around with the knuckler when Gene Lamont wasn't around. "When it rained, we couldn't work out on the field because of all the mud," Candiotti recalls. "So I'd teach guys the knuckleball in the motel parking lot."

The Milwaukee Brewers noticed his pitching efforts, selecting him in the Rule 5 draft in December and assigning him to Double-A El Paso of the Texas League. "I pitched very well in the minor leagues for the Milwaukee affiliate in '81," Candiotti recalls. With El Paso, he posted a 7–6 record. Candiotti also finished second on the club in wins, third in ERA (2.80) and innings (119), and led in complete games (six).

Throughout his time in the minors in the early 1980s, Candiotti stayed positive. "Sure, it was tough being in Double-A and Triple-A," Candiotti says. "But I wanted a chance to make it to the big leagues. To reach that goal, I was willing to make all the sacrifices. You know, all of the bus rides, all of the stops at McDonald's for every meal because we couldn't afford anything else.... When I did make it in 1983, I thought I was going to be pitching in the major leagues [from that point on]. But I had to start all over again by the following spring."

# 4

## *Minor Leagues, Little Prank,*
## *Big Leagues: The Knuckleball*

After an impressive 1983 campaign and a solid spring training in 1984, Tom Candiotti expected to be a part of the Milwaukee rotation at the start of the '84 season. If he could win 19 games in 1983—combining his regular-season efforts in the majors, minors, and in winter ball—with his off-speed pitches, how many games could he win if given a shot in the Brewers' starting rotation?

However, Milwaukee had too many pitchers and Candiotti wasn't going to win a spot on the team given the fact the others ahead of him had much more major league experience. As the *Milwaukee Journal's* Tom Flaherty noted before the season, new manager Rene Lachemann had as many as 14 qualified pitchers with big league experience battling for 10 spots on the staff, making it "one of the biggest battles the Brewers have ever had in spring training."[1]

Veteran righthanders Rollie Fingers, Don Sutton, and Pete Vuckovich were already assured of roster spots. Also part of the staff were Mike Caldwell, Moose Haas, Pete Ladd, and rookie Jaime Cocanower. Throw in Tom Tellmann and Jerry Augustine, two relievers who had done the job for Milwaukee in 1983, and veteran Rick Waits, and that made it 10 pitchers with big league experience. Chuck Porter, who won seven games—completing six—as a rookie in 1983, deserved a shot as well. Where exactly did that leave Candiotti? Lamented the *Journal's* Bob Wolf on March 25, a week before Opening Day: "You would think a performance like [his 1983 campaign] would give Candiotti a big edge going into the 1984 season. Not so. The way it looks now, all he will get out of it is a return ticket to Vancouver."[2] The move became official three days later, when Candiotti and righthander Bob Gibson were optioned to the Triple-A Canadians, meaning they would start the season in the minors.

A dejected Candiotti took the news hard. He was in tears as he shook hands with his teammates in front of his locker before leaving the major league camp, realizing he wouldn't begin the season in Milwaukee. "It's somewhat of a letdown," Candiotti said then. "I was a real success with Milwaukee last year, and I had a great winter league season in Puerto Rico. I was 8–0, had a no-hitter for eight innings, and made the all-star team. Everything looked great.... Then I get to camp here and I don't even have a job secured. Everybody says we don't have enough pitching, yet we have too many pitchers. It's a numbers problem rather than an ability problem."[3] General manager Harry Dalton, meanwhile, admitted it was indeed a numbers game. As Dalton explained, the Brewers "have 14 people who have pitched to some extent in the major leagues.... Tom Candiotti did well for us down the stretch. That's 13, 14 [pitchers on the staff]. It's going to be a tough staff to cut," especially with several of the veterans coming back from injuries.[4]

Years later, Candiotti admits he understood why he was sent down. "I was in great shape and ready to go in 1984," he says. "But it just became a numbers game. A lot of times as a young player, you don't think about that. You think if you're one of the 10 best pitchers in the organization, you should be in the big leagues. You don't understand the numbers sometimes. Guys that are out of options or guys that are under contract ... those guys don't get sent down. They could send me down without losing the rights to hold me."

When the Triple-A season began, Candiotti started the Canadians' season opener in Vancouver. He pitched two-hit ball over six innings and defeated Tucson, 7–1. Despite pitching with tendinitis in his right arm, Candiotti would win several more games for the Canadians. In 15 starts, he went 8–4 with a 2.89 ERA and four complete games. The Brewers finally rewarded Candiotti for his efforts midseason, calling him up on July 13.

Alas, 1984 was a lost year for Milwaukee, which at the time was 40–48 and 19 games behind first-place Detroit. A big blow was the loss of third baseman Paul Molitor, who played only 13 games before missing the remainder of the season with a torn muscle. Rollie Fingers, meanwhile, was pitching again but would miss the final two months with back problems. Then there was Pete Vuckovich, who wound up missing the entire season after an operation to remove a bone spur. Milwaukee would finish the year with an AL-worst 67–94 record.

As for Candiotti, that year was very painful for him physically. "I did well down in Triple-A, got called up, but then hurt my arm," Candiotti recalls. "I had tendinitis on my shoulder. I went on the disabled list, had to make a couple of rehab starts, but my arm just wasn't strong enough. I was just a mess that year." On August 2, Candiotti was a last-minute scratch before his start at Yankee Stadium and was placed on the disabled list with recurring shoulder soreness, which turned out to be tendinitis. Though he was ready to come off the DL in mid–August after being able to throw without any pain, the Brewers kept him deactivated until the rosters expanded from 25 to 40 players on September 1. (To put Milwaukee's woes in perspective, from July 6 to August 10— a span of 33 games—Candiotti and Don Sutton were the only two Brewers starting pitchers to register victories.)

In his eight big league appearances in 1984, Candiotti went 2–2 with a 5.29 ERA. "It was tough for me not being in the big leagues for much of that year," says Candiotti. "Not only that, I remember after that season, I needed toe surgery. I had a bone chip on my right big toe, so I was a mess. There were a lot of times when I was really frustrated. It seemed I had arm injury after arm injury, and then that toe injury. Unfortunately, I ended up falling out of favor with the Brewers' organization. Because the Brewers had several young pitchers coming up, they didn't think I was a prospect anymore, so they basically gave up on me."

More bad news was on the way for Candiotti in the offseason. All he had to do was follow the Brewers' off-season transactions to realize he was getting phased out. At the winter meetings, the club traded Don Sutton to Oakland for righthander Ray Burris, who had the AL's ninth-best ERA and was a former post-season star with the 1981 Expos. Then, just before spring training, Milwaukee acquired righthander Danny Darwin from Texas and righty Tim Leary from the Mets. The 34-year-old Burris (13–10, 3.15 ERA) and 29-year-old Darwin (8–12, 3.94 ERA), who combined to post a 3.56 earned run average in 435.1 innings over 60 starts in 1984, were essentially replacing the 40-year-old Sutton and 36-year-old Mike Caldwell (who was released) in the Brewers' rotation. Burris, Darwin, and Leary were joining a staff that already included Moose Haas and Pete Vuckovich, and Milwaukee was also expected to look at rookies Bill Wegman, Chris Bosio, Juan Nieves, and Teddy Higuera.

New manager George Bamberger admitted when Darwin and Leary were acquired that it would be "very, very competitive" among the pitchers during spring training. "Guys who had jobs last year might not make the club this year," Bamberger said. "I'm going to hate like hell to have to sit in that office and tell some of those guys they didn't make it."[5] One of "those guys" was Candiotti, who would instead spend the 1985 season in Double-A El Paso and Triple-A Vancouver, going 10–13 with a 3.75 ERA between the two teams. The Brewers, who inadvertently discovered his knuckleball one spring afternoon, told him to concentrate on developing that pitch the whole season in the minor leagues.

That came about when, during spring training, Bamberger saw Candiotti throwing knuckleballs in the bullpen. "I was throwing knuckleballs as a joke just to beat up the catcher, Bill Schroeder," Candiotti recalls. "[The Brewers] were going to release me. That's when they offered me a minor league pitching coach job. But I was messing around that day, throwing knuckleballs to Schroeder. It was funny. Knuckleballs were bouncing off Bill's shoulder and his mask. Next thing I knew, I turned around and Bamberger was watching me."

Bamberger wanted a word with the pitcher, and Candiotti thought he was in big trouble. To Candiotti's surprise, though, the Brewers' skipper began the conversation by saying, "Kid, we didn't know you throw a knuckleball."

Candiotti responded with a shrug, "Well, I do. I've done it my whole life. I throw it once in a while to get some guys out."

"Listen, you've got a great knuckler," Bamberger continued. "You've gotta throw it more often. It might mean a new career for you. I've been around the game a long time. I've seen [knuckleballers] Hoyt Wilhelm and Wilbur Wood, and your knuckler's as good as any of them."

The Brewers decided that Candiotti needed to master that knuckleball before he could return to the major leagues. "So," says Candiotti, "they wanted me to throw the knuckleball down in the minor leagues that season. Instead of releasing me, they sent me down to start working on the knuckler."

The term "knuckleball" is a misnomer. Sure, when the pitch was first invented by Eddie Cicotte and Nap Rucker in 1905, it was thrown with the knuckles. Knuckleball pitchers in those days threw the pitch by pressing the knuckles of the hand against the seams of the baseball. By the time the 1940s rolled around—when the Washington Senators famously had four knuckle-ballers in their starting rotation—the ball was gripped with the fingertips or fingernails. Since then, knuckleball pitchers have gripped the ball using the fingertips and not the knuckles.[6] "It's really a fingertip ball," broadcaster Tim McCarver once said about the knuckleball. "But it's too hard to call it that. It's kind of awkward. So 'knuckleball' is much easier for announcers to say. So really announcers call it a knuckleball."[7]

Even then, there is a tendency for many people to think all knuckleballers throw the same way. Former Indians general manager Joe Klein says the belief couldn't be more wrong. "Even though knuckleball pitchers throw the same pitch," explains Klein, "they don't throw it the same way. First of all, they don't grip the ball with their knuckles. Second, they don't even hold the ball the same. Take Candy, for example. He threw it with three fingers, but Phil Niekro threw it with two."

Nowadays, knuckleballers grip it with two or three fingers—not the knuckles—dug into the ball. The ball is then pushed toward the plate instead of thrown. It has little movement and doesn't rotate, dancing toward the plate at a very slow speed to confuse the batter and oftentimes the catcher. Nobody knows where the pitch is going, not even the pitcher throwing it. A knuckleball, usually clocked in the 50–60 mph range, frustrates even the best hitters in the game. "I'd rather face a guy who throws 100 miles an hour than one of those guys," Red Sox Hall of Famer Ted Williams once said, convinced he had much more success against conventional pitchers. "If the pitcher doesn't know where it's going, how in the hell am I supposed to know?"[8]

It's also not a pitch that managers like. It isn't a pitch that scouts like, as they prefer pitchers with 100-mph fastballs. "Scouts don't go out looking for knuckleball pitchers," says former Dodger general manager Fred Claire. The perception is that pitchers trying to learn the knuckleball are guys that have lost their fastball and aren't able to get a big league job if they don't come up with a new pitch. Young pitchers do not need that pitch because if they can throw 90 mph, they can get to the majors. Jim Kaat, who won 283 major league games, once referred to the knuckler as a "pitch of desperation."[9] There are other negative words associated with that pitch: knuckleballers aren't athletes; they can't throw the ball with velocity; they're old; they're washed up. Who needs guys like that? "Knuckleball pitchers don't get a lot of attention," Claire admits, but adds that it takes skill to learn the pitch. "One thing not a lot of people realize is that it's not as easy as it looks. It's a very difficult pitch to throw. It's just as difficult to hit."

Though many big leaguers mess around with the knuckleball during warm-ups, there are only a handful of pitchers who can throw it successfully in the majors. "Al Nipper came to Cleveland for one season in 1990," recalls Candiotti of the righthander who logged a 6.75 ERA in nine games with the Indians. "Nip tried to throw the knuckleball. You play catch with Nip, and he can throw it. But it's a bit more difficult when you get on the mound and there's an umpire back there and a guy with a bat, and 50,000 people in the stands. It's a very difficult pitch to throw, and there are no pitching coaches teaching it."

But once a pitcher has the technique of the knuckleball mastered, it can prove to be a lengthy stint in the majors. A 20-year career is certainly possible. "Look at the three knuckleball pitchers around when I first got to the big leagues," Candiotti says. "Phil Niekro pitched until he was 48. Charlie Hough and Joe Niekro both pitched into their 40s. These guys threw the knuckleball well enough to have pretty lengthy careers. A good knuckleball is tough to hit. A really good one moves so much that it's tough to catch and it's tough to hit."

Conversely, a poorly thrown knuckleball can get smoked. "There are going to be times," says Claire, "when that ball doesn't break at all. Well, that ball's going to be hit harder than anybody who ever throws a baseball." And on a bad day, a knuckleballer won't be able to throw it for a strike. Walks, dropped third strikes, wild pitches, and passed balls are expected when he doesn't have his bread-and-butter pitch working. Baserunners will take advantage by running because the pitch moves slowly to the plate and it's difficult for a catcher to handle the ball and then try to throw anybody out.

There's also the fact nobody seems to love knuckleballers. People are simply more impressed with pitchers who throw 95 mph and rack up big strikeout totals. Not just the scouts and managers, but also the media and fans. Everyone would rather see Nolan Ryan and his fastballs and strikeouts. Meanwhile, a knuckleballer? The perception is he isn't good enough to get hitters out with conventional pitches, so he has to resort to a trick pitch to hang around. Sure, he can throw plenty of innings, but he doesn't *look* very impressive while doing it. He can't throw the ball by anybody. He doesn't have any knee-buckling breaking balls. Just knuckleball, knuckleball, knuckleball. Once a reporter asked Candiotti during a post-game interview session what pitches he had working that afternoon, and teammate Kevin Gross wryly interjected by uttering those exact words: "Knuckleball, knuckleball, and knuckleball."[10]

Adrian Brijbassi, a long-time baseball fan and journalist, recalls the time his beloved Blue Jays acquired Candiotti for the 1991 stretch drive. Torontonians, says Brijbassi, were yawning because the team didn't get anyone "sexy" like a hard-throwing Jack Morris—even though Candiotti by then had become the majors' best knuckleballer. Candiotti, in fact, had the AL's third-best ERA at 2.24 midway through that season, but to many in Toronto, it was disappointing to get a guy who "tried to trick you" with that knuckleball.

Candiotti, however, disagrees with the notion that the knuckleball is a trick pitch. "Is the knuckler any more of a gimmick than, say, the splitter?" Candiotti asks. "A lot of teams don't want to deal with having a guy with a knuckleball. You hear about the wild pitches and passed balls, but it's really a stereotype and not accurate. A guy that throws a knuckleball will pitch 200 innings, give up fewer hits than innings pitched, have a good ERA, and have a 2–1 strikeout-to-walk ratio—and I did those things throughout the course of my career. When that knuckleball was working, it really was a devastating pitch for hitters."

Tim Wakefield, a knuckleballer made his big league debut in 1992, once said, "Sometimes, I feel like knuckleball pitchers don't get the respect they should."[11] Knuckleballer Charlie Hough, one of baseball's winningest pitchers in the 1980s, could relate to that. From 1984 to 1989, his 90 victories were the ninth-most in the majors. However, journalist George Will suggested that the name "Hough" somehow didn't fit on the list of baseball's elite. In *Men at Work: The Craft of Baseball,* in a chapter discussing righthander Orel Hershiser's success, Will noted that the Dodger ace had just eight more wins than the Texas knuckleballer, but "Hough is hardly a byword for glamour, or even a household word, even in the homes of baseball fans."[12] As author Rich Westcott noted, knuckleballers are simply viewed as freak shows. "The knuckleball is really a freak pitch that thrives on abnormal behavior," wrote Westcott. "[Because the knuckler] lacks the macho stature of a 95 mph fastball, knuckleball users are kind of like the Rodney Dangerfields of the pitching fraternity. They get no respect. They're treated more like the sideshow performers at a circus."[13]

For Tom Candiotti, respect or not, the knuckleball was his last shot at returning to the majors. Initially, Candiotti was assigned to Double-A El Paso, where he was 1–0 with a 2.76 ERA in four starts. But he didn't want to throw the knuckleball there, not when the scores of some of the games resembled football contests (for example, when the Diablos outlasted the Beaumont Golden Gators 35–21 in 1983). "El Paso is one of the worst places to work on a new pitch," Candiotti recalls. "Balls just flew out of that park. So I didn't want to throw the knuckler there. How are you supposed to experiment with a new pitch in a ballpark like that? But then I got sent to Triple-A Vancouver after about three weeks [when Jim Kern was called up to Milwaukee] and I started to throw the knuckler."

Candiotti threw the knuckleball in Vancouver but wasn't happy with his results. "It was terrible for me those first few weeks in Vancouver," he says. "The ball was moving too much. When I first started throwing it, there were some long days, very frustrating days. I was walking a lot of hitters in the first half of the year, but things got better around midseason." What Candiotti did was begin throwing strikes with the knuckleball, and when he got ahead of hitters with the knuckler, he threw his curveball or fastball. The hitters were baffled. They never knew what was coming.

Meanwhile, Candiotti also found that he was on his own. There was nobody in Vancouver that could mentor him. Manager Tom Trebelhorn and pitching coach Mike Paul didn't know what to tell him because they had never coached a knuckleballer. "It was all trial and error for me," says Candiotti. "It was all part of the learning process. There was nobody who could teach me the knuckleball. It wasn't like teaching a curveball or a slider, where anybody could teach it. And it was totally different when you got on the mound and you weren't throwing on flat ground. There were times the catcher couldn't handle the pitch, [resulting in] a lot of wild pitches and passed balls. I was out there alone most of the time because nobody could give me any advice."

Numbers-wise, 1985 was the worst season of Candiotti's pro career. He went 9–13 in 24 starts in Triple-A, and his 3.94 ERA was a full run higher

Though he spent only parts of two seasons with Milwaukee, Candiotti always pitched well at home in a Brewers uniform. In his nine outings at County Stadium from 1983 to 1984, Candiotti went 5–2 with a 2.18 ERA over 53.2 innings while throwing mostly 80-mph fastballs and off-speed pitches, including slow curveballs and the occasional knuckleball (courtesy Milwaukee Brewers).

than any season he'd had in the minors. He still rebounded in the second half and kept his walk total down, issuing only 36 bases on balls in 150.2 innings with Vancouver. And though that knuckleball began working better later that year, realistically one minor league season just wasn't enough time to perfect the new pitch. "It really wasn't a lot of time to try and master a pitch like a knuckleball," laments Candiotti. "It's just not something that you can master overnight."

As it turned out, Milwaukee had no plans for Candiotti to pitch again. In late September, he was called up for a workout to show George Bamberger his knuckleball. One problem: Bamberger never put him on the active 40-man roster for the Brewers' remaining games. Candiotti didn't get in one game, not even for one pitch. "For the two weeks I was there, I'd throw every other day and George would watch," recalls Candiotti. "But because I got hit by a line drive in the [PCL] playoffs and had to leave that start, they didn't officially activate me and I never pitched for Milwaukee in '85."

Still, you have to wonder. If the Brewers were in a pennant race and didn't want to lose any games on a knuckleball that bounced to the backstop, it was understandable why they wouldn't activate Candiotti. But at the time, they were in sixth place in the seven-team AL East, 30 games behind first-place Toronto. They weren't even in danger of suffering the embarrassment of finishing last; with a week left in the season they were 11 games ahead of cellar-dwelling Cleveland. Milwaukee wasn't going to improve its positioning in the standings either, being 10.5 games behind fifth-place Boston. The club had nothing to play for during the season's final weeks, other than to give prospects more playing time so that they would be ready for 1986.

At the time, Brewers pitching coach Herm Starrette thought Candiotti would get a shot, suggesting that his experiment with the knuckler was progressing well. "He's the only pitcher I've seen who throws it like Phil Niekro," Starrette said in late September. "He's building up confidence in it. He just needs to learn how hard he has to throw it."[14] By that time, though, Starrette might have been among the minority in the organization who thought highly of Candiotti's knuckleball. Following the season, Bruce Manno, the Brewers' minor league director, advised Candiotti that he had bottomed out as a prospect. "They were going to release me in 1985," Candiotti recalls. "Bruce Manno wanted me to be a pitching coach in the organization. But I told him, 'No. I can still get hitters out. I'm not going to retire.'"

Even if Milwaukee had kept him, though, Candiotti knew he had no future there. "I'd fallen out of favor with the organization," Candiotti explains. "I couldn't throw the ball that hard. I had tendinitis. At the same time, they had these other kids that were starting to come up [through the minor league system]. Guys like Teddy Higuera, Juan Nieves, Dan Plesac, Bill Wegman. I was older than them and didn't have as much potential in their eyes. I saw the direction [the Brewers] were going. I wouldn't have been given the chance to develop my knuckleball in the majors. So, for me, it was time to move on."

Baseball people would say Milwaukee was doing the right thing. It was no sure thing Candiotti's knuckleball would work in the big leagues. And with all of those young arms in the organization, where exactly would Candiotti fit in? Joe Coleman, a former big league pitcher who won 142 games from 1965 to 1979, once offered his thoughts on whether or not an organization should develop a knuckleballer. "I've been told by people who should know that it takes three to four years to develop a knuckleball," Coleman said. "I mean develop it to where you can throw strikes and have control. Now you're talking about a lot of guys you draft during that time, a lot of prospects. Can you afford to keep trying to develop a knuckleballer over those prospects? ... How many good knuckleballers have there been?"[15]

Joe Niekro, who mastered the knuckleball midway through his career during the 1970s, agreed that it wasn't easy to learn the pitch. "It's a very tedious pitch," Niekro said in 2003. "There's not many guys who can take a baseball, throw a knuckleball and get the spin off of it. There's a lot of guys who can take a baseball and throw a curveball and a slider and a half-speed, but not too many guys can take the spin off of it. When you become a knuckleball pitcher, there's two things you have to do. Take the spin off of it, then you have to get it close enough where the hitter's going to swing at it."[16]

The Cleveland Indians figured Candiotti would be able to do those two things with his knuckleball. While Milwaukee—or any other team, for that matter—wasn't willing to take that gamble with him, Cleveland certainly was. And it was thanks to a man by the name of Orlando Gomez, a manager in the Indians' farm system.

Candiotti did not pitch in the majors in 1985, but it wasn't a lost year. Chiro Cangiano, the owner of the Puerto Rican League's Ponce Lions, phoned him in September to offer him a spot on the Lions' pitching staff in the 1985–86 winter league season. Cangiano remembered Candiotti's two victories with Mayagüez against Ponce in the Puerto Rican League finals two years earlier, and wanted him on the Lions this time around. Candiotti accepted the offer, and headed to Puerto Rico after the major league season. While with Ponce, he led the league with 53 strikeouts and threw his knuckleball for strikes consistently.

It was there in Puerto Rico where his knuckler got noticed. Orlando Gomez, one of the Ponce coaches and also a minor league manager in the Cleveland organization, saw Candiotti throw the knuckleball and was so impressed that he phoned Joe Klein, the Indians' vice president of operations and general manager. Gomez persuaded Klein to head to Puerto Rico to watch Candiotti pitch, and the rest, as they say, is history.

On December 12, 1985, Cleveland signed Candiotti as a minor league free agent and invited him to spring training as a non-roster player with the understanding that he'd use the knuckleball to try and make the club. The Indians, losers of 102 games in 1985 and having traded away quality starters like Bert Blyleven, Rick Sutcliffe, and John Denny in recent years, were desperate for any kind of pitching after compiling a major league-worst 4.91 ERA. Even a guy like Candiotti, who'd won just six career games and was now throwing a knuckleball. "We think he can win for us," Klein said two months later at the Indians' spring camp in Tucson.[17]

To this day, Klein still smiles when thinking back to Gomez's insistence that he take a chance on Candiotti. "What happened was Orlando Gomez set up a bullpen [session] for us with Tom," Klein recalls from his office in Camden, New Jersey, where he's currently the executive director of the Atlantic League. "When I saw Tom throw the bullpen, I saw potential with the knuckleball. Part of my history is I had [knuckleballer] Charlie Hough in Texas, when I was director of player personnel for the Rangers. Charlie really had his best big league production when he was with the Rangers, and from what I saw from Tom, I really thought there was potential with Candy and his knuckleball."

Candiotti knew then he had to throw the knuckler as one of his main pitches in order to return to the majors. "Without the knuckleball, I would've been always on the bubble, a pitcher who was the sixth starter of a five-man rotation," Candiotti reflects. "But the knuckler really helped me become a number one or two starter in my best seasons."

# 5

# *Revival in Cleveland*

In the winter of 1985, there was no way to predict how Candiotti's career would have turned out even with the knuckleball. His major league resume included just six wins, a 3.99 ERA, and 88 innings. He'd gone through a series of stints on the disabled list, elbow and shoulder problems, and the Tommy John elbow reconstruction surgery. Then during the spring of 1985, Milwaukee informed him he needed to develop the knuckleball in the minor leagues to continue in the organization.

Candiotti worked on the knuckler in Triple-A Vancouver, but the Brewers were not interested in keeping him after the 1985 season. Cleveland, though, was impressed enough with how his knuckleball moved in winter ball, and the Indians offered Candiotti a contract in December.

Out of around 300 pitchers in the majors in 1985, only Charlie Hough, Phil Niekro, and Joe Niekro threw the knuckleball. Not only did Candiotti become the fourth practitioner of the knuckleball in 1986, he also emerged as Cleveland's top pitcher while leading the team in wins, ERA, starts, complete games, shutouts, innings, and strikeouts. Candiotti attributes that success to two factors. "I threw the knuckler 95 percent of the time in Vancouver," he says. "I had to throw the knuckleball in every situation, and it got better as the season went on. I had a better feel for it. Then when I signed with Cleveland, the Indians also brought in Phil Niekro to help me out, which really helped with my development with the knuckler."

While it looks easy to throw a knuckleball, in reality, it isn't. Candiotti had always thrown the knuckler just for fun, having picked it up while playing catch with his father as a kid. He also threw it once in a while in a game to surprise a hitter. And to fans watching from the stands—many of whom would jeer when the hitter swung and missed on a knuckler—it looked like the easiest pitch in the world to throw. Throwing it on the sidelines as a mess-around pitch is different than throwing it consistently on a major league mound. Throwing it under 10 percent of the time in a game is different from using it as a primary pitch. "A lot of guys can throw it for fun," explains Candiotti. "But to go out there and throw it to a hitter, with a catcher trying to catch it and an umpire trying to call it, and 50,000 people watching you, is different. It's not a pitch that anybody can go out there and start throwing."

Candiotti made it look easy as he became the Indians' best pitcher overnight. No one could have foreseen that type of success in the spring, especially when opposing coaches rolled their eyes when rumors surfaced he was actually going to make the team. And he went from a pitcher that no other team wanted, a 28-year-old who'd already been given up by the Kansas City and Milwaukee organizations, a guy who was asked to retire and become a pitching coach, to a staff ace in Cleveland.

Unlike baseball executives from other clubs, general manager Joe Klein had a different view when he saw Candiotti throw his bullpen session for the Indians. "What we saw in the bullpen made him a high-priority pitcher for us," recalls Klein. "We didn't think anybody else knew about him, that he might be coming up with the knuckleball, despite clubs going down there and watching games in Puerto Rico."

Klein saw enough potential in Candiotti to want him in Cleveland, and instructed Dan O'Brien, the club's business manager, to get a deal done. Recalls Klein, "When I talked to Dan O'Brien about it—Dan signed a lot of the players on the Indians—I said, 'I don't care how you do it, but make sure that we get him.' So Dan went to Candiotti and his agent with a progressive minor league contract that would pay him something like $3,000 a month in Triple-A in April, $4,000 in May, $5,000 in June, $6,000 in July, and so on. They said, 'Why do you want to do that?' Dan's answer was, 'Because we think by May, you're going to be in the big leagues.' So that got Candiotti and his agent's attention. From day one, we wanted Candy to mix his curveball in, but we wanted him to throw his knuckleball."

As it turned out, Candiotti was ahead of schedule. He made the Indians' big league club out of spring training and began the season in the majors. "There were other teams that talked to me," recalls Candiotti. "But all of them wanted me to begin the year in the minors and then call me up if I pitched well. With the Indians, however, they told me I had a chance to win a big league job if I pitched well in the spring."

With Milwaukee, Candiotti had worn uniform number 49. Now with Cleveland, he again wore 49. Texas knuckleballer Charlie Hough wore that same number, and major league knuckleballers traditionally have worn 49. But

Candiotti had made it to the majors *without* the knuckleball, so why that number? When he pitched in the 1991 AL playoffs, a field reporter for the CBS broadcast told the television viewers that Candiotti wore 49 because of his love for the San Francisco 49ers football team.[1]

But that wasn't the actual reason. "I was with the Brewers in 1983 and they just gave me number 49," says Candiotti. "I don't remember ever wearing another number. Then I went to camp with Cleveland in 1986, and there must have been someone on the team that was number 49 because my number was 62 in the spring. And then either the guy didn't make the team or he was released—I don't even know—but when I made the Opening Day roster, number 49 was in my locker. So I've always had 49 everywhere I went. It wasn't because of the 49ers. It was because that's what was given to me. And once you have a number, it's like, 'Okay, sure, I'll keep my number.'"

Luckily, veteran knuckleballer Phil Niekro, who was signed by Cleveland before the 1986 season following his release from the Yankees, had always worn number 35 throughout his career. When Niekro got to Cleveland, he also wore number 35. "Knucksie was a great mentor for him," remembers Joe Klein. "They'd always talk to each other about the knuckleball." Klein recalls sitting in the dugout watching and eavesdropping on Candiotti and Niekro discuss how they gripped the ball.

"This is how I hold my knuckleball," said the pupil while showing off his grip. "How do you hold yours?" The pupil was holding the ball with his right thumb on the bottom of the ball while his index and middle fingernails gripped the ball on top. "I don't want to show you mine," replied the mentor, "because it might mess you up."

"That," says Klein, "is how individual that pitch is."

Candiotti acknowledges that he and Niekro didn't throw the knuckler the same way. "Phil was more of a pusher when it came to throwing the knuckleball," says Candiotti. "I didn't push, I let it go, and I found that the knuckleball worked best when I threw it hard. For a knuckleball pitcher, you want to take the spin off the ball. It was easier for me to take the spin off when I threw hard."

For Candiotti, it was an adjustment year. Throwing the knuckleball meant he had to go through a different set of routines during his off-days. He had to, for instance, cut his nails a certain length to make sure he could grip the ball effectively. "I had to keep my nails long enough," he says, "so that they could dig into the ball, but not too long to have them bend back and break. There were other things like timing, positioning of the hands and fingers, and shifting [of] body weight." With the knuckleball, Candiotti also saw a lot of strange things. "Wild pitches for strike threes, passed balls, a lot of walks, and all that," he continues. "It was frustrating because the ball would go all over the place."

Fortunately, Niekro was there to mentor him. "Having him sitting down with me in Cleveland teaching me the knuckleball was a great learning experience for me," adds Candiotti. "Here I was, trying to make the knuckler my main pitch, and I had Phil around. It was like talking to Thomas Edison about lightbulbs and electricity. He really accelerated my learning process with that pitch."

Doc Edwards, who was Cleveland's bullpen coach in 1986, says the signing of Niekro was huge in the development of Candiotti. "That was a great advantage for Candy," says Edwards. "It really worked out well, because Candy had a master of the knuckleball to be his mentor." But even before the Indians signed Niekro on April 3, Candiotti was doing well in the spring with his own knuckleball. Against San Diego in mid–March, for instance, he tossed four shutout innings, allowing three hits and only one walk with five strikeouts. "I gave up something like four earned runs in 20 innings that spring," Candiotti recalls. "I struck out a dozen batters—and 10 of them came on the knuckleball—and I walked just two guys."

The game that impressed Klein the most came on March 19, when Candiotti threw five shutout innings with five strikeouts and no walks against Milwaukee in Tucson.[2] "I remember I was sitting with [Brewers executives] Sal Bando and Harry Dalton," Klein recalls. "They couldn't wait to know who was pitching for us. They said, 'Who's your pitcher?' I said, 'Candiotti.' A couple of hours later, we'd beaten them and Candy had pitched great. When I left, those two guys were talking to each other, like, 'Why didn't we do something with him? Why didn't we stick with him?' That's when I saw the other people shaking their heads. I just happened to run by [Brewers players Paul] Molitor and [Robin] Yount, and they said, 'This guy's not a flash in the pan, Joe. I know he's [almost] 30 years old, but he's going to be able to handle it.'"

Candiotti, who was throwing as much as 80 percent knuckleballs during that spring, also impressed manager Pat Corrales. "He's moved to the head of the class," Corrales said, referring to Candiotti's streak of 16 scoreless innings late in the spring.[3] The performance against Milwaukee went a long way to Candiotti securing a rotation spot to begin the season, according to Klein. "We were going to have him in Triple-A at first," Klein says. "But Tom went out and pitched a game like that, it was like, 'Wow.' I thought he'd be up in the big leagues by summer time—and that was why we gave him that progressive Triple-A contract." The Indians, however, knew they simply couldn't send Candiotti down, not when he could pitch in Cleveland right away.

Candiotti made his Indians regular-season debut in Cleveland's third game of the year at Baltimore's Memorial Stadium on April 10, allowing three hits over six innings with five strikeouts. The only run off him came in the fifth when he threw a high fastball to Rick Dempsey, who promptly homered to tie the game 1–1.[4] The Orioles won, 5–1, scoring four runs off the Indians' bullpen. "That was the first time where I was using the knuckler as my main pitch in a major league game," Candiotti adds. "It was a cold and windy night in Baltimore, and the wind made the knuckler move a lot. I threw my slowest knuckleball 45 mph, and you could see from the frustration of the hitters. When I struck out Eddie Murray and Cal Ripken—two future Hall of Famers in their lineup—I knew that if I threw the knuckler over the plate, nobody was going to hit it. Before that, I wasn't really sure that pitch would work against major league hitters. But I knew I had something when I threw it against Murray. He took three swings that weren't even close, so it was like, 'Wow, even a great hitter like Murray misses this pitch.' It was a great confidence booster."

That knuckleball was almost unhittable on April 21, when Candiotti blanked Baltimore, 7–0, on a three-hitter with 10 strikeouts—his second career major league shutout—on a cold, rainy night in Cleveland. Orioles shortstop Cal Ripken, Jr., who'd averaged 27 homers and 98 RBIs the past four seasons, had the key at-bat in the fifth but struck out with the bases loaded and Baltimore trailing, 3–0. "It seems like he mixes pitches more so than other knuckleball pitchers," said Ripken, acknowledging his teammates were baffled by Candiotti's assortment of pitches that night. "He throws a knuckleball that the Niekros and Charlie Hough would be proud of."[5]

It was an adjustment for Candiotti throwing the knuckler on more of a full-time basis. "When that season began," he says, "I was throwing maybe 50 percent knuckleballs. Before, I threw just 10–15 in a game. It became tough because I hated walking hitters. But with the knuckleball, there were days when it was moving so much that you couldn't throw it over the plate. Then when you got behind in the count, you didn't want to walk the hitter, so you came in with your other stuff. By the end of the year, though, I was throwing a lot more knuckleballs. And before I threw the knuckleball, I was probably averaging two walks every nine innings. Once I started using it, I was walking maybe four, five guys per game. Pat Corrales, the manager, said he didn't care if I walked guys. He just wanted me to throw the knuckleball because nobody could hit it."

Even if Candiotti threw strikes, it didn't necessarily mean he would be successful. He still needed a catcher who could catch the knuckleball. On April 25 at Yankee Stadium, for instance, Candiotti threw three straight knuckleballs to start the game that both leadoff hitter Rickey Henderson and catcher Andy Allanson flailed at in vain. Henderson struck out but reached base when the third strike eluded Allanson and went to the backstop. Candiotti blames himself, not Allanson. "I used to throw these super-nasty knuckleballs that nobody was ever going to hit," he recalls. "Unfortunately, when I threw it, the ball would always go to the backstop because the catcher couldn't catch it either. Phil Niekro sat me down and told me that I had to throw a knuckleball that the hitter would try to hit, the catcher could catch, and the umpire could call. But when I first started, I tried to throw it so that nobody could hit it and nobody could catch it. That was no good."

Candiotti was especially good when he pitched against his former club. On May 21, he pitched in Milwaukee for the first time since leaving the Brewers. He'd faced them in the spring—tossing five shutout innings in Tucson in an Indians' victory—but this was the real thing. Though Milwaukee scored two runs in the first two innings, Candiotti settled down as he mixed in his curveball with the knuckler and retired 22 of the final 23 batters—getting 11 on groundball outs in that stretch—in going the distance. Cleveland scored four runs off rookie Bill Wegman (who matched Candiotti with five shutout innings in that spring game in Tucson) and won, 4–2.

Ironically, Wegman was one of the heralded pitchers the Brewers thought highly of and a reason Candiotti was no longer in Milwaukee. Both pitched in Vancouver in 1985 and posted very similar numbers: Candiotti was 9–13 with a 3.94 ERA; Wegman 10–11 and 4.02. But Wegman was also five years younger and had more of an upside, the Brewers decided. Two months into the 1986 season, though, Wegman was 0–4 with a 5.07 ERA in nine starts while Candiotti already had three complete-game victories with a 3.33 ERA.

As Brewers second baseman Jim Gantner noted, Candiotti "has got a great knuckler," adding those knuckleballs could make hitters look foolish. "He's the type of guy [that] can make you look bad swinging," Gantner said. "If he gets that knuckleball over, he's tough. The last few innings, they were really dropping."[6] Charlie Moore, meanwhile, thought it was Candiotti's curveball that set up his knuckler so well. "He put the curveball over any time he wanted to. I think he threw the curveball more than the knuckler," the Brewers' catcher said. "It kept us off balance. I couldn't hit most of them with a boat paddle."[7] Said Phil Niekro that day about Candiotti's outing: "It was outstanding. It was fun to watch. I was really enjoying it."[8]

Candiotti was tough even when he had to change the way he gripped the ball. On June 19, he defeated Seattle, 8–1, with a complete-game five-hitter with nine strikeouts, losing his shutout in the eighth when Bob Kearney homered on a 3-and–1 fastball. The performance was surprising, because just before the game he'd split a fingernail while warming up in the bullpen. Candiotti had to retreat to the clubhouse to cut the nail off and apply some hardener on it. When the game began, Candiotti used the tip of his index finger to hold the ball instead of gripping it with his fingernails. "When you throw a knuckler, you stick your nails and fingertips into the ball," he explains. "A broken nail for me is like a normal pitcher having tendinitis."

On June 30, Candiotti made a triumphant return to Oakland Coliseum—the A's ballpark was about 20 miles from Concord, where he grew up—by defeating the Athletics, 8–3. It would be the beginning of an eight-week stretch where Candiotti was virtually unbeatable, as he went 8–3 in 12 starts with a 3.17 ERA from June 30 to August 29. He remembers his battle with A's third baseman Carney Lansford, who went 1-for-4. "I played against Carney in Little League in 1969," Candiotti recalls. "On my team I was the best pitcher and I played shortstop. The team that beat us in the tournament, Santa Clara, had a pretty good pitcher: Carney Lansford. Carney was the one who beat us, and they then went on to play in the Little League World Series that year.

"Carney got to the big leagues before I did. When I finally made it, he was with the A's. I remember coming into Oakland, and somebody did a story about how ironic it was that in Little League, Carney was his team's best pitcher while I was the best shortstop and hitter. But here we were in 1986, and Carney was Oakland's best hitter [he'd finish second on the A's with a .284 average] and I was Cleveland's best pitcher."

Politician Guy S. Houston, a former teammate of Candiotti's at St. Mary's, remembers the knuckleballer's friends and family were all there for him in his Bay Area return. "When he was with the Indians and he came back to Oakland to pitch, people went to the game to see him," recalls Houston. "Everybody was rooting and cheering for Tom. When you saw him, he was very humble. When he saw you, he recognized you. He appreciated all the guys at St. Mary's. Tom was a great pitcher at St. Mary's, and he did well when he got to the big leagues. He was somebody that everybody wanted to succeed."

Early on in 1986, whether or not he would succeed was a big question. Sure, Candiotti looked great against Baltimore and Milwaukee but was awful against the Yankees. That eight-week run, beginning on June 30 in Oakland, though, improved his record to 13–9 with a 3.63 ERA entering September. Candiotti should have been an AL All-Star that year, says general manager Joe Klein. "We recommended to the league that they take him," Klein recalls. "We said, 'If you take a pitcher, take Candiotti.' Candy quickly became the ace of the Cleveland pitching staff, and deserved to be an All-Star." Alas, the league didn't take Klein's suggestion. The Indians' All-Star representatives were third baseman Brook Jacoby and pitcher Ken Schrom (10–2, 4.17 ERA at the break).

Despite the All-Star snub, Candiotti still won plenty of games in the second half. So much so that newspaper scribes were talking about the fact that his 12th victory on August 18 against Milwaukee put him ahead of Niekro's pace at the start of his career. Niekro, with 309 victories by then and pitching in his 23rd season, had begun his career with a 6–6 record through his first three years, from 1964 to 1966. As a 28-year-old in 1967, Niekro went 11–9 for a 17–15 career mark before his 29th birthday. Candiotti, meanwhile, was also 6–6 as of his 28th birthday in 1985. With a 13–9 record in August of 1986, Candiotti was already 19–15 before reaching 29 years of age. "Tom is just starting to scratch the surface as a pitcher," said Niekro. "He has some advantages over me at the same period. He has a team that believes in him, two guys in Chris Bando and Andy Allanson who can catch him. He couldn't be in a better situation."[9]

Tribe rooters thought they couldn't be in a better situation with the emergence of Candiotti and the hitting of Joe Carter, Pat Tabler, and Cory Snyder. And could it be? For a few months in 1986, Cleveland was relevant in the pennant race. People were excited about Indians baseball once again, something that hadn't been seen for nearly 30 years as the Tribe had not won a pennant since 1954. In 1985, the Indians drew 655,181 fans. With an exciting ballclub in 1986, that total soared to 1,471,805, the most in Cleveland since 1959.

With the decades of losing—Cleveland had won just three pennants and two World Series titles even though it was one of the American League's eight charter franchises when the league was founded in 1901—fans had come to expect that the Indians would fall out of contention early every year. But many were ready to embrace the 1986 Indians, who gave everyone hope that they were ready to win. "It's been discouraging, no question about that," said Clevelander Morton Klein, an Indians supporter for nearly 60 years. "But you become complacent and you don't expect them to win the pennant. I don't. It's discouraging, but we've gotten so we don't expect anything anymore. We go crazy if in July the team is still in contention."[10]

But when the '86 team was contending, fans finally came out to the ballpark, just as a different generation of fans had done 40 years earlier when the club was relevant. In the Indians' World Series-winning 1948 season, they set a major league record for the highest single-season attendance with 2,620,627.[11] They then drew 2,233,771 fans the following year. For the first half of the 1950s, when the Indians were competitive, they were one of baseball's top drawing teams, averaging more than 1,456,000 per year. Things changed later that decade, however, when Cleveland had the AL's second-worst attendance for three consecutive seasons, from 1956 to 1958. In the 1960s, the Indians became perennial losers, finishing over .500 only twice in the decade, and never once reached the 1,000,000 mark in attendance, averaging only 758,750 fans and having the league's worst and second-worst attendance four times. In the 1970s, Cleveland finished below .500 eight times, and was also in the bottom third in league attendance nine times.

"We came within $25,000 to $50,000 of breaking even for the whole year," general manager Joe Klein says of the success at the gate in 1986. "Cleveland had lost money, basically, all through the 1950s. After the 1954 World Series, it was quite a downtime in Cleveland. The team just lost money." But the sudden rejuvenation of the Indians made fans flock to the ballpark for the first time in decades. "We got recognized by major league baseball that year," Klein continues. "They gave us a bonus of some sort to show the Indians made a profit in 1986."

For Klein, the most memorable 1986 moment came on August 1, when 64,934 fans packed Cleveland Stadium for a doubleheader against the Yankees—the largest crowd ever for a twi-night doubleheader in Indians history.[12] "We just came from nowhere and actually made a run," Klein says. "[That] August night, we ended up with a walk-up crowd of 50,000 in a twi-night doubleheader against the Yankees. It was one of my more incredible nights in baseball. That was the definitely the high point in the old ballpark in Cleveland until [1994 when] they got the new ballpark [Jacobs Field]." On August 2, the Indians defeated the Yankees, 6–5, closing to within five-and-a-half games back of first-place Boston. Unfortunately, they'd then lose their next five contests to fall out of contention.

Still, Cleveland would finish a respectable 84–78, rebounding from its 102-loss debacle from a year earlier.

While Candiotti was only 3–6 in early June, he won 10 of his next 15 starts to build his record to 13–9 going into September. During the course of the season, Candiotti notched victories over future Hall of Famers Bert Blyleven and Tom Seaver, as well as such tough opposing starters as Frank Viola, Mike Boddicker, Jose Rijo, Mike Flanagan, Dennis Leonard, and Mike Moore. "The Indians gave me a chance to start every fifth day, and the more I threw the knuckleball throughout the season, I suddenly gained more confidence in the pitch," Candiotti says in explaining the reason for his success in the latter half of the 1986 campaign. "That season was supposed to be a learning experience, but all of a sudden, halfway through the season it wasn't a learning experience at all. I was expected to win ballgames, and I realized that the knuckleball was the best pitch in baseball if I threw it over the plate. You throw your best knuckleball, and nobody's going to hit it."

After winning only once out of five starts in September, Candiotti got his 15th victory—and 16th complete game—on October 1 in Minnesota by tossing an eight-hitter with no walks in Cleveland's 12–3 win. He also entered the Indians' record books by striking out a career-high 12 batters, which was a rare feat in the annals of Cleveland pitching. From 1970 up to 1986, Sam McDowell, Steve Dunning, Gaylord Perry, Dennis Eckersley, Len Barker, and Bert Blyleven were the only Indians pitchers with 12 or more whiffs in a game.[13]

Candiotti even became the first Tribe pitcher since 1976 to have a 12-strikeout, zero-walk game—just the ninth time since 1916 that the feat had been accomplished by a Cleveland hurler. "We quickly found in Cleveland that his control of his breaking ball, when he was behind in the count, was so good that he could throw a curveball for a strike," says Joe Klein, noting he wasn't surprised at the number of low-walk, high-strikeout games Candiotti threw. "He'd never give them a fastball when he was behind in the count two balls and no strikes. He learned very quickly how to get hitters out, whether it was with his curveball or his knuckleball.

"I can't tell you the number of called strike threes he got, because it was big every game. It was always in situations where there were runners on the bases and he'd get a called third strike. Sometimes it was a 65-mph knuckleball, 72-mph curveball ... and all of a sudden he'd throw an 88-mph fastball in on a hitter and he'd get a strikeout also. Whatever he threw, he'd get a strikeout in a big situation."

Candiotti thought his season was done after his 15th victory, as Cleveland had only three games remaining and he wasn't scheduled to make another appearance. Pat Corrales, however, approached him in the clubhouse before the season finale against Seattle and asked him to pitch. "It was the final day of the season," Candiotti recalls. "We weren't going to the playoffs. The biggest thing on everyone's minds was when the bus to the airport was leaving. I was just going to spend the day in the dugout watching the game. But Corrales said, 'Candy, you're pitching today. And you're going to finish the game, no matter what.'"

When Candiotti hesitated upon hearing the news, Corrales said, "C'mon, why not? It's a chance for you to get another win, and get another complete game!" The knuckleball pitcher reluctantly answered, "Okay, if you really need me to pitch, I'll go out there." Candiotti figured that Corrales wanted him to win the AL complete games title. Entering the season finale, he was tied with Minnesota's Bert Blyleven (who pitched for Cleveland from 1981 to 1985) with 16 complete games, tops in the league.

"Bert wasn't going to pitch on the last day of the season," says Candiotti years later. "I wasn't supposed to either, but Corrales perhaps wanted me to win the complete games championship. It wouldn't have mattered if I gave up 10 runs. He would've left me in the game just so I could finish ahead of Blyleven."[14] Candiotti went the distance in winning, 4–2, his second straight start without allowing a walk, and won the complete games title. With 17 of them, Candiotti even recorded more complete games than seven entire major league clubs in 1986. By going beyond the sixth inning on that final day, Candiotti also entered the Indians' record books. From June 13 to October 5, he pitched at least six innings for 22 consecutive starts, the longest such streak in Tribe history since Wayne Garland's 28-game run in 1977–78, according to Baseball-Reference.com. In 1995, Cleveland's Dennis Martinez would match Candiotti's streak, but no pitcher has since surpassed it in an Indians uniform.

As Candiotti admits, that 17th complete game felt just like an exhibition contest. "I got to the ballpark and I was all packed up and ready to go home," he says. "It'd been a long season, and I was just going to watch the game and get out of there as soon as it was finished. But an hour before the first pitch, Corrales told me I was starting. And it turned out to be a quick game. Two hours later, it was over. I think everyone just swung at the first pitch because they wanted to get it over with."

# 6

## *Success in the Big Leagues*

Candiotti finished 16–12 in 1986, but the victories he remembers most are those against Milwaukee. "I really wanted to beat the Brewers whenever I pitched against them," says Candiotti. "It wasn't because of the organization, but it was because of one person. Sure, the Brewers told me I wasn't good enough to pitch in the majors. The organization felt I was expendable because of the other young pitchers they had coming up. But I understood that and I respected that. After all, the Brewers' organization took care of me and I was okay with that.

"But then there was a coach for the Brewers by the name of Andy Etchebarren."

Etchebarren, a former catcher with Baltimore, California, and Milwaukee, had caught Hall of Famers Jim Palmer and Nolan Ryan during his 15 big league seasons. He had the distinction of being the last man to ever bat against Sandy Koufax in the majors when he hit into a double play to end the sixth inning in Game Two of the 1966 World Series. Etchebarren had become a coach after his playing career, first as the Brewers' minor league catching instructor from 1982 to 1984 before being promoted to their big league club as first base coach in 1985. A two-time All-Star with Baltimore early in his career, Etchebarren was never much of a hitter—owning a .235 batting average in 2,618 at-bats—but he knew all about pitchers. In Etchebarren's mind, Candiotti wasn't a good one. The ex-catcher had seen enough of him during their time together in the Brewers' organization, and knew why the team didn't want him back.

Etchebarren was still coaching first base for Milwaukee in 1986 when the Indians traveled to Chandler, Arizona, for a spring training game in late March with the regular season slated to begin in a few days. The coach had a front-row seat as Candiotti started that game. Cleveland led, 3–1, through four innings, but everything unraveled in the fifth. Pitching with cracked fingernails, Candiotti hit a batter and gave up two walks and two stolen bases as the Brewers scored five runs in that fifth inning en route to a victory that afternoon.

"I'd pitched well in spring training and was going to be the number three starter for the Indians," recalls Candiotti years later. "But that day against Milwaukee, I broke my fingernails. I didn't know what to do because it was the first time that I'd cracked a nail during a game. I figured it was because of the dry weather in Arizona that caused my nails to break. The Brewers scored a few runs and I had to come out because of my nails. For a pitcher throwing a knuckleball, your fingernails are crucial because you have to dig your nails into the ball. And when I couldn't throw the knuckler, I really struggled out there."

Candiotti had thrown five shutout innings against Milwaukee less than two weeks earlier in Tucson but was ineffective after breaking his fingernails in the rematch in Chandler that particular afternoon. With the Brewers having their way against him in that game, Etchebarren figured it was time to take some shots at him. Says Candiotti, "During that game, Etchebarren was yelling at Bobby Bonds, the Indians' first base coach, 'If he's one of the starters in the Indians' rotation, then you really have a bad team!'"

When Bonds told him what Etchebarren had said, Candiotti became furious. "That a coach would actually say that about a player out there," Candiotti says, "I thought was a lousy thing for anyone to say. So when I had a chance to pitch against the Brewers, I turned it up not a notch, but I turned it up 10 notches. I always took it a little personal. It wasn't because of the organization. I loved the Brewers. I really liked Harry Dalton, the general manager; he was really great. Bud Selig, the owner at the time I was there, was great. So I never had any hard feelings towards the organization. It was only because of Andy Etchebarren, who told Bobby Bonds about my ability. Put it this way: it made it special for me when I did beat the Brewers."

That season, Candiotti was always motivated when facing Milwaukee, a ballclub with good hitters like Paul Molitor, Robin Yount, and Jim Gantner. In three starts, Candiotti was 2–0 with a 3.38 ERA, fanning 18 with eight walks over 24 innings, and tossing two complete games. (Beating Milwaukee during that era wasn't easy. Knuckleballer Charlie Hough had a stretch from 1982 to 1989 where he was 0–9 with an 8.21 ERA in 13 starts versus the Brewers. For his career, Hough would be 2–12 with a 6.10 ERA against them, walking 60 and striking out 61 in 121 innings. At County Stadium, the numbers would be 1–7 and 5.85.)

Another memorable outing in Milwaukee came on August 24, 1988, one week before Candiotti's 31st birthday. Despite battling a sore throat and cough, the knuckleballer insisted on making his scheduled start and allowed one earned run over six innings in Cleveland's 7–2 victory. "Candiotti's had the real hard flu the past few days," manager Doc Edwards noted afterward. "We were lucky to get six innings out of him today, to be honest."[1] Candiotti, who also struck out Brewers number two hitter Jeffrey Leonard three times, reached double digits in victories for the second time in three years with the win.

One other game against his old team that stood out came on August 2, 1989, when he had just come off the disabled list a few weeks earlier and was pitching in Milwaukee. Because his arm was well rested—and because he was facing the Brewers—Candiotti threw plenty of fastballs over eight innings in a 1–0 victory over Chris Bosio. No Brewer got a hit in the first four innings, and all six hits off Candiotti were singles. "I took harder stuff to the mound today than usual," Candiotti said that afternoon, when his fastest pitch was clocked at 80 mph. "They know my best pitch is the curve. They were all looking for curveballs today, so I had to vary my pitching around."[2]

Milwaukee loaded the bases with one out in the sixth, and that was when Candiotti used the fastball to set up the curveball to record the game's biggest out. With the count 2-and-2, Glenn Braggs was probably looking for the knuckler or curveball—but Candiotti threw a waste pitch, a fastball up and in for ball three. With the count full, Braggs was lost. What was coming next? Fastball? Knuckleball? Instead, Braggs swung and missed on a curveball for the second out, and Candiotti went on to record his second 1–0 victory in 12 days. "We've been a good knuckleball-hitting team in the past," said Braggs. "He had us off balance all day. He kept us looking for it but he never really threw it."[3] (According to the *Wisconsin State Journal* in 1989, Milwaukee had a reputation as a team that hit knuckleballers well. The starting lineup that afternoon had a .328 lifetime batting average against Candiotti going in, led by Robin Yount's .389 and Paul Molitor's .345.[4])

How many knuckleballs did Braggs actually see? "He didn't throw me one knuckleball all day," Braggs said of Candiotti. "It surprised me. I know he has a lot of different pitches, but by my third time up I was thinking to myself, 'Geez, this guy hasn't thrown me one knuckleball yet.'"[5] According to the pitching chart kept by Milwaukee, Candiotti's curveball was clocked between 52 and 56 mph that day, and the odd slow knucklers that he did throw averaged 64 mph.[6] It was another one of his ways of getting back at the Brewers, letting the organization know that velocity wasn't everything and that he shouldn't have been let go. "I remember that game even though it was a long time ago," recalls Edwards years later. "Candy just had all of his pitches working. He gave us a really big lift because we were in a pennant race at the time."

On May 12, 1988, at County Stadium, Candiotti threw 146 pitches in

Cleveland's 3–1 victory. While Juan Nieves—one of the pitching prospects the Brewers kept in favor of him—allowed only three hits, Candiotti was tattooed for five doubles and 10 hits. Though Milwaukee had runners in scoring position in seven separate innings, Candiotti allowed just one run to lead the Indians to the win. "In the ninth, they put the leadoff guy on second base," he recalls. "Even though I'd thrown over 130 pitches by then, Doc Edwards still let me continue. With two outs, I got Paul Molitor to strike out looking to end it. He might've been looking for a knuckleball but I threw a fastball and it just froze him."

"Candy wasn't afraid to throw his fastball," recalls Edwards. "There were a lot of times those hitters just froze because they weren't expecting to see his fastball. But Candy could throw it for a strike all the time, and the umpire was calling a lot of his pitches [28 of them in that 1988 game] for strikes. When he threw that final one, Molitor didn't even swing because he was looking for the knuckleball. It just seemed Candy threw a lot of strikes with all his pitches whenever he needed them."

Molitor might have made a gaffe in looking for the wrong pitch, but as ESPN's *SportsNation* noted in 2006, Milwaukee made a mistake in letting Candiotti go, listing that particular decision as one of the top five biggest blunders in franchise history.[7] From the Brewers' point of view, it was particularly ironic when Candiotti would return to County Stadium and routinely outpitch the youngsters the club kept ahead of him—like Bill Wegman, Chris Bosio, and Juan Nieves—and doing it with curveballs and fastballs, no less.

As knuckleballer Charlie Hough once admitted, it was normal for Milwaukee to want to keep those young pitchers, regardless of how good or bad they were. Not that he agreed with it, but that's the reality in baseball. "It took me 12 years to start," Hough said about his own experience with the Dodgers. "There were guys given shots ahead of me who weren't nearly as good. A knuckleball pitcher in the minor leagues has to win, where a guy with a good arm has to show that he has a good arm."[8]

The 1986 Cleveland Indians led the majors in batting (.284) and runs scored (831), and were first in the AL in steals (141). The pitching staff was a different story, despite Tom Candiotti's 16 wins and 3.57 ERA, as Cleveland finished with the third-worst ERA in the league at 4.58. Rookie Scott Bailes had 10 wins and seven saves but compiled a 4.95 ERA. Closer Ernie Camacho, making a comeback from elbow problems, recorded 20 saves but blew 10 other opportunities and had a 4.08 ERA. (The bullpen blew five of Candiotti's leads in the late innings—3–2, 4–3, 6–3, 7–6, and 4–1—including three by Camacho.) Every reliever had an ERA over 4.00 except 29-year-old rookie Doug Jones, a September call-up.

Sometimes manager Pat Corrales just didn't have much confidence in the bullpen. On July 27 in Texas, Candiotti led, 8–2, in the seventh inning but had trouble getting the third out. Corrales marched out of the dugout for a conference on the mound. "Look, you're not coming out of this game," the skipper said, pointing to the bullpen area. "See who's warming up right now? I'm not bringing that son of a bitch in because he's gonna screw this game up. You're pitching out of this yourself." With that, Corrales turned around and returned to the dugout. Candiotti retired the next hitter on a pop-up, and Cleveland went on to win the game.

Candiotti led the AL in complete games and also finished in the top 10 in ERA (3.57), wins (16), innings (252.1), starts (34), and shutouts (three). "Who knew the knuckleball would've worked out so well?" Candiotti reflects. He laughs when thinking back to his confrontation with Gene Lamont, his manager in Double-A Jacksonville, who warned him not to throw the knuckler. "That turned out to be a really smart decision, didn't it? Pretty intelligent, wasn't it?" Another intelligent decision was Milwaukee letting Candiotti go. Juan Nieves (11–12, 4.92), Bill Wegman (5–12, 5.13), and Chris Bosio (0–4, 7.01), three young pitchers that the team kept and had high hopes for, combined to win the same number of games that Candiotti did.

From 1986 to 1993, Candiotti would use that knuckleball to average 32 starts, 220 innings, and 143 strikeouts a year, to go along with a 3.38 ERA—numbers fitting for a number one or two starter. Three times—in

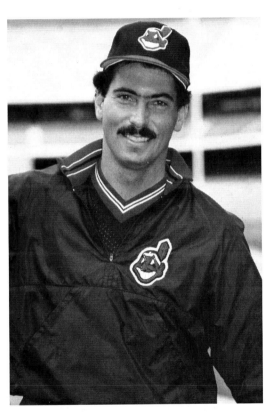

Candiotti had reason to be happy in 1986. That season with Cleveland, he threw the knuckleball on a full-time basis and led the American League with 17 complete games while notching a career-high 16 victories. The Indians' best pitcher in 1986, Candiotti also finished in the top 10 in the league in ERA, wins, innings pitched, games started, and shutouts (National Baseball Hall of Fame Library, Cooperstown, New York).

1987, 1988, and 1990—he'd be picked to start on Opening Day (although the 1990 opener didn't count as an official game because it was called due to poor weather after only four innings, with all the stats from that contest wiped out). Entering the 1986 season, though, many baseball people snickered at Cleveland's signing of a pitcher who had a 6–6 career record. Milwaukee thought Candiotti couldn't succeed, and first base coach Andy Etchebarren echoed that sentiment during spring training, questioning his ability during a game in which he was struggling. "I always told myself that I could do it," reflects Candiotti. "When you hear people questioning your ability, you don't forget. You want to show those guys they're wrong about you."

Candiotti recalls a story from his rookie year in 1983, when California second baseman Bobby Grich ripped him to reporters after he'd shut the Angels out, 7–0. Says Candiotti: "The next day, it came out in the papers that Bobby Grich was quoted as saying something like, 'You'll probably never see this guy again. That was the worst stuff I've ever seen in the league.' It was funny for a guy to make this remark, especially since his team had just gotten shut out." (Grich's exact quote, according to newspaper accounts, was: "I was not impressed with his pitching. He shut us out but we were just not swinging well. His pitching is not something to be impressed with."[9] To which Brewers catcher Ned Yost responded, "Candiotti had great stuff. He was throwing his curve and slider for strikes all day and he had a great cutting fastball. He really knows how to spot the ball."[10])

Brewers veteran pitcher Pete Vuckovich, who saw those comments in print, made sure the young Candiotti never forgot about what was said. In the locker room, Vuckovich asked him, "Hey, did you read the paper today?" Candiotti answered, "Yeah." Vuckovich held the paper in his hand, and said, "Did you read THIS?" He showed Candiotti the quotes from Bobby Grich. Candiotti again answered, "Yup."

"Don't you EVER let him get away with that kind of trash talk. You'd better do something about it," said Vuckovich.

Replied Candiotti, "Yes, sir."

Candiotti didn't face California again until the following spring in Sun City, Arizona. "I pitched a couple of innings, and Bobby Grich happened to come up to bat against me," says Candiotti. "I threw one that knocked him down, and he was just staring at me. So, the situation was addressed pretty good."

Though Candiotti had gotten his payback, in his mind the incident wasn't over. "I had bad feelings toward Bobby Grich for a long time," Candiotti admits. "I never really saw him again—he was out of baseball after 1986 as my career was taking off—until 15 years or so later when I was playing in a celebrity golf tournament up in the Boston area. I got paired with Bobby Grich that afternoon. In fact, [former hockey player] Mike Eruzione, Bobby, and I were the threesome that went out that day. Bobby and I both played baseball. You'd think we would meet each other beforehand and say, 'Good luck out there today.' But we didn't talk to each other for 10 holes. That's two-and-a-half hours. We didn't talk to each other. Finally, we were walking down the fairway, and he goes, 'You had a pretty good career.' I go, 'Oh yeah? Well, thanks.'

"So we talked about that situation, and he goes, 'You drilled me.' I said, 'Well, that's what you get for saying what you said.' He was laughing, and he said, 'Yeah, that was good!'"

After that exchange, Candiotti and Grich were finally on speaking terms. "It was great after that," Candiotti continues. "We were talking. We sat down for dinner at the table together that night. He even called me a year later to try and get reservations at a golf course in Scottsdale, Arizona. So this was a guy that I really couldn't stand because of the remarks he made about my performance against the Angels. [I threw] a curveball that they couldn't hit, and he was frustrated they couldn't get a run off me. He just didn't feel like giving me any credit."

Grich's comments came in 1983, but not all of the teams that Candiotti beat that season were sour grapes. After Candiotti defeated New York for his fourth major league victory, the losing club had nothing but praise for him. "I like him a lot [as] a pitcher," Yankee shortstop Ron Smalley said. "It seems he can throw any of his pitches any time for a strike. He certainly isn't overpowering, but he sure can pitch."[11] Yankee catcher Rick Cerone agreed. "I was impressed with him," he said, while adding, "but watching his fastball will put you to sleep."[12]

Even if watching Candiotti's fastballs put people to sleep, it was a pitch that at least the manager expected. In 1984, new Brewers skipper Rene Lachemann thought Candiotti was being disrespectful of the game of baseball because he didn't throw a fastball. Lachemann had been with the Mariners as their manager for parts of the previous three seasons, and since he was new to the Milwaukee organization, he didn't know Candiotti's repertoire. Candiotti did throw a few knuckleballs against Seattle late in the 1983 season, but by then Lachemann was no longer with the Mariners, having been fired two months earlier. "I went to camp with the Brewers in 1984 and pitched in the team's first intrasquad game," explains Candiotti. "Lachemann was the home plate umpire that afternoon. It was his first year managing the team, and he was ready to go, have a good spring and good season."

Things got off to a rocky start between Candiotti and his new manager, however, when he threw the slowest pitch in his repertoire. "Rick Manning was up to hit, and I threw a knuckleball," Candiotti recalls. "Lachemann went absolutely nuts when he saw that. He ripped his mask off and just started cursing at me, saying how I was making a mockery of the game when we were supposed to be preparing for the season. I said, 'But I throw the knuckleball once in a while!' Even Manning said, 'Hey, Skip, Candy's got a pretty good knuckler.'"

Candiotti and Lachemann worked their differences out quickly (sooner than the feud with Grich, at least). It took five years, but they eventually were on good terms after having a little chat in Cleveland one afternoon, after both of them had left the Brewers. By then, Candiotti was with the Indians. Lachemann, who was let go by Milwaukee after the 1984 season, remained in the game as a coach in the Boston and Oakland organizations.

In 1986, Lachemann was the third base coach in Boston. Though the Red Sox were running away with the AL East in late August, Candiotti pitched well against them twice in a span of seven days in the final week of that month. The Indians won both of those starts against Lachemann's Red Sox by scores of 5–4 and 7–3. Candiotti got the no-decision in the contest in Cleveland—when the bullpen blew his 4–1 eighth-inning lead—but earned the win over future Hall of Famer Tom Seaver in the game at Fenway Park.

By 1989, Lachemann had become the Athletics' third base coach. On September 18, the A's were in town, and Candiotti faced Oakland ace Dave Stewart, who was 19–9. The Indians' knuckleballer was fired up that night, knowing Lachemann was watching from the third base coach's box. Things didn't start off well when Candiotti allowed three straight singles to begin the game, but he then went with his hard knuckleballs and baffled the A's the rest of the way. He ensured Lachemann would be lonely in the coach's box, allowing only three baserunners to reach third after the first inning. Candiotti threw eight innings of two-run baseball, and Cleveland denied Stewart his 20th victory.

By then, Lachemann had changed his mind about Candiotti. The two men ran into each other in the weight room at Cleveland Stadium. "At first, we didn't say anything to each other," recalls Candiotti. "But then he finally goes, 'All right, I guess you know better than I do.' For a knuckleball pitcher, it was tough, because managers really wanted nothing to do with that pitch. Managers just don't understand the pitch, which was probably what happened with Lachemann. But he and I were fine after that chance meeting in the weight room."

Ironically, Lachemann would become the first manager in the history of the expansion Florida Marlins in 1993, and his Opening Day starter was none other than knuckleballer Charlie Hough.

There was a lot of optimism for Cleveland entering the 1987 season. The

Indians put together a successful year in 1986, winning 84 games to finish with their best record since 1968. They also drew 1.47 million fans, their highest attendance total since 1959. Cleveland was expected to be even better a year later. There might have been doubts about the pitching, but everyone knew the Indians could hit. So much so that prognosticators were jumping on their bandwagon, with publications everywhere picking Cleveland to win the AL East.[13] In fact, both *Sports Illustrated* and *USA Today* picked them to win the AL pennant, predicting they'd reach the World Series for the first time since 1954.

Candiotti further added to that optimism as he had his knuckler dancing throughout the spring. On March 15, he began with five perfect innings—and finished with a two-hit, six-inning performance—in a 5–1 victory over California. Following that outing, manager Pat Corrales named Candiotti the Indians' Opening Day starter. "He's throwing his knuckleball even better than last year," Corrales said.[14] On March 27, Candiotti threw only 85 pitches in a complete-game four-hitter with no walks, beating Oakland, 1–0. For the spring, his ERA was 2.81 in 32 innings—including 0.90 in 20 innings over a three-start span where he allowed just 10 hits and four walks—even though the thin Arizona air in the spring training stadiums isn't conducive to making a knuckleball dance.[15] "Absolutely amazing," noted Indians batting coach Bobby Bonds. "You might never see a knuckleball pitcher go nine innings on 85 pitches as long as you live."[16]

"I remember that afternoon," Joe Klein says, thinking there might never have been a 1–0 ballgame in Tucson before, not when the light Arizona air isn't conducive to pitching duels. "An hour and 40 minutes later, he'd beaten them. He threw 79 or 80 pitches. Can you believe that? He pitched a complete game in spring training. I was blown away, as was everybody in the ballpark."

Candiotti downplays the significance of that feat. "It was just spring training," Candiotti says. "And we were also training in Tucson. It was a two-hour drive [for teams playing in Scottsdale to get there], so no teams liked to go down there. We were the only team there in Tucson because everybody else was in Scottsdale. So it was just a long day for the players. A lot of times, the players would be like, 'Let's just get this game over with. Let's swing at the first pitch.' That's probably what was happening." However, Oakland did try to extend the game at the end. Through eight innings, Jose Canseco had the A's only two hits. After Candiotti recorded the first two outs in the ninth, Terry Steinbach and Rob Nelson had back-to-back singles, with Steinbach racing to third on Nelson's infield hit. Stan Javier then tried to tie the game by bunting for a hit. Thankfully, Javier was thrown out at first, and both teams were happy to walk off the field that afternoon.[17]

Candiotti would also make history for Cleveland during the 1987 season, accomplishing a feat that only some of the best pitchers in the club's long history had been able to pull off. And he did it against a pair of teams trying to win the AL East title, not against clubs trying to swing at bad pitches on purpose. On August 3 in Cleveland, Candiotti pitched a one-hitter against the Yankees, a team which at the time had the AL's best record. On September 2 in Detroit, he one-hit a Tigers squad that went on to finish with a major league-best 98–64 record. With those two games, Candiotti entered the Indians' record books by becoming one of just a handful of pitchers in club history to throw two one-hitters in a single season, joining six-time All-Star Sam McDowell (1966) and Hall of Famers Addie Joss (1907), Dennis Eckersley (1977), and Bob Feller (1939, 1940, 1946, and 1947).[18]

"Those were two very well-pitched games," recalls Indians outfielder Cory Snyder of Candiotti's two one-hitters. "Those were tight games too. They were probably two of the closest games I was actually in [where a pitcher was trying for a no-hitter] and being able to watch. What I remember from those games was he kept the guys off balance. He threw good pitches. When that happens, you play good defense, you do everything you can to try and keep it for him. There weren't a lot of no-hitters thrown [back then] and you tried everything to preserve it for him. Those were great games that you were happy to be a part of."

The night of Candiotti's first one-hitter, Yankee manager Lou Piniella noted, "He looked like a 20-game winner."[19] In an ideal world, Candiotti going for no-hitters late in the season should have come at a time when Cleveland was chasing a pennant and when he was chasing 20 wins. Unfortunately, the '87 Indians were a disaster. By the All-Star break, they were 23 games out of first place. The one-hitter against Piniella's Yankees in August, meanwhile, was just Candiotti's *fourth* win. He *lost* the one-hitter against Detroit.

"It was a year where nothing went right," says Candiotti. "We lost 101 games. There just wasn't a whole lot to cheer about that season."

# 7

# *There's Bad, and*
# *Then There's the Indians*

From minor league non-prospect to Opening Day starter. That's how far Tom Candiotti had gone in two years. He went from spending all of 1985 in the minors to two years later being an Opening Day starter for a club that was a trendy pick for the World Series. A guy who had to redefine himself in Triple-A with a knuckleball, a guy who wasn't on any club's 40-man roster entering spring training a year ago. A guy who'd come out of nowhere to lead the American League in complete games in 1986, poised for an encore in 1987. Now Candiotti was the ace on an up-and-coming team trying to win its first pennant since 1954. His ascent to the top—as well as the revival of the Cleveland Indians—seemed like a wonderful fairy tale.

However, the dream came to a crashing halt right off the bat, as Opening Day in 1987 in Toronto was a disaster. Candiotti never got the feel for the knuckleball in the rain at Exhibition Stadium, and instead threw more curveballs and fastballs. The result was five-plus innings, six extra-base hits, and a 7–3 Indians loss. "My knuckler didn't work in the rain, and I was behind the count on every hitter," recalls Candiotti. "The wind and the cold, especially the rain, really affected the knuckleball, which really is a feel pitch. You lose the feeling in your fingertips and it makes the ball spin. I had to throw other pitches because the knuckler just didn't work in the rain. But that day, nothing was working. It was just an ugly day for everything."

Early on, nothing was working for Cleveland, which stumbled out of the gate with a 1–10 start, 10 games out of first place. Even when Candiotti threw a shutout—beating Toronto's Jimmy Key, 5–0, on April 21—things weren't right. "My elbow began to hurt in Baltimore [in my third start of the year]," he recalls. "My next start, I had a shutout against the Blue Jays but the elbow hurt a lot ... on every pitch I was throwing. I had the Tommy John surgery five years before that, and I didn't have any elbow problems again until 1987. I had to miss two weeks because of that."

The Indians, meanwhile, continued to struggle. On May 17, following an 8–4 loss to Detroit, their 12th defeat in 14 games, they dropped to 11–26 and were 13 games out of first place. They never recovered. They were 21 games back on June 30, and 26-and-a-half games out on July 31. By season's end, Cleveland finished 37 games behind the AL East-winning Tigers. To several members of the Indians, the collapse was hardly a surprise. "I never thought the '87 team would win the pennant," outfielder Joe Carter said years later. "We knew we didn't have enough pitching. We had plenty of hitting, but that was all."[1] Even though the '86 Indians had the majors' best hitting, their pitching ranked 24th out of 26 big league teams—and they were also the AL's worst-fielding team. In 1987, everything was magnified because their pitching was the worst in baseball, compiling a 5.28 ERA that was the highest in the majors in 31 years.

"I wasn't surprised we didn't contend for the pennant in 1987," says Doc Edwards, who started that season as the bullpen coach before taking over as manager at the All-Star break. "I knew when we left spring training that we didn't have enough pitching to win a pennant. We were really about four pitchers short." Edwards laments the fact the Tribe had traded away pitchers Rick Sutcliffe and Len Barker in previous seasons to get more offense, leaving the club short in that department.

As Edwards recalls, Candiotti was one of the pitching staff's lone bright spots. Though he was just 1–6 with a 5.65 ERA over the first two months, Candiotti did have some bad luck. On May 14, he allowed only four hits with seven strikeouts in Chicago, leaving with a 3–2 lead. But the bullpen slipped up in the final two innings, and Cleveland lost, 4–3. Against Milwaukee on May 30, Candiotti left with a 5–3 lead and the Indians were one out from winning. Alas, the bullpen let that one slip away when Paul Molitor drove in the tying run with two outs in the ninth.

The bullpen was Cleveland's Achilles' heel, and everyone knew it. "It's one of those things," laments Cory Snyder. "When you're a player, you have a good idea coming out of spring training of what kind of team you have. That year, Joe Carter and I were on the cover of *Sports Illustrated*. There was a lot of hype. People were saying, 'This is Cleveland's year.' And we had a very solid team. We hit the ball. We averaged [about] five runs a game. We had a good pitching staff. We had a good closer. But what hurt us that year was our middle relief and things like that. It was just one of those things. We did the best we could but it just didn't happen for us."

Edwards remembers a game from April 10 that season, when Cleveland scored 11 runs but still fell, 12–11, to the Orioles. "One night, I [stole] the signs from the bullpen of the other team," says Edwards. "I was the bullpen coach then, and I relayed the signs to Pat Corrales, the manager. With this offense we scored a lot of runs, but Baltimore beat us. That was how bad our pitching was. On the pitching staff we had about five or six who were really good, like Candiotti, [left-handed starter Greg] Swindell, and [closer Doug] Jones, but you gotta have a full load when you go to war. We just never had the depth in the pitching staff to carry us all the way."

The lack of pitching depth certainly cost Cleveland in 1987. Indians starters would fail to pitch at least five innings in a major league-high 51 games.[2] There was also bad defense, which cost Candiotti several games. In his 32 starts, he allowed 25 unearned runs. On May 25 in Boston, he was chased after just 2.2 innings, with first baseman Pat Tabler's first-inning error leading to three runs. Carter, the Indians' other first baseman, also cost him two games against Detroit thanks to misplays in both contests, as Candiotti lost, 2–1 and 4–3, to Jack Morris. Carter and Tabler combined for 24 errors while platooning at first base, and Cleveland finished with an AL-worst 153 errors. As Carter would tell the *USA Today* the following season, he figured he cost Candiotti "three or four ballgames myself" in 1987 because of his unfamiliarity at first base.[3]

But with the questionable pitching and defense, why were the so-called experts on the Indians' bandwagon before the season started? As Tabler remembered years later, they were also picked to win for very strange reasons. "We were on the cover of *Sports Illustrated*," said Tabler, "with the prediction that we were going to win the pennant in 1987—and the knuckle-headed reason was that five or six years in a row [from 1981 to 1986], a different team had won the American League East. So *SI* figured it was our turn, because we had a young, up-and-coming team.... [The] sad truth was, we just weren't ready."[4]

With Cleveland languishing in last place in the second half, general manager Joe Klein traded 328-game winner Steve Carlton to AL West-leading Minnesota (July 31) and 318-game winner Phil Niekro to AL East-leading Toronto (August 9). While both veterans were dealt to contenders, Candiotti was the one guy staying put. And there was no way anyone was getting their hands on the knuckleballer with Klein in charge. "When a team falls out of the pennant race like ours, contending teams come to you asking for your best players," says Klein. "But I wasn't going to trade Candiotti because he was a winner and I knew he was going to continue winning for us."

Meanwhile, hitters knew Candiotti was going to continue walking them if they waited out his knuckleball in 1987. In the first half, he averaged 5.10 walks per nine innings, and the Indians lost 14 of his 17 starts. Ironically, he walked a career-high 10 batters on June 5 in Oakland—and still defeated the Athletics, 4–3, by pitching three-hit ball over seven innings. Twice—in the third and fifth innings—he walked the bases loaded, but both times retired future Hall of Famer Reggie Jackson to escape trouble. "You have to let the knuckleball guys pitch their way out of jams," manager Pat Corrales said of watching Candiotti from the dugout. "There are times I just close my eyes. They drive me crazy."[5]

Against Oakland, Candiotti fell one walk shy of equaling a club record originally set in 1903 by Gus Dorner. (Apparently, some people were disappointed Candiotti fell short. The headlines in the June 6 weekend edition of the *Miami News* read: "Candiotti Blows Chance for History," as though it were a bad thing he didn't tie the mark.) Even Indians greats Bob Feller, Herb Score, and Sam McDowell had walked 10 or more batters in a Cleveland uniform. Feller, for example, once walked 11 in seven innings against the Yankees in 1938, and issued double digit free passes five other times. McDowell walked 10 or more three times, including an 11-walk, 12-strikeout game in 7.2 innings in Chicago in 1964. "Fortunately, I changed speeds with my knuckleball and was able to get Reggie out twice with the bases loaded and win the game," says Candiotti.

Ironically, Reggie Jackson probably didn't mind facing Candiotti that night. "Sal Bando taught me how to hit a knuckleball," Jackson once said. "He told me to just stand at home plate and follow the speed of the ball to get it timed." Noting that knuckleball pitchers typically threw every pitch at the same speed, Jackson added, "When I faced a knuckleballer, I'd just stand there with the bat on my shoulder and not get into a hitting position until the guy released the ball. I always got a good home run cut against knuckleballers."[6] Candiotti's knuckleballs, however, came at several speeds, and Jackson went 0-for–4 with two strikeouts against those knucklers while stranding nine runners on base before being pinch-hit for in the ninth inning.

Part of the reason Candiotti struggled in 1987 was manager Pat Corrales's insistence that he keep throwing the knuckleball. In Texas, Corrales had managed Charlie Hough, who'd thrown the knuckler exclusively and successfully enough to become the Rangers' staff ace. Why shouldn't Candiotti just keep throwing it all the time? "Corrales told me to throw nothing but knuckleballs," Candiotti recalls. "But with the knuckler, it's a game-to-game challenge. Sometimes, an inning-to-inning challenge. Sometimes, I'd be struggling early in games trying to get the feel of it, and then if I found it after the first couple of innings, I'd have a good game. Really, I didn't just depend on the knuckleball. I needed my curveball and my fastball too. If I was ahead of the hitter, I'd throw the knuckler. The knuckleball was part of my repertoire, but I had to use my other pitches too."

Corrales didn't buy it. "Just keep throwing the knuckleball," the manager said. "Throw it against a wall if you have to, just to keep the feel of it. Keep throwing it so that you can get better with it." At that point in Candiotti's career, though, he couldn't always throw the knuckler for strikes, and had to pitch from behind the count frequently. The results? Candiotti posted a first-half ERA of 5.57 in 97 innings, registering 55 walks and 53 strikeouts.

"I was always behind in the count 2-and–0 or 3-and–1," Candiotti explains. "In 1986, I was always pitching ahead because I also used my fastball and curveball. That was really my repertoire. I had to use my other pitches along with the knuckler to get hitters out. In '86, I was getting ahead of the hitters with my curveball. But then Pat told me that if there were runners on base, I had to throw the knuckler. The thing is, I couldn't throw strikes 75 percent of the time with it because I still hadn't mastered the pitch, so I was pitching behind the count all the time. I wasn't successful when I kept throwing knuckleball after knuckleball after knuckleball. I wanted to throw the knuckler maybe 50 or 60 percent of the time and use my other pitches."

When Doc Edwards replaced Corrales as Indians manager at the All-Star break, he allowed Candiotti to use all of his pitches. Candiotti got strikeouts with his curveball and fastballs. His ERA went down. He walked fewer hitters—3.27 per nine innings compared to 5.10 during the Corrales era. "Tom would start some people off with ball one, maybe ball two, but he could then throw that curveball for a strike," recalls Edwards. "And that really gave him an edge over most knuckleball pitchers because they normally throw the knuckleball because they don't have other good pitches. Tom was different. He wasn't a knuckleball pitcher, but a good pitcher with a knuckleball. He used that curveball and the fastball to go with the knuckler, and he was successful doing that."

Candiotti also pitched without worrying about upsetting the manager. In a complete-game 7–2 victory against Boston on August 29, he couldn't get the feel for the knuckleball, and threw only three of them after the fourth inning. Recalls Candiotti: "I was thinking later, 'I don't know if Pat would've liked that too much. If I gave up a hit on a curveball, he would've been mad.' Whenever I allowed a hit on curveballs or fastballs, I felt like I was doing the wrong thing. I felt a lot of pressure to throw knuckleballs. It became very draining mentally. And walking guys and having men on base constantly. To me, I thought it was crazy to just walk everybody with the knuckleball when I knew I had trouble throwing it for strikes—and I was told to keep throwing it."

Edwards's hiring, which gave Candiotti freedom to throw all of his pitches and not strictly knuckleballs, was one reason he began to pitch better in the second half in 1987. The other reason was Rangers knuckleballer Charlie Hough, who worked with him just before the All-Star break, and suggested to Candiotti that he change his mechanics when throwing the knuckler. Candiotti straightened out his wrist as he threw, and the ball was able to float up and down in the strike zone as opposed to moving laterally.

From July 23 to August 14, Candiotti went 4–1 in five starts with a 2.63 ERA and three complete games, allowing just seven walks over 41 innings. Included in that stretch was a 3–1 win over a Toronto ballclub that was 21 games over .500, a victory that, at the time, knocked the Blue Jays out of first place. Also, two victories over the Yankees, including a 2–0 one-hitter on August 3 that would be the start of a slump that would knock them out of first place within a few days. After posting two complete-game victories with a 0.50 ERA in the first week of August, Candiotti was named the AL Player of the Week as he beat out Milwaukee's Paul Molitor—who batted .393 with 11 runs scored during that week to extend his hitting streak to 25 games—for the award.[7]

The August 3 one-hitter came against a Yankees team that was 23 games above .500 with an AL-leading 64–41 record. Led by Don Mattingly, Dave Winfield, and Mike Pagliarulo—a trio which combined for 89 homers and 299 RBIs—New York had a two-and-a-half-game lead over second-place Toronto and a 26-and-a-half-game advantage over Cleveland. With Pagliarulo's 32 dingers leading the way, the Yankees as a club would sock 196 homers, fifth-best in the league.

Candiotti, though, held New York hitless over seven innings while throwing a mix of knuckleballs, fastballs, curveballs, and changeups. He'd retired 21 of 22 hitters up to that point, and the only baserunner was Winfield, who walked on a 3-and-2 pitch to lead off the second.[8] "He was great that day," recalls manager Doc Edwards. "He got ahead in the count. He was in the strike zone. He had his good curve and went to his knuckleball. When he was ahead in the count, he was going for the strikeout. He was just like a conventional pitcher. He was kind of pitching backwards because a fastball pitcher throws fastballs—his best pitch—whereas Tom wasn't always throwing his knuckleballs. But Candy still pitched great."

Alas, Mike Easler began the eighth with a bloop single to right field, breaking up the no-hitter. The near no-hitter isn't mentioned as a part of Cleveland sports lore like the more infamous plays that symbolize near-misses that have plagued the city such as "The Catch," "Red Right 88," and "The Drive," but it might as well have been. Easler, a Cleveland native, wasn't even in New York until seven weeks earlier. He played for the Yankees in 1986—going 3-for-12 off Candiotti—but was traded to Philadelphia during the offseason. The Yankees then re-acquired Easler on June 10 to be their primary designated hitter. "It was a 3-and-2 count to Easler," Candiotti recalls. "I didn't want to walk him and have the tying run come up. So I threw him an inside fastball, and he just got enough of it. Brett Butler came charging in from deep center field but had no shot at catching it. It fell in between Butler and [second baseman] Tommy Hinzo."

On September 2 in Detroit, Candiotti took another no-hitter into the eighth—striking out seven Tigers—only to lose, 2–1. "I had a no-hitter with two outs in the eighth inning," recalls Candiotti, "but Matt Nokes broke it up on a 3-and–1 pitch. He hit the ball just over Tommy Hinzo at second base to break up that no-hitter." Candiotti didn't catch any breaks against the Tigers, who scored an unearned run in the fifth. With Chet Lemon aboard via a walk, first baseman Joe Carter booted a grounder to put runners on first and second. A sacrifice and a groundout later, and Cleveland was losing, 1–0. Nokes's eighth-inning single—Detroit's only hit of the night—drove in the second run, as the Indians dropped a 2–1 decision after managing only one run in the top of the ninth.

It was only the 20th time since 1916 that a major league pitcher had tossed a complete-game one-hitter (of at least eight innings) and lost. Had Candiotti retired Nokes—and Cleveland not gotten its run in the ninth—he would have been the first major leaguer since the Chicago Pirates' Silver King in 1890 to throw a complete-game eight-inning no-hitter and still lost.[9] (An eight-inning no-hit game wouldn't be considered a no-hitter today, but it would've counted as one according to the rules interpretation in 1987.) Candiotti's knuckleball was moving so much that even opposing pitcher Jack Morris thought he'd get that no-hitter. "I really thought the guy was going to get it," Morris said afterward, "but that we would win 1–0."[10]

Candiotti finished 7–18 with a 4.78 ERA, but Indians outfielder Cory Snyder believes he should have won more games. "He really pitched well in the second half that year," says Snyder, "but it was just one of those years where everything went wrong. In the first half he struggled a little bit, but he turned it around after the All-Star break. As far as we were concerned on the club, Candy was a winner. He knew how to pitch and he really kept us in the game most nights."

In 1987, Candiotti gave up 93 walks and 28 home runs, numbers that were mediocre. But the knuckleballer pitched into the seventh inning 23 times out of 32 starts and threw seven complete games. He allowed fewer hits (193) than innings pitched (201.2). With his numbers, Candiotti felt he deserved better. "I went 7–18, sure," he said the following spring. "But I can easily count seven more wins if the bullpen had mopped up, or if it hadn't been for the defense. You look at guys with higher ERAs and they've got 17 wins. All you can do is ask yourself what's going on?"[11]

Baseball historian Bill James, when analyzing pitchers' performances by looking at cheap wins versus tough losses, figured that Candiotti deserved a 12–13 record in '87; however, the knuckleballer was only 6–5 in games where he pitched well, skewing his overall numbers.[12] For instance, on May 9 against Kansas City, Candiotti pitched valiantly despite a sore elbow but was betrayed by his defense (four errors and a passed ball) and lost, 4–0. On June 17 against Boston, he allowed one run through the first seven innings but received no support in a 4–0 loss. The hitting, which was supposed to be the Indians' strength, struggled. Cleveland finished 12th out of 14 AL teams in runs scored, and gave Candiotti the second-poorest run support (3.69 runs per game) for an AL pitcher.[13] He received two runs or fewer 10 times, and only three runs seven other times.

Candiotti pitched better after the All-Star break, when he threw the knuckleball over for strikes more consistently. In August, he notched quality starts against defending AL champion Boston as well as Toronto and the Yankees, with the latter two clubs in first place when Candiotti faced them. He pitched quality starts in Minnesota and Detroit in September, against the two eventual AL playoff teams. His ERA in eight post-break starts against those five teams was 2.65 over 68 innings, and he averaged more than eight innings per start.

As Candiotti continued to develop his knuckleball after the 1987 season, it would prove to be a tough pitch for batters to hit deep. In 1988, for instance, he allowed only 15 homers over 216.2 innings. "It doesn't surprise me that Candy had a lot of success during those years," says Tribe outfielder Cory Snyder when told of the fact Candiotti had a low home run rate. "He always knew how to pitch and mix up his pitches. He had a great knuckleball and curveball, and for a few seasons, was one of the best pitchers in baseball. He was real tough. A lot of hitters didn't want to face him because they just couldn't hit him."

In 1989, Candiotti allowed only 10 home runs in 206 innings. In a three-month stretch that summer, he surrendered just one round-tripper in a span of 124.2 innings over 19 starts! From May 9-August 13, Seattle's Jeffrey Leonard was the only hitter to take him deep, in a game on June 9, the first homer Candiotti allowed in 53 innings. California's Devon White would be the next hitter to take him out of the ballpark, on August 18.

Then in 1991, Candiotti gave up 12 homers over 238 innings, almost none coming off of the knuckleball. Nearly every one came on a curveball or fastball, in situations where he didn't want to pitch around hitters and opted to go right after them with runners aboard. That season, according to newspaper accounts, he gave up homers on fastballs to Joe Carter, Mike Greenwell, Kevin Maas, and Juan Gonzalez and a grand slam on a slider to Robin Ventura.

(Candiotti allowed only three bases-loaded homers over 451 career major league games.) Tom Brunansky and Carlos Martinez hit curveballs into the seats. In the postseason, he allowed one homer, which came on a curveball to Kirby Puckett.

"There were some years where I didn't give up any home runs on knuckleballs," Candiotti says. "Usually, they came on curveballs, when I was trying to throw a strike. I pitched really well during those years, and kept my team in every game I pitched. Even though we had some bad teams in Cleveland, I always gave them everything I had. We just didn't win a lot of games with the Indians."

# 8

## *The Pitcher with the Knuckleball, Not the Knuckleball Pitcher*

When baseball fans opened up the sports section in the newspapers to look at the pitching matchups on Opening Day in 1988, they were probably rolling their eyes when they saw the probables for the Indians-Rangers game in Texas. In that game, it was Tom Candiotti versus Charlie Hough. True, Candiotti had tossed eight strong innings against San Francisco in his final spring start of 1988—retiring 15 of 16 Giants batters in one stretch—but he had gone 7–18 the year before, suggesting his knuckleball just wasn't good enough.[1] And he was going up against another knuckleballer. Not the best Opening Day matchup, certainly not Jack Morris against Roger Clemens (the matchup in the Detroit-Boston contest). Who really wanted to see two knuckleballers in the same game?

As journalist and baseball fan Adrian Brijbassi says, people think knuckleball pitchers are all the same. They don't throw fastballs or unhittable sliders. All they do is trick the ball by hitters. "Fans just don't want to see a game on Opening Day pitched by a couple of knuckleballers," Brijbassi explains. Those who watched Tom Candiotti up close and personal, however, realize he wasn't a "pure" knuckleballer. In fact, he was very different from Hough, as Candiotti's knuckler, for example, wasn't his slow pitch. He threw a hard knuckleball and used his curveball as his slow pitch, unlike Hough, who threw knuckleballs almost exclusively.

"Charlie threw the knuckleball 95 percent of the time," Candiotti says when comparing his pitching style to Hough's. "For me, though, I also threw curveballs and fastballs. I really mixed things up. Sometimes I threw the knuckleball only 30 percent of the time in a game. I often threw it less than 50 percent because I used my other pitches during the course of a game."

And it wasn't as though both pitchers were ineffective on Opening Day in 1988. Candiotti threw 6.1 innings and allowed one earned run, while Hough gave up three runs over eight innings. Texas, aided by two errors in the seventh, won the contest, 4–3. (In fact, that season Candiotti and Hough pitched against each other twice in a span of three weeks. In those two starts, Candiotti compiled a 1.17 ERA with 12 strikeouts in 15.1 innings. The Indians' knuckleballer hit only one batter and threw one wild pitch, while Cleveland catcher Andy Allanson was charged with one passed ball, proving that knuckleball duels aren't always about wild pitches, passed balls, and walks.) Also, as Candiotti points out, he and Hough were completely different types of pitchers. Sure, Hough threw the knuckleball 95 percent of the time and Candiotti didn't, but at the end of the day, both needed the knuckler to be successful, didn't they? Well, looking at the scouting reports didn't really help to understand each pitcher. Here are a few excerpts from *The Neyer/James Guide to Pitchers* by Bob Neyer and Bill James containing scouting reports of pitchers who threw the knuckleball during the 1980s:

> TOM CANDIOTTI (p. 155)
> **Pitch Selection, 1983–84:** 1. Slow Curve 2. Slow Slider 3. Fastball
> **Pitch Selection, rest of career:** 1. Knuckleball 2. Slow Curve 3. Fastball
> **Sources:** *The Scouting Report* (1983 and 1990 editions)
>
> CHARLIE HOUGH (p. 247)
> **Pitch Selection:** 1. Knuckleball 2. Fastball 3. Slider
> **Source:** *The Scouting Report: 1990*
>
> PHIL NIEKRO (p. 325)
> **Pitch Selection:** 1. Knuckleball 2. Fastball 3. Slider
> **Source:** *The Sporting News* (9/9/1972, Wayne Minshew)

At first glance, the scouting reports make sense. After all, a knuckleballer doesn't throw knuckleballs exclusively. Perhaps he'll throw them 95 percent of the time—like Hough—and throw an 80-mph fastball here and there when he needs a strike, such as when the count is 3-and-0 or even 2-and-0. Otherwise, it's just knuckleball, knuckleball, knuckleball. Right? Not quite, according to Indians manager Doc Edwards. "When you say knuckleball," Edwards says, "most people assume they're all alike, but they're not. They're definitely different. Joe Niekro would throw a lot of fastballs. He still threw a 90-mph fastball and a hard slider, and then he'd throw a knuckleball to strike you out. His brother, Phil Niekro, was a regular everyday knuckleball pitcher who made his living with that knuckleball. As for Candiotti, he'd probably throw you a curveball unless he was trying to strike you out on a 1–2 pitch."

And here's the scouting report for Joe Niekro, who was discouraged from using the knuckleball earlier in his career before using it as his main pitch in the late 1970s.

JOE NIEKRO (p. 324)
**Pitches, 1967–1971:** 1. Slider 2. Fastball 3. Curve
**Pitches, 1972–1975:** 1. Fastball 2. Knuckleball 3. Slider 4. Curve 5. Change
**Pitches, 1976–1988:** 1. Knuckleball 2. Slider 3. Fastball 4. Curve (occasional)
**Sources:** *The Sporting News* (8/20/1977, Harry Shattuck; and 7/28/1979, Shattuck); *The Scouting Report* (1983, 1985, and 1987 editions)

With Phil Niekro no longer pitching—he retired after the 1987 season—there were only three practitioners of the knuckleball in the majors. However, two weeks after Candiotti defeated Hough, 2–1, in Cleveland on April 20, the fraternity of knuckleballers grew even smaller when Joe Niekro, with a 10.03 ERA in five appearances, was released by Minnesota.

Still, Twins slugger Tom Brunansky didn't consider Candiotti a knuckleballer, especially when he was still getting hitters out with his slow curve, fastball, and even the slider. "You expect to see curveballs and knuckleballs," said Brunansky following Candiotti's 3–1 victory over Minnesota on April 14, "but then he came up with a couple nasty sliders out of nowhere. When he comes out with his fourth-best pitch and beats you with it, you've got to tip your hat to the guy."[2] As Candiotti says, he wasn't really a knuckleball pitcher. "I had four pitches going, where I'd throw a knuckleball and curveball [while mixing in] a fastball and slider," says Candiotti. "It really confused the hitters because they weren't sure what I was going to throw. In 1986, I threw more curveballs. Then in 1988, I threw a lot more fastballs. I was really mixing those pitches in. I wasn't really a knuckleball pitcher, but a pitcher with a knuckleball."

White Sox catcher Carlton Fisk, who hit .174 off Candiotti in 23 career at-bats, didn't know what he would throw. "He's a tough pitcher," Fisk once said. "He's one of those guys who gets such a large-breaking curveball. You wouldn't think the guy would have such good control with a big breaking pitch like that. With the knuckleball, you'd think he might have control of one or the other.... Then he threw some fastballs, he threw a couple of sliders, had that knuckleball around the plate all game and was able to throw that big curveball for a strike when he was behind in the count. That's tough. He's a tough pitcher."[3] Wade Boggs, a five-time AL batting champion in the 1980s, agreed. "[Candiotti] throws it a little harder than Hough," the Boston third baseman noted. "He has a slider, a fastball, a curve and you don't know if he's going to throw it 80 percent of the time, or 20 percent of the time. You have a lot more in your head than, 'Okay, here comes the knuckler.'"[4]

Candiotti was even confusing play-by-play guys, according to Doc Edwards. "Candy had a great curveball before he even learned the knuckleball," says Edwards. "I used to laugh watching it on television because announcers would say, 'Wow, look at that great knuckleball move,' [when] it was actually a curveball. It was a slow breaking curveball that he could throw for a strike any time he wanted to. But a lot of the broadcasters kept calling it a knuckleball. He started out sometimes with the knuckleball but he started a lot of times with the curveball. And everybody called it a knuckleball! When he got ahead, he'd go to the knuckleball. So he wasn't just messing up the hitters, but he was doing it to the broadcasters also!"

Long-time Yankees outfielder and broadcaster Bobby Murcer, who retired as a player before Candiotti made his major league debut, was never confused from the broadcast booth. He once noted you just never knew what Candiotti would throw. "You can be up there so zoned in on that knuckleball," Murcer said. "The next thing you know, he throws you a curveball or one of those 85 mile-an-hour fastballs, and you're not able to pull the trigger."[5]

As broadcaster Tim McCarver once estimated, a knuckleball is so unpredictable that it was like 15 different pitches.[6] But when Candiotti started mixing in curveballs, fastballs, and sliders, it seemed he had at least 20 pitches. According to Indians outfielder Cory Snyder, Candiotti's specialty wasn't the knuckleball. "He had an incredible knuckleball," says Snyder from his home in Hawaii, "and, to be honest, he probably also had one of the best curveballs that was kind of a 'get-it-over' pitch. When it was two balls and no strikes, he could get that curveball over for a strike instead of just throwing a fastball. He threw those three pitches but he threw hard enough and he had a good idea how to get people out with it. There aren't that many knuckleball pitchers with that ability to get that done. I played with Phil Niekro, another knuckleball pitcher, but Candy had really good stuff. But his curveball was very, very good also."

Baseball people on Candiotti, the pitcher with the knuckleball, not the knuckleball pitcher:

• Cal Ripken (Orioles shortstop), 1986, after seeing a 3-and–2 curveball from Candiotti with the bases loaded in a close game: "He seems to be able to throw that [curveball] for a strike anytime he wants to. It's not like facing [Phil] Niekro or someone like that, a guy you know is going to stick pretty much with the knuckleball."[7]

• Pete Incaviglia (Rangers outfielder), 1986: "I hate to say it, but [Candiotti] fooled me good. It was like going downhill in a roller coaster in the dark. It made me nauseous.... He was supposed to throw knucklers, but those curves really did us in."[8]

- Tom Kelly (Twins manager), 1986: "He uses his curveball the way other pitchers use their fastball. He [sets] up the knuckler with his curve, and that's effective."[9]
- Marty Barrett (Red Sox second baseman), 1987: "Candiotti throws a very good curveball. That's his best pitch because he can't get his knuckleball over like the other knuckleballers."[10]
- Tony Muser (Brewers hitting coach), 1989, on how Candiotti kept hitters off balance by throwing different pitches: "Nobody in the league throws a 52-mph curveball. It's all variation of speeds. With a 50-mph curve and a fastball in the high 70s, you're talking a 30-to-35-mph difference."[11]
- Doug Rader (Angels manager), 1990, after Candiotti induced three double play grounders: "Candiotti throws a lot of breaking balls, so hitters are going to be out in front of a lot of pitches and hit them into the ground."[12]
- Tom Brunansky (Red Sox outfielder), 1990: "It wasn't so much his knuckleball as it was his other stuff. He also threw a lot of slow curves and sliders to keep us off balance. If all he threw was knuckleballs like Hough, it would be different."[13]
- Kelly Gruber (Blue Jays third baseman), 1991: "He has at least three different kinds of breaking pitches. And he can throw two different knuckleballs—hard and slow. He's a tough, tough pitcher."[14]
- Chuck Knoblauch (Twins second baseman), 1991: "He's got a great knuckleball but he's got a really good curveball, too. He sets up his knuckleball—I think everybody goes up there looking for the knuckleball—and he surprises them with a curveball."[15]
- Mike Gallego (Yankees second baseman), 1992: "The man is definitely a student of the game, as far as setting hitters up."[16]
- Tony Gwynn (Padres outfielder), 1992: "He's tough.... Not only is a knuckleball tough to hit, but then Candiotti mixes in a regular slider, a regular curveball. He's always keeping you guessing."[17]
- J.T. Snow (Giants first baseman), 1997: "[The ball] was dancing around a lot.... What makes it tough, though, against him is in addition to his knuckleball he throws a slow curve and then zips a fastball in there."[18]

In 1988, Cleveland started out 16–6 and finished April in first place. The pitching was one of the keys for the early-season success, as Candiotti (4–0, 2.13 ERA) and lefty Greg Swindell (5–0, 2.53 ERA) were undefeated in April. The Indians, who were the league's worst-fielding team in 1986–87, had also become a better defensive club after acquiring first baseman Willie Upshaw from Toronto. The addition of Upshaw allowed Joe Carter and Pat Tabler to move to center field and designated hitter, respectively, instead of platooning at first base. Shortstop Julio Franco was moved to second to allow rookie Jay

Bell—an excellent fielder—to take over the shortstop position. "No one is out of position now," noted Carter. "We come out each day knowing where we're going to play and what we have to do to improve at that position. It's made a big difference."[19]

But even with the good pitching and improved defense, the Indians' strong start wouldn't last. They fell out of first place for good on May 3, and proceeded to lose 24 of 33 games from the second week of June to plummet from a half-game out to fifth place, eight-and-a-half games behind, by mid–July. Candiotti, meanwhile, continued to roll. On May 18, the knuckleballer beat Chicago, 2–1, with seven strikeouts and no walks—his major league-leading sixth complete-game win—to improve to 6–1 with a 2.04 ERA.

With the victory over the White Sox, Candiotti was 5–0 with five complete games in six home starts, averaging 7.44 strikeouts while allowing one earned run or none five times. Early on, he was going the distance often, allowing manager Doc Edwards to rest his bullpen. But with a 162-game schedule, Edwards knew he couldn't keep his starters out there too much. And without a strong bullpen other than closer Doug Jones, Edwards often had to go from Candiotti straight to his stopper—even if it meant bringing Jones in earlier. "Doug Jones saved 37 games that one year," says Edwards. "A whole bunch of them were two-and-a-third-inning saves only because when I got past Candiotti and those guys, I never had a guy to pitch the seventh and the eighth to get to the ninth. Candiotti would be going good and you want to relieve him after six. I wanted to bring in Jones in the seventh inning [sometimes]. If I pitched somebody else in between Candiotti and Jones, we might not have a lead when we get to the ninth."

Because of his repertoire, even Candiotti could be burned out like a conventional pitcher. "The most number of pitches I ever threw in a game was 175 in 1986," he recalls. "But out of those pitches, maybe only half were knuckleballs." In 1988, Candiotti was again mixing his pitches. He averaged 122 pitches through his first 15 starts, throwing knuckleballs, curveballs, fastballs, and sliders. Throwing that many pitches took its toll on Candiotti. "At the time I started having a stiff shoulder and I was also nursing a sore right knee," he says, "but I kept pitching through it for three months because we were contending in May and June that year, and I wanted to help the team win ballgames."

Other teams didn't feel sorry for him. Certainly not A's pitching coach Dave Duncan. "I don't consider it pitching," Duncan once said of the knuckleball in general, likely referring to pure knuckleballers such as Charlie Hough and Phil Niekro. "It's a trick pitch: the same thing every time. You don't go inside, outside, change speeds."[20] A knuckleballer simply didn't set a hitter up, other critics argued, the way a conventional pitcher did. It was always the same thing every single time: knuckleball, knuckleball, knuckleball. Baseball fans felt the same way. Wrote one Blue Jays blogger years later: "Candiotti himself never worked a hitter *in his life*. Really! He just floated knuckleball after knuckleball up there, without much of a clue as to where it was going."[21]

Those who faced Candiotti, though, knew he didn't throw the same thing every time. He changed speeds with his knuckler, and sometimes used different arm angles. Outfielder Dave Martinez, who batted .300 in 20 career at-bats off him, once said: "He doesn't just go up there, throw it and hopes it does what it's supposed to do. He knows what he's doing up there."[22] Pitcher Bud Black, teammates with Candiotti from 1988 to 1990 in Cleveland, once estimated that the knuckleball pitcher threw 15 different speeds of knuckleballs.[23]

Candiotti confirms his knuckleballs came at several different speeds. "The hard one that I throw—my power knuckleball—the movement of the ball takes place near the end of the flight," Candiotti explains. "When I throw it slower, the ball doesn't break as erratic and it's more tantalizing to the hitters. They want to swing at the slow knuckler. A lot of times the hitters won't swing at the hard knuckler unless they have to." Throwing strikes for a knuckleball pitcher isn't very difficult once he has the mechanics down. "You just aim for the catcher's mask, and the knuckleball—most of the time—will break into the strike zone, either down to the left, down to the right, or straight down," Candiotti elaborates. "We just like to mess with the hitters, saying we don't know where it's going. Hitters will think, 'If the pitcher doesn't know where the ball's going, how will I know?'"

Edwards doesn't agree with the criticisms toward knuckleballers and specifically toward Candiotti, especially since he often threw really slow knucklers to set up his biting curve and his 80-mph fastball. "Tom didn't throw the same thing every time," Edwards says. "He started [hitters] out sometimes with the knuckleball but he started a lot of times with the curveball. When he got ahead, he'd go to the knuckleball, which was harder to hit, [even] if you were trying to look for it. And Tom would start some people off maybe ball one, ball two, and they'd sit on a knuckleball or a fastball. But Tom would throw a curveball.

"[Because] he could throw a curveball for a strike anytime he wanted to— he could come out on Christmas and throw a strike with that low curve—that really gave him an edge over most knuckleball pitchers. The other knuckleball pitchers normally throw the knuckleball because they don't have other good pitches. Not Tom, though. Tom always mixed it up. He had a great aptitude, great instinct, something you can't teach. Tommy had it."

Yankees slugger Jack Clark knew Candiotti was tough—going 0-for-12 off him with six strikeouts—noting his knuckler wasn't the same every single time. In fact, Candiotti would gradually master the knuckleball well enough that it appeared he could control its path to the plate. "He's got a different type of knuckleball," Clark once said. "It's more along the lines of a forkball. It's the type of pitch he can get over at any time. He can control it, throw it inside and outside and change speeds."[24]

Candiotti even recalls numerous times throughout his career where he won without the knuckleball. When he didn't have the knuckleball working early in a game, he'd throw the fastball until he got a feel for the knuckler. Then, when he had a good knuckleball, he would throw it for a few innings. If it wasn't moving well for the final few innings, he'd switch to the curveball. On July 11, 1986, for instance, Candiotti threw primarily curveballs against Texas, and still pitched a complete-game 7–2 victory. "The hitters were expecting to see the knuckleball, but I never threw it," Candiotti recalls. "It was one of those afternoons when I couldn't control the knuckler so I threw the curveball 90 percent of the time, pretty much the entire game."

Even in his late 30s with the Dodgers, Candiotti wasn't just a knuckle-baller. There were times when he never felt in control of the knuckleball and had to throw other pitches. One example came on July 18, 1993, against Montreal, when Candiotti threw mainly curveballs and fastballs the entire game. He still went seven innings and threw 125 pitches in the Dodgers' 2–1 victory, beating an Expos team that would win 94 games. "In my 40s, I still didn't think of myself as a knuckleball pitcher," Candiotti adds. "In my final season in the big leagues, I got guys like Cal Ripken, Manny Ramirez, and Jim Thome out on fastballs. Hey, you get pop-ups in those situations, it's a great pitch. And hitters told me my curveball was my toughest pitch. My knuckleball wasn't even my number one pitch. For several years there in Cleveland, I was really a tough pitcher ... one who happened to throw a knuckleball."

Even with the knuckler, it wasn't a simple matter of floating "knuckleball after knuckleball up there." An example came in Candiotti's 8–3 victory versus Detroit on May 14, 1989. Candiotti was tired after throwing 131 pitches and was pulled in the ninth before he could get that final out. "We had a [six-run] lead by the [fifth] inning," he says. "With a big lead like that, as a pitcher, all you want to do is throw strikes. You want to go right after hitters. So I threw more fastballs and curveballs. By the final inning, I was tired. Throwing a lot of pitches like that wore me down."

There are also mechanics, pre-game routines, in-game adjustments, pitching, and other things that Candiotti dealt with, which essentially made him similar to a conventional pitcher. Indians pitching coach Mark Wiley played a key role in helping him with mechanics in 1991. Even after compiling a 3.34 ERA from 1988 to 1990 using the knuckleball as a main pitch, Candiotti still

strived to improve. At spring training in 1991, he worked with Wiley to formulate a game plan. One adjustment Candiotti made was getting his upper
body to go more toward the plate. The change gave him a more consistent
delivery with the knuckleball, which he attributed to the reason he threw more
strikes than usual.[25]

After being traded to Toronto in midseason, Candiotti also worked with
Jays pitching coach Galen Cisco in adjusting his pre-game routine. On September 2 against Baltimore, Candiotti allowed four runs in the first two innings
before tossing five shutout frames after that. Since it takes an inning or two to
develop the feel for the knuckleball, Cisco suggested Candiotti adjust his
warm-up pattern by throwing two innings in the bullpen before a start. Candiotti would simulate a game, throwing 25 pitches, sitting for 10 minutes, and
then getting up and throwing again. On September 7 in Cleveland, in his first
start with the extra warm-up, he took a shutout into the ninth. Candiotti followed that up with seven scoreless frames against Oakland on September 14,
the equivalent of a complete-game shutout. On September 18 in Seattle, he
took a 1–0 lead into the eighth—the same as tossing another shutout, with
the two bullpen innings—en route to a career-best 2.65 ERA in 1991.

On occasion, some in-game advice helped Candiotti. On April 26, 1998,
while he was with Oakland, he allowed four first-inning runs against Baltimore.
"Pitching coach Rick Peterson told me after that inning that I needed to get
out over my front leg," says Candiotti. "I tried that in warm-ups and it felt
fine. I tried that in the next inning and it got me right back in sync." Candiotti
allowed only two baserunners after that, retiring 18 of his final 20 batters in
pitching seven innings of five-hit ball, winning that game, 12–4.

On July 10, 1999, with Cleveland, Candiotti allowed seven runs against
Cincinnati. Afterward, bullpen coach Luis Isaac noted he didn't keep a stiff
wrist when throwing the knuckler. "Luis told me I'd gotten away from my normal delivery from my first stint with the Indians in the 1980s, so we made that
adjustment," recalls Candiotti. In his next three outings, all in relief, he went
back to his normal delivery and didn't allow any hits while striking out five
batters in four innings of work.

Candiotti even used video and technology to help him. For two months
in the winter of 1987, Candiotti watched videotapes of his starts from that
season, wanting to understand which of his pitches were getting hit. "I took
notes on what I was doing out there on the mound, how certain players were
hitting against me ... and I entered each hitter onto my computer," explains
Candiotti. "I entered in what pitches I threw against him and how he reacted
to it, if I got him out or if he got a hit off me, that sort of stuff."

The following season, if Candiotti was pitching against Baltimore, for example, he would look up the information on his computer and go over what he did against each Orioles hitter. "I'd formulate a game plan and figure out what I would throw to each hitter," explains Candiotti. "I would figure out what pitches to throw to Cal Ripken on a certain count, things like that. It's amazing how video really helped me succeed in the big leagues."

In 1988, Candiotti finished 14–8 with a 3.28 ERA over 216.2 innings. He started out 6–1 with a 2.04 ERA over his first nine starts, and ended on a 7–0 run with a 2.22 ERA in his final 10 outings. But in between, he lost five straight starts while receiving only 10 runs of support. (In fact, in Candiotti's eight losses in 1988, he received only 18 runs of support.)

Candiotti broke the five-game losing streak on June 19 by beating New York, 11–3, tossing a six-hitter with 10 strikeouts and no walks. His no-walk, 10-strikeout complete game was only the 17th time since 1916 that a pitcher had accomplished that feat while going the distance against the Yankees, according to Baseball-Reference.com.

Though the 0–5 skid cost Candiotti a spot on the All-Star team, he was still having a better season compared to 1986, his first year throwing the knuckleball in Cleveland. Four months into the 1988 campaign, Candiotti had 102 strikeouts with 36 walks in 147.2 innings, a 2.8 strikeout-to-walk ratio. At that same point in 1986, he had already issued 67 walks (with 103 strikeouts).

In 22 starts by the end of July, Candiotti also had 10 complete games, tied for the major league lead. His record, though, was just 8–8 with a 3.68 ERA. Things got worse when he was a last-minute scratch on August 2 in Baltimore because of a weak shoulder muscle. "When I was warming up in the bullpen that night, my shoulder was really stiff and I couldn't get loose," Candiotti recalls. "I'd experienced the shoulder problem for almost three months. It just got to the point where I didn't wanna really hurt my arm, so I ended up going on the DL."

After Candiotti returned from the disabled list, everything he threw worked. In his first game back on August 19, he beat Kansas City's Bret Saberhagen, 4–2, allowing only one hit and one walk over five innings. It was the first of six consecutive triumphs for Candiotti, who would go 6–0 with a 2.25 ERA to end the season. During the streak, he also defeated Detroit's Frank Tanana, 4–0, and beat AL East-winning Boston twice. In his 31 starts, Candiotti went the distance 11 times. He narrowly missed his second complete-games championship, finishing three complete games behind AL co-leaders Roger Clemens and Dave Stewart.

And while he was establishing himself as a solid pitcher—not knuckleball pitcher, but pitcher, period—others were more impressed with Candiotti the person. During an era in which ballplayers were beginning to make millions of dollars and adopting a "me first" attitude, Candiotti was very much a throw-back player. "Tommy's a class act, on and off the field," says Doc Edwards. "He's a first-class human being. The way he carries himself, and Tom has class. If he was by your son, he's everything you want your son to be." Candiotti also made time for fans after ballgames. "He signed autographs for everybody wait-ing for him," says Mark Mazza, a childhood friend of Candiotti's. "He was that kind of guy. He'd sign for every single person that waited for him, even if it took more than an hour to sign for everyone waiting there."

On the mound Candiotti was as good as any pitcher during the second half. Over his final 60 innings of 1988, he allowed only 43 hits and 16 walks with 30 strikeouts. Despite his strong year—as well as Greg Swindell's 18 vic-tories, John Farrell's 14 wins, and Doug Jones's 37 saves—Cleveland still fin-ished sixth in the AL East with a 78–84 record, 11 games out of first place. Nonetheless, this marked the Indians' best showing in the standings since 1959, when they finished five games behind pennant-winning Chicago.

The 1989 season was another strong year for Candiotti. Pitching 206 innings but receiving an average of only 3.36 runs of support from the Indians, Candiotti finished 13–10 with a 3.10 ERA. He allowed 188 hits and only 10 home runs while recording 124 strikeouts with 55 walks. But there were some concerns before the season when Candiotti pitched only 15 innings during spring training as he missed time because of a sore arm and bad back.

Candiotti was not hampered by the lack of spring innings. On May 29, following a victory over Toronto, he was 6–2 with a 2.96 ERA in 10 starts. But once again, Candiotti would be at his best following a stint on the disabled list. He was placed on the DL on July 2, one day after leaving a start against Oakland with a weak shoulder.

As it turned out, the two weeks off to rest that shoulder would work wonders for Candiotti. He returned on July 17 and would not lose a game until September 3, going 5–0 with a 1.36 ERA in his first nine starts after coming off the DL. He should have been 7–0, but closer Doug Jones coughed up his 2–0 and 1–0 leads on July 17 and August 29, respectively. In that stretch, Candiotti gave up only 44 hits, two home runs, and 11 walks in 66.1 innings, recording 36 strikeouts. (In a five-start span, Candiotti was 4–0 with a 0.47 ERA. In 38.1 innings, he allowed two earned runs, six walks, and just 19 hits.) Over the previous two summers, Candiotti was 11–0 with a 1.78 ERA after coming off the DL—including 6–0 with a 2.25 ERA in 1988.

Cleveland, 10 games out of first place on July 18, crept back into the AL East race behind first-place Baltimore and second-place Toronto by late July, thanks in part to Candiotti's resurgence. "When I came back from the sore shoulder," Candiotti says, "I didn't lose for two months, and we started winning and somehow got back into the race because nobody in the division was running away with it, so it was like every team had a chance. But the Blue Jays got hot and ended up winning the division, and they went to the playoffs."

Though Cleveland would finish 73–89 and in sixth place, the team stayed in contention until mid–August. And while Toronto might have been the division's best team down the stretch, the top pitcher in the East was from Cleveland. Led by Candiotti, the Tribe closed to within one-and-a-half games of first on August 4. "In Cleveland, we didn't always have good pitching," recalls manager Doc Edwards, who felt confident every time Candiotti took the ball as the Indians remained in the pennant race. "But when Candy and [Greg] Swindell were on the mound, you knew we were always going to have a chance to win. And when Candy was on his game, it didn't matter who he was pitching against—he was just capable of beating ANYBODY."

During Candiotti's undefeated streak, he beat Boston's Roger Clemens, 3–2, and also recorded two 1–0 victories. Edwards has fond memories of the second 1–0 game on August 2 in Milwaukee, as Cleveland was within striking distance of first place. "The Brewers had a good lineup with Paul Molitor and Robin Yount—who was the MVP that year—but Candy beat them that afternoon," recalls Edwards. "He was really dealing that day with the curveball and that knuckleball. If it'd been a playoff game, it would've been remembered for a long, long time. He was that good that afternoon. Candy was just superb."

On August 8 at Yankee Stadium, Candiotti threw only 30 knuckleballs out of 101 pitches through 7.1 innings in beating New York, 3–1. "That year," Candiotti says, "when I came back from shoulder tendinitis, my arm felt strong. I really went back and forth between being a knuckleball pitcher and a conventional pitcher at that time. I felt I could throw my fastball by people. I was throwing a lot of fastballs, which would surprise the hitters. Then once they began catching up to my fastballs, I'd go to the knuckleball to mess up their timing."

Candiotti went undefeated in July and August of 1989, and the other members of the Indians' starting rotation—Greg Swindell, Bud Black, and John Farrell—did well. But without a strong offensive lineup, Cleveland lost 24 of 35 games from August 5 to September 10 to fall out of contention. With the team 65–78 and 14-and-a-half games out of first place on September 10, Edwards was fired and replaced by special assignment scout John Hart.

Despite Cleveland's collapse, there were still some memorable moments for Candiotti. His 13 victories gave him 50 wins from 1986 to 1989, tying him for the most by an Indians pitcher with Len Barker (1980–83) in that decade. Candiotti could have finished ahead of Barker, but his offense didn't always cooperate. For instance, Candiotti allowed just three singles through 5.1

innings before leaving with an injury on June 25 in Texas, trailing, 1–0. The Rangers won, 4–2, behind Nolan Ryan, who took a no-hitter into the eighth inning and also surpassed his 4,900th career strikeout.

After the game, however, Rangers pitching coach Tom House still sought out Candiotti, who had suffered a shoulder injury and was on his way to the disabled list. "Candy, congratulations," House said. The Rangers' pitching coach explained to Candiotti that he'd just surpassed 100 innings and was headed for his fourth straight 200-inning season. "You're now just the 20th pitcher in the history of the game to become a full-time knuckleballer for at least four years in the big leagues," House explained.

When Candiotti went on the DL a week later, righthander Rod Nichols was called up from Triple-A Colorado Springs. Nichols would go 4–6 with a 4.40 ERA, notching victories at Fenway Park and Yankee Stadium in back-to-back starts in August. Candiotti, though, remembers Nichols more for his helping set up a competition against closer Doug Jones—not an intense competition to see who could hit triple-digits on the radar gun, but to see who could throw *slower*.

Nichols was charting one of Candiotti's starts when he noticed the knuckleballer had achieved a rare feat that afternoon. "We had the radar readings in the dugout," Candiotti recalls. "I was pitching a game one time, and Rod was charting my game. He had to chart the radar readings along with the game charts. He said that I hit every speed from 84 mph, which was the top, all the way down to 49 mph with my knuckleball during the course of that one game. I hit 49, 50, 51, 52, 53, and all the way up to 84." With Candiotti normally throwing three "zones" with that knuckleball, he could throw it at any speed he wanted to. "The mid-knuckleball was about 63–64 mph," he says. "When I threw my hard knuckler—which I threw if I wanted a strikeout—it was up to 72. And that day, I got my slowest one down to 49."

Jones overheard the conversation, and boasted he could throw slower than Candiotti. He then marched out to the mound and started throwing his slowest pitches. "Jonesie went out there and threw one 55," Candiotti recalls. "We'd get the readings, and I think he finally got one down to 50 mph. But he couldn't beat my lowest speed. So I ended up beating Jonesie by one mile per hour because I got one down to 49, throwing a really slow one there."

American League hitters knew all about Candiotti's slow pitches, including Milwaukee outfielder Terry Francona. "He looks like Nolan Ryan after seeing some of that other [slower] stuff," noted Francona about Candiotti's 80-mph fastballs and 52-mph curveballs.[26] Though the Indians' knuckleballer's best fastballs were only 80 mph, his numbers were on par with baseball's best fireballers. Entering September, Candiotti had a 2.85 ERA, striking out 100 batters while walking only 46. Over a 35-start stretch from July 27, 1988 to August 29, 1989, Candiotti was 19–6 with a 2.67 ERA over 239.2 innings while allowing 188 hits and 63 walks.

Unfortunately, Candiotti couldn't catch any breaks in his final four starts of 1989 despite a 2.35 ERA over 30.2 innings while allowing only six walks (and no homers). On September 13, he lost, 3–1, to Detroit's Jack Morris despite allowing just two earned runs and two walks over 6.2 innings. On September 18, Candiotti battled Oakland and Dave Stewart for eight innings but left trailing, 2–1, and came away with a no-decision. On September 29, he carried a one-hit shutout into the sixth but lost, 2–1, in Chicago.

The 1989 Indians couldn't hit, wasting the fine efforts of a pitching staff that ranked fifth in the AL in ERA (3.65) and third in shutouts (13). The top three starters—Candiotti (13–10, 3.10), Swindell (13–6, 3.37), and Black (12–11, 3.36)—had ERAs under 3.50 and each won two 1–0 games, but none exceeded 13 victories. John Farrell (9–14, 3.63) pitched 208 innings and led the team with seven complete games and 132 strikeouts but lost 14 games. The staff even issued the fewest walks (452) in the majors, the first time Cleveland ranked number one in that category since the 1954 pennant-winning team featuring Hall of Famers Bob Feller and Bob Lemon. Had the 1989 Indians had a more formidable offense—like the 1986 edition that led the league in runs, triples, batting average, total bases, slugging percentage, and stolen bases—Cleveland might have had a shot.

Not only did Cleveland finish last in the AL in runs scored (604), it also ranked last or second-to-last in several other offensive categories, including batting average (.245), stolen bases (74), on-base percentage, total bases, and slugging percentage. Joe Carter led the club with 35 homers with 105 RBIs but batted only .243 with 112 strikeouts. Cory Snyder's 18 homers ranked second on the team, and Brook Jacoby was second in RBIs with only 64. "That year we needed Joe and Cory to get the big hits for us in order to have a chance to win the pennant," Doc Edwards laments. "We needed offense, but we really didn't get that much, and we really fell out of it in August."

# 9

# *Staff Ace*

Tom Candiotti had proven in 1989 that he was among the American League's best pitchers. Though he finished just 13–10, he could have had 18 victories had he pitched on a better club than the 73–89 Indians. In 1990, Cleveland—with former AL Manager of the Year John McNamara now managing the team—was expected to contend for the AL East, especially with Candiotti at the top of a rotation that also included Bud Black, Greg Swindell, and John Farrell.

Candiotti (15–11, 3.65 ERA), Black (11–10, 3.53), and closer Doug Jones (5–5, 2.56) were the team's top pitchers in 1990, combining for 31 victories and 43 saves (although Black was traded to Toronto in September). While that trio did their jobs, the same couldn't be said for the others as the Indians' staff collectively allowed a major league-high 163 round-trippers. Swindell got off to a slow start and went just 2–5 in his first 15 starts with a 5.14 ERA, and Farrell spent time on the disabled list with an elbow injury and started only 17 games. The fourth and fifth starter spots were a mess, with nine different pitchers getting at least one start—and delivering awful results.

The Tribe's hitting was much better than the 1989 edition, even though Cleveland had traded slugger Joe Carter to San Diego in December in exchange for outfielder Chris James and rookies Sandy Alomar, Jr. and Carlos Baerga. While Carter had hit 35 homers in 1989, he was booed regularly by Indians rooters because there were rumors that he had no interest in staying and wanted to be traded out of town.[1] The revival in the Indians' offense had little to do with 36-year-old first baseman Keith Hernandez, who was signed to a two-year deal worth $3.5 million. The former Mets All-Star was expected to provide some left-handed power in the Tribe lineup but batted .200 with one homer and eight RBIs in 43 games in an injury-plagued 1990 season.

Cleveland, though, received contributions from Alomar (.290, nine HRs, 66 RBIs), James (.299, 12 HRs, 70 RBIs), Brook Jacoby (.293, 14 HRs, 75 RBIs), and newcomer Candy Maldonado (.273, 22 HRs, 95 RBIs), more than offsetting Hernandez's mediocre production.

On the morning of June 29, Cleveland was seven-and-a-half games behind first-place Boston. That night, the Indians began a 25-game swing against the tough AL West and would go 11–14 during that stretch. Miraculously, they gained ground in the Eastern Division race at the end of the 25 games and were only four-and-a-half games out of first place on July 25. After surviving the tough stretch, though, they had nothing left. Cleveland began an eight-game home stretch in late July but proceeded to drop six of eight to fall out of contention, finishing 11 games out by season's end.

In Candiotti's five full seasons on the club, even though he was 65–59, Cleveland finished either sixth or seventh in the seven-team AL East three times and never placed higher than fourth. The 1990 Indians finished fourth but registered a sub-.500 record for the eighth time in nine seasons. On a team that was victorious only 77 times, Candiotti won 15 games. It also proved to be his final full season in Cleveland, as the club wasn't interested in giving him a long-term deal even though he was clearly the ace of the pitching staff. "They were looking to get younger," Candiotti says. "We had a pretty good offense in 1990 but we didn't have enough pitching. And the next year, they started trading away everybody to get younger players."

Candiotti got out to a fast start in 1990, winning four of his first five starts. Even a stint on the disabled list in May—due to inflammation of the right elbow—didn't slow him down, as he improved his record to 9–3 with a 3.52 ERA by June 30. Including his late-season run in '89, he was 15–7 with a 2.91 ERA over his last 188.2 innings while allowing only 170 hits—and 15 homers—and 48 walks with 114 strikeouts.

Though Candiotti was 9–4 with a 3.59 ERA in the first half, he wasn't selected to the All-Star Game. Instead, reigning Cy Young winner Bret Saberhagen of Kansas City was named to the team, even with a 5–7 first-half record. Seattle's Randy Johnson, 9–3 with a 3.68 ERA (including a no-hitter on June 2) but 59 walks over 110 innings (4.83 per nine innings), was also an AL All-Star. A hard-luck home loss against Seattle on July 5—where Candiotti allowed two runs on seven hits and two walks over eight innings—prevented the knuckleballer from winning 10 games before the All-Star break.

While Candiotti was winning in 1990 early on, the other Indians starters were not. When he defeated the Red Sox, 4–0, in Boston on June 10, it ended a six-game losing streak for Cleveland. Candiotti was also the only Tribe starter to be victorious over a 20-game span, going back to May 19. The knuckleballer was 2–2 with a 3.24 ERA, while the rest of the starters—Bud Black (0–2, 5.04 ERA), John Farrell (0–3, 4.15 ERA), Jeff Shaw (0–1, 9.00 ERA), Greg Swindell (0–2, 6.66 ERA), and Sergio Valdez (0–2, 10.61 ERA)—were 0–10 with six no-decisions and a 5.90 ERA. At that point, the Indians were a middling 24–30 but only six-and-a-half games behind the front-running Red Sox. Had they had better pitching, they might have been relevant in the AL East, a mediocre division that was certainly up for grabs. Unfortunately, Cleveland wasn't pitching well enough to be a factor.

The Indians went on to post the AL's second-worst team ERA at 4.26, but finished second with a .267 team batting average and fourth in runs scored. One of their best hitters was catcher Sandy Alomar, Jr., who hit .290 en route to winning AL Rookie of the Year honors. More importantly, Alomar could handle catching the knuckleball, and he had great mobility and blocked balls in the dirt well—preventing would-be passed balls. "Sandy and [backup catcher] Joel Skinner were both great catchers who could catch the knuckleball very well," Candiotti says. "Both could throw extremely well, which is very important for a knuckleball pitcher on the mound, because it stopped the running game. Most teams are going to want to run because the catcher normally can't handle the knuckleball. But both Sandy Alomar and Joel Skinner were excellent in being able to catch and throw."

Alomar would tell reporters that Candiotti "helped me win a Gold Glove [in 1990] because I had only eight passed balls with his knuckleball."[2] But when Candiotti was traded in 1991, Alomar was the happiest player in the Indians' clubhouse. "When he left," recalled Alomar years later, "I said, 'Candy, I love you. I loved having you on the team and I'm glad you're going to a contender. But I'd rather not catch you ever again.'"[3] Recalls Candiotti, "When I went to pick up my stuff in the clubhouse, Sandy took his knuckleball glove [the oversized mitt used specifically for catching knuckleballs] and he threw it at me. He said, 'Take this out of here with you! I don't ever want to see it again!'"

The Indians finished 77–85 but were still relevant as late as July 25, when they were 46–50 and only four-and-a-half games out of first place. With 12 consecutive games on deck against two last-place clubs—the Eastern Division's Yankees (34–60) and the Western Division's Royals (45–50)—they had every reason to be optimistic. The Indians, though, lost four of five at home to the Yankees, with Candiotti getting their only victory in that series. They dropped two of three at home to Kansas City, with Candiotti needing to come on in relief in the first game. They then lost three of four in New York—plummeting to nine-and-a-half games in back of first-place Boston—despite Candiotti's near-no-hitter in the series opener. "We were a couple of pitchers short," Candiotti says. "[Fourth starter] John Farrell was hurt, and that whole month we didn't have any success with our fifth starters. Who knows what would've happened if we pitched a little better that year?" The Indians' relievers were also scuffling. For a three-week stretch in July, the bullpen—with the exception of closer Doug Jones—was roughed up for a 5.54 ERA in 26 innings.[4]

On July 28, Candiotti held the Yankees to four hits in a 2–1 win. Two nights later, Candiotti made his second relief appearance in July, replacing an ineffective Jeff Shaw in the sixth inning against Kansas City. Candiotti threw 3.2 scoreless innings to finish that game—a 7–6 Indians loss—allowing three hits with no walks and five strikeouts. Incredibly, he threw 62 pitches on just one day of rest following his 99-pitch outing against New York.

The fact that the Indians called on Candiotti twice to pitch in relief in July spoke volumes about their mediocre staff, as the pitchers outside of the Candiotti-Swindell-Black trio were horrible. While those three starters combined to go 9–6 that month, Cleveland was missing quality starts from the other two rotation spots. With John Farrell on the disabled list, manager John McNamara used *seven* other starters in July alone—Jeff Shaw, Al Nipper, Sergio Valdez, Charles Nagy, Rod Nichols, Cecilio Guante, and Mike Walker. Those seven pitchers combined for 13 starts in July, going 1–12 with an 8.53 ERA, with the lone victory coming in their first try on July 3 when Nipper defeated Seattle. In fact, during the entire season, nine different pitchers were used for the numbers four and five rotation spots. Valdez (5–5, 4.97), Walker (1–6, 6.07), Shaw (3–4, 6.18), Nagy (2–4, 5.73), Nipper (2–3, 5.98), Kevin Bearse (0–2, 12.91), Nichols (0–2, 7.45), Steve Olin (1–0, 2.57), and Guante (0–1, 12.00) made 53 starts, and their numbers included 265.1 innings, 333 hits, 127 strikeouts, 126 walks, 42 homers, 27 losses, and a 6.00 ERA.

Entering August, Cleveland's pennant dreams had already been dashed. Still, Candiotti provided one more highlight on August 3 at Yankee Stadium, where he had allowed just 11 hits in 21.1 innings with a 1.27 ERA in his previous three starts. Through seven innings on this night, Candiotti didn't allow a hit despite a rough beginning to the game. Exactly three years earlier—on August 3, 1987—he tossed a one-hitter against the Yankees while allowing just two baserunners. In this no-hit bid in 1990, though, Candiotti gave up two baserunners and two runs—on zero hits—in the very first inning. With one out, he hit rookie Jim Leyritz with a pitch. Oscar Azocar, another rookie, then reached on second baseman Jerry Browne's two-base error, putting runners on second and third. A wild pitch allowed Leyritz to score, and Mel Hall followed with a groundout to drive in Azocar.

Over the next six innings, the only Yankee to reach base was Matt Nokes in the fourth, and that came about because of Candiotti's own throwing error. The knuckleballer took his no-hitter and a 4–2 lead into the eighth. "I played

Candiotti enjoyed his finest major league success in a Cleveland uniform, going 72–65 with a 3.53 ERA from 1986 to 1991 while pitching 45 complete games and seven shutouts. With the Indians, Candiotti took a no-hitter into the seventh inning four times, and in 1987 tossed a pair of complete-game one-hitters. The knuckleballer also pitched 7.2 innings of one-hit ball in a 6–4 loss at Yankee Stadium in 1990. Candiotti was traded to the Toronto Blue Jays in June of 1991 and eventually returned to the Indians during the 1999 season (National Baseball Hall of Fame Library, Cooperstown, New York).

with Candiotti for four years [actually, three] and that's the best I've seen his knuckleball," Hall, his former teammate in Cleveland, said afterward.[5] Candiotti retired the first two batters in the eighth—retiring 21 of 22 batters since the opening inning—and was four outs away from history. The only pitchers to ever toss nine-inning Yankee Stadium no-hitters were New York's Monte Pearson (1938), Allie Reynolds ('51), Don Larsen ('56), and Dave Righetti ('83), as well as Cleveland's Bob Feller ('46) and Detroit's Virgil Trucks ('52).

With two outs in the eighth, Steve Sax walked before shortstop Felix Fermin couldn't handle Leyritz's grounder in the hole. It was ruled an error, Cleveland's third of the game, and there were now two runners on with Azocar at the plate. On Candiotti's 110th pitch—an 0-and-1 knuckleball—dreams of the no-hitter bounced up the middle, just beyond the reach of second baseman Browne, and the score was 4–3. "No big deal," said Azocar, who'd been a pitcher in the minors before switching to the outfield in 1987. "I broke up two no-hitters in the minor leagues."[6] With Candiotti's no-hitter gone, McNamara summoned Doug Jones to close out the inning. But Hall ripped Jones's first-pitch fastball into the upper deck in right field, giving Candiotti a 6–4 loss.

While Cleveland finished 77–85 in 1990, Candiotti went 15–11 with a 3.65 ERA over 202 innings, marking the fourth time in his five seasons that he led the Indians in victories. He became the first Indians pitcher to register five consecutive 200-inning seasons since Sam McDowell from 1967 to 1971.[7] Candiotti also became the first Tribe pitcher with at least 13 wins in three straight seasons since Rick Waits from 1978 to 1980. During the 1970s, Dennis Eckersley (1975–77) and Gaylord Perry (1972–74) were the only Indians to accomplish the feat of 13 or more victories three years in a row. "It's gotten to the point," McNamara said, referring to the fact Candiotti simply won no matter how bad the team was, "that you can predict what's going to happen when he pitches."[8]

Even though Candiotti was the ace in Cleveland, the club was in no hurry to sign him to a long-term deal. He was eligible for salary arbitration at the end of the 1990 season, and would enter free agency the following year. But he'd also expressed interest in remaining with the Indians—provided he was given a four-year contract. "At the time," Candiotti explains, "pitchers were starting to get four-year contracts. It wasn't so much the money as it was the security."

Candiotti was referring to the fact that pitchers with inferior numbers were getting big contracts that offseason, led by Brewers southpaw Teddy Higuera, who parlayed an 11–10 record and a 3.76 ERA into a four-year, $13 million deal. The fact that Higuera had a history of injury problems didn't stop Milwaukee from giving him that contract. Bud Black, 13–11 with a 3.57 ERA in 1990 while splitting time with Cleveland and Toronto, was given a four-year, $10 million contract by the Giants.

Candiotti figured he deserved more, especially since he was a lock for 200 innings every year with his knuckleball (as he'd done in each of his five seasons with Cleveland). He was willing to sign for an amount below the market value for pitchers, as long as he had that fourth year. Unfortunately, Cleveland didn't do four-year deals. "I made it very clear to the Indians that I wanted to stay," Candiotti says. "The fans loved me. I thought I could probably spend the rest of my career there. Playing in Cleveland was like a homecoming for me because my mom and her family are from nearby Youngstown, Ohio. It was awesome to pitch in front of them wearing that Indians uniform. Cleveland was also where I learned how to pitch. I really, really wanted to stay there."

But Candiotti also wanted to receive a contract comparable to the one that Black had received from San Francisco. From 1986 to 1990, Black was 42–42, averaging 150.2 innings. Candiotti, on the other hand, was 65–59 during that span while averaging 215.2 innings. If Black had gotten a four-year deal worth $10 million, Candiotti figured he deserved at least what the left-hander signed for, if not more, and rejected Cleveland's offer of three years for $7.2 million. Instead of a long-term contract that would have kept him in town for likely the rest of his career, both parties finally agreed to a one-year deal worth $2.5 million in February 1991 to avoid salary arbitration—meaning Candiotti would become a free agent at the end of the '91 season.

Ohio's other team, the Cincinnati Reds, did not mess around with their right-handed ace, locking up 1990 World Series MVP Jose Rijo to a three-year contract worth $9 million on the same day Candiotti signed his one-year deal. Rijo, who could've become a free agent after the '91 season, became the 16th pitcher in baseball history to earn at least $3 million annually.[9] The members of the $3 million pitchers club: Roger Clemens, Dave Stewart, Bob Welch, Doug Drabek, Nolan Ryan, Mark Davis, Teddy Higuera, Mark Langston, Bruce Hurst, Dennis Martinez, Tom Browning, Mike Boddicker, Dennis Eckersley, Bobby Thigpen, Jack Morris, and Rijo.[10]

Although Rijo had just led Cincinnati to a World Series sweep over Oakland, he had never had a 200-inning season. From 1986 to 1990, Rijo was 45–40 with a 3.51 ERA in 157 games, averaging 149 innings per season. Plus, he'd been on the disabled list for the third straight year in 1990. Candiotti, in that period, averaged well over 200 innings and had 20 more victories with a comparable ERA (3.66) in 161 games. "You don't want to take less money than guys whose stats aren't as good as your own," Candiotti said as he continued to see pitchers with lesser numbers getting compensated by their organizations far more than what happened with him in Cleveland. "It doesn't make you feel good."[11]

Candiotti was most upset, though, at the contract that Mike Witt, a four-time 15-game winner with California in the 1980s who had a 114–113 career record, received that offseason, which made him the highest-paid pitcher in New York Yankee history.[12] The former Angels righthander, traded to New York in May of 1990, was 5–9 with a 4.00 ERA for the season while missing two months with a sore elbow. "Mike Witt got $8 million for three years," Candiotti told reporters, adding he felt cheated by the Cleveland organization. "The Indians offered me $7 million."[13]

Candiotti would have even harsher words for John Hart, the Indians' personnel director and general manager-in-waiting who handled the contract talks. "The negotiations were bad [in the winter of 1990]," he said. "I understand. John Hart was a rookie. They can't screw around. This isn't the time to say I'm 34, that I throw a freak pitch and whatever other excuses they used."[14] Some 20 years later, Candiotti reflects in a different light. "The Indians ended up trading me in June of 1991," he says. "When I talk to John Hart now, we're really cordial now. He admits he didn't really want to trade me but he goes, 'It was one of those business things. We just had to.' They just had to get younger. John had a chance to get Mark Whiten and Glenallen Hill, who were really high prospects at the time. They were trying to assemble guys that could in a couple of years turn into really good players."

While Candiotti wasn't happy with his contract situation then, old-timers weren't impressed with the contracts handed to the modern players. Ballplayers were never well paid before the free-agency era and needed part-time jobs in the winter to keep food on the table, but the game had evolved to a point where players were pulling in million dollar salaries. Indians Hall of Famer Bob Feller could only shake his head when salaries skyrocketed in the 1990s. "Pitchers had better arms when I played because we had to go to work in the offseason. The closest thing some of the players today come to manual labor is to swing a golf club. Players in my era had to go to work in the coal mines or the factories in the offseason," Feller said in 1991. "To me, a guy like [Boston ace righthander Roger] Clemens is a good pitcher, but not great. I don't think [Oakland ace righty Dave] Stewart is that great, either."[15]

Cleveland, which had great hitting in 1990 but was derailed by a lack of dependable fourth and fifth starters, adopted a new strategy for 1991. During the 1990 season, outfielder Alex Cole made his big league debut on July 27 and became a terrific leadoff hitter, batting .300 with 40 stolen bases (with ranked fourth in the AL) in 63 games. His outstanding half-season prompted the Indians to move back the outfield fences at Cleveland Stadium by 15–20 feet, with general manager Hank Peters figuring they would try to win with speed and defense, primarily Cole's. The new dimensions would also help out the pitchers, as deep flyballs now became long outs instead of home runs, as the club looked to take advantage of the fact Cole and the Indians outfielders were more apt at chasing long flyballs than hitting them.

It didn't work out. Cole fell coming out of the batter's box during spring training and dislocated his shoulder. He was never the same again. In 1991, the fleet-footed outfielder would steal just 27 bases in 122 games—and be described as "tentative" and "so lost" on the basepaths by a Cleveland scribe, who noted Cole "just doesn't run the same" after the shoulder dislocation.[16] The team would finish 57–105 while ranking last in runs scored (576) and home runs (79), and third-to-last in steals (84). So, while the Indians moved the fences back, they also moved further back in the standings. "We were really close to having a good team," Candiotti laments. "Candy Maldonado had a good year [with 22 homers and 95 RBIs in 1990] and he really wanted to come back, but they didn't re-sign him after that season. When they traded Buddy Black and then didn't re-sign Maldonado, you could see the direction that they were going in."

The fences at Cleveland Stadium would return to their normal positions for the 1992 season, and Cole would be traded midseason. Candiotti was gone by then, having been dealt to Toronto in June 1991. When Candiotti reflects on the Indians' strategy of moving the fences specifically for Cole, he quips, "Dumbest thing in the world. For Alex Cole? Who the heck is Alex Cole?" The knuckleballer had a point. Cole had been a rookie the year before. Which other club would move its fences for a player who had a grand total of two months' worth of major league experience? Only in Cleveland.

"I think what happened," Candiotti elaborates, "was that they knew we had no offense and we were at most going to score two or three runs, and the way we were going to win was have the pitchers throw shutouts. They tried to make [the ballpark] more pitcher-friendly and also make it so we could use team speed. We didn't have power other than Albert Belle, really. But the whole experiment was just a total disaster. They couldn't get things right there, but when John Hart took over [as the general manager], you started to see change happening."

Gone were high-priced veterans like Candiotti and Greg Swindell. Cleveland would build a farm system that began to produce major league prospects, the front office would lock up those promising young players—like Charles Nagy, Sandy Alomar, and Carlos Baerga—to long-term contracts that eliminated arbitration years while signing several veterans who'd contribute on the field, and a brand new ballpark replacing Cleveland Stadium would be ready for 1994. The Indians would start winning ballgames and drawing fans to the new ballpark—at one point recording 455 consecutive sellouts from 1995 to 2001, at the time a major league record. By 1995, Cleveland would transform into a perennial pennant contender, having added veterans Dennis Martinez, Orel Hershiser, and Eddie Murray to go with a talented roster that already included youngsters like Alomar, Baerga, Belle, Kenny Lofton, Jim Thome, and Manny Ramirez.

Joe Klein, the former Indians GM, adds that when brothers Richard and David Jacobs bought the team from the Steve O'Neill estate in 1986 for $35 million, they rescued the struggling franchise. "The Indians were not a profit-making organization," says Klein. "When Steve O'Neill passed away, he left the team in trust. The commissioner's office, in concert with the Steve O'Neill estate, had to sell the franchise. The sale of the club to the Jacobs brothers was the impetus for the new stadium because they were realtors and commercial business people. [Soon enough,] they started winning and they had quite a run starting in the mid–1990s. Cleveland baseball became revitalized at that time. They became a model baseball franchise and things got better for them."

On June 2, 1991, Candiotti was 7–2 with a 2.25 ERA for an Indians team that was only 19–27. He was on his way to being the first pitcher ever to post four straight winning seasons for a losing team, according to sportswriter Peter Gammons later that month. With a 49–35 record in 1988–91 for Cleveland, his .583 winning percentage in that span was .151 higher than the Tribe's .432 in other games.[17]

Candiotti's 3–2 victory over Detroit on June 2 gave him a 72–61 record with Cleveland, an accomplishment he to this day is proud of. "You get dis-credited sometimes," Candiotti says, "because you throw a knuckleball. But when I was with the Indians all those years, when they were a really bad team, I won more games than I lost. People look at my career record and say, 'Oh, this guy doesn't know how to win' or 'Oh, this guy throws a knuckleball,' but I always won in Cleveland. Those were the best years of my big league career." That 72nd triumph made Candiotti just the fifth Indians pitcher since 1955 with that many victories, joining Sam McDowell (122), Gary Bell (96), Luis Tiant (75), and Rick Waits (74).

By midseason, there were already rumors about Candiotti (or another top-flight starter like Greg Swindell) being traded to the first-place Blue Jays, who seemed vulnerable to second-place Boston after losing ace Dave Stieb to an injury (initially a shoulder problem, but later also a sore back).[18] The Blue Jays were also lacking a consistent fifth starter. They had already tried Denis Boucher, Jim Acker, Willie Fraser, and Juan Guzman, all of whom had failed (though Guzman would get another shot after going 0–2 in his first two starts). Toronto was in Cleveland on June 11–13, and slugger Joe Carter was receptive regarding the possibility of the knuckleballer joining the Jays. "I've always been a Candiotti fan," Carter said. "Before the game we were joking that he didn't know if he'd be pitching to me or to [Indians designated hitter] Chris James. He'd be a welcome acquisition."[19]

What everyone knew, though, was that Candiotti wouldn't see much offense in Cleveland. As one AL scout noted, the Indians "don't have a number three, four or five hitter. What they have is a lot of leadoff hitters and number six, seven, eight and nine hitters."[20] Candiotti allowed three hits with two walks and nine strikeouts in a complete-game effort against Toronto on June 12, but lost, 1–0, to rookie Mike Timlin, who was auditioning as the Blue Jays' fifth starter. Timlin was making his first start since 1989 in Class A and had a subpar 3.92 ERA over 41.1 innings in 26 career big league relief appearances but took a no-hitter into the sixth inning, teaming up with three relievers to blank Cleveland.

It only got worse from there for Candiotti. Despite allowing just one walk with seven strikeouts over six innings in Chicago on June 18, Candiotti lost, 6–5, as shortstop Felix Fermin's sixth-inning error led to four unearned runs. On June 23 in Toronto, Candiotti allowed two runs in six innings but still lost, 3–1, as Timlin tossed five shutout innings and rookie reliever Bob Mac-Donald worked 2.1 hitless innings for his first big league victory. "My first major league win was over Cleveland and Candy was on the losing end of it," MacDonald recalls, adding Candiotti was very tough that year. "I know no hitter likes to hit a knuckleballer as they can start slumps that last weeks."

It was Cleveland's bats that had been slumping. Since June 7, Candiotti had gone 0–4 despite a 2.22 ERA in 28.1 innings with 24 strikeouts and seven walks. As for Timlin, who'd go on to register 74 career relief victories in the majors? While he was unscored upon when opposing Candiotti—in major league starts numbers one and three—he'd struggled in his second start on June 18, allowing three runs in 3.2 innings in a 4–2 loss to New York. Timlin's fourth and final big league start would come in 2002 with St. Louis, when he allowed four runs in 4.1 innings in Milwaukee and took the loss. Thus, in his two non–Candiotti starts, Timlin was 0–2 with a 7.88 ERA. In two starts against the knuckleballer, he was 1–0 with a 0.00 ERA.

Despite a 2.24 ERA through 15 starts on June 23, Candiotti was just 7–6 while losing games by scores of 2–1, 2–0, 1–0, 3–1, 8–1, and 6–5. In his two no-decisions: two runs (one earned) on five hits and one walk in seven innings at Texas on April 26, and one run on three hits with seven strikeouts over six innings at Seattle on May 7. With better support, Candiotti could have been 13–2. To put things in perspective, Minnesota's Scott Erickson was 11–2 with a 1.51 ERA, receiving eight-plus runs of support five times in his 14 starts. Boston's Roger Clemens was 9–4 with a 2.13 ERA.

Regardless, Candiotti was still proving to be one of the top pitchers in

Indians history. His outing on June 23 in Toronto marked his 172nd start in a Tribe uniform, and at the time, he had started the 15th-most games in the 90-year history of the franchise (1901–1991). His Cleveland resume also included the following numbers, along with his ranking in the Indians' team record books at the time:

- 176 appearances, 36th all-time in club history
- 45 complete games, 40th all-time
- 72 wins, tied for 22nd all-time
- 753 strikeouts, 16th all-time
- 3.53 ERA, 18th all-time for Indians pitchers with at least 1,000 innings
- 5.71 strikeouts per nine innings, sixth all-time for Indians pitchers with at least 1,000 innings (just behind Indians legend Bob Feller's 6.07)
- .526 winning percentage, 19th all-time for pitchers with at least 1,000 innings

But as it turned out, Tom Candiotti wouldn't continue to further etch his name into the club's record books. The veteran knuckleballer, 72–65 in his five-and-a-half seasons with Cleveland, would be traded to Toronto on June 23, 1991.

# 10

## *From Worst to First*

Tom Candiotti had heard the rumors throughout the spring of 1991. The Blue Jays, Red Sox, Athletics, and Cubs had all been talking with Cleveland about acquiring him in a trade.[1] Even the fourth-place Yankees were inquiring about him in June after completing an 8–4 homestand to close to within three-and-a-half games in the AL East.[2] A subsequent six-game road losing streak, though, brought New York back to reality. The other teams also eventually backed off, but the Toronto rumors wouldn't go away.

The Blue Jays had long been seeking a fifth starter, and with veteran ace Dave Stieb sidelined with a sore back, their starting rotation had two big holes.[3] Though Toronto was in first place with "only" Jimmy Key, Todd Stottlemyre, and David Wells, missing two starters could cripple the team's chances. The 1990 Indians, for instance, faded because they didn't have a fourth and fifth starter, despite the contributions of the top three guys Candiotti, Greg Swindell, and Bud Black. Seven different pitchers filled in for the last two spots in July and combined to go 1–12, and Cleveland fell out of contention.

Wanting to fill the void left by Stieb, Toronto pulled the trigger on June 27, trading lefthander Denis Boucher and outfielders Glenallen Hill and Mark Whiten to Cleveland for Candiotti and minor league outfielder Turner Ward. "I think it's a good deal for both teams," Blue Jays manager Cito Gaston said the day the trade was announced. "I know they got some good players and we got a quality pitcher. If he pitches for us the way he pitched against us, this will really help our staff."[4]

The acquisition of Candiotti also allowed Mike Timlin to return to the bullpen, where the rookie's relief innings were missed during the time he filled in as a starter. With Timlin and lefthander Bob MacDonald working in middle relief and hard throwers Duane Ward and Tom Henke closing games out, the

Toronto bullpen was back to being a dominant force. "Anytime an organization is willing to make a move to better the team," recalls MacDonald, "it's a positive thing. The thing is GM Pat Gillick made the move to make the team better, so we were happy about the move."

While the Blue Jays were happy about the trade, the man who originally gave Candiotti a shot in Cleveland was not. Joe Klein, who had moved on to Kansas City by 1991, was the Indians' GM who'd signed the knuckleballer in the winter of 1985. "I was sad [that the trade] happened," says Klein. "When you're the Cleveland Indians, especially at the trading deadline, everyone comes asking you for your best players. They'd try their best to get you to give a price on them. 'What'll it take to get them?' Once we found Tom, we weren't in a hurry to trade him because I thought he'd be a quality pitcher in the big leagues for a very long time. So it was sad to see him getting traded at the time."

Meanwhile, in Cincinnati, there was outrage that the defending world champion Reds didn't seriously pursue Candiotti. With the club fading because of its pitching woes, closer Rob Dibble ripped general manager Bob Quinn, saying, "We definitely had enough guys to get Candiotti ... but our management let him get away."[5] At one point during a four-week stretch, Cincinnati's third, fourth and fifth starters were a combined 2–10 with an ERA approaching 7.00. "Candiotti would have been the perfect complement to all our hard throwers in the bullpen," added Dibble.[6] The *New York Daily News*' Bill Madden agreed. "The Reds blew it on Tom Candiotti," wrote Madden. "[H]is dancing knuckler would have been the perfect complement to all that bullpen heat of theirs."[7]

In Toronto, where the Blue Jays had already made the postseason twice without winning a single series (losing the AL Championship Series in 1985 to Kansas City and in 1989 to Oakland), expectations were high. With the Candiotti acquisition, they were now supposed to win the AL pennant. "It was all over the newspapers and on television," Candiotti recalls. "There were very high expectations that the Blue Jays were now supposed to go to the World Series."

Boston manager Joe Morgan merely scoffed at that notion, suggesting that Toronto "gave up too much" in acquiring the knuckleballer. "Candiotti might not win five games," Morgan said. "Now they'll probably have to go get a catcher."[8] He had a point. How were the Blue Jays going to fare without a catcher who could handle a knuckleball? Neither one of their catchers—Pat Borders and Greg Myers—had any experience with that pitch. "He gave me nightmares," Borders would say of Candiotti and that knuckler the following spring. "Besides just trying to catch the thing, it is practically impossible to throw anybody out at second and, with a guy on third, that's all he ever wanted to throw."[9]

The game that best exemplified Borders's comments came on July 16 in

Kansas City, three weeks after the trade. But it was Myers feeling the frustration with "the thing." Toronto led, 1–0, in the ninth inning with Candiotti trying to complete the shutout. Alas, with a runner on third, a knuckleball eluded Myers for a passed ball, tying the game. In the 10th inning, Myers made a bad throw when Bill Pecota took off from second trying to steal on another Candiotti knuckler, and Pecota scored the winning run as the ball scooted away in left field.

Myers's misadventures showed everyone just how difficult Candiotti's knuckler was to handle. How could a team in a pennant race rely on a knuckleball? This trade was no guarantee. Boston third baseman Wade Boggs, referring to the Blue Jays' late-season collapse in 1990 even after acquiring two veteran lefthanders, noted, "Last year, when they got Bud Black and John Candelaria, everybody said they were going to win the division."[10] This time Toronto had given up Mark Whiten and Glenallen Hill—two outfield prospects who could hit with power, run, and throw—as well as lefty Denis Boucher. "With Whiten and Hill gone," continued Boggs, "what happens if somebody goes down in their outfield?"[11] Added Boston general manager Lou Gorman: "I'll tell you in October whether it was a good deal."[12]

The Red Sox, despite their bravado, had their own issues. The fifth-place Yankees had just swept them at Fenway, dropping them to three-and-a-half games behind Toronto. In that series, Boston ace Roger Clemens was pounded for six runs by a Yankee ballclub that was a mediocre 28–37 going in. Clemens, who was battling a stomach virus, had allowed at least four runs in each of his last three starts, losing two of them. The rest of the rotation was also limping, as Mike Gardiner (5.1 IP, 5 R) and Tom Bolton (3.2 IP, 8 R) both faltered against New York, with Gardiner being placed on the disabled list after that start. To make matters worse, the two big free agents pitchers Boston had signed during the offseason, Matt Young and Danny Darwin, were sidelined with injuries for a huge chunk of the year.

While Boston thought its rivals had given up too much to get Candiotti, some AL scouts didn't think so. Some said, for instance, Boucher was still pitching Class A Advanced ball a year earlier. Plus, he was an off-speed pitcher, not a strikeout guy. Hill's attitude and strikeout ratio were questioned, with one AL personnel director going as far as saying Hill was nothing more than "a platoon player" and Boucher "a little overrated."[13] Whiten might be the best of the trio, but as another baseball executive was quoted in the papers as saying, he wasn't a sure thing, either. "You're gambling on Whiten's bat," the executive said. "Will he hit enough to be a big-time player?"[14]

Wrote the *New York Daily News*' Bill Madden, general manager Pat Gillick "gave up no one who figured big in the Blue Jays' future. Of the three, only Whiten, a switch-hitting outfielder with speed, has gotten high ratings from the scouts. But he has yet to show he can hit at the major league level and as one scout said of him this week: 'He's got great tools, but I think the Blue Jays did a great job of overrating him.'"[15] Madden added the deal "has all but clinched the AL East pennant for Toronto.... In Candiotti, the Jays get a durable, 200-inning starter with the third-lowest ERA (2.24) in the AL, a veritable ace. And with Dave Stieb sidelined with a back injury (not to mention his history of being anything but an ace in September), Candiotti was the one commodity the Blue Jays needed to assure themselves of playing in the postseason."[16]

Toronto rightfielder Joe Carter suggested a fifth starter was still needed with Boucher gone and nobody else able to do a credible job in that role. "We still don't have a number five starter because this guy is like a number two," Carter said of Candiotti.[17] Before the trade, Toronto had veteran lefthander Jimmy Key and two younger starters in Todd Stottlemyre and David Wells. Rookie Juan Guzman, tried out as the fourth starter, was 0–2 with an 8.31 ERA in his first two major league starts in June, with both outings against last-place Baltimore (which at 21–38 was the worst team in baseball). Guzman didn't last five innings in either of those two starts, and walked six Orioles—all of whom scored. Meanwhile, Boucher, Jim Acker, Mike Timlin, and Willie Fraser had all had turns in the number five spot. Boucher (0–3, 4.58) and Fraser (0–1, 18.00 as a starter) were gone, and Acker (1–2, 7.52 as a starter) looked awful. Timlin, who'd been a closer in the minors, was best suited to pitch in relief.

At the time, Toronto desperately needed a veteran starter to step in to anchor the rotation. A 200-inning pitcher every year since 1986, Candiotti was that starter. He was going to take pressure off the bullpen and the younger starters. "We're just not too certain how [injured] Stieb is," Gillick said then. "At this point, we had Timlin and Guzman in the rotation, and we needed a fourth guy. [Candiotti] was available. We talked about a lot of players, and we just felt this was the way to go. We've got an opportunity to win the division."[18]

The Blue Jays had already made three major acquisitions in the offseason with the 1991 AL East title in mind, getting Devon White from California to solidify the center field position and trading for Carter and Roberto Alomar from San Diego to land a proven RBI man and a talented, young All-Star caliber infielder, respectively. With those new pieces, Toronto was in first place. With Stieb sidelined, another starter was needed, and Candiotti was regarded as the answer. "Tom was a little bit different style of pitcher and the rest—or the most—of the people we had were fastball pitchers," recalls Gillick. "As far as their styles of pitching, they had very different styles. Wells was a hard thrower. Guzman was a hard thrower, which was one reason we liked to have Tom on the club, was the variation of styles. And he was a workhorse capable of delivering 200-plus innings, something he'd done [in each of the previous five seasons]."

For Gillick, the Candiotti trade was his latest attempt in trying to bring a pennant to Toronto. Under Gillick's watch, the Blue Jays hadn't had a losing season since 1983—the only major league club which could boast that feat—while winning AL East titles in 1985 and 1989. However, they had not won a post-season series in two tries. Not that Gillick hadn't made deals to try and put his club over the top. Over the past few seasons, he had made mid- or late-season deals for pitching, trying to win that elusive pennant. Those trades just never panned out. For instance, in 1990, Gillick acquired John Candelaria and Bud Black down the stretch from Minnesota and Cleveland, respectively, but the two lefthanders combined to go 2–4 with a 4.86 ERA and Toronto missed the postseason. In 1987, lefthander Mike Flanagan was obtained from Baltimore and went 3–2 with a 2.37 ERA in seven starts but Toronto fell short, failing to make the postseason.

Then there was Cleveland's Phil Niekro, acquired that same season in 1987. But the ancient knuckleballer was 0–2 with an 8.35 ERA in three starts before earning his release. "Pat Gillick loves knuckleball pitchers," says Joe Klein. "Phil Niekro went there at the end of 1987. Pat was looking for a starter for three or four games and he didn't want to bring anyone up from the minor leagues. And I thought Niekro would be a good change of pace for him. And then Pat later took a shot at Candiotti. The one in Chicago was probably the one Pat wanted. Charlie Hough. But Pat tried Candy up there and Tom gave it a good effort."

Did Klein ever bug Gillick about his penchant for picking up knuckle-ballers? "I remember seeing Pat at the winter meetings later on," Klein says. "I smiled and kind of gave him the knuckleball sign. He said, 'If I keep trying, I'll find one.' He never did get Charlie Hough, though. But Candy did real well for him."

According to journalist Adrian Brijbassi, the fans and media weren't thrilled that the team's newest pitcher threw a knuckleball. "Candiotti was the type of guy Gillick wanted to get, but he was a knuckleballer," says Brijbassi. "Automatically, there was that perception. It wasn't as sexy as getting, say, a Jack Morris, a hard thrower and a big-time winner. Candiotti threw a knuckleball. He tried to trick you. He wasn't a charismatic guy or a particularly good-looking guy like [fellow knuckleballer] Tim Wakefield [who'd go 8–1 as a rookie with Pittsburgh in 1992]. I don't think people were all that excited about him. They just felt, 'Okay, this guy's just here. He may be at the top of the rotation but we still love Jimmy Key more.' And they had Juan Guzman, who was your hard-throwing righthander. As far as Candiotti goes, he was your classic rental player. You just felt he was probably past his prime. His prime was in Cleveland. You weren't going to invest a whole lot, either emotionally or as a fan, into him."

Despite Brijbassi's comments, Candiotti was actually having a good year in 1991, aside from wins and losses. From May 27-July 23, Candiotti had a 1.76 ERA over 11 starts—six with Cleveland and five with Toronto—but received more than three runs of support just twice, resulting in a 4–7 record in that span. For the season, he was 9–9 with a 2.09 ERA. In his first five Blue Jays starts, he had a 1.65 ERA while allowing nine walks with 27 strikeouts over 38.1 innings. Yet he was only 2–3, suffering 3–1, 2–1, and 3–2 losses. In his last few starts with Cleveland, he'd lost games by scores of 1–0, 2–0, and 3–1.

Candiotti was victorious, though, in his second and third starts with Toronto on July 3 and July 11, stymieing Minnesota, 4–0, and Texas, 2–0.[19] Both the Twins and Rangers were in first place in the AL West at the time he faced them, but Candiotti was tough, striking out 17 batters over those two games. His victory over Texas gave the Blue Jays their 16th win in 19 games, allowing Toronto to move six-and-a-half games ahead of Boston. "Even prior to the trade, we felt we had the best team from top to bottom," recalls Bob MacDonald. "Adding Candy only solidified the team even further. I wouldn't say he put us 'over the top' in that regard, though he certainly added another 'bullet' in the Toronto gun that we felt was pretty loaded to begin with."

The trade also allowed Candiotti to be reunited with former Indians teammates Joe Carter and Pat Tabler. On July 14, he saw another familiar face in town as the Jays acquired ex–Tribe outfielder Cory Snyder from the White Sox. "I knew Candy, Carter, and Tabler from Cleveland," Snyder recalls. "It was kind of weird how we all went to Toronto for a little bit. But it was exciting to be able to play for a team that had a chance to go to the playoffs." Then on August 9, Toronto traded for Brewers outfielder Candy Maldonado, who played for Cleveland in 1990. Ex-Indians outfielder Turner Ward, acquired in the Candiotti trade, was still in Triple-A but would be called up later in the season.

"It felt like we were still in Cleveland, with all of the ex-teammates there," recalls Candiotti. But in reality, being with Toronto was nothing like what he'd experienced with the Tribe. For example, the last time Candiotti pitched at Cleveland Stadium on June 12, only 8,089 fans were on hand. But in the victory over Minnesota on July 3 at SkyDome, he was pitching in front of a crowd of 50,071, a total that bumped the Blue Jays' attendance figure to 2,039,708 for the year. It was the fastest 2,000,000 in big league history, something the club had achieved in only 42 home dates.[20]

Buck Martinez played for Toronto during the Exhibition Stadium era in the 1980s but was a broadcaster and manager at various times for the franchise after SkyDome opened in 1989. Fans were coming to SkyDome in droves, noted Martinez, because the Blue Jays were winning and people were excited about the team and the new ballpark. "Toronto fans had become very loyal," he once said about the state-of-the-art stadium, "very quickly and with the Blue Jays getting better and better by the year ... and Blue Jays games were the place to be. It became a national thing. People from all across Canada bought into it, and even internationally, people were coming from all over the world to see the stadium because it was so unique."[21]

The Indians, meanwhile, had drawn more than 2,000,000 fans just twice in their entire history—and that was back in 1948 and 1949.[22] Cleveland never contended for a pennant after its 1954 World Series loss, and people stayed away from the ballpark for decades, with fewer than 1,000,000 fans in attendance in 22 of the last 31 years. In the 1980s, Cleveland had baseball's second-worst attendance (10,144,299), just ahead of Seattle (9,839,630). The Tribe finished in the bottom three in the league in attendance in four of Candiotti's five full seasons on the team. In 1988, even when Cleveland had the best record in baseball in April, fans stayed away. In 13 home games that month, the team averaged under 13,500 fans per game. In one stretch of eight games at Cleveland Stadium in April, an average of only 5,562 fans showed up, and this was during a time when the Indians were on their way to a 16–6 start. In 1990, Cleveland averaged an AL-worst 15,126 fans per home game in a ballpark with a capacity that exceeded 70,000.

"It was just that the old atmosphere was very tough," Indians catcher Sandy Alomar, Jr. noted about Cleveland Stadium. "It was cold, it was right next to the lake, and it's so old."[23] The ballpark, located just south of Lake Erie, was known for the biting cold winds that would blow into the stadium during much of the spring and fall. During hot summer nights, the artificial lights from the stadium would attract swarms of annoying insects like midges and mayflies from the lake.[24] It was hardly a ballpark for anybody to be excited about. "Their 60-year-old stadium, a dreary, cavernous edifice, works against the team, psychologically and economically," *New York Times* sportswriter Murray Chass once noted.[25] Added Reds general manager Bob Quinn, who'd spent 13 years working in the Cleveland organization, about the Indians' ballpark: "The stadium is a gloomy place."[26]

Interestingly, the Blue Jays hit like the Indians when Candiotti was pitching for them. He received only 2.33 runs per game in his first nine starts with Toronto, resulting in a 2–5 record despite a 2.60 ERA. Even the manager would joke about Candiotti's hard luck. On days Candiotti was starting, Cito Gaston would announce to the players, "Candy's pitching today, so I guess we're not getting any runs," or "By the way, you guys better score some runs for Candy or he might not be back next season."

The Blue Jays were certainly pleased that Candiotti was averaging more than seven innings per outing in his first nine starts. Prior to Candiotti's arrival, the fifth-starter rotation of Jim Acker, Willie Fraser, Denis Boucher, and Mike Timlin made 15 starts with a 2–7 record and 5.40 ERA, and averaged fewer than five innings per outing. "The guy's done everything we've asked of him but he's just had bad luck pitching for us. We've never got him any runs," said Gaston.[27]

Most of the time the bullpen wasn't needed when Candiotti took the mound, says Bob MacDonald. "When he went out there, Candy always had a chance to complete a game," recalls MacDonald. "So our feeling as relievers when Candy took the mound is that he always had a chance to complete a game and never got us involved. Duane Ward was a reliever who was putting up 100-plus innings from the bullpen. He needed the days off, if at all possible." With Candiotti able to take pressure off the bullpen every fifth day, it helped everybody on the staff, thereby benefitting the team. "He probably didn't win as many games as he should have with the way he pitched," Key said about Candiotti, "but he did exactly what the club needed him to do. He pitched a lot of innings and kept us in games. He took a burden off the other starters because when he pitched, you knew he'd go seven or eight innings. That meant the bullpen would be rested for the next game. He's a staff saver."[28]

In Toronto's 4–0, 14-inning loss to Detroit on August 8 at SkyDome, Candiotti tossed four-hit ball over seven innings and tied his career high with 12 strikeouts. That night, with the knuckler working from the get-go, Candiotti fanned the game's first two batters before walking Dave Bergman. Cecil Fielder then struck out but reached base as catcher Greg Myers dropped the third strike. Another passed ball by Myers advanced both runners before Mickey Tettleton walked. Incredibly, the Tigers had struck out three times and hadn't gotten a hit but had the bases loaded. Candiotti, though, got out of the inning unscathed.

"It was tough for Myers and [Pat] Borders to adjust to me midseason," reflects Candiotti about the catching situation. "They'd never caught a knuckleball before. Because I threw the knuckleball, I normally spent more time with my catchers than other pitchers. People don't realize this—even the guys in the media—but not having spring training to work with them made a big difference." Candiotti's 12 strikeouts also equaled a single-game Blue Jays club record shared by Pete Vuckovich (1977), Jim Clancy (1988), and Dave Stieb (1988). But he didn't get a chance to set the record as he was pulled after seven innings. He didn't get the victory, either, as Toronto couldn't score the entire evening and Detroit won it with four runs off Tom Henke in the 14th.

From July 16 to August 13, Candiotti compiled a 3.22 ERA—allowing 17 walks and 39 hits over 44.2 innings—but Toronto lost all six of his starts. In his last 13 outings, he was 2–9 with a 2.49 ERA. On August 13, Candiotti had an American League-best 2.38 ERA but a 9–11 record overall, 2–5 with the Blue Jays. The team was struggling, too, losing seven straight contests in the second week of August. On August 14, second-place Detroit had clawed to within two games of Toronto, with third-place Boston only five-and-a-half games back.

Still, general manager Pat Gillick knew Candiotti was doing the job. "He rests the bullpen, he helps a staff in a lot of ways that statistics don't show," Gillick noted.[29] Before pitching in the finale of a big three-game series on August 18 at Tiger Stadium, Candiotti lamented that his record wasn't indicative of his pitching. "I don't think I can ever recall pitching this well—there are only four games I shouldn't have won," said Candiotti.[30] His good pitching would continue in Detroit. When the Jays arrived in town for their series on August 16–18, they had a slim two-game lead in the AL East.

|           | W-L   | GB  |
|-----------|-------|-----|
| Toronto   | 63–53 | —   |
| Detroit   | 61–55 | 2.0 |
| Boston    | 57–58 | 5.5 |

The two teams split the first two contests, meaning Toronto still had a two-game advantage and would leave Detroit in first place, regardless of what happened in the finale. Candiotti pitched the Blue Jays to a 4–2 victory anyway, tossing three-hit ball over seven innings, and Toronto headed home with a three-game lead in the division.

On August 28, Candiotti was at it again. In his 12th start with Toronto, Candiotti came through with one of the greatest clutch—yet most underappreciated—pitching performances in team history. He tossed an eight-inning one-hitter in Baltimore, giving the Jays some breathing room in the standings. Toronto began the day with a one-game lead over Detroit, which had Bill Gullickson—who had a majors-best 16 victories—pitching that night against last-place California. The Jays, meanwhile, were trying to complete a three-game sweep in Baltimore with Candiotti pitching—but it was a tall task as they'd never swept a series at Memorial Stadium. Then there were the lifetime batting averages against Candiotti by the numbers one, two and five hitters in the Orioles' lineup: Mike Devereaux at .375, Joe Orsulak at .529, and Randy Milligan at .444.

With the Tigers trotting out their best pitcher against the Angels, it was plausible that they'd win their game and be tied with Toronto atop the East by the end of the night. But somehow, even with Gullickson tossing a complete-game five-hitter, Detroit still lost, 1–0. The turning point in the Blue Jays-Orioles contest, meanwhile, came in the first inning when Baltimore threatened against Candiotti—but couldn't score.

With one out, Orsulak lined an opposite-field single off the glove of third baseman Kelly Gruber. A groundout moved Orsulak to second before Glenn Davis walked. A passed ball moved both runners into scoring position for Milligan, a .444 career hitter against Candiotti. The Toronto knuckleballer, however, struck him out swinging on a full-count pitch to escape the jam unscathed. Baltimore got nothing else the rest of the night as Milligan's strikeout marked the first of 22 straight outs recorded by Candiotti, who held the Orioles to just that one Orsulak hit over eight innings.

With Toronto ahead, 3–0, hitting coach Gene Tenace sent closer Tom Henke into the game to start the ninth. (Manager Cito Gaston had been hospitalized a week earlier with a sore back. During Gaston's 33-game absence, Tenace took over as the interim manager.) Henke proceeded to toss a 1–2–3 inning to complete the one-hitter, as the Jays moved two games ahead of Detroit. "With the bullpen we've got, there's no sense in forcing a guy to go back out there when he's done his job," Tenace said of Candiotti, who threw 110 pitches on the humid night.[31] As for Baltimore's lone hit, the Orsulak liner that went off the tip of Gruber's glove? Gruber felt he should've caught it. "I could've had it and I should've had it," the third baseman lamented. "I don't know how I missed it."[32]

Candiotti, meanwhile, continued to roll as he notched 4–1 and 6–0 wins over Cleveland on September 7 and Oakland on September 14. The victory over the A's, Candiotti's 13th of the year, improved his record to 35–1 lifetime when he received six or more runs of support. He also lowered his major league-leading ERA to 2.26 and recorded his 25th quality start, prompting the Associated Press to call him "the best 13–11 pitcher in baseball."[33] On September 18 in Seattle, Candiotti took a three-hit shutout into the eighth inning—the eighth time in 16 Blue Jays starts that he began a game with at least seven scoreless innings—but had just a slim 1–0 lead. The Mariners tied it in the eighth before Toronto prevailed, 5–3, in 12 innings to snap a three-game losing streak and remain two-and-a-half games ahead of Boston, which had gone 28–10 since August 9. "I should've had at least 18 wins by then," Candiotti reflects. "My strikeouts were up. My walks were down. I had the best ERA in the league. It was my best season ever."

And Candiotti was doing it with his team in the pennant race. Though the Blue Jays' lead in the AL East had shrunk to two games in mid–August, they wouldn't relinquish their position in the standings, thanks in part to their knuckleballer's 4–0 record and 1.72 ERA from August 18 to September 18, with Toronto winning all seven of his starts.

But as it turned out, Candiotti wouldn't win another game in 1991.

# 11

## *"You've gotta throw more knuckleballs..."*

On the morning of September 23, 1991, Tom Candiotti had a major league-leading 2.23 ERA over 31 starts, just ahead of Boston's Roger Clemens (2.43) for the American League ERA race. In his 226.1 innings, Candiotti had allowed only 186 hits, 66 walks, and 12 homers while recording 162 strikeouts. In his 16 starts since being traded from Cleveland to Toronto, the knuckleballer's ERA was 2.21. Over his last nine outings, it was 1.60. With two weeks remaining in the season, Candiotti was on pace to post the AL's sixth-best ERA since the advent of the designated hitter in 1973:

| | |
|---|---|
| Ron Guidry (1978) | 1.74 |
| Roger Clemens (1990) | 1.93 |
| Dave Righetti (1981) | 2.05 |
| Jim Palmer (1975) | 2.09 |
| Bret Saberhagen (1989) | 2.16 |
| Tom Candiotti (1991) | 2.23 |

Unfortunately, disaster struck that night in California. Though Candiotti was suffering from an abscessed tooth and had received injections to reduce the pain before the game, he still took the mound against the Angels. He retired the first two batters, but California loaded the bases on two singles and a walk. Max Venable lined a three-run triple to right, and Ron Tingley doubled home two more runs after a bunt single by Luis Sojo. The Angels then re-loaded the bases before Candiotti was pulled, and Dave Gallagher smacked a two-run single on a 1-and-2 pitch off rookie David Weathers to make it 7–0. Toronto valiantly fought back against Chuck Finley, only to lose the game, 10–9.

With those seven earned runs, Candiotti's ERA jumped to 2.50, now second in the AL to Clemens's 2.43. (Had Weathers retired Gallagher, Candiotti would've been charged with "only" five earned runs and his ERA would've been 2.42.) "We went into Anaheim and I was having lunch with David Wells," Candiotti recalls. "As I was eating, I bit into a chip and I almost fell off my chair. Something happened to my tooth. I was like, 'What in the world happened?' And then I was pitching that night. I called the trainer out to look at me when I got to the ballpark. They had to call a dentist to come down and examine me. He came in and looked at me, and he thought I cracked a tooth or something happened with the nerves. So they shot me with six shots of Novocain in my mouth. And they gave me some Tylenol and said, 'Go get them.' My mouth was swollen like a chipmunk."

Soon after, interim manager Gene Tenace and pitching coach Galen Cisco went into the clubhouse to check on his status. "Can you pitch?" they asked. Candiotti could barely talk but didn't want to let his team down. "Yeah," the knuckleballer countered, "I can pitch. Sure."

Everyone was happy with the answer. "Good," said Tenace, "because we need you to pitch tonight."

Candiotti responded firmly, "Okay, I'll give you everything I got." And that was that. He was getting the ball that night.

"So I threw my warm-up pitches," Candiotti recalls, "and they gave me two more shots before I went out in the first inning. So I had eight shots altogether in my mouth. I went out there and next thing you know, I gave up seven runs. It didn't have anything to do with the knuckleball. It was more me pitching all injected up. The next day I had to go to the dentist and, of course, have a root canal done. It was a fractured tooth. But that one game against the Angels cost me that ERA title because I [eventually] lost it by three-hundredths of a point to Roger Clemens."

Would a pitcher today make that start to jeopardize losing the ERA title? Candiotti thinks not. "Can you imagine somebody doing that nowadays?" he asks rhetorically. "Most people would've said, 'No, I can't pitch. I've just been injected eight times in the mouth.' They wouldn't have made the start. Of course I couldn't pitch. I didn't have my normal pre-game and I wasn't really ready to pitch. But back then, when you're in the pennant race and when the manager and pitching coach say, 'Hey, listen. We need you,' it was like, 'Okay, I'll give you what I got.'"

On September 28 against Minnesota, Candiotti outpitched Jack Morris through four innings, retiring eight straight batters in one stretch while the Twins' righthander had allowed at least a hit in every inning. But disaster struck in the fifth when Brian Harper hit an easy double-play grounder to first baseman John Olerud. Recalls Candiotti, "Olerud flipped the ball—it wasn't a good flip—into the base, into the runner, and I had to grab the ball and it made me go into the baseline. [Harper] came down, right on, just missed my Achilles tendon on my right foot. He cut it really bad. [Unfortunately] the ball, [Harper], and myself, all got to the bag at the same time. If the ball got to me sooner, I could catch it and then look for the bag. I go in [to the dugout] and the guy looks at it and he stitches it. I get five stitches in my right foot. And I still go out to pitch. But it was bad. It was ripped open, and my sock was bloody."

Though Candiotti could barely push off the rubber, he tried to continue pitching. But he wasn't the same after being spiked by Harper, the only player on the field wearing spikes. Minnesota scored four runs off the knuckleballer in that inning to break open a scoreless game, and went on to win, 5–0. Candiotti's ERA climbed to 2.60, a distant second behind Clemens's 2.38. But while Clemens (who defeated Baltimore, 2–1, on September 26) was leading the ERA race, his Red Sox were fading. The same day Morris beat Candiotti, Boston lost for the fifth time in six games and remained three-and-a-half games behind with only eight to play. Fast forward to October 2, when Toronto began the day with a four-and-a-half-game lead and gave the ball to Candiotti against the California Angels at SkyDome. It was a historic night as the Blue Jays became the first team in big league history to reach 4,000,000 in attendance for the season. Toronto also had a chance to clinch its third AL East title in seven seasons with a victory.

To understand Candiotti's impact in Toronto, one only needs to look at its opponents in the division-clincher, the 1991 Angels. California had three 18-game winners in lefthanders Mark Langston, Jim Abbott, and Chuck Finley, but spent most of the final two months of the season in last place. On July 3, the Angels were 44–33 and tied atop the AL West standings, but a seven-game losing streak (which included four shutout defeats) dropped them to fifth place. They were out of contention by July 31, falling to eight games out and in the sixth spot.

Part of California's problem was an offense that ranked second-to-last in the AL in runs and home runs. Another was the back end of its rotation; fourth starter Kirk McCaskill went 10–19 with a 4.26 ERA while the number five spot was a total disaster. The Angels used several pitchers in that spot, but none delivered. Scott Lewis was 2–5 with a 6.83 ERA in 11 starts; Mike Fetters was 0–4 with a 5.74 in four tries; Joe Grahe, 2–7 and 5.37 in 10 starts; and Kyle Abbott, 1–2 and 4.58 in three starts. Even ex–Dodger ace Fernando Valenzuela got in two starts, going 0–2 with a 12.15 ERA.

Ironically, it was California visiting SkyDome in Toronto's potential division-clincher, which should serve as a reminder that the Blue Jays' fortunes could have been the same as the Angels' if not for Candiotti. Like California, Toronto struggled offensively as it ranked 11th out of 14 AL teams in runs scored while lacking production from its DH spot throughout the season (.248, five HRs, 57 RBIs, with one of those homers an inside-the-park job).[1] Like California, the Jays were down to three starting pitchers in May and June—Jimmy Key, Todd Stottlemyre, and David Wells—as their parade of fourth and fifth starters weren't getting it done. Without Candiotti—who'd averaged over 6.2 innings in his 18 starts while compiling a 2.92 ERA with the Blue Jays—Toronto might well have collapsed. (Set-up man Mike Timlin might have moved to the rotation, taking a valuable arm out of the bullpen and forcing the other starters, including rookie Juan Guzman, to pitch deeper into ballgames.)

But in the season's final week, Toronto was about to win its division while California was struggling to finish above .500. One more victory—or one more Boston loss—meant the Jays would clinch the East. After six innings they led, 4–3, and when Candiotti began the seventh by striking out Kevin Flora, they were just eight outs away. At that juncture, Candiotti was pulled with one out and nobody on, having thrown 108 pitches. Though California got runs off Wells and Timlin to go ahead, 5–4, Toronto rallied in the bottom of the ninth and won it on Joe Carter's RBI single, setting off a big celebration at SkyDome.

As Carter reflected, it was a great story for both himself and Candiotti. The two of them had experienced the lean years in Cleveland, and were now division champions in Toronto. "I thought about how far we had come the night we won the division," Carter said a few days later. "Candiotti was on the mound at the start and I got the hit in the bottom of the ninth that won it. It was like a fairy tale, a dream come true."[2] And was it different at SkyDome compared to old Cleveland Stadium? "Yeah, it's different to go from where there's nobody in the stands to where you draw 4,000,000," added Carter.[3]

Outfielder Cory Snyder, who didn't play in the division-clincher, concurs years later. "There's a huge difference," says Snyder, who in 2014 was a coach with the Tacoma Rainiers of the Pacific Coast League. "I loved Cleveland. There were some great fans and great people there. But when you're playing—and it doesn't matter where you're at—when you're playing in front of a packed house and there are a lot of fans, it's awesome. Even though ballplayers play hard, there's an extra incentive for ballplayers to really play harder for the team because of all the people out there supporting you. It was just kind of a different atmosphere [in Toronto]. They had some good teams. They had some winning ways. So it was a good time."

As left-handed reliever Bob MacDonald recalls, it was the best of times in Toronto. "Sold out every game from mid–May on," says MacDonald when reflecting back on the atmosphere at SkyDome. "Fifty thousand every game, the stadium was brand new, you were a celebrity in the city, and the team was winning. In the years that followed, all *four* of those things were never matched with the other organizations I played with [the Tigers, Yankees, and Mets]. It was truly something special."

When 1991 ended, Candiotti led the majors with 27 quality starts and finished with the AL's second-best ERA at 2.65, just behind Roger Clemens's 2.62. His Toronto ERA of 2.98 led all Blue Jays starters, as did his three complete games. Candiotti's total of 167 strikeouts was more than any other Toronto pitcher, and his 6.32 strikeouts per nine innings was second on the team. Eighteen times in his 34 starts he allowed one earned run or none while pitching at least six innings. It was the AL's highest single-season total since Ron Guidry had 20 in 1978, according to Baseball-Reference.com. Candiotti also allowed two runs or fewer while working six or more innings a total of 22 times in 1991. Since 1916, the AL's highest single-season total was 27, a record held by Bob Feller (1946), Denny McLain (1968), and Wilbur Wood (1972).

Still, because Toronto averaged just 3.12 runs in his 19 starts, Candiotti went only 6–7. Rightfielder Joe Carter, though, knew that the knuckleballer did his job as the Blue Jays desperately needed his quality innings with ace Dave Stieb sidelined since late May. "We needed that guy who could

Candiotti pitched effectively for the American League East champion Blue Jays during the 1991 season, logging a 2.98 ERA with a team-leading three complete games. Even though the mid-season trade to Toronto didn't give the Blue Jays' catchers a lot of time to adjust to his knuckleball, Candiotti still recorded 14 quality starts in his 19 regular-season appearances. He also received the Blue Jays' Pitcher of the Month honor in August, voted by the Toronto Chapter of the Baseball Writers Association of America. However, a lack of run support yielded Candiotti a losing record of six wins and seven losses in his 19 starts (courtesy Toronto Blue Jays).

go out ... every fifth day, pitch seven, eight, nine innings, and keep us in a game," Carter said of Candiotti, who recorded 14 quality starts for Toronto. "He makes everybody in the rotation better because he takes a strain off the bullpen when he pitches."[4]

The Jays advanced to the AL Championship Series against Minnesota. If Candiotti was being considered to start Game One at the Hubert H. Humphrey Metrodome, it would have been one of the logical choices. Statistics aside, Candiotti was also a veteran who wouldn't be rattled by the boisterous Metrodome crowd, and his knuckleball worked best in a domed stadium, where there were no elements to affect the pitch. That knuckler was precisely the reason Cito Gaston (who rejoined the team after missing 33 games recovering from his bad back) picked him for Game One. As far as the skipper was concerned, Candiotti's knuckleball could upset the Twins hitters' timing and put them in a slump. "When I was a hitting coach," Gaston said of Candiotti, "I used to hate seeing him start the first game of a three-game series because he'd throw the hitters off for two or three days. Hopefully, he can do that here."[5]

"That sounds like Cito," Joe Klein chuckles when told about Gaston's theory. "It kind of makes sense. In Texas one year [in 1979], when I was the farm director of the Rangers, we had Fergie Jenkins, Steve Comer, Doc Medich, and Doyle Alexander, four average-fastball righthanders. We got beat in [August] when we lost [22 of 31 games]. By the third game of a series, when a team sees too many average-fastball righthanders, they're able to hit them. [Teams] just beat the daylights out of us that one year."

Klein brings up the 1979 Rangers to illustrate the point about the philosophy behind having a variety of pitching styles in a rotation. Texas finished third in the AL West that year, five games behind division-winning California. Klein believes the Rangers faded because they had the same type of pitchers. Sure, lefthanders Jon Matlack and John Henry Johnson made starts at various points during the year, but the four righthanders were getting the majority of them. Without a different style of pitcher to give opponents a different look, Texas was at a major disadvantage. Opposing batters were seeing the same pitches every night, and were hitting them. "That goes back to what Cito was talking about, having different kinds of guys," says Klein. "That's why Cito's idea was good. In Cito's case, hey, maybe it didn't work, but it was a good plan. Separate the hard-throwers with soft-tossers."

Gaston's rotation gave Toronto that precise strategy. Start off with the knuckleballing Candiotti, then the hard-throwing Juan Guzman, followed by the finesse pitching of Jimmy Key, and back to hard-throwing Todd Stottlemyre. If the series was extended beyond four games, then it was back to Candiotti, Guzman, and Key. Unfortunately, it wasn't so simple. All of the excitement over the division title in the city of Toronto was great, but the expectation this year was for the Blue Jays to win the World Series. Torontonians had been through several late-season collapses since 1985, and felt that 1991 was their year. No excuses. No alibis. These Jays had to win. The big question entering the ALCS was: Who would start Game One? When it was announced Candiotti was getting the start, second-guessers surfaced immediately in the Toronto papers.

Long-time Dodgers general manager Fred Claire doesn't want to get into whether a knuckleballer should start a post-season series opener but does share Gaston's sentiments that such a pitcher could upset a hitter's timing. "There are advantages [with knuckleball pitchers] because first of all, they are very rare, so hitters aren't accustomed to seeing knuckleballs," Claire says. "It's a very difficult pitch to throw, and it's just as difficult to hit. So once you have someone who can establish some command with a knuckleball, you have someone who can fit into a staff. You don't have to worry about being overloaded from the standpoint of having opposing teams face three or four right-handed pitchers in a row—or three or four left-handed pitchers in a row. So, a knuckleball pitcher really breaks up the rotation of what the opposing hitters are seeing, and hitting is timing. Anytime you can throw off timing, you've got a chance to be successful."

Joe Carter, teammates with Candiotti from 1986 to 1989 in Cleveland, was happy with the arrangement of the rotation. "In a big game, I want to see him on the mound," Carter said of the knuckleballer the day before Game One, calling him "a gamer" and even thinking it was fitting they'd both be in the starting lineup.[6] "This has been a long time coming for us," Carter added. "With Candy on the mound, I know it's destiny."[7] Cory Snyder, who was left off the 1991 post-season roster, believes starting Candiotti in Game One was the right decision. "Candy was a great pitcher," Snyder says. "I don't know why you wouldn't want him on the mound for a big game because he was a great pitcher. For anybody at all to think that it was wrong for him to [pitch] the first game, in my opinion, is wrong. I don't care when Tom threw, he had a great chance. Every time he was on the mound, I felt, as a team we felt, we had a great chance to win that night. When you have that feeling out of a starting pitcher—which we had with Tom—there's nothing better."

"I don't know if [the series is] going to go the distance," said centerfielder Devon White prior to Game One. "I think we'll take it before that. Maybe five games. We'll be satisfied if we get away with one in here [in Minnesota] because we're pretty tough at home."[8] White made this prediction knowing the pitching rotation, essentially counting on Candiotti to close out the series in Game Five. Third baseman Kelly Gruber, who'd been with the Jays for all of their near-misses in the 1980s, liked the rotation setup of Candiotti and Guzman in the first two games. "This is a changed team," Gruber said. "White, Alomar and Carter are three of the best players in the game and we've got them now, along with a rookie pitcher like Guzman and, of course, Tom Candiotti."[9] Bill Madden of the *New York Daily News* stated back in July that while the off-season acquisitions of Carter, Alomar, and White helped Toronto get to first place, it was the addition of Candiotti that essentially clinched the AL East. Madden called Candiotti "a veritable ace" who was capable of giving the team many quality innings.[10]

Everything suggested the decision to start Candiotti in Game One was logical. Except in the eyes of the Toronto scribes and fans. "I do remember that," says journalist Adrian Brijbassi, referring to the heavy criticism Cito Gaston received for his decision. "The [Jays pitchers] didn't get the run support against Minnesota in '91. That probably had to do with the [series] loss more than anything. Guzman was unproven, and you could make the argument for Jimmy Key for sure. But Key didn't particularly have a good second half [going 6–8 with a 4.02 ERA]. The Twins were loaded with right-handed hitters like Kirby Puckett, Dan Gladden, Chuck Knoblauch, Shane Mack, and Brian Harper—they had Chili Davis, too, a switch-hitter—so Key might not have been the best guy to send out there. And you figure if Candiotti's knuckleball was on, he might be able to win."

Could rookie Guzman have started Game One? Ironically, the last post-season game at the Metrodome had featured a rookie opposing starting pitcher—Cardinals lefthander Joe Magrane, who started Game Seven of the '87 World Series. Magrane was 9–7 with a 3.54 ERA that season, but compiled an 8.59 ERA in two World Series starts, both at the Metrodome. In Game One, Minnesota hammered him for five runs in the fourth inning en route to a 10–1 victory. Magrane was then chased in the fifth inning in Game Seven, as the Twins won, 4–2. In the 1987 postseason, Magrane was 0–1 with an 8.74 ERA in three starts. In fact, no rookie starting pitcher had won a post-season game since Philadelphia's Charles Hudson in Game Three of the 1983 NLCS. But then again, Hudson—8–8 with a 3.35 ERA in 26 starts that year—went on to lose both of his starts in the 1983 World Series with an 8.64 ERA as the Phillies fell to Baltimore in five games.

Starting rookie pitchers in post-season play, especially in a Game One situation? Not exactly a sure thing, especially at the Metrodome. "The thing I do remember is Guzman was unproven," Brijbassi says, reflecting back on the series objectively, "so you don't know what you were going to get out of him. Key was, at the time, on the downside. His last great year was probably 1988." Brijbassi does have a point when talking about the veteran Toronto lefthander, who'd struggled in 1989–90. Key went 13–14 in 1989 with a 3.88 ERA, and was 13–7 with a 4.25 ERA the following season. In both years, he gave up more hits than he had innings pitched.

But others at the time weren't quite as objective. Not in a city where the Blue Jays had already lost the ALCS in 1985 and 1989, and had narrowly missed making the postseason in 1987 and 1990. The team had to win it all in '91; otherwise, the season would be labeled a failure. In fact, the ALCS had already been deemed a lost cause even before it started. Armchair managers throughout the city declared the rotation of Candiotti-Guzman-Key-Stottlemyre was a mistake, with most observers wanting Guzman or Key in the opener. Fans questioned the decision to start Candiotti in Game One. Some players, according to the papers, grumbled privately about the call.[11] Toronto newspaper scribes, meanwhile, added more fuel to the fire by essentially calling the decision a mistake.[12]

Never mind the recent failures of rookies in post-season play. The argument for Guzman (10–3, 2.99 ERA) to start Game One was simple: he won 10 straight decisions from June 22 to October 1, and the *Toronto Star* reported whispers that the Twins were afraid of seeing his nasty slider and hard fastball three times in the series.[13] Meanwhile, Key (16–12, 3.05 ERA) seemed upset at being bumped to Game Three; the lefthander stated he "would have loved to have been the one" to get the Game One assignment, and hinted he deserved the opportunity. "I figure, in setting a rotation, you look at how a guy's pitched lately, how he's done against the team you're up against. I think my numbers are there," Key said, likely referring to his career ERA of 2.86 against Minnesota compared to Candiotti's 3.31.[14]

Several Toronto players, according to the papers, were privately saying Key, their best "big-game pitcher," should have gotten the start.[15] (Interestingly, in the 1991 NLCS, Pittsburgh had arguably its hottest pitcher, lefthander John Smiley, start Games Three and Seven against Atlanta—not Game One. Smiley, a 20-game winner, went 7–0 with a 2.58 ERA down the stretch.) Before Gaston announced the rotation, the *Toronto Star* had assumed the lefty was the logical choice for the opener, stating that "Jimmy Key clearly seems tabbed for Game One."[16] The *Hamilton Spectator* called Key "a proven big-game pitcher" who had the experience to pitch out of trouble in the biggest moments.[17] But with Candiotti chosen for Game One instead, the scribes weren't so confident of Toronto's chances. The title of *Star* writer Dave Perkins's column the day before the series began—"Settled Rotation Gives the Twins Big Advantage"—said it all. The order of the Jays' rotation "leaves them open to some serious questioning," noted Perkins.[18]

"More than a few players' eyes are being rolled when the rotation is mentioned," added Perkins. "The only way Key gets [the Twins] twice is if the series goes to a seventh game and this is what a few players are grumbling about; they think Key is their big-game guy and they'd like to see more of him."[19] However, that wasn't the manager's version of the players' reaction. "I think the guys [the pitchers] were all happy enough when I explained the setup to them," Gaston told reporters.[20] But leave it to the scribes to criticize his decision. Publish stories to suggest the players didn't agree with the manager! The team's veteran lefthander was upset! (Key was quoted in the *Star* as saying, "I know they had a lot of choices ... but I don't get paid to understand why they do things," a sign he didn't endorse Gaston's decision publicly.[21])

All of the grumbling came before the series began. The critics suggested that pitching Candiotti in Game One was risky because of his unpredictable knuckleballs and his late-season slip-up in California, forgetting Toronto had won five of his seven starts after September 1 with the knuckleballer going 2–2 with a 3.83 ERA. Key, meanwhile, had compiled a second-half ERA of 4.02 but was still called the team's "proven big-game pitcher" and "big-game guy" in the papers.[22] In September, his ERA was 3.68, with Toronto losing four of his six starts. And Key, a finesse pitcher with only 125 strikeouts in 209.1 innings, wasn't overpowering. Another overlooked fact was his lack of pitching deep into ballgames; he averaged only six innings per start in the second half, meaning the bullpen had to be heavily relied on during his outings.

Second half, 1991:

|  | GS | CG | IP | H | ER | HR | BB | SO | ERA | W-L |
|---|---|---|---|---|---|---|---|---|---|---|
| Key | 16 | 0 | 96.1 | 101 | 43 | 9 | 21 | 54 | 4.02 | 6–8 |
| Candiotti | 17 | 3 | 116.2 | 100 | 40 | 5 | 40 | 71 | 3.09 | 5–6 |

Las Vegas bookmakers didn't think the two pitchers were that much different, labeling Toronto underdogs against Minnesota because of "the recent struggles of starters Tom Candiotti and Jimmy Key" among other things.[23] As Michael Roxborough, operator of Las Vegas Sports Consultants, explained, "Candiotti's last three starts haven't been too good ... [and] Key hasn't really been in full stroke lately either."[24] Somehow, the scribes had overlooked Key's second-half performance—as well as his history in big games. At the time, Key's post-season resume included an ugly 4.91 ERA in three starts. He also faltered down the stretch in each of the past two seasons. In 1990, Key had a 5.59 ERA over his final three starts as the Blue Jays finished two games behind first-place Boston. He had a 4.78 ERA in September 1989, and lasted only four innings against Baltimore in the season's penultimate game with Toronto trying to clinch the division. Yet, Key's big-game struggles were all but forgotten by the time the 1991 playoffs began.

In Torontonians' minds, their team was going to win the 1991 ALCS—provided Guzman or Key started Game One. In the regular season Toronto had gone 8–4 versus Minnesota, including 5–2 at the Metrodome. "I thought they were going to beat the Twins," admits Toronto-based journalist Adrian Brijbassi. "Everyone in the city thought that." It wasn't that simple, though. What's been forgotten by Torontonians was the fact the Metrodome was an extremely tough park for visiting teams in the postseason. In the 1987 ALCS, the Western Division champion Twins (85–77) faced the best team in baseball, the Detroit Tigers (98–64), and hosted the first two games at the Metrodome. Though Detroit had veteran aces Doyle Alexander (9–0, 1.53) and Jack Morris (18–11, 3.38) starting the first two contests, Minnesota still won, 8–5 and 6–3, en route to a five-game series victory.

Whitey Herzog, manager of the heavily favored 1987 Cardinals team that lost the World Series to the Twins because St. Louis dropped all four games in Minnesota, knew how tough the Metrodome was in post-season play. In those days, home-field advantage in the World Series was predetermined, and alternated between the AL and NL team every year. In odd years (like 1987 and 1991), it was the AL champion that had the extra home game in the Fall Classic. Not only that, in odd years, the AL West had home-field advantage in the ALCS as well, regardless of the teams' records.

In 1987, Minnesota had home-field advantage against Detroit in the ALCS despite a mediocre 85–77 record. The Twins—who had a .358 road winning percentage—lost all three games at Busch Stadium in the World Series, but won all four contests at the Metrodome to upset the Cardinals. For the entire postseason, they benefited from starting each series at the Metrodome, and went 6–0 at home. With 1991 being an odd year, the AL West champion Twins would begin the ALCS at home, and if they got that far, they would get the extra home game in the World Series again.

As Herzog once explained, the Metrodome was tough for visiting teams in the postseason for several reasons. "It was like nothing I ever saw," the ex–Cardinals manager noted. "The ball and the roof are the same color, so every popup is a flight to the Bermuda Triangle. There's 55,000 fans in one room, all of 'em waving hankies and hollering so loud you can't hear the ball hit the bat."[25] There was a tendency for fielders to lose flyballs in the roof when playing at the Metrodome. There was the challenge of the dome's artificial turf, which was different from the other AL ballparks. There was the daunting task of trying to concentrate in an environment with all of the crowd noise, which made communicating between fielders all but impossible. Then there was the fact the 1991 Twins, at 95–67, had finished with the best record in the AL. And with 54,000 hankie-waving fans at every home game, there was no guarantee they could be beat.

Still, Torontonians had the series won. Their Blue Jays had fallen short in the 1989 ALCS to an Oakland A's juggernaut that won 99 games. This time, it was different. Noted *The Globe and Mail's* Stephen Brunt, "No unbeatable team emerged from the American League West to stand in the way of a first trip to the Series. With that kind of pitching staff and with the Minnesota Twins emerging as the first post-season opposition, it looked very much like the breakthrough was at hand."[26]

The only way the Jays could lose, in the eyes of the Toronto fans and scribes, was if Candiotti messed up in Game One. But even if he couldn't win the first game, the team still had Juan Guzman in Game Two to try and earn the split. It was somewhat presumptuous to think Toronto would sweep the first two games in the Metrodome, given the fact Minnesota had never lost a post-season game on that field. Look at how the '87 Twins handled the Cardinals and how they pounded Tigers veterans Doyle Alexander and Jack Morris, who went a combined 0–3 with an 8.47 ERA in the '87 ALCS.

On Minnesota's side, manager Tom Kelly had some tough decisions to make with his lineup in the 1991 ALCS. Before the series, there was talk that reserve first baseman-rightfielder Gene Larkin might replace veteran leftfielder and leadoff hitter Dan Gladden in Minnesota's starting lineup.[27] The switch-hitting Larkin batted .389 against Toronto during the season and hit .320 in September—but had no place to play with first base occupied by Kent Hrbek (.284, 20 HRs, 89 RBIs) and right field by Shane Mack (.310, 18 HRs, 74 RBIs). Gladden, who had the worst season of his nine-year career in 1991, seemed like the logical choice to be benched. He batted .205 after July 31—and .121 over the final two weeks of the year—finishing with a .247 average in 461 at-bats. Against Toronto pitching in 1991, Gladden hit just .200. He also stole a career-low 15 bases during the season and was thrown out nine times.

Kelly ultimately stuck with Gladden as the leadoff man, and the move paid immediate dividends in the opening inning of Game One. After Candiotti started Gladden with two quick strikes, the Twins' leftfielder grounded the 0-and–2 pitch through the hole past shortstop Manuel Lee, and Minnesota was in business. Chuck Knoblauch followed by hitting the very next pitch on the ground, which also got through the hole at short, and suddenly there were two men on and the Metrodome was going crazy. "They managed to hit balls that found the hole and got through the infield," says Candiotti. "It wasn't the best way to start the game, but the groundballs they hit just got past Manuel Lee. Unbelievable."

People covering the team could have believed it. Lee's range at shortstop was not regarded as one of the club's strengths. Early that season, third baseman Kelly Gruber recalled a telephone conversation he'd had with former Toronto shortstop Tony Fernandez the night in December 1990 when Fernandez was traded to San Diego. Gruber wondered how well Lee, who'd started his career as a shortstop but had spent the majority of his time in the big leagues at second, would adapt to playing shortstop again with Fernandez gone. "I wanted to know if I would have to 'cheat' toward my left because I wondered if Manuel would show the range that Tony had over the years," noted Gruber in his biography.[28] The *Philadelphia Inquirer*'s Dick Polman, meanwhile, offered this scouting report of the shortstop position during the ALCS: "The Jays' incumbent, Manuel Lee, hits ninth in the lineup (for good reason), and fields his position with a minimum of range." He also speculated that Toronto was probably looking to sign Dick Schofield, a good defensive shortstop, in the offseason to replace Lee.[29]

With two on, Candiotti struck out Kirby Puckett looking and retired Kent Hrbek on a flyball, and was on track to get out of the inning unscathed. The next batter was Chili Davis, who'd never driven in a run in the postseason. In his only previous playoff series, Davis batted .150 in San Francisco's seven-game NLCS loss to St. Louis in 1987. Against Candiotti, it looked like the drought would continue as he hit a pop-up to left field on a 3-and-2 knuckleball. "It was just a softly hit ball, just a little blooper," recalls Candiotti. However, that blooper was hit to no man's land in short left field, dropping in to score both runners, sending the Metrodome into a frenzy. "I was just trying to put the ball in play somewhere," Davis explained afterward. "He gave me a pitch that was kind of in on me, but I managed to knock it over the third baseman's head."[30]

To this day, Candiotti still can't believe Davis's pop-up fell in for a hit. "In that inning, I gave up two groundball singles, just seeing-eye groundball hits," Candiotti recalls. "Then Chili Davis's hit. The ball hit the very end of his bat and barely went over Kelly Gruber's head at third base. It was hit so softly that Kelly was going back to try and get it. But it just squibbed over his head. Both runners scored, and Chili had his hands over his face like he couldn't believe that had happened." Davis told Candiotti as much following the game. "Candy, I've never seen a guy with the kind of luck you have," Davis said. "You gave up a bunch of groundball hits that just happened to find the right holes. If Manny Lee had even gotten to one of those balls.... It was ridiculous." Added Toronto catcher Pat Borders of Candiotti: "He didn't have any luck. He threw some good pitches up there that the Twins just put in play—and they found holes."[31]

Minnesota struck again an inning later. Shane Mack hit a hard groundball single that went off Candiotti's leg, stole second, and moved to third on a line-out to right field. Three singles later, the Twins were ahead, 4–0. More bad luck came in the third. With a runner on second base, Candiotti seemed poised to get out of the inning unscathed when Mack hit a two-out line drive to right field. But Joe Carter misplayed the liner for a double, making it 5–0. Toronto valiantly fought back in the middle innings, but Minnesota hung on and prevailed, 5–4.

Though Candiotti's linescore—2.2 IP, 8 H, 5 R, 5 ER, 1 BB, 2 SO—was horrendous, he maintains that many of those hits weren't hard-hit balls. "The media will look at the numbers and say, 'Oh no, he got clobbered,' but baseball people will look at how hard the ball was hit and realize there weren't a lot of hard-hit balls that night," Candiotti says. "Shane Mack hit a groundball that struck me right in the shin—and almost broke my shin. Other than that, there were probably four or five groundballs that just found holes and got through the infield. It was ridiculous. And Cito Gaston comes out and says, 'You've gotta throw more knuckleballs.' But I didn't pitch a bad game. The balls weren't hit hard. That's how you analyze your performance as a pitcher. You look at how many hard-hit balls there were. You look at the line drives you gave up. Were the balls good pitches they hit, or were they bad pitches I grooved? When I analyzed that game, yes, those were bad results, but I can recall only one hard-hit ball. That was it."

But in Toronto, the fans and scribes felt they were proven right in saying Candiotti shouldn't have started Game One. Noted *The Globe and Mail's* Stephen Brunt, pitchers like Candiotti who threw "a gimmick pitch" did so because "their basic repertoire of curves and fastballs and sliders isn't good enough to get anyone out."[32] Worst of all, he didn't even get beat on his best pitch. "We were trying to get him to throw a few more knuckleballs," an irritated Cito Gaston remarked. "They hurt him on curveballs."[33] Brunt added that Candiotti "looked to all the world like a knuckleball pitcher afraid to throw his knuckleball."[34] The *Toronto Star's* Dave Perkins noted Candiotti was "scared" of throwing his best pitch in a big game.[35] "Candiotti's lack of confidence in Borders behind the plate was obvious," Perkins continued. "He didn't want to throw the knuckleball to him. It was his curveball that he kept throwing and the Twins kept killing."[36]

Former Cleveland manager Doc Edwards doesn't think the adjectives "scared" and "afraid" describe Candiotti at all. "Tom Candiotti was fearless when he went out there to the mound," says Edwards. "He had no fear of anybody or anything. He was a pitcher who'd try to throw his knuckleball into the strike zone at any time with the attitude of, 'I'm gonna throw it in there and I'm gonna let it move. You [the catcher] take care of it.' [Unfortunately], it darts and moves and jumps so much. You gotta find a [catcher] that can handle him, [otherwise] you could have five passed balls in the first two innings."

What Edwards says about the necessity of having a catcher being able to catch a knuckleball pitcher, coupled with the fact Candiotti wasn't a true knuckleballer, made it easy to see why he was throwing more curveballs. "Even during my time with Cleveland, I'd thrown a lot more curveballs than I did in that playoff game," Candiotti says years later, while remembering that former Indians manager Pat Corrales also pressured him to throw more knuckleballs. "I remember Cito Gaston telling me, 'You gotta throw more knuckleballs.' With Cito and Pat, I look at them as frustrated managers who wanted results. They were trying to help me without really knowing what I was doing out there on the mound. Take Cito Gaston, for instance. Little did he know, I probably struck a hundred guys out on curveballs. That was a pitch I had great command of. Now he's saying, 'You're not allowed to throw a curveball now,' even though I've got a hundred strikeouts on curveballs!"

Candiotti also laments the fact Borders and Greg Myers were constantly being rotated during the regular season, meaning neither catcher had an opportunity to get used to the knuckler. "One time Borders would catch, the next time Myers would catch," Candiotti explains. "You just didn't know. When we got to the playoffs, Borders [became the starting catcher but he] hadn't caught me that much, and my knuckleball was moving pretty well against Minnesota. There were [several balls] that he missed. I mean, if he couldn't catch the ball, how was I going to keep throwing knuckleballs? They were going to swing and miss, and he was just going to miss the ball again!"

Interestingly, most Toronto observers expected Candiotti to throw strictly knuckleballs, forgetting that during the season he sometimes threw the knuckler only 30–40 percent of the time. "He has the knuckleball," said Pittsburgh third baseman Steve Buechele, who faced Candiotti from 1986 to 1991 in the AL, "but I wouldn't call it his bread-and-butter pitch. His bread-and-butter pitch is his curveball."[37] Seattle manager Jim Lefebvre noted the following of Candiotti: "He's a slow curve pitcher with a knuckleball."[38] Added Billy Beane, an advance scout for Oakland in the early 1990s: "He's not a knuckleballer, he's a curveball pitcher with a great knuckler. Everything he does works off his extraordinary curveball."[39] Broadcaster Tim McCarver, who knows all about Candiotti's repertoire, once said in the late 1990s: "Tom Candiotti, yes, he's a knuckleball pitcher. But he's more than that. His curve is his strike pitch. In other words, if he falls behind a hitter, he'll throw the curveball instead of the fastball for the strike. But if he's ahead, the knuckler's coming."[40]

Toronto rooters weren't buying it. After Candiotti had lost Game One, everyone was quick to point out how badly he'd choked. But then again, in the hockey-mad city of Toronto, it seemed anything short of a championship for the baseball team was considered a failure. That appeared to be how the fans and the media viewed the Blue Jays; if they didn't win the World Series, their season was a disaster. To this day, there are sports talk show hosts in Toronto who have consistently maintained that the Jays haven't played any meaningful games in the month of September since 1993 (the last time they appeared in the postseason).[41] This assertion is made even though the team was in contention for a playoff spot from 1998 to 2000.

David Wells, who pitched for the Jays from 1987 to 1992 and 1999–2000, would in his autobiography *Perfect I'm Not* refer to Toronto fans as being "surly" and "cluelessly negative," among other things.[42] Recalling the 2000 season in which the team was just two games back of a wild-card berth with 10 games remaining but wouldn't draw well at home, Wells lashed out at them: "Though we Jays are still smack in the middle of a pennant race, we're averaging less than 20,000 fans per game. We Jays are young, we're exciting, we're playing good ball ... and nobody seems to care.... Baseball fans in Canada simply don't understand what they're watching. I've seen these people boo players for moving up a runner with a well-hit sac fly.... It's ridiculous."[43] In the season's final weeks, the fans wouldn't let up. "[When the Jays lost three of four at home] the hometown fans boo this team, top to bottom," Wells noted. "Honest to God, the Toronto fans suck.... Even though [the team] is right in the thick of the hunt, right into the last week of 2000, these [fans] have *no* idea what we've accomplished."[44]

Wells's displeasure with Toronto fans dated back to 1991. "You get 30, 40 thousand people booing at you, I don't like that at all," Wells said during the ALCS. "People getting down on us and we're trying to win.... When [reliever] Jim Acker comes in and the whole stadium is booing him ... man, you got to pull for the guy instead of making him feel like crap!"[45] Players were booed when they were struggling. The team was booed after a loss, even during a successful 1991 season. "This is a great city and a great facility. But it would make it easier if the fans could try having just as much fun as we do," Wells continued.[46]

Off the field, Wells and Candiotti certainly had their share of fun. "One night, David and I bought a bunch of stink bombs," recalls Candiotti. "They were little sulfur capsules that were plastic caps and if you stepped on them, it was the worst sulfur smell in the world." Candiotti and Wells would set them off in hotel rooms during road trips. "We'd say, 'All right, let's go get Tom Cheek,'" says Candiotti, referring to the team's veteran radio broadcaster. "David and I got our hands on a room service menu. We smash this thing outside his room, slide it underneath the door, and we'd run down the hallway [to hide]. Tom Cheek would come out in his pajamas and go 'Ahhhhhhh!' wondering what the heck the smell was! We were cracking up!" Sometimes they even took on unsuspecting Torontonians in the public. "I squished one of these things in a McDonald's at the mall downtown one time and everyone just started leaving," Candiotti recalls. "We did that all the time. We did it in restaurants, in malls, in team hotels, in elevators, everywhere!"

The fans and media, though, were more interested in wins and losses, not how much fun the players were having. Essentially, for 1991 to be considered a success, Toronto had to win the World Series. Even before the AL East title had been clinched, it was suggested in the papers the division crown meant little. "[The] reality is that, in terms of this city's history in baseball," wrote a Toronto scribe one day before the division was won, "winning yet another divisional title means next to nothing. Diddly-squat, you might say.... A warning: 1991 will be recorded as just another failure [like 1985 and 1989] if they don't get past the western representatives from Minneapolis and compete creditably afterward in the World Series."[47]

Wrote Steve Fainaru of the *Boston Globe* on the differences between Boston and Toronto: "The media is almost as skeptical as in Boston, although, unlike here, the fans really haven't a clue what's going on. They are drawn like sheep to the magnificent SkyDome, where, if they flashed, 'GET UP AND GET A BEER' on the all-seeing Jumbotron, there probably would be a run on the concession stand.... Blue Jays fans are told when to cheer and when to laugh. And most important, they are told not to take it too hard."[48] Journalist Adrian Brijbassi, who grew up in Toronto, offers some perspective. Torontonians weren't dumb; they just wanted to see a winner. Brijbassi recalls that in 1987, shortstop Tony Fernandez (elbow) and catcher Ernie Whitt (rib) suffered season-ending injuries in the campaign's final weeks, and the Blue Jays blew a three-and-a-half-game lead with seven games remaining. "So, 1987 was the first one, the first heartbreak for the fans, where you could relate to a Red Sox fan as a Jays fan," explains Brijbassi. "Everyone thought the Jays were going to win the World Series. They were in first place going into the final week of September. But it was just one bad thing after another."

To this day, the players and fans believe Toronto should have won the division in 1987. "We'll never forget the last series that we played," Fernandez recalled in 2010. "That was right [after] I broke my elbow for the first time at Exhibition Stadium. Ernie Whitt went down also with an injury. We believe that cost us the pennant that year."[49] As the years went by, Blue Jays fans grew frustrated seeing the club keep falling short. By 1991, they wanted a World Series team. "In 1987, all the media was saying the Jays were the team to beat in all of baseball," continues Brijbassi. "When they didn't do it, and the way they didn't do it, just a collapse at the end, everyone felt devastated. The city wanted a winner, they wanted the Jays to close the deal, and you could see everyone really started becoming critical of them."

Following its Game One loss in the 1991 ALCS, Toronto bounced back with a 5–2 victory in the second game as Juan Guzman and relievers Tom Henke and Duane Ward held the Twins to just five hits. However, Minnesota won the next two at SkyDome by 3–2 and 9–3 scores as neither Jimmy Key nor Todd Stottlemyre could pitch the Blue Jays to victory, and Toronto was on the cusp of extinction.

With the Blue Jays trailing three games to one, the fans and the Toronto media were hoping that Cito Gaston would skip Candiotti's turn in Game Five and instead bring Guzman back on short rest. But Gaston chose to stick with the knuckleballer. Candiotti, for his part, was happy to get the call. "I was glad they gave me another start," Candiotti reflects years later. "People were saying Juan Guzman should've started that game but I didn't let it bother me. When you go out there on the mound to compete, you don't think about what's being said in the papers. You just go out there and pitch. And I really felt like I pitched a good game. I felt I redeemed myself."

# 12

## *From First to Worst*

With Toronto facing elimination in Game Five of the 1991 ALCS against Minnesota, Blue Jays fans didn't want to see Tom Candiotti on the mound and were instead hoping to see rookie fireballer Juan Guzman. When the starting lineups were announced, though, it was indeed Candiotti listed as the starting pitcher—much to the disappointment of the 51,425 spectators at Sky-Dome—as the Jays didn't budge from their original plan. Many settling into their seats were thinking that Toronto would be eliminated that afternoon, while going down without sending its best pitcher out to stop the Twins.[1]

Manager Cito Gaston's decision to start Candiotti was simple. "Even if Guzman wins, we still have to win two more," Gaston explained. "That keeps everybody on the same rotation and I prefer to go that way."[2] Dodger manager Tommy Lasorda and CBS broadcaster Jim Kaat understood the decision, pointing out during the pre-game telecast that Gaston made the right call. As Lasorda put it, "Candiotti was one of the pitchers who got them there," and definitely should be the fifth-game starter.[3] According to Kaat, starting Candiotti was the "logical choice" and the "best choice."[4] If Candiotti won Game Five, which Lasorda predicted, Toronto would be in good shape, as Kaat pointed out, with two well-rested starters (Guzman and Jimmy Key) going in Games Six and Seven.[5]

No one else at the ballpark was buying it. Blue Jays fan Larry Grossman, who attended Game Five, noted in *A Baseball Addict's Diary: The Blue Jays' 1991 Rollercoaster*, nobody in the city of Toronto was optimistic about team's chances with Candiotti taking the mound. Everyone figured the knuckleballer was going to lose. "It was sad," wrote Grossman. "It was also unnecessary. Rumors had floated around after [Game Four] that Cito might actually play to win and start Guzman instead of Candiotti. But when we arrived an hour early at 3:00 p.m. it was Candiotti, all right. The mood was somber. Restrained. Genuine nervousness."[6]

That was the atmosphere inside SkyDome in the first inning, as Minnesota jumped ahead, 1–0, when Kirby Puckett drove a 2-and-1 curveball into the seats. Though it was the first homer allowed by Candiotti in 30.2 innings, going back seven starts, the scribes in the press box were already busy writing Toronto's obituary while snickering with the "I-told-you-so" looks. An inning later, Chili Davis ripped a first-pitch curveball to center field for a single. With Candiotti now throwing knuckleballs, it became a nightmare for Borders with Brian Harper at the plate. A knuckler eluded the catcher for a passed ball, advancing Davis to second. Unfazed, Candiotti struck Harper out on a 1-and-2 knuckleball, but that pitch got past Borders also for a second straight passed ball. Instead of a runner on with one out, there were two runners aboard with nobody out. Shane Mack smacked a single to right for a 2–0 lead, but Minnesota couldn't tack on any more runs as Candiotti bounced back and got the next three outs, including a strikeout of Dan Gladden, to end the inning.

In the third inning, Puckett swung and missed on a 2-and-2 knuckler with one out but reached first base when the ball got past Borders—the second straight inning in which Candiotti struck a hitter out only to have him get on base. Before Candiotti's arrival in Toronto, Borders had never caught a knuckleball. After the trade was announced, he'd had a little humor with the daunting assignment when reminded that Candiotti threw the knuckler only half of the time. "I guess I'll only drop about 50 percent [of the pitches]," the catcher quipped.[7] It might've been funny then, but it was no laughing matter now in the postseason. With Puckett aboard, Candiotti bailed Borders out by retiring Kent Hrbek and Davis to end the inning. In the press box, meanwhile, the Toronto media were busy snickering even as the knuckleballer was on his way to getting out of that frame. "Candiotti can't afford to strike anyone else out" was the consensus, as two of his three strikeouts up to that point ended up putting the hitter on base with Borders dropping the third strikes.[8]

The Blue Jays' bats finally woke up in the bottom of the third, when they struck for three runs on Roberto Alomar's RBI single, Joe Carter's run-scoring double, and John Olerud's RBI groundout. An inning later, Alomar delivered a two-run single with the bases loaded for a 5–2 Toronto lead. In the top of the fifth, Minnesota loaded the bases with two outs on two singles and a walk, but Candiotti retired Harper on a grounder to shortstop on his 93rd pitch.

With four innings to go, Toronto appeared ready to extend the series, with Duane Ward (who hadn't pitched in three days and was well rested), Tom Henke, and David Wells ready to come on in relief. But Candiotti was sent back out in the sixth, and Shane Mack looped a broken-bat, leadoff single

While Blue Jays fans questioned the team's decision to start Candiotti in Game One of the 1991 American League Championship Series, Toronto rightfielder Joe Carter endorsed the move. "In a big game, I want to see him on the mound," Carter was quoted as saying of the knuckleballer prior to the series. As it turned out, though, the Blue Jays lost that first game, 5–4, en route to a five-game defeat against the Minnesota Twins. For the series, Candiotti had an 8.22 ERA over 7.2 innings in two starts (courtesy Tom Candiotti).

that dropped in front of rightfielder Candy Maldonado. Mike Pagliarulo followed with a single to center on Candiotti's 102nd pitch, ending the knuckleballer's day. As he walked off the mound, Dick Stockton announced on the CBS telecast that "Candiotti has delivered in a big game for the Blue Jays," adding he'd given his team a "big effort."[9]

Instead of the hard-throwing Ward entering the game, though, it was struggling rookie Mike Timlin, who'd surrendered a 10th-inning homer to Pagliarulo to lose Game Three and then allowed two more runs in Game Four. Timlin had also faded in the latter half of September and into October. Over his final eight regular-season appearances, despite a 0.00 ERA and 10 strikeouts over 10.1 innings, he'd allowed eight of nine inherited runners to score. Now, two days after losing Game Three, Timlin was back out there in Game Five.

Timlin quickly retired Greg Gagne on a pop-up as runners held at first and third. One out. He then induced a routine grounder off the bat of Gladden to third baseman Kelly Gruber. With a three-run lead, the safe play was to get the sure out at first, conceding the run. Gruber, however, opted to throw home to cut down the lead runner. "A high chop, no time to get a double play," he said afterward, "so you just get it out of your glove as fast as you can and give [catcher] Pat [Borders] a chance at the plate."[10]

The throw was wide to the left of home plate, and Borders had to reach out and catch it. While holding the ball in his glove, Borders tagged Mack, who came home from third, not with the ball but with his bare hand. Borders was charged with an error, Mack was safe, and the score was 5–3. It only got worse from there for Toronto. Chuck Knoblauch followed with a two-run double down the right-field line off Timlin, and the game was suddenly tied. Two innings later, Minnesota struck for three runs off Ward and Wells, and clinched the pennant with an 8–5 victory.

For Candiotti, Carter, Timlin, and the other newcomers to the postseason, it was a disappointing loss but they looked at it as the team having a good season that just ended too early. As Carter noted, Toronto was able to win the division even though there were many new faces on the club, which was no small feat. "Twenty-two clubs were sitting home and watching," Carter reflected after Game Five. "I look on it as a productive season for myself and the team."[11]

But for the rest of the veteran players who'd been through past late-season and playoff failures—like Key and Henke—losing their third ALCS in seven years was unacceptable. For the fans and the media, the talk was about how the team had choked yet again. Carter would admit a year later it wasn't fun to be reminded constantly about the team's reputation as post-season losers. "You definitely get tired of hearing about it," Carter noted in 1992. "I wasn't here in

1987. I wasn't here in 1985. I wasn't here in 1989. They dwell too much on the negative and don't talk much about the positive."[12]

After Game Five, the Toronto newspaper scribes didn't care that Candiotti had pitched into the sixth inning with the lead. Instead, they were grumbling about why Guzman and Key each started just once in the series—and lamenting the fact Ward was charged with the loss. "The saddest part of the day," wrote one scribe, "was Ward, the Jays' most valuable pitcher, going into his third inning and sucking up the loss. There ain't no justice."[13] Another Toronto scribe used the word "unjust" when referring to "that one final 'L' beside Duane Ward's name."[14] Journalist and long-time Toronto fan Adrian Brijbassi was one of those who felt sorry for Ward, noting Candiotti simply hadn't been in town long enough and wouldn't be sticking around. "Tom Candiotti was a rental player," Brijbassi explains. "You knew he wasn't going to stay. As soon as the free agency period began, you knew he was gone. With a guy like Ward, everyone liked him. He was a big part of the Blue Jays' bullpen with Henke. Everyone rooted for those guys."

Candiotti remembers the standing ovations he received at SkyDome. Things changed, though, after the ALCS loss. "People loved me there," Candiotti says. "I pitched my heart out for those Blue Jays, and every time I took the mound there, I felt like I was super welcomed. I always got a great response from the crowd. The people in Toronto were just great. They'd follow me around when I left the SkyDome Hotel to grab a bite. [But] then I didn't pitch well in the postseason—I didn't get a lot of breaks, either—and they were upset. They were mad because we didn't win."

Cito Gaston, meanwhile, also had other tough questions to deal with. Was he even the right manager for the Blue Jays?[15] Why was John Olerud, 3-for–19 with no extra-base hits in the series, batting cleanup? Why did Toronto lose an unprecedented three straight home games in LCS play? "No way I thought they could sweep us here [at SkyDome]," said Kelly Gruber. "I really felt we were going to the World Series.... We could have won the first three games, but we missed a lot of golden opportunities."[16] Absolutely. A sacrifice fly here, a hit there (the Blue Jays went 1-for–9 with runners in scoring position in Game Three), a flyball that traveled a few more feet (Maldonado's drive to the warning track in Game One), a baserunner who didn't slow down while rounding third (Alomar being thrown out at home in Game One), and who knows?

Candiotti knows the team didn't choke; Toronto simply lost to a better club. "I did the best I could for the Blue Jays," Candiotti says, "and I think I did a good job. We lost the first game, 5–4, but my second game wasn't that bad. I left that game with a possible win, but we ended up losing the game.

After that game, Chili Davis came into the Blue Jays' clubhouse to congratulate us on a great season. He came up to Joe Carter and myself, and we exchanged hugs. Chili said, 'You guys aren't chokers. You guys aren't losers. You guys played great this year. You could've been there just as well as us.'"

Candiotti was having a beer by his locker thinking about the loss when Davis entered the clubhouse. After they exchanged hugs and before Davis was about to leave, he pointed at Candiotti's arm and said, "Throw me a fastball once in a while." Candiotti smiled, and poured the rest of his beer over Davis's head.

After the 1991 postseason, Tom Candiotti became a free agent. Early on, there were rumors in the Cleveland newspapers about him returning to the Indians—the *Akron Beacon Journal's* Sheldon Ocker suggested that the return of Candiotti would be "the most significant public relations move since sewing numbers on uniforms"—although both sides dismissed the notion that he was going to return.[17]

By then, ex–Indians general manager Joe Klein had moved on to Kansas City to become the Royals' director of player personnel. Though Klein had always been a Candiotti fan, there wasn't any room on the small-market Royals. "We were kind of in a different place when I went back there to Kansas City," Klein says. "We were at the end of the [Bret] Saberhagen-[Danny] Jackson-[Mark] Gubicza pitching staff. There were some young pitchers the Royals were already committed to, so it really wasn't a good fit there."

Toronto wanted Candiotti back, but the knuckleballer was seeking a four-year deal while the club's policy for pitchers was to restrict contracts to a maximum of three years. "About 1980–81, a lot of teams were getting into five-year contracts and we determined it was not good business principles," said team president Paul Beeston. "Teams were paying a lot of guys who were not playing."[18] As Beeston reasoned, it wasn't a smart move to start handing out long-term deals to pitchers, as they historically either went through injuries or had bad seasons after getting big contracts. A recent example was the Chicago Cubs signing lefthander Danny Jackson—who had a 72–74, 3.66 ERA career mark—to a four-year deal worth $10.5 million after the 1990 season. In 1991, Jackson went 1–5 with a 6.75 ERA while appearing in only 17 games (14 starts) for Chicago. The contract seemed a big gamble given Jackson's history with injuries; the southpaw landed on the disabled list three times in 1990 with a bruised left forearm and stiffness in his left shoulder, and had had arthroscopic surgery on the same shoulder the year before that.

Then there was the contract the Brewers gave Ted Higuera, who'd undergone surgery for a herniated disc and missed several weeks of action in 1989. Ankle and chest injuries had soon followed, but he bounced back to make 27 starts in 1990 with an 11–10, 3.76 ERA mark. Despite his history of injuries, Milwaukee re-signed Higuera to a four-year deal worth $13 million that off-season.[19] In 1991, he appeared in only seven games and had to undergo reconstructive shoulder surgery after tearing his rotator cuff. There were more examples. Tom Browning, who re-signed with Cincinnati for four years and $12.48 million plus an option after the 1990 season, lost 10 of his last 14 decisions in 1991 to finish 14–14 with a subpar 4.18 ERA.[20] And, of course, Toronto let Bud Black go to San Francisco by not offering him a four-year contract. Black wound up losing an NL-high 16 games with a 3.99 ERA.

Agent Rocky Lucia, however, viewed Candiotti as a vastly different pitcher. "Tom had a history of being durable, going out there and giving teams a lot of innings," recalls Lucia. "At the time Tom was one of only five guys who'd started 25 games with 200 innings for the last [six] years [along with Bob Welch, Frank Viola, Mark Langston, and Roger Clemens]. There were a lot of pitchers getting four-year deals at that time, when free agent salaries were starting to escalate. And because Tom threw the knuckleball, it put less strain on his arm and he was going to pitch for a very long time. He was a guy whose track record showed that he could pitch to a 3.50 ERA and log 200 innings every year."

Toronto, though, wasn't prepared to do any four-year deals with any pitcher, period. "A number of years ago," general manager Pat Gillick said then to reiterate the club's policy and echo Beeston's sentiments, "we went back and did some research, looking at the mortality rate among pitchers. I don't think it is a good gamble to go beyond three years."[21] There was another factor, says Candiotti. "People looked at me differently because I threw a knuckleball," he recalls. "Every team we talked to, they all said, 'Well, you're a knuckleballer.' I was discredited for throwing the knuckleball."

From 1986 to 1991, Candiotti ranked fourth among AL pitchers in complete games (48), sixth in ERA (3.48) and innings (1316.2), eighth in starts (191), and was tied for ninth in wins (78)—but not everyone was convinced he deserved a four-year contract. "If this costs them Tom Candiotti," wrote one scribe, "well, so what? There are always 13-game winners available.... The Jays do not change their policy for Tom Candiotti."[22] But the knuckleballer's ERA was more indicative of his pitching. Candiotti had a 2.43 ERA in his eight no-decisions, and if he'd allowed one fewer earned run over his 34 starts he would have won the ERA title (at 2.61 over Roger Clemens's 2.62). As sports analyst Michael Salfino noted years later, Candiotti in 1991 had the second-unluckiest season ever—based on his win total and how his ERA compared with the league average—behind only Philadelphia Athletics pitcher Lefty Grove's 13–13 season with a 2.51 ERA in 1926. (Candiotti's earned run average was 57 percent better than the league average.)[23]

Candiotti met with the Los Angeles Dodgers in early December and received a four-year, $15.5-million contract offer almost immediately. But Candiotti, hoping to remain in Toronto, gave the Blue Jays one more shot to offer a fourth year. On the afternoon of December 3, 1991, Rocky Lucia called Gillick to ask if Toronto would match the offer. "With my track record and the 200 innings I could guarantee every year, I thought it warranted a four-year contract," says Candiotti. "I was really, really close to signing with the Blue Jays. Pat Gillick came out with Paul Beeston two different times. They said they put their best offer on the table, $10.7 million for three years. I said I'd like to get a four-year contract and we'd wait to see who was interested. The Dodgers took our offer just like that, but before we even accepted it, we called the Blue Jays back and gave them an opportunity to match. But they said they couldn't do it."

On November 27, a week before Candiotti signed with the Dodgers, Los Angeles traded for Cincinnati outfielder Eric Davis, a two-time NL All-Star who could hit for power and steal bases. "This club is going to be very competitive, have a very good chance of winning in 1992," Dodger manager Tommy Lasorda said after Candiotti was signed.[24] Rightfielder Darryl Strawberry felt the Dodgers already were improved from the 1991 team that finished 93–69. "I feel we're better," Strawberry said. "You lose a guy like [first baseman] Eddie [Murray] who drives in 90 runs [before opting for free agency to sign with the Mets] but you replace him with Eric [Davis], who can do that and hit 30 homers and is the right-handed hitter we needed.... I'm real thrilled about it."[25]

*Baseball Digest* called the 1992 Dodgers the favorites to win the NL West, citing the following reasons: "great outfield, speed boosted, defense tighter, sound starting rotation, excellent catching, [and] offense potent."[26] The magazine called their outfield a "modern 'dream' outfield" and predicted that "pitching strength and improved power should put the Dodgers across this season. After all, they finished only a game behind [NL champion] Atlanta in '91 with a lesser cast."[27] In Steve Delsohn's *True Blue,* Bill Plaschke of the *Los Angeles Times* would be quoted as saying he thought the 1991 Dodgers were a championship-caliber team: "In 1991, I felt the Dodgers could have won the World Series. I thought they were that good."[28]

Others, however, weren't so sure, particularly with the Candiotti signing. According to Giants president Al Rosen, the Dodgers' knuckleballer would have difficulty holding baserunners in the NL. "The speedsters in this league will be going every time he cocks his arm," noted Rosen.[29] The Toronto newspaper scribes didn't have kind words either. Noted *The Globe and Mail*'s Stephen Brunt, Candiotti's leaving the Blue Jays "hardly seemed a significant loss" because of his "non-performance in the playoffs."[30] The *Toronto Star*'s

Candiotti officially inked a contract with Los Angeles in December of 1991, signing a four-year deal to pitch for his childhood team. Candiotti—shown here with agent Rocky Lucia, Dodger general manager Fred Claire, and team lawyer Sam Fernandez—would go on to lead the Los Angeles starters in ERA in both the 1992 and 1993 seasons. The knuckleballer, who grew up in the Bay Area but rooted for the rival Dodgers in his youth, would also lead the club in victories in 1992 and in strikeouts in 1993 (courtesy Fred Claire).

Dave Perkins scoffed at Claire's comment about Candiotti being "a winning, competitive pitcher and person." Wrote Perkins: "Candiotti is a flat-out winning competitor? Which AL playoff series were you watching, Fred? ... He pitched scared when it counted. He was scared to throw his best pitch, so he got beat with his curveball. That's not my definition of a winner."[31]

Opinions didn't change over time. Wrote Perkins a decade later, the decision to "rely on the terrified Tom Candiotti" in the playoffs "was a disaster."[32] Wrote Scott Radley of *The Hamilton Spectator* in 2006, the trade "that brought Tom Candiotti and Turner Ward for super-prospects Glenallen Hill, Mark Whiten and journeyman Denis Boucher turned into a fizzle all-round."[33] Cito Gaston even labeled Candiotti "the most disappointing" pitcher he'd ever had in his years as a manager.[34] "We traded for a knuckleballer and all he did was throw his curveball," Gaston said. "If he had gone out and thrown his knuckleball, we would have been in the World Series. You should never, ever get beat on your second-best pitch."[35]

Pat Gillick, meanwhile, only reflects on the positives when discussing Candiotti today. "In the playoffs against Minnesota," the Toronto general manager recalls, "I don't think Tom had a particularly good series. But, all in all, we were happy with Candiotti in the way that he performed and conducted himself.... The thing about Tom is he was really the ultimate professional. He was someone who set a standard on our club by example, not only by pitching by example but by the way he conducted himself in the clubhouse, on the field.... He set a great example for the other players on the club."

At the time, Claire expressed his admiration for Candiotti for not being afraid to throw the knuckler. "To have the courage to throw a knuckleball, you have to have a lot of confidence in yourself," Claire said then. "It's like staring at a 20-foot downhill putt and believing you are going to put it in."[36] To this day, Claire still stands by the decision to sign Candiotti. "The signing of Tom Candiotti was never a mistake in my eyes," he says. "He always was prepared to pitch and always gave a professional effort. Tom is a *great* competitor and anyone who knows him knows that to be true. He has the heart and mind of a winner."

Candiotti made his NL debut on April 9, 1992, in San Diego in the Dodgers' third game of the year, and defeated the Padres, 6–3. Candiotti's outing—six hits, two walks, seven strikeouts over 7.1 innings—marked the first time that a knuckleballer had appeared in an NL game since 1987. Interleague play didn't exist then, so the NL hitters who hadn't played in the AL had never faced Candiotti. "It was strange for those hitters, but the same for me too," Candiotti recalls. "When I faced the Mets for the first time that spring, it was weird pitching against all those unfamiliar faces, guys I'd never seen before. But Eddie Murray was in the Mets' lineup, and I'd faced him many times when he was with Baltimore. He got a hit off of me, and I went over to first base and told him, 'Eddie, you never hit me that well in the American League!'"

Nobody hit Candiotti well in his next two starts, when he won, 6–2, in Houston on a complete-game six-hitter (April 14) and followed that up by going the distance in a 4–2 victory over Atlanta (April 19). After three NL starts, he was 3–0 with a 2.49 ERA and was the NL Player of the Week for April 13–19. Candiotti's victory against Atlanta also gave the Dodgers three wins in that particular four-game series, dropping the defending NL champion Braves to last place in the Western Division. At that time, things looked great in Los Angeles. "I really thought 1992 was going to be a special year," says Candiotti. "With Darryl Strawberry and Eric Davis hitting in the middle of the lineup, I figured we'd score a lot of runs."

However, by season's end, Los Angeles would sit 35 games behind Atlanta in the standings, as the club was betrayed by injuries, bad hitting, and horrendous defense. While the Dodgers of the 1980s had been able to overcome sloppy fielding to challenge for pennants—including the 1988 World Series-winning club led by Cy Young winner Orel Hershiser and Most Valuable Player Kirk Gibson—the '92 team was not only defensively challenged but also crippled by the injuries to its top two sluggers, as Strawberry and Davis appeared in the lineup together only 30 times.[37]

In 1992, Strawberry underwent back surgery and was essentially lost for two seasons, while Davis was hurt on and off all year.[38] The two sluggers combined for a .232 average, 10 homers, and only 57 RBIs in 423 at-bats. The Dodgers finished last in the majors in runs scored (548), home runs (72), and doubles (201), with rookie first baseman Eric Karros's 20 homers and 88 RBIs leading the club. Amazingly, no other Dodger hitter had more than 39 RBIs or more than *six* home runs. The defense, meanwhile, committed a major league-worst 174 errors, 43 more than the NL's next-closest team (Philadelphia). Dodger shortstop Jose Offerman led the majors with 42 errors, while second baseman Lenny Harris finished second with 27.

On May 31, the Dodgers were 22–23 and remained within striking distance at three-and-a-half games out of first place. But they then went 9–18 in June—including 10 straight losses—and fell to last place by month's end. They never recovered, and finished the season with 99 losses, the most ever for a Dodger team in LA. Their last-place finish was the first in franchise history since 1905, when the club was in Brooklyn and known as the Superbas. The last time the team lost at least 99 games came in 1908, when the Superbas finished with 101 (and in seventh place, just ahead of last-place St. Louis).

The only time the 1992 Dodgers were over .500 was April 9, after the third game of the season when they were 2–1 following Candiotti's victory in San Diego. The last time they were as high as third place was April 25, when they were 9–9 and only a game-and-a-half back after Candiotti struck out nine in a 7–6 win in San Francisco. In early June, with the Dodgers in fifth place, Candiotti white-washed first-place Cincinnati, 1–0, to pull them to within four-and-a-half games back in the NL West. But the Dodgers just kept on losing. On June 19, they dropped to last place with a 26–36 record despite Candiotti's seven-inning effort against Houston, losing, 2–1, in 12 innings. The Dodgers would stay in the basement from that point on.

Candiotti began the season 3–0, but the Dodgers' mediocrity caused him to go 8–15 the rest of the way even though his ERA from May onwards was 2.89. The team scored one run or none seven times for him, and he lost games by scores of 3–2, 3–0, 1–0, 2–0 (twice), and 3–1 (twice). The Dodgers couldn't handle groundballs and flyballs. Candiotti's 3.00 ERA led all Dodger starters (rookie Pedro Astacio had a 1.98 ERA but made only 11 starts); his

1.178 WHIP led the team, as did his six complete games and 11 victories. His 152 strikeouts was second-most behind Kevin Gross, and he surpassed 200 innings for the seventh straight season.

The best way to demonstrate Candiotti's hard luck was to look at the pitchers with the worst ERAs in both leagues, both of whom finished with *winning* records. Montreal's Mark Gardner, who had an NL-worst 4.36 ERA, went 12–10 while reaching a personal high in wins. The Yankees' Scott Sanderson, with the majors' worst ERA at 4.93, finished 12–11. Candiotti, meanwhile, had 11 outings in which he pitched quality starts in 1992 but didn't get the victory, going 0–7 with four no-decisions while logging a 1.96 ERA. Six times he allowed one earned run or none while pitching at least six innings but was 0–3 with three no-decisions. Mike Morgan, a righthander for the Cubs, was one who knew about Candiotti's hard luck. "Candiotti and Gross, all those guys I know, they were 11–15 [and 8–13, respectively]," Morgan said. "The media and fans say, 'Look at their numbers,' but they were just as good as guys who won 17 games."[39]

For Candiotti, there were some memorable moments in 1992, including his first visit to Pittsburgh's Three Rivers Stadium. Because he'd only pitched in the AL during his first eight seasons and interleague play didn't exist then, he had never faced NL teams or been to NL ballparks until he became a Dodger in 1992. "I'd always listened to Dodger games on the radio as a kid," Candiotti recalls. "When they were playing at Pittsburgh's Forbes Field, somebody there had some sort of 'Green Weenie jinx.' I didn't like how the guy used it against my Dodgers, so my mom got a hot dog out of the fridge and dyed it green. I'd stick that green hot dog up against the radio whenever the Dodgers were playing in Pittsburgh."

Candiotti was referring to 1966, when LA outlasted Pittsburgh and San Francisco to win the NL pennant. (Before 1969, baseball had no division within the two leagues, with the only post-season competition being the World Series itself.) That July, Pirates broadcaster Bob Prince introduced to the baseball world the "Green Weenie," a plastic green frankfurter that Pirates fans pointed at the field whenever the team needed a rally. Legend had it that Prince saw Pirates trainer Danny Whelan with a green rubber hot dog hanging from the dugout railing in a July 23 game in Houston.[40] During the eighth inning that day, Whelan shouted at Astros pitcher Bob Bruce, "You're going to walk him!" while waving the hot dog in the direction of the pitcher's mound.[41] Bruce walked the hitter, and Pittsburgh—trailing, 3–0, at the time—scored four runs and prevailed, 4–3.

Prince later asked Whelan about the green hot dog, and soon enough, the Green Weenie jinx was born, as Prince started talking about it on his broadcasts and the gimmick was revealed to the rest of America. When shaken at an opposing team, the Green Weenie—just a green plastic hot dog—was supposed to jinx them. Prince would wave it whenever he wanted the Pirates to rally in the late innings. For example, on July 29, Pittsburgh trailed Philadelphia, 3–1, before Prince finally waved the Green Weenie for the first time that day in the eighth inning. The Pirates responded with four runs and won, 5–3, to move ahead of San Francisco atop the NL standings. "Never," the Pirates broadcaster said, "waste the power of the Green Weenie."[42] On July 25, Prince waved a Weenie at Giants ace Juan Marichal; the following day Marichal caught a finger of his pitching hand in a car door and missed two scheduled starts.[43] The hex was probably used from August 1 to 4 when the Dodgers lost three of four at Forbes Field to temporarily fall out of first place.

"Going into Pittsburgh in 1992 brought back those memories of hearing about that jinx and the green hot dog," reflects Candiotti. But by then, the Green Weenie was no longer a tradition in Pirates baseball. There was nobody waving any green frankfurters at Three Rivers Stadium on June 2, but there was no offense either from the Dodgers with Candiotti pitching. What everyone saw instead was the Dodger hitters waving their bats feebly against Pittsburgh's Randy Tomlin, as Candiotti lost a 1–0 heartbreaker despite allowing just five singles over seven innings.

That defeat was one of seven starts in 1992 where Candiotti allowed one earned run or none without getting the win—as he lost four of those games with three no-decisions. He held the opposition to two earned runs or fewer 18 times, but was only 8–6 in those starts. From June 2 onwards, Candiotti compiled a 2.74 ERA in 141.1 innings, allowing 122 hits with 104 strikeouts and 45 walks—but went just 6–12. Those numbers were shades of 1991, when he was 6–11 from June 7 onwards despite a 2.85 ERA in 158 innings with 105 strikeouts while allowing 140 hits and 52 walks. "It was real tough during those years," Candiotti continues. "I'd pitch well but have nothing to show for it. It was tough."

# 13

## *Not Past His Prime*

Tom Candiotti was always at the wrong place at the wrong time. He pitched for the Indians in the 1980s and left the organization in 1991, just before Cleveland became a perennial powerhouse beginning in the mid–1990s. He also pitched for a low-scoring Blue Jays team in '91, but wasn't around when Toronto became an offensive machine in 1992–93 while winning back-to-back World Series.

When Candiotti got to Los Angeles in 1992, he thought he had gone to a team on the verge of winning a championship. But the Dodger teams of the 1990s couldn't score runs and were mediocre defensively, resulting in a poor won-lost record for the knuckleballer. "My career was on the upswing in the early 1990s and into the mid-'90s," Candiotti laments of his 95–110 won-lost mark in that decade. "My first years with the Dodgers, I pitched better than I pitched with Cleveland. But they just didn't score when I pitched. The defense was really lousy with Jose Offerman at shortstop. My first four years in Los Angeles, I should've had just the same numbers, if not better, than I'd had with the Indians."

The numbers backed up Candiotti's assessment; in his first four Dodger seasons (1992–95) his ERA was 3.38 but he was hurt by the fact that he received either the worst or second-worst run support of any major league starter in three of those four years. From 1991 to 1995, even with the eighth-best ERA (3.21) in the majors, Candiotti had a 46–59 mark.

| | G | GS | IP | H | BB | SO | HR | ERA | W-L |
|---|---|---|---|---|---|---|---|---|---|
| 1986–89 CLE | 130 | 128 | 876.2 | 840 | 307 | 539 | 71 | 3.67 | 50–48 |
| 1992–95 LA | 118 | 114 | 760.2 | 705 | 246 | 550 | 52 | 3.38 | 33–46 |

In his first two Dodger seasons in 1992–93, Candiotti was only 19–25 despite a respectable 3.06 ERA. In 1994, he had more complete games than Dodger ace Ramon Martinez (five to four) and a similar ERA (4.12 to 3.97), but finished with five fewer wins (seven to 12). In 1995, Candiotti was 7–14, even with a 3.50 ERA, while Martinez was 17–7 with a 3.66 ERA. With the Dodgers unable to hit or field on a regular basis for Candiotti, he wound up not posting a winning record in those seasons.

Things looked good for Candiotti initially in Los Angeles, though, when he led the Dodgers in almost every significant pitching category in 1992. Through 11 starts on June 7, he had a 2.99 ERA with four complete games, including two shutouts. With a 6–4 record at the time, Candiotti was on pace for 18 wins. That did not last, as the Dodgers slumped badly after June 1, losing 10 consecutive games at one point. And though Candiotti had a 3.02 ERA after June 7—allowing only nine homers and 111 hits over 125.1 innings and having a 2-to–1 strikeout-to-walk ratio (95 to 40)—he still lost 11 of his 16 decisions.

August might have been Candiotti's unluckiest month in 1992. On August 1, he pitched five shutout innings in a 7–2 win over San Diego but had to leave the game after being hit in the ankle by a line drive off the bat of opposing pitcher Andy Benes on the final out in the fifth. On August 8, a bruised left knee forced Candiotti out of a game in Atlanta, and he was placed on the disabled list a day later.[1] Then on August 21, *Los Angeles Times* writer Bill Plaschke suggested either Candiotti or righthander Kevin Gross (who'd just no-hit San Francisco on August 17) would be the logical choice to be taken out of the LA rotation in September in favor of rookie Pedro Astacio, who'd thrown two shutouts in his first four big league starts. As Plaschke noted, Candiotti and Gross were "the only two Dodger starters whose arms and mental makeup" were suited for relief work.[2] At the time of the comments, Candiotti had the fewest walks among LA starters, was the co-leader in victories and strikeouts, and was leading the staff in ERA:

|  | GS | IP | H | BB | SO | HR | ERA |
|---|---|---|---|---|---|---|---|
| Candiotti (9–10) | 22 | 147.2 | 125 | 46 | 115 | 12 | 3.11 |
| Hershiser (9–10) | 25 | 158.2 | 155 | 52 | 92 | 11 | 3.86 |
| R. Martinez (8–10) | 24 | 148.2 | 136 | 67 | 100 | 11 | 3.93 |
| Gross (6–12) | 22 | 144.1 | 131 | 59 | 115 | 8 | 3.37 |
| Ojeda (6–5) | 22 | 129.2 | 127 | 65 | 77 | 7 | 3.40 |

*Opposite*: **After having a successful run with the Indians in the 1980s, Candiotti continued to pitch well in the first half of the 1990s with the Blue Jays and Dodgers. Candiotti, shown here in his Toronto uniform in 1991, logged a 3.21 ERA from 1991 to 1995—which was the eighth-best in the major leagues—while notching 46 victories with 20 complete games in that period (courtesy Toronto Blue Jays).**

Former Indians manager Doc Edwards thinks Candiotti was better used as a starter, adding the only true knuckleball reliever was Hoyt Wilhelm. "The knuckleball [is a pitch that] breaks so funny, gets past the catcher, and goes to the backstop," Edwards says. "You got the bases loaded in the ninth inning, the ball gets by the catcher, the game's over. So most managers are reluctant to use knuckleball pitchers in relief situations. With Tom, he won a lot of ball-games for us in Cleveland. We had other guys on the team who were pretty good pitchers, too. But at times Tom was the guy who was winning and the guy who was doing the job. When you're doing that, you had to be the number one."

In August, Candiotti led the Dodgers in wins, ERA, and strikeouts. But he lost a pair of 2–0 heartbreakers immediately upon his return from the disabled list, to Pirates knuckleballer Tim Wakefield on August 26 and to Cubs ace Greg Maddux on August 31. In the matchup against Wakefield, Candiotti won the battle for throwing the slowest pitch—with his slowest of the night clocked at 53 mph while Wakefield's came in at 58 mph—but lost the game, 2–0, with both runs coming after shortstop Jose Offerman made bad throws to first base.[3]

On his 35th birthday, on August 31, at Wrigley Field, Candiotti wasn't supposed to pitch. The knuckleballer got the call because scheduled starter Ramon Martinez had a sore elbow. "Pitching coach Ron Perranoski and I were both joking that Ramon had 'Maddux-itis' because Greg Maddux was pitching for the Cubs that night. [The extent of Martinez's elbow problem would be serious; he'd miss the rest of the season.] But for me, though, I really wasn't ready to pitch," recalls Candiotti. "I didn't find out until only half an hour before game time." Through the first 6.2 innings, though, Candiotti allowed only two baserunners—via a first-inning walk and a third-inning error by second baseman Eric Young—while recording his 1,000th career strikeout (Rey Sanchez in the third). He retired 20 of the first 22 Cubs, including 14 straight, as Steve Buechele came up to bat with two outs in the seventh with the game still scoreless.

Buechele, who began the year in Pittsburgh but was now the Cubs' every-day third baseman, lined a 2-and–1 knuckleball to right-center field that fell in for a single, breaking up Candiotti's no-hitter. Buechele stole second and scored when rookie first baseman Eric Karros muffed Derrick May's grounder, with the routine groundball bouncing off his glove and into right field. May then stole second and came around to score on Dwight Smith's line-drive single to left. Candiotti finished with a complete-game two-hitter, allowing no earned runs with seven strikeouts and one walk. "Stuff-wise, I don't think I've thrown a better game than that," Candiotti noted afterward.[4]

Though Candiotti had outpitched Maddux—who tossed a five-hitter with one walk and six strikeouts—and lowered his ERA to 2.95, he still saw his record drop to 9–12. At 53–78, the Dodgers had the worst record in baseball. It was just Candiotti's luck. In 1991, when he was pitching for first-place Toronto, he went 6–7 with a 2.98 ERA because those Blue Jays couldn't score runs. What if Candiotti was pitching instead for the 1992 Jays, who on August 31 were sitting atop the AL East at 75–57? Jack Morris, signed by the team after Candiotti went to the Dodgers, was 17–5 despite a 4.22 ERA. And just four days earlier, Toronto had acquired Mets righthander David Cone, and would have Morris and Cone as the top two starters in the 1992 postseason. "No Tom Candiotti nonsense this time around," noted a Toronto newspaper scribe.[5]

Unfortunately, nobody cared that Candiotti had performed well during the 1991 season to get the Jays to the playoffs. He was viewed as a pariah in Toronto, a playoff choker, but Cone and Morris would forever be highly regarded as heroes. "That's true," admits journalist Adrian Brijbassi, a long-time Jays fan. "You can't just say it's because of what [Cone and Morris] did with the Jays. You look at their whole careers, and at what they did outside of Toronto. Candiotti had been just a guy in Cleveland who never won anything. He might've had a good ERA, but he never closed the deal in a big situation."

Though Toronto would defeat Oakland in six games in the 1992 ALCS, Cone was pounded for six runs in Game Five. The Blue Jays then upset the Braves in six games in the World Series, but the outcome didn't seem possible initially, especially when the former Mets righthander was ineffective in Game Two in Atlanta. Cone gave up four runs over 4.1 innings, walked five, threw a wild pitch, and allowed four stolen bases. Toronto trailed, 4–3, entering the ninth inning, and appeared destined to go down 2–0 in the series. Morris—the Game One loser—and Cone looked like non-factors in what appeared to be another disappointing October for the Blue Jays. However, Ed Sprague smacked a two-run pinch-hit homer off Jeff Reardon, giving Toronto the victory.

There were no such Sprague heroics for Candiotti in the 1991 ALCS. "Candiotti never closed the deal against Minnesota," says Brijbassi. "You can say Morris and Cone didn't either against Atlanta. But they did close the deal at some point during their careers. Cone had a pretty good resume with the Mets and later with the Royals, and he was considered one of the best pitchers in the American League for a few years. After [Roger] Clemens, people would say Morris was right up there as the best pitcher in the 1980s. And he won the World Series with Detroit and Minnesota, and then with Toronto."

Still, Blue Jays general manager Pat Gillick remembered Candiotti's con-

**TOM CANDIOTTI**

In his first season in the National League, Candiotti was the best pitcher on a Los Angeles team that lost 99 games in 1992. The knuckleballer led all Dodger starting pitchers with 11 victories, six complete games, and a 3.00 ERA. Though Candiotti's main pitch was the erratic knuckleball, he still led the team with a 2.4 strikeout-to-walk ratio, walking 63 batters while striking out 152. He also tossed two complete-game shutouts, beating the New York Mets, 2–0, on May 16 and blanking the Cincinnati Reds, 1–0, on June 7 (courtesy Tom Candiotti).

tributions. "I don't think we would have won it [the 1991 AL East title] without Candiotti," said Gillick the day of the Cone trade. Toronto led the division by two-and-a-half games when the Candiotti deal was made, and eventually won it by seven. "His record indicates he didn't do too much, but he gave us a lot of innings and quality innings," Gillick told the *New York Times.*[6]

    To this day, Gillick is still appreciative of what the knuckleballer brought to the Jays. "When we had him in '91," Gillick recalls today, "Tom was a real professional on the field and so consequently he had an impact on a number of players on our club. He was always a very positive, upbeat person, and the ultimate professional. Unfortunately, we got knocked out of the playoffs by Minnesota, whom I thought we matched up well against. But I thought we actually had a better team in '91 than we had in '92. We didn't play as well in the '91 playoffs as we had during the season, but it was a thrill, not only for me but the players and the fans, to go back to the playoffs after being out of it for a year in 1990."

There was no thrill in Los Angeles in 1992, as the Dodgers finished 63–99. It certainly wasn't Candiotti's fault for the team's failures, as he posted a 3.00 ERA and allowed only 13 homers in 203.2 innings. Still, it seemed he didn't always get a lot of respect. For instance, sportswriter Bill Plaschke suggested in mid–August that rookie call-up Pedro Astacio deserved a spot in the rotation, and that one possible solution was to move Candiotti to the bullpen.

Was the apparent lack of respect because of that knuckleball? Candiotti thinks it was a factor. "If you didn't know I threw a knuckleball and you looked at the stats, the ERA, hits per nine innings, WHIP—I was right up there [among the league leaders] and I pitched 200 innings every year—you'd want me on your team," he explains. "But when you find out I throw the knuckleball, it's like, 'He's a knuckleball pitcher? I don't want him on my team.'" As the *Arizona Republic*'s Doug Haller once lamented, the knuckler can be a very effective pitch because it frustrates hitters, but big league clubs don't embrace it. "To put it simply," Haller wrote, "the knuckleball annoys organizations. It's a dial-up modem in the age of high-speed Internet, a mosquito at a toddler's outdoor birthday party. The knuckleball produces wild pitches, passed balls, stolen bases, mammoth home runs and ugly baseball."[7]

But even with that knuckleball, Candiotti led the Dodgers in ERA, was second in strikeouts (152), and issued the lowest number of walks among the regular starters (63). He allowed the fewest hits per nine innings (7.8) and walks per nine (2.8). Still, Candiotti lost 15 games. "Three runs a game is a good average to have in the National League," Atlanta's Tom Glavine once said, referring to what a solid ERA should be for a starting pitcher. "On average, if you give up three runs in the National League, your team will score three or four runs on most nights. So you have a chance to win."[8]

Candiotti gave the Dodgers a chance on most nights. He even recorded more strikeouts than Orel Hershiser and Ramon Martinez. Didn't that qualify the knuckleballer as the staff ace? Joe Niekro, who won 221 major league games from 1967 to 1988, would have agreed. "If you're a knuckleball pitcher and you can get people out, why not?" Niekro said in 2003. "My brother [Phil Niekro] was the ace of the Braves for three years and me and Nolan [Ryan] were sort of aces on the Houston staff."[9]

Tom Candiotti did enough to be that on the 1992 Dodger staff.

In 1993, Los Angeles finished with an 81–81 record, just one year after the 63–99 disaster. For Candiotti, though, nothing had changed in terms of his luck. He had the NL's seventh-best ERA at 3.12, marking the fourth time in eight years that he had finished in the top 10. In 17 of his 32 starts, Candiotti gave up two runs or fewer while pitching at least seven innings. Five other times, he allowed three runs in six or more innings. However, the Dodgers averaged 2.81 runs in Candiotti's starts—2.23 while he was in the game—resulting in an 8–10 record and 14 no-decisions.

From May 31-August 25, Candiotti's 17 starts included 123.1 innings, 87 hits, 94 strikeouts, 34 walks, six homers, a 1.53 ERA, but just six victories. Over a 75-day span that began on June 12, the knuckleballer made 15 starts and didn't lose a single one of them, allowing just 19 earned runs. Over 106.1 innings in that stretch, Candiotti allowed 79 hits and 28 walks with 81 strikeouts, posting a 1.61 ERA. Ten of those 15 games, though, resulted in no-decisions. Some of Candiotti's no-decisions in 1993 included the following:

- One run over eight innings against St. Louis; left trailing, 1–0.
- Two runs—one earned—over eight innings in San Francisco; left with the game tied, 2–2.
- Two runs over eight innings against the expansion Colorado Rockies; left trailing, 2–1.
- Eight innings of four-hit ball against Pittsburgh; left trailing, 1–0, against rookie Paul Wagner (who had a 5.23 ERA at the time).
- Worked five innings against the Mets while pitching on two days' rest; left trailing, 1–0.
- Two runs on six hits and no walks over seven innings in St. Louis; left trailing, 2–0, against rookie Rene Arocha. (Los Angeles scored six runs the night before off Braves ace lefthander Tom Glavine, and would score eight runs a night later.)
- One run over seven innings against Atlanta; left trailing, 1–0.

Candiotti also suffered some hard-luck losses in 1993:

- Three runs—one earned—over eight innings against San Francisco; the Dodgers' two fourth-inning errors led to a 3–1 loss.
- One run (which came on a sacrifice fly) over eight innings against Atlanta; Dodgers lost, 2–0. (They'd won, 5–4 and 5–1, earlier in the series, defeating Cy Young winners Glavine and Greg Maddux.)
- Three runs over eight innings against the expansion Florida Marlins; Dodgers lost, 3–2, after stranding 11 baserunners against six Marlins pitchers, including two runners in the first, third, fourth, eighth, and ninth innings.

Candiotti even threw five shutout innings during the Dodgers' postseason goodwill series in Taipei, Taiwan, but LA lost, 1–0, to the Taiwanese all-stars.[10] Including that outing as well as spring training back in America,

Candiotti had a 2.80 ERA in 247.2 innings. "We just couldn't score any runs," Candiotti reflects. "I had a stretch of [17] straight starts where I allowed three runs [or fewer]. It was ridiculous." Indeed. In 11 of his 32 starts, Candiotti received zero runs while he was still in the game. During the pennant race with San Francisco in late August, meanwhile, Atlanta's Glavine said that the Braves' pitchers knew if they were able to "hold the other team to three runs, we'll win nine of every 10."[11] And it wasn't as though the 1993 Dodgers couldn't score runs. They averaged 5.22 runs for Kevin Gross (13–13, 4.14), 4.53 for Orel Hershiser (12–14, 3.59), and 4.34 for Pedro Astacio (14–9, 3.57).

Candiotti's strong 1993 season began in spring training. In his first five spring starts, he allowed four runs—three earned—in 22 innings. First, it was a run over three innings against Houston, followed by a run in four innings versus Kansas City, and then four scoreless innings against the Mets. Next up, five shutout innings of two-hit ball versus the Mets on March 18. In his fifth start, facing the Mets on March 27, it was two runs—one earned—in six innings.[12] But Candiotti saved his best for his final spring start, allowing one hit and two walks in seven innings in a 6–0 win over California at Dodger Stadium. He began the game with 4.1 perfect innings and didn't allow a hit until Chad Curtis opened the seventh with a single. "The knuckleball was moving great all night," Candiotti said then. "I've been in that zone, it's been like that all spring."[13] He struck out his sixth, seventh, and eighth batters after the Curtis single before calling it a night, wrapping up the spring with a 0.93 ERA (three earned runs in 29 innings).[14]

When the regular season began, though, Candiotti was 0–3 with a 6.55 ERA in April while pitching with a cracked fingernail. Traditionally, he had been unbeatable in the season's first month (even though the knuckler isn't known to flutter in the early-season cold weather), posting an April record of 14–2 with a 2.96 ERA (149 IP, 49 ER) from 1988 to 1992. Not so in 1993. "I had to put acrylic on my nails to harden them," Candiotti recalls. "It wasn't until late May that I pitched without anything on my nail. For a knuckleball pitcher, a broken fingernail's like a regular pitcher having tendinitis."

When April ended, the Dodgers had the majors' worst team batting average at .227. They also had the NL's worst record. At 8–15, the Dodgers were behind the two first-year expansion teams—Colorado (8–14) and Florida (10–13). Just a year earlier, the Dodgers had gone 9–13 in April—last in the NL West—en route to their historic 99-loss season. Even then, they were only three games out of first place. In 1993, they were already six-and-a-half games out.

Things got no better after April. Not only were sluggers Darryl Strawberry and Eric Davis dealing with various ailments, Todd Worrell—signed in the offseason to be the team's closer—was also sidelined with a sprained fore-arm.[15] Even with the injury-depleted lineup—with Strawberry (back), Davis (rib cage), and Tim Wallach (back) out—Candiotti won his first game on May 1, beating Philadelphia, 5–1, with eight innings of five-hit, nine-strikeout ball. Beginning with that victory, in fact, the knuckleballer would go on to compile a four-month stretch where he logged a 1.85 ERA and lost just twice in 22 starts. In that span from May 1-August 25, Candiotti allowed only 43 walks and six homers with 120 strikeouts over 155.2 innings. However, he'd go just 8–2 while recording 12 no-decisions in that stretch.

Back in 1987, Twins lefthander Steve Carlton had commented on Can-diotti's luck following a 3–1 loss in Minnesota, the knuckleballer's ninth defeat where he received two runs or fewer during a trying season. "Candy, you're the unluckiest guy I've ever seen," said the future Hall of Famer. Candiotti, though, responded defiantly, "No, things will turn around. If I pitch long enough, my luck will change." If only Candiotti knew.

Despite the Dodgers' sloppy fielding and inconsistent hitting in 1993, Candiotti went 3–1 with a 2.61 ERA in May. The knuckleballer capped off the month with a dominant 5–1 victory in St. Louis on May 31, tossing a four-hitter where three of those hits never left the infield. The Cardinals didn't even get a hard-hit ball until the ninth.[16] Candiotti was even better in June, com-piling a 1.80 ERA in five starts, recording 33 strikeouts over 35 innings while allowing only 11 walks and 24 hits. Remarkably, he went 0–1 with four no-decisions. That lone June decision was a 2–0 loss to Atlanta's John Smoltz on June 6, when Candiotti allowed one run on four hits in eight innings. On June 23, Candiotti pitched four-hit ball in eight-plus innings to outduel Houston's Doug Drabek, but the Dodger bullpen blew his 3–2 lead in the ninth. On June 28, Candiotti pitched eight shutout innings against San Francisco, but it was Dodger reliever Pedro Martinez getting the victory when Dave Hansen's grand slam won it, 4–0, in the bottom of the ninth.

Candiotti again pitched well once the calendar turned to July, compiling a 1.49 ERA in six starts. On July 4 in Montreal, Candiotti tossed seven shutout innings of two-hit, no-walk, six-strikeout ball—in the Dodgers' 1–0, 11th-inning victory—but got his eighth no-decision in 16 starts. "In the 1990s, bullpens started becoming a little more prevalent," Candiotti says, recalling that the Dodgers wouldn't let him stay longer in ballgames to pick up more victories. "It seemed like Tommy Lasorda was saving Pedro Martinez, who threw so hard, to come in after me. Of course, Pedro was great even without following a knuckleball pitcher, obviously. [In games Martinez followed Can-diotti in 1993, his ERA was 1.35 in 26.2 innings with 34 strikeouts. In other games, Martinez's numbers were 3.02 in 80.1 innings with 85 strikeouts, according to Baseball-Reference.com.] But the Dodgers just kind of liked that combination, of a hard thrower coming in after me."

Then there was also the catching part of the equation. "We played a lot of close games because we didn't have a good offense," Candiotti says. "And when you had a one-run game [in the final inning].... I think the Dodgers were always scared of stolen bases, so if they could get me out and have a guy like Pedro in, that could stop the running game." Against Houston, for example, Candiotti had a four-hitter through eight, but walked the fleet-footed Steve Finley to open the ninth. "For Lasorda, it was an easy decision," continues the Dodger knuckleballer. "The guy has a chance to steal and get into scoring position, and then there's a chance for a passed ball or wild pitch, and you don't have a catcher who can throw.... So, you bring in a hard thrower to finish off the game."

Outfielder Cory Snyder recalls that Candiotti simply was unlucky. "Sometimes you don't get run support for certain guys," says Snyder. "Sometimes as a position player, you try to do too much, [and] sometimes it backfires on you. In '93, it was one of those years [where] we were trying a little too hard instead of going out there and just trying to play the game. I think sometimes the media makes it out to be as, 'Oh, Tom's on the mound, so he probably won't get any runs today,' and then it kind of becomes a mental thing and you try too hard to get him runs. It was one of those years that just didn't happen for him. It didn't faze him because he was a great pitcher. He still went out and did the job for us. He still threw well that year."

It was in July where Candiotti made two starts in the same series, with the Dodgers playing five games over four days on July 8–11 at Shea Stadium, including a doubleheader on the first day. Candiotti's feat was necessitated because Kevin Gross (first game of the July 8 doubleheader), Orel Hershiser (July 9), and Pedro Astacio (July 10) were already scheduled to pitch in the series, and Ramon Martinez was serving a five-game suspension. Pitching on three days' rest, Candiotti worked six innings against New York on July 8 (second game of the doubleheader), and he then returned on two days' rest to pitch five innings on July 11. "That's one of the advantages of having a knuckleball pitcher," he says. "We recover quickly. When the Dodgers wanted me to start on short rest, I could've done it every time because the knuckleball put very little strain on your arm." Unfortunately, he received a total of only three runs of support and settled for no-decisions in both games, extending his streak to eight straight starts without a victory despite his 1.87 ERA over 53 innings in that span (along with 36 hits and 45 strikeouts). Naturally, the Dodgers scored 23 runs in the three games in the Mets series that Candiotti did not start.

Candiotti, just 3–5 despite a 3.02 ERA in 18 starts, tried to find humor in his situation. Take the Dodgers' three-game series in San Francisco from

July 26 to 28, for instance. In the first game, LA scored three runs on four hits off Bryan Hickerson in the first inning en route to a 15–1 victory for Hershiser. In the dugout, Candiotti told Gross, "That's all the runs we'll see this series." He was close. The following night, the Dodgers managed just three hits off John Burkett as Gross lost, 3–2. In the series finale, Candiotti also received only two runs. Fortunately, the knuckleballer won, 2–1, holding Giants sluggers Will Clark, Matt Williams, and Barry Bonds to one hit in 10 at-bats. "I always joked that I wasn't getting more than two runs because Hershiser was getting all of them!" Candiotti recalls.

While the big story for the 1993 Dodgers was rookie catcher Mike Piazza's season (.318, 35 HRs, 112 RBIs), another was how they pounded Giants rookie Salomon Torres on the season's final day to eliminate San Francisco from the postseason. What wasn't a story but became a recurring theme was how the team struggled against rookie hurlers when Candiotti was pitching. He saw that for three straight starts, from August 20 to September 1, as the Dodgers made three consecutive rookies look like Cy Young. On August 20, Candiotti allowed six hits over seven innings with no walks in St. Louis, but left in favor of a pinch-hitter, trailing rookie Rene Arocha, 2–0. Though LA rallied for three ninth-inning runs and won, 3–2, Candiotti was left with his 12th no-decision in 25 starts.

On August 25 against Pittsburgh, Candiotti allowed one run on four hits over eight innings, fanning seven with one walk. He retired his final 13 batters—and 17 of the last 18—and lowered his ERA to a major league-best 2.43. Unfortunately, the Dodgers couldn't touch rookie Paul Wagner, who tossed 6.1 shutout innings after having compiled a 7.09 ERA over his last nine appearances. LA finally tied the score in the eighth—before losing, 2–1, in 12 innings—giving Candiotti his 10th no-decision over his last 15 starts (where he was 5–0 with a 1.61 ERA). In each of his last 19 starts, Candiotti had allowed three earned runs or fewer, and he averaged only 2.5 walks per nine innings—better than his career 2.9 average (580 walks in 1,786 innings).

Entering September, Los Angeles was already out of contention at 66–64, 18-and-a-half games behind NL West-leading San Francisco. But Candiotti had a shot at the ERA title with his 2.43 earned run average. Things changed on September 1 in Pittsburgh, when Candiotti opposed rookie lefthander Steve Cooke, who had a 5.03 ERA over his last eight starts and was coming off a 4.1-inning, six-run disaster against lowly San Diego (49–78) on August 27. He'd then go 4–11 with a 5.02 ERA in 1994 and be out of the majors four years later. In the Dodger game, though, Cooke spun his second career complete game, defeating Candiotti and LA, 5–1.

The game was decided in the first inning, when Candiotti walked Jay

Bell and Jeff King ahead of Dave Clark's two-out RBI single and Al Martin's three-run homer. "I'll never forget this one," Candiotti says. "I had two strikes on Jeff King [with two outs], but Eric Gregg—the umpire—called the next pitch a ball instead of strike three. If you looked at the replay, there was no question it was a strike." King eventually walked, prolonging the inning, and moments later Pittsburgh had four runs on the board. After that, Candiotti allowed only one more run over the next five innings, but the damage had been done. When the game ended, his ERA had climbed to 2.60—knocking him out of the major league lead behind Jose Rijo (2.53) and Greg Maddux (2.56)—and his 15-start undefeated streak was over.

Though he would fall out of the ERA race thanks to a subpar September, Candiotti's two best starts of that month came against the two best teams in baseball. The first occurred on September 6 at Dodger Stadium, when Candiotti shut down the red-hot Atlanta Braves, winners in 21 of their previous 25 games. The Braves, who had gone from nine-and-a-half games behind San Francisco to only two-and-a-half games back during their hot streak, were trying to catch the Giants in the NL West with only three weeks remaining. "For the Dodgers, we felt like we were really playing for something because we all wanted to beat Atlanta," says Candiotti. "For us, it was a different kind of intensity level because we wanted to ruin their season. It felt like that again in the final weekend when the Giants came to Dodger Stadium to end the season. I pitched just as well against them too."

Against Atlanta, Candiotti allowed five hits over seven innings, with the only run off of him coming on a fourth-inning sacrifice fly. The Dodger knuckleballer set down three of the first four Braves on strikeouts, before finishing with six punchouts and two walks. Unfortunately, when Candiotti was pulled for a pinch-hitter he was trailing, 1–0, marking the third time in four starts that he'd departed losing either 1–0 or 2–0. This time, LA rallied off John Smoltz for a 2–1 victory, giving Candiotti a no-decision.

Candiotti's ERA in his 28 starts was 2.55, with 144 strikeouts and 159 hits over 190.2 innings. It was the 18th time that he had pitched at least seven innings—the ninth time in his last 10 outings. Yet Candiotti had just an 8–6 record. But he wasn't the only frustrated pitcher. In the losers' clubhouse, Smoltz expressed the same about his 13–10, 3.41 ERA mark. "I find sometimes I can't pitch any better, but the results aren't there," lamented Smoltz.[17] Of course, the Braves' pitchers expected—and normally received—plenty of support. "We're a lot more relaxed because we know we'll get a lot of runs," said Braves lefthander Tom Glavine, who was 14–5 with a 3.32 ERA in 25 starts since May 1 while allowing at least three runs 13 times during that stretch. "We know that if we hold the other team to three runs, we'll win nine of every 10."[18]

Candiotti had a strong season for Los Angeles in 1993, leading the major leagues with a home ERA of 1.95. From May 1 to August 25, Candiotti lost only twice in 22 starts while logging a 1.85 ERA with 120 strikeouts and 43 walks over 155.2 innings. Going into the final month of the season, the Dodger knuckleballer had a major league-best 2.43 earned run average, but a subpar September ended up costing him the 1993 National League ERA title (National Baseball Hall of Fame Library, Cooperstown, New York).

In 13 of Candiotti's 28 starts, meanwhile, LA had scored *two runs or fewer.* Since May 1, he was 8–3 in 24 starts despite a 2.03 ERA. And when Candiotti allowed three runs over eight innings against Florida on September 11, he lost a 3–2 decision. As if the poor run support wasn't bad enough, the Dodgers even took a start away from him (as well as Pedro Astacio) in the final week of September so that rookie reliever Pedro Martinez could get in two starts of his own.[19]

Entering the final weekend in 1993, Candiotti was 8–9 with a 3.19 ERA. He was no longer in contention for the ERA title but still had a shot at playing spoiler in his final start. San Francisco, battling Atlanta for the NL West crown, was in town for a season-ending four-game series with Candiotti starting the opener. "This was before the wild card, where only the two division winners in each league made the playoffs," Candiotti recalls. "Either the Braves or the Giants would be eliminated on that final weekend. We had a chance to knock the Giants out of the playoffs. The Dodgers had such a huge rivalry with the Giants, and we just wanted to knock them out."

The Giants, with their 100–58 record, arrived at Dodger Stadium one game behind Atlanta (101–57) with only four to play. In the opening game, Candiotti allowed seven hits over eight innings and limited the Giants' trio of Will Clark, Matt Williams, and Barry Bonds to two hits in 11 at-bats. But Los Angeles collected only four singles—and committed three errors—as San Francisco won, 3–1, behind 20-game winner Bill Swift to move into a first-place tie with the Braves, who had lost to Houston earlier in the evening. "Tom Candiotti pitched well for the Dodgers and we were fortunate to be able to take advantage of their errors," noted Swift.[20]

In the fourth inning, Bonds was on second with two outs when shortstop Jose Offerman booted Royce Clayton's routine grounder for his major league-leading 37th error, prolonging the inning. Kirt Manwaring promptly singled to right, scoring Bonds. But when Cory Snyder's throw from right field skipped into the Dodger dugout, Clayton scored as well. Back in spring training, Dodger righthander Kevin Gross had high expectations for 1993. Recalling the 1992 disaster, he'd said, "The [pitching] staff did a pretty good job about [keeping the Dodgers close despite the errors]. We all knew the guys were struggling. That's a tough job. I can't play shortstop. But this year if somebody isn't doing the job, they'll have them out of there. We'll make a move, something."[21] But no move was made, and Candiotti was losing, 2–0.

With the score 2–1 in the sixth, the Dodgers threatened with two on and one out, but Swift retired both Mike Piazza and Eric Karros. The Giants made it 3–1 in the eighth off Candiotti, but even that run was tainted. Centerfielder Brett Butler misplayed Matt Williams's line drive by making an ill-advised diving attempt on the ball that went for a one-out triple. Williams then scored on an infield hit by Willie McGee, a two-out single off Karros's glove at first base.[22]

With the loss, Candiotti finished with an 8–10, 3.12 ERA mark. For the third straight year, he posted a sub–3.20 ERA while surpassing 30 starts, 200 innings, and 150 strikeouts. For the second time in three seasons, Candiotti was the major league ERA leader at one point in September. But in those three years, he was 13–13, 11–15, and 8–10. Candiotti allowed one earned run or none in 18 of his starts in 1993, but got three runs of support or fewer 22 times. In his four starts against San Francisco, he logged a 0.84 ERA over 32.1 innings and allowed no home runs while striking out 26 Giants with 12 walks—and won just *once*.

One night after Candiotti's 3–1 loss, the Dodgers scored seven against the Giants. The first five Dodgers reached base against 21-game winner John Burkett—giving LA a quick 3–0 lead—before the Giants righthander recorded the first out. But San Francisco hammered Ramon Martinez for six runs—with Barry Bonds slugging two homers—as the Giants won, 8–7. In the third game, the Dodgers chased starter Bryan Hickerson after two-plus innings, and Brett Butler and Mike Piazza each finished with three hits. San Francisco, though, won, 5–3, as Dave Martinez drove in three runs, including a seventh-inning, two-run double off Orel Hershiser. After 161 games, San Francisco was tied with Atlanta atop the NL West with identical 103–58 records.

On the season's final day, Atlanta defeated Colorado, 5–3, behind left-hander Tom Glavine in an early contest, meaning San Francisco had to win in Los Angeles again to stay alive. But the Giants fell flat, getting crushed, 12–1, as the Dodgers pounded 21-year-old rookie righthander Salomon Torres (who'd begun the year in Double-A and was making just his eighth big league start) and the bullpen for six extra-base hits, including four homers.[23] The Giants, despite winning 103 games in 1993, missed out on the postseason.

While people today still remember the Braves-Giants pennant race, not many remember Candiotti's 1993 efforts. He thinks he could have been better remembered had he won the '93 ERA title. He laments two incidents in particular that cost him that championship. "We were in Pittsburgh," Candiotti says, referring the Eric Gregg game on September 1. "Jeff King was the hitter, and Eric Gregg was the umpire. It was a 2–2 count with two outs, I threw a knuckleball which was right there, and Jeff took it. After Jeff took the pitch, he walked across the plate like it was called strike three, to go back to the dugout. But Eric didn't call a strike. So Jeff stopped, turned around and went back to the batter's box. I yelled at Eric, 'Hey, where the hell was that pitch?

Even he thought it was strike three!'" Three pitches later, King reached on a walk and the Pirates went on to score four runs in the inning.

"Then we were in Colorado, where the knuckleball didn't work," Candiotti continues, referring to a 12–3 loss on September 17 at Mile High Stadium, which was located 5,280 feet above sea level. "The elevation in Denver, the high altitude.... It was sucking all of the moisture out of the balls, making them lighter and harder. And curveballs didn't break ... they hung in the strike zone." Baseballs travel faster in Denver because there's less resistance in the thinner air—and when Candiotti threw his knuckleball and curveball that night, the balls crossed the plate faster and had less time to break. The result: 1.2 innings, seven runs, nine hits. "I came into September leading the National League in ERA, but those two events, that one especially with Eric Gregg and the Pirates, and then the game against the Rockies, cost me the ERA title," adds Candiotti.

Candiotti, who also lost a bid for an ERA championship in the final two weeks of the 1991 season, went 0–5 with a 6.50 earned run average in September of 1993 to fall out of the race for the ERA title this time around. However, he refutes the notion that his knuckleball became less effective once the calendar turned to September, when the summer weather gave way to autumn. "Yes, a knuckleball moves really well when it's humid," Candiotti says. "Anywhere that's humid, it's like, 'Wow, that pitch moves really well all over the place.' [But] in '91 when I lost the ERA title, it was that one game in Anaheim when I had eight shots of Novocaine. Then in '93 it was the two events that hurt. It wasn't because the knuckleball wasn't working in September."

Baseball historian Bill James once wrote, "The analogy that seasons are to careers as months are to seasons, it seems to me, has one major flaw, which is that it doesn't account for pennant races. A pennant is a real thing, an object in itself; if you win it, it's forever. If a pitcher goes 7–0 in June and puts his team into first place, that's just June; if he then goes 1–5 in July and the team slips to fourth place, the end result is pretty much the same as if the hot streak had never existed."[24]

However, that's probably not a fair way to look at a pitcher's impact. What if the season was never played to the end, say, because it was cut short by a players' strike? It doesn't mean his accomplishments "never existed." Led by Mike Piazza's 24 home runs and 92 RBIs as well as Tim Wallach's 23 homers and 79 runs batted in, the Dodgers sat atop the NL West at the time of the strike on August 11. But the team's first-place standing was also thanks in part to Tom Candiotti's seven wins and team-high five complete games. He allowed only nine home runs in 153 innings, giving him the best rate (0.53 per nine innings) among Dodger pitchers. Though Candiotti's 4.12 ERA was subpar (his career ERA was 3.41 entering the season), it was a broken fingernail that led to his two worst outings. Erase his start on May 9 against Houston with the broken nail—seven earned runs in 2.1 innings—and his ERA would have been 3.76, better than Dodger ace Orel Hershiser's 3.79. In 14 of his 23 outings (22 starts), Candiotti went at least six innings while allowing three earned runs or fewer. Unfortunately, the bullpen blew four of his late-inning leads and the offense scored just 12 runs in his seven losses.

In his first three starts, though, Candiotti received good support. On April 6, he defeated Florida, 3–2. On April 12, Candiotti won, 7–3, on a four-hitter in St. Louis, becoming the first Dodger with back-to-back complete games to start the season since Hershiser in 1986. Then on April 17, a 19–2 victory in Pittsburgh, thanks to Cory Snyder's three homers. Though Candiotti began the year 3–0, there were some concerns. "I started having trouble with my fingernails soon after," the knuckleballer says. "Because of that, I really couldn't throw the knuckleball effectively in the next few starts."

Another concern was the Dodgers' record when Candiotti wasn't pitching. They had won all three of his starts but had lost eight of the other nine games started by everybody else, and had a mediocre 4–8 record even after the blowout victory in Pittsburgh. Through the first 12 games none of the other Dodger starters had recorded a win, and the bullpen had already suffered four losses. The other starters would be a combined 0–4 with eight no-decisions before Hershiser was victorious in LA's 16th game.

After the slow start, though, the Dodgers won 12 of 18 games from April 24 to May 14 to stay within striking distance of first place. When Candiotti defeated San Diego, 7–1, on May 15—on a five-hitter with seven strikeouts and one walk—it put LA in the top spot in the NL West for the first time, tied with San Francisco. The Dodgers would stay in first place from that point on in 1994, helped out by a hot streak that month when they went 11–2 in one stretch and the fact that the rest of the division was fairly mediocre.

Their ascend to the top was improbable, especially since the hard-hitting Giants resided in the division. Because of realignment in 1994, the NL West was left with only San Francisco (103–59 in 1993), Los Angeles (81–81), San Diego (61–101), and Colorado (67–95). Cincinnati and Houston were transferred to the newly created NL Central while Atlanta, winners of three straight Western Division titles, moved to the NL East. With the Braves gone, it was a foregone conclusion that the Giants—who had strengthened their starting rotation by signing righthander Mark Portugal (18–4, 2.77 ERA with Houston in 1993) in the offseason—would win the West. "By getting us out of this division," Braves lefthander Tom Glavine said that April, "it might open up a door for [the Dodgers] as far as the wild-card spot goes. It's certainly not derogatory to them, but I would think that San Francisco would be the class of that division."[25]

The Giants spent the first 41 days of the season alone in first place, from April 4 to May 14, thanks mainly to the mediocrity of the rest of the division early on. Then on May 15, San Francisco lost, 9–6, to Cincinnati despite scoring six runs off Reds ace Jose Rijo and dropped its record to 20–17. That defeat, coupled with Candiotti's 7–1 victory over the Padres, meant the Giants and Dodgers (20–17) now shared top spot. Three days later, San Francisco would relinquish its share of the division lead, and would not get back to the top again for the rest of the year.

But while the Dodgers remained in first place from May 15 onwards, they stopped hitting for Candiotti, who went just 3–5 in 13 appearances despite a 3.35 ERA from May 20-July 27. On May 20 in Cincinnati, Candiotti pitched eight innings of five-hit, two-run ball, but the Dodgers lost, 3–2. On June 21 in San Diego, he allowed two runs over seven innings but LA lost, 4–3. Six nights later, Candiotti lost, 3–2, to San Francisco as catcher Mike Piazza struck out with the bases loaded in the third and ended the game by hitting a pop-up with the tying runner on third base. The winning run was also made possible when Piazza's passed ball advanced Barry Bonds to third, and the Giants' slugger eventually scored on an easy groundout. On July 7, Candiotti lost, 3–0, to the Mets in lefthander Jason Jacome's second big league game. (Jacome would pitch just *one* more shutout in 135 starts in his professional career after that season, *none* in the majors.)

While the Dodgers might have been an improved club, their Achilles' heel was their relief pitching. In the first half, the bullpen blew three saves for Candiotti, coughing up late-inning leads of 4–3, 6–5, and 9–4. That 9–4 blown lead, an 11–10 Dodger defeat on June 6 in Florida, was the most excruciating. With two outs and none on in the seventh, the Marlins struck for seven straight hits to tie the game, with rookie Darren Dreifort and veterans Jim Gott and Al Osuna failing in relief. "Unbelievable ... nobody on, and we can't get one guy to get one out," noted manager Tommy Lasorda. "It took us four pitchers to get one out."[26] Todd Worrell, who had struggled since returning from the DL two weeks earlier, didn't pitch that night. But he got the ball two days later and blew his fourth straight save opportunity as Florida scored three ninth-inning runs and won, 5–4.

The bullpen's struggles were one of the reasons LA went just 46–42 in the first half. In the season's first two months, Dreifort, who began his pro career in the big leagues without ever pitching in the minors, was 6-for-9 in saves while compiling an 0–5, 6.21 ERA mark. The Dodgers would send him to Double-A on June 23. Worrell, who would register 30-plus saves in each of his first three seasons from 1986 to 1988 while with St. Louis, had been dealing with injuries to his elbow, shoulder, forearm, and rib cage since 1990. He would record just 19 saves from 1990 to 1994 while landing on the DL five times. In the first half of 1994, his second year with the Dodgers, Worrell recorded seven saves while blowing six other opportunities. Then there was veteran righthander Gott, whose first-half ERA was 5.13.

At the All-Star break, the Dodgers still sat atop the NL West standings, owning a five-game lead over Colorado and a seven-and-a-half-game edge over San Francisco. A 13-game post-break road trip followed, and that was where Candiotti repeatedly bailed out the Dodgers. He gave the club a quality outing each time out when nobody else seemed capable of providing even five innings. He pitched on short rest and in relief. After a six-inning four-hitter in a 3–2 victory in Philadelphia on July 15, Candiotti returned on two days' rest in relief because of the ailing staff. On July 18 in New York, rookie Ismael Valdez was an emergency replacement for Orel Hershiser—who had a strained left rib cage muscle—but left the game after recording just three outs because of a blister. In came Candiotti on two days' rest, and he tossed seven relief innings of three hit-ball as LA won, 7–6, in 10 innings (after Todd Worrell blew the knuckleballer's 6–3 lead in the bottom of the ninth).

Once again, it was another example of Candiotti coming up big for the team. For the third straight game, a Dodger starter hadn't lasted past three innings. First, it was Hershiser removing himself from a game in Philadelphia during his warm-up pitches because of a muscle strain. (Ramon Martinez, the emergency starter, was clobbered for nine runs in 4.1 innings.) The following day, Pedro Astacio allowed six runs in 2.1 innings, as the Dodgers lost three of four to the Phillies. Then the Valdez game against the Mets where the rookie had to leave in the second, with Candiotti providing seven relief innings.

On July 23, Candiotti pitched seven innings of six-hit, two-walk ball in a 2–0 loss in Montreal, giving the bullpen some much-needed rest—as the relievers had worked nine innings over the previous two games thanks to back-to-back short outings by starters Martinez and Astacio. Candiotti then returned on three days' rest for the finale of the Dodgers' 13-game road trip in San Francisco on July 27. Pitching for the fourth time in 13 days, he had a four-hitter and a 1–0 lead entering the eighth inning. With the bullpen having allowed 10 runs in the previous two games, manager Tommy Lasorda opted to allow Candiotti to continue pitching. "Give me what you've got," was the message from Lasorda even with Candiotti tiring in the eighth.[27] The Giants—who'd made up eight games in the standings by winning 13 of their last 16—erupted for four runs and won, 4–1. Los Angeles finished 3–10 on the trip and its lead over San Francisco—which had been as many as nine-and-a-half games on July 6—was suddenly down to a half-game.

While the bullpen was a disaster during the trip—Todd Worrell (15.75 ERA), Jim Gott (9.39 ERA), Roger McDowell (9.82 ERA), and Omar Daal (5.40 ERA) all pitched poorly—the starters weren't getting it done either. Astacio went 0–2 in his two starts with a 22.85 ERA while lasting a total of 4.1 innings. Martinez was 1–2 with a 5.19 ERA in his three starts; Kevin Gross, 0–2, 6.11 in three starts; Hershiser pitched only once, getting rocked in San Francisco for five runs in five innings in a 12–5 loss; Ismael Valdez, normally a reliever, made one start and lasted one-plus inning. Candiotti, though, wasn't part of the problem, logging a 2.60 ERA in four games and working at least six innings each time. Two of LA's three victories came in games in which he had pitched.

However, Candiotti struggled when August began, getting pounded for five runs over 2.1 innings against San Diego and then for five more runs over 3.2 innings in Cincinnati. The 5–3 loss against the Reds on August 9 dropped Candiotti's record to 7–7 with a 4.12 ERA. Despite his subpar numbers, he was still the team's most durable and effective pitcher since joining the Dodgers in 1992. Candiotti's 570.1 innings, 13 complete games, and 3.35 ERA from 1992 to 1994 led the club. On the Dodgers, his 409 strikeouts and 6.45 strikeouts per nine innings trailed only Gross's 432 and 6.89. And in 1994, Candiotti was the only starter who was winning in April—going 3–1—when LA began the season slowly. (Astacio, Hershiser, Martinez, and Gross combined to go 2–4 in 18 April starts.) Candiotti was the one who pitched well when the other starters were struggling on the road trip that began the second half.

The Dodgers had a three-and-a-half-game division lead on August 11 but would not make the postseason. Nobody would, as baseball's labor dispute wiped everything out. The players went on strike after games played on the night of August 11, and the rest of the season would eventually be canceled. The strike would last 232 days and would not end until 1995.[28]

# 14

## *The Great Run by a Knuckleballer on the Other Coast*

The 1995 season should have been known in the baseball annals as the year of the knuckleball revival. But thanks to the Dodgers' lack of offense for Candiotti and the September slump of Boston's Tim Wakefield, it didn't turn out that way. At least Wakefield received a lot of accolades along the way for his fine pitching for three months. When the season began, though, who would've thunk it?

Wakefield, who in 1993–94 went a combined 14–31 with a 5.94 ERA in both the minor leagues and major leagues, was released by Pittsburgh before the 1995 season. He'd spent the 1994 season with Triple-A Buffalo, leading the league in losses, walks, and homers allowed. Nevertheless, the Red Sox gave Wakefield a chance, and the knuckleballer made his '95 season debut on May 27 and defeated the Angels, 2–1, in Anaheim. Wakefield then returned on two days' rest to win, 1–0, in Oakland. Next up, a 2–1 home victory over Seattle on June 4. He would win 10 straight starts at one point, and on August 13, was 14–1 with a 1.65 ERA. Though Wakefield proceeded to go 2–7 with a 5.60 ERA to end the season, he was named the *Sporting News'* AL Comeback Player of the Year.

Out West, Candiotti compiled a 3.50 ERA for the first-place Dodgers. Unfortunately, he received very little support and finished just 7–14. In a nine-start span in the first half, Candiotti posted a 0.97 ERA while allowing two earned runs or fewer each time out—but went only 3–3. In five of those starts, he didn't allow a single earned run, but in three of them the Dodgers were shut out. Beginning with a 3–0 shutout at Shea Stadium on May 25, Candiotti had a stretch of 20 starts where he allowed three earned runs or fewer 18 times.

Erase a four-inning, 10-run mess in San Francisco on August 4, and Candiotti's season ERA would have been 3.09, good for seventh in the NL.

Two other knuckleballers made their big league debuts in 1995. Milwaukee's Steve Sparks, who blanked Texas, 1–0, in his first start on May 19, won nine games with a 4.63 ERA. Philadelphia's Dennis Springer made his debut in mid–September, going 0–3 in four starts but pitched into the sixth inning three times. Quite a comeback year for the knuckleball. But Wakefield was the one everyone was talking about. As Bob Ryan of the *Boston Globe* said a decade later of Wakefield, that '95 season was magical indeed. "[F]or two months, he put on the best exhibition of knuckleball pitcher ever seen on this, or any other, planet. No one currently drawing a breath ever again will see anything like the Tim Wakefield of May, June, and July in 1995. That is the lock of all locks. A knuckleballer going 14–1 again? Nah."[1] However, Candiotti's 1.53 ERA over a 17-start stretch in 1993 from May 31-August 25 was right up there. His numbers included 123.1 innings, 87 hits, 34 walks, 94 strikeouts, and just one loss. And from May 1 to the end of August, Candiotti lost only twice, allowed six homers, and held the opposition to one earned run or none 15 times in his 22 starts. But Candiotti's pitching has all been forgotten, as his efforts garnered very little media attention.

Interestingly, while Wakefield was 14–1 with a 1.65 ERA from May 27-August 13 in 1995, Candiotti wasn't that far off that same summer as he notched a 2.58 ERA during that same span. In fact, from May 25 to July 28—the equivalent of two full months—the Dodger knuckleballer posted a 1.74 ERA in 13 starts. Had Candiotti received better support, he might have had a gaudy record too, as he was almost as good in those two months in 1995:

| | GS | W–L | IP | H | BB | SO | HR | ERA | |
|---|---|---|---|---|---|---|---|---|---|
| Wakefield | 17 | 14–1 | 131.0 | 98 | 37 | 79 | 12 | 1.65 | (May 27–Aug. 13) |
| Candiotti | 16 | 5–7 | 111.2 | 97 | 35 | 82 | 8 | 2.58 | (May 25–Aug. 14) |

As Wakefield noted, it wasn't all his glory. "But it wasn't just me," he once noted about the difficulty of duplicating his magical season. "The defense was great. I got runs. It's easy to win that way."[2] Candiotti, meanwhile, did not get any defensive or offensive support. And the reason his ERA from late May to mid–August was over 2.50 was because of one bad start. On August 4, Candiotti allowed 10 runs on a night where he was pitching with a ripped fingernail, which hampered the effectiveness of his knuckleball. Erase that four-inning disaster, and his ERA in that span would have been 1.84.

The revival of the knuckleball indeed.

Candiotti was simply an afterthought on the 1995 Dodgers. Eric Karros, Mike Piazza, and Raul Mondesi, the team's young sluggers, were the obvious stars in Los Angeles. Closer Todd Worrell had 32 saves and was an All-Star. Ramon Martinez won 17 games and threw a no-hitter in July. Ismael Valdez went 13–11 with 150 strikeouts in his first full big league season. There was also sensational Japanese righthander Hideo Nomo, who won Rookie of the Year honors after going 13–6 while striking out an NL-leading 236 batters with his famed "tornado" windup.

Candiotti, meanwhile, had a solid 3.50 ERA in 190.1 innings over 30 starts, registering 141 strikeouts. His 21 quality starts were tied for third-most in the majors, trailing only Seattle's Randy Johnson (23) and Atlanta's Greg Maddux (22), the Cy Young Award winners in the two leagues. Unfortunately for Candiotti, the Dodgers couldn't hit or field on days he was pitching.

The pattern began on May 1 in a 7–0 loss in San Francisco where they couldn't hit lefthander Terry Mulholland, who would go 5–13 with a 5.80 ERA in 1995. In the fourth inning, LA committed four errors, an inning in which Candiotti had to strike out the side to ensure he could return to the dugout. "It was frustrating, because I felt I had a real good knuckler today," he noted. "I thought I had some of my best stuff."[3] On May 9, the Dodgers could not capitalize on five walks (in six innings) issued by San Diego's Scott Sanders, as Candiotti suffered a 9–2 loss. But the big story was Jose Offerman tying a dubious record in the fourth. The Dodger shortstop committed three errors in one inning—equaling a Los Angeles record—as the Padres exploded for three runs to go ahead, 5–1, and cruised to the victory.

On May 14 against the Cardinals, it was two errors by third baseman Garey Ingram—filling in because veteran Tim Wallach was sidelined with a back injury—that cost Candiotti a win.[4] Though Candiotti allowed only two earned runs on five hits and a walk over seven innings, St. Louis still won, 6–5. The offense and defense again betrayed Candiotti on May 30, when he lost, 5–0, to Phillies rookie Tyler Green. Philadelphia scored four unearned runs in the third inning—thanks to centerfielder Roberto Kelly's three-base error and catcher Tom Prince's passed ball. With two outs and the bases loaded in the seventh and LA still down, 4–0, Kelly had a chance to atone for his error but instead grounded out, and Green went on to complete the shutout.

On June 10, Candiotti lost to Green again, 3–0, despite allowing just a sacrifice fly and a solo homer. One year earlier, Green had gone 7–16 with a 5.56 ERA with Triple-A Scranton/Wilkes-Barre and led the International League in losses (16), runs allowed (110), and hit batsmen (12), while setting club records for most earned runs, hits allowed, homers, and hit batsmen. He surrendered 179 hits in 162 innings while walking 77 with just 95 strikeouts. Amazingly, Green threw two complete-game shutouts against Candiotti in a span of 11 days without ever tossing one in his 59 minor league starts. Green wouldn't pitch another shutout in the majors. "We're facing a pitcher—at least on paper—who looks like he's struggling. Not tonight. He pitches a nine-inning shutout," lamented Candiotti. "It just doesn't make sense."[5]

On June 16, Candiotti threw eight scoreless innings against Chicago— in his 300th major league start—and had a no-hitter until two outs in the sixth. The knuckleballer allowed just three hits (all singles) with five strikeouts before leaving in the ninth for a pinch-hitter. The Dodgers still lost, 2–0— their third shutout defeat in Candiotti's last four starts—as Howard Johnson drilled a two-run homer off Rudy Seanez in the bottom of the ninth. "I had a good knuckleball and I was changing speeds with it," Candiotti said. "I had two or three pitches working."[6] But the Dodger bats had nothing working against Steve Trachsel, who in his previous three starts had gone 0–3 with an 8.62 ERA. And this game happened at Wrigley Field, where he'd had very little success. In his first three home starts in 1995—all Cubs losses—Trachsel logged a 6.89 ERA. From 1993 to 1995, his first three big league seasons, Trachsel would be 3–16 in 28 starts at Wrigley, including 2–8 with a 6.19 ERA in 1995. Against Candiotti, though, seven scoreless innings.

Over a nine-start stretch from May 25-July 6, Candiotti compiled a 0.97 ERA—allowing him to end the first half with a 2.82 earned-run average— but went only 3–3 thanks to a lack of support as the Dodgers were shut out four times in that span. His numbers during that stretch: 65 innings, 43 hits, seven earned runs, 18 walks, 44 strikeouts, only one homer allowed, and a .185 opponents' batting average. "With the knuckleball, I began throwing it in the big leagues in 1986," reflects Candiotti. "But it took a few years to really master that pitch. In the 1990s, I started having better command of it when I was using the knuckleball more, maybe 80 percent of the time in some games compared to 40 percent before. The more I threw it, the better it got. By the time I was with the Dodgers, I was throwing the knuckler real well, having better command of it every year. In the mid–1990s, and especially in 1995, I really felt as though every time I went out on the mound, my knuckler was moving better than the last start. I felt like I was locked in as good as I could be locked in. And also, a knuckleball moves really well in places like Wrigley Field in Chicago, Busch Stadium in St. Louis, and Memorial Stadium in Baltimore, where it's hot and humid, because the ball will move a lot if the air is humid. The humidity in those places was really conducive for the knuckleball."

The 1995 Dodgers got off to a 22–25 start before a 9–1 run beginning in mid–June vaulted them into first place. From late June to the end of the season, they battled Colorado for the NL West title, with the two teams flip-flopping back and forth in the standings throughout the second half. But along the way, the Dodgers' defense continued to struggle, as LA was last in the NL in fielding percentage. "We don't execute and our defense stinks," first baseman Eric Karros said during the All-Star break. "It's not just bad, it stinks. You can't hide it. It's not just the errors, but the plays we should make and don't make. I mean, we can't catch the ball."[7]

Along the way, the Dodgers stumbled on days Candiotti was pitching, as he went 4–6 despite a 1.74 ERA during a 13-start stretch from May 25-July 28. On June 4, he allowed two runs in seven innings against the Mets, but the bullpen coughed up his 3–2 lead in the eighth. On June 21, Candiotti finally got some support in a 10–1 victory in St. Louis, but saw three different Dodger infielders commit errors in the third inning before he fanned Ray Lankford with the bases loaded to escape the jam unscathed.

On June 25, Candiotti struck out 11 Giants over eight innings in a 3–2 triumph while pitching on three days' rest, completing LA's first four-game sweep of San Francisco since 1980. Even in the victory, the Dodgers struggled offensively against William VanLandingham (who'd go 13–21 with a 5.25 ERA in 1996–97, his final two seasons in the majors), again illustrating how unlucky Candiotti was on nights he was pitching. The Dodgers, meanwhile, had won the first three games of the series by scores of 7–6, 7–2, and 7–0. In the opener, Ramon Martinez allowed five runs on 12 hits, but the Dodgers battered Jose Bautista for six runs by the fourth inning in the victory. In the next two contests, they hammered Mark Portugal (5–1, 3.28 ERA going in) for seven runs, and then Giants ace Mark Leiter and reliever Dave Burba for seven more.

It only got worse for Candiotti. On June 30 against Colorado, He allowed four singles with seven strikeouts and two walks over seven innings but lost, 2–1. Both runs off him were unearned, coming after Tim Wallach booted a groundball at third base. The offense, meanwhile, couldn't solve Kevin Ritz (who went in with a 16–27, 5.37 ERA career mark) and only broke the shutout in the ninth. It was the fourth time in Candiotti's career that he'd lost a start despite not allowing an earned run, with the pitcher allowing just 10 hits and 10 walks with 23 strikeouts over 26.2 innings in those games.

In June, Dodger rookie Hideo Nomo went 6–0 with a 0.89 ERA and was named the NL Pitcher of the Month. Candiotti, by the numbers, was the Dodgers' second-best starter that month. On June 29, Nomo blanked Colorado, 3–0, on a six-hitter. Against those same Rockies the following night, Candiotti lost, 2–1, despite allowing just four hits over seven innings. He fell to 2–2 in June with a 1.43 ERA in six starts. The knuckleballer's June record matched Martinez's 2–2 mark—even with an ERA 3.75 runs lower.

Stats of Dodger starters, June 1995:

| | IP | H | R | ER | BB | SO | HR | ERA | BA | (W–L) |
|---|---|---|---|---|---|---|---|---|---|---|
| Nomo | 50.1 | 25 | 7 | 5 | 16 | 60 | 2 | 0.89 | .143 | (6–0) |
| **Candiotti** | **44** | **32** | **9** | **7** | **11** | **32** | **1** | **1.43** | **.198** | **(2–2)** |
| Valdez | 47 | 37 | 14 | 13 | 14 | 37 | 4 | 2.49 | .216 | (5–1) |
| Astacio | 26.2 | 25 | 17 | 15 | 7 | 21 | 4 | 5.06 | .250 | (0–4) |
| R. Martinez | 33 | 44 | 21 | 19 | 1 | 18 | 3 | 5.18 | .328 | (2–2) |

On July 6 in Atlanta, Candiotti tossed eight shutout innings of three-hit ball (all singles) with no walks and five strikeouts—and still couldn't get a victory. Candiotti carried a perfect game into the fifth inning and retired 24 of his 27 batters, before leaving for a pinch-hitter in the top of the ninth. Alas, three-time reigning Cy Young winner Greg Maddux allowed five hits with no walks in his eight shutout innings, and the Dodgers went on to lose, 1–0. It was the fifth time in Candiotti's 15 starts that the Dodgers had been shut out. "You really have the worst luck of any pitcher I've ever seen," Atlanta right-hander John Smoltz told Candiotti afterward. Replied the knuckleballer: "I have the worst run support in the history of baseball. I really do. But what am I gonna do?"

On July 13 in Los Angeles, Candiotti lost, 4–0, to Florida southpaw Chris Hammond, the knuckleballer's third straight outing in which he received zero runs when he was still in the game. As the *South Florida Sun-Sentinel* noted, the Dodger lineup that faced Hammond had seven of the eight position players hitting over .300 against lefties, and yet they couldn't touch him.[8] Manager Tommy Lasorda, baffled by the six shutouts pitched against Candiotti, simply said, "You can't explain it. How do you explain it?"[9]

When July ended, Boston knuckleballer Tim Wakefield was 11–1 in 14 starts with a major league-best 1.58 ERA. Candiotti, meanwhile, wasn't getting any breaks in Los Angeles. Despite eight strikeouts and six-hit ball over eight innings on July 28, he still lost, 3–2, to Cincinnati's John Smiley, who held Raul Mondesi and Mike Piazza—the Dodgers' number three and four hitters—hitless in eight at-bats. Following the defeat, Candiotti was 5–9 with a 2.98 ERA. Over his last 13 starts, Candiotti had a 1.74 ERA, but a lowly 4–6 record.

1995 Stats, Pitchers' previous 13 starts through July 30

| | GS | IP | H | R | ER | BB | SO | HR | ERA | (W–L) | BA |
|---|---|---|---|---|---|---|---|---|---|---|---|
| Candiotti (LA) | 13 | 93 | 72 | 26 | 18 | 28 | 71 | 4 | 1.74 | (4–6) | .213 |
| Wakefield (BOS) | 13 | 101.1 | 81 | 24 | 18 | 28 | 65 | 8 | 1.60 | (10–1) | .220 |

Wakefield slumped down the stretch, going 2–7 with a 5.60 ERA after August 13. He was then roughed up by Cleveland for seven runs in Game

Three of the ALDS. Can-
diotti, meanwhile, finally had
a rotten outing on August 4
after being nearly unhittable
for two months. The Giants
pounded Candiotti for 10
earned runs over four innings
—his worst major league start
ever—in a 15–1 Dodger loss in
San Francisco. "I broke my fingernail while warming up in
the bullpen," he recalls. "But I
didn't say anything because the
Dodgers really needed me to
pitch that night [with the
bullpen being overworked in
the previous series in Col-
orado]. So I went out there,
and without my best pitch, I
got hit hard. It was ugly when
I couldn't throw the knuckler
... just a bad game."

Candiotti compiled a 3.50 earned run average in
190.1 innings in 1995 for the Dodgers, including a
1.74 ERA over a 13-start stretch from May 25 to
July 28. However, the veteran knuckleballer
endured some tough luck during that season. Even
though Candiotti logged a 3.35 ERA in his 15
home starts—allowing only 29 walks over 102
innings—he recorded just a 3–9 record at Dodger
Stadium (courtesy Tom Candiotti).

    Following that outing,
though, Candiotti pitched
well down the stretch, logging
a 3.30 ERA over his final 10
starts of the season as the
Dodgers went on to win the NL West title over the Rockies. Unfortunately,
Candiotti often pitched without any offensive or defensive support, resulting in
a mediocre 2–4 record over those final seven weeks of the year. For the season,
Candiotti was only 7–14 but had a respectable 3.50 ERA with 141 strikeouts
in 190.1 innings. His earned run average was comparable to some of the big
winners in baseball, most notably teammate Ramon Martinez, who had a 3.66
ERA and an NL-leading 81 walks over 206.1 innings (with 138 strikeouts)
but went 17–7. Though Candiotti allowed two or fewer earned runs 18 times,
he often found himself losing a lot of those games (five losses with six no-
decisions). LA plated three runs or fewer 17 times in his 30 starts, and he again
received the majors' worst support—3.34 runs per nine innings. Then there
was the porous Dodger defense, which committed 28 errors behind him, most
in the majors against a pitcher.[10]

In the 1995 postseason, Candiotti was scheduled to start Game Four of the best-of-five Division Series against Cincinnati—but the Dodgers were swept, 3–0, and he never got to pitch. Martinez was rocked for seven runs in Game One as LA fell, 7–2, the Dodgers lost, 5–4, in Game Two, and the Reds prevailed, 10–1, over Hideo Nomo in Game Three. "I was supposed to start the fourth game," Candiotti reflects. "But Nomo and Ramon didn't pitch well in that series, and it was three-and-out. We had a pretty good team in 1995, but we just couldn't get it done in the playoffs when we got there."

Though it was a frustrating season, Candiotti did get the respect of his peers and his bosses. "The fact that he survived a stretch like that is because he is one hell of a class guy and a competitor," manager Tommy Lasorda said, knowing his knuckleballer didn't receive much help from the Dodger offense.[11] Candiotti, meanwhile, still recalls the comments of some of the game's best players. "I remember the Astros' Jeff Bagwell and the Giants' Barry Bonds always told me I was a tough pitcher to hit against," Candiotti says. "Pitchers like John Smoltz, Tom Glavine, and Ramon Martinez all told me I had the worst luck they ever saw. I never got the run support or defense, but I definitely had the respect of my teammates and opponents."

"A pitcher's record is always going to be reflected by the support he receives," says general manager Fred Claire. "Tom had an incredibly good year for us but those things tend to balance out, so the bottom line is, you look at him and the years he had in the major leagues. He had a very respectable earned run average for his career. He went on to win over 150 games and pitch 16 seasons in the big leagues. That's a significant accomplishment. The bottom line is Tom was a consistent winner in his career."

Candiotti certainly had been consistent over the previous six seasons, posting the majors' eighth-best ERA among pitchers with at least 1,000 innings from 1990 to 1995 with his 3.28 earned run average over 1200.2 innings pitched. (The seven ahead of him: Greg Maddux, 2.47; Jose Rijo, 2.74; Roger Clemens, 2.94; Dennis Martinez, 3.02; Kevin Appier, 3.11; David Cone, 3.20; and Tom Glavine, 3.26.) The knuckleballer's 6.33 strikeouts per nine innings during that span ranked ahead of the strikeout rates of conventional pitchers like Doug Drabek (5.98 strikeouts per nine innings), Todd Stottlemyre (5.91), Charles Nagy (5.78), Jack Morris (5.76), Greg Swindell (5.72), Orel Hershiser (5.64), Tim Belcher (5.64), David Wells (5.59), Jimmy Key (5.44), and Dennis Martinez (5.38).

On December 15, 1995, the Dodgers re-signed Candiotti to a two-year contract worth $6 million. "I liked the West Coast," the knuckleballer says in explaining why he decided to return to Los Angeles, "and I was happy where I was at. And by 1996, the Dodgers looked like they were on the verge of becoming a force in the National League—we could've competed with anybody in the league—and I wanted to be there to win a championship with them. We were really the class of the National League West at that time. It would've been tough leaving the Dodgers at that point."

From Fred Claire's perspective, re-signing Candiotti made sense. During the knuckleballer's four Dodger seasons, his ERA was 3.38, fifth-best in the NL (behind Greg Maddux, Jose Rijo, Tom Glavine, and John Smoltz). He led the Dodgers in innings and ERA from 1992 to 1995. "With Tom, you had a pitcher who could take his turn, produce a lot of innings and give your bullpen a chance to rest on many occasions," Claire reflects. "Tom always was viewed as a professional pitcher and a pitcher with the makeup to win big games."

On November 30, the club signed free agent shortstop Greg Gagne to solidify its defense. Gagne, an 11-year AL veteran who'd earned a reputation while with Minnesota and Kansas City as one of baseball's best fielding short-stops, would be taking over for Jose Offerman. In his four years as the regular Dodger shortstop from 1992 to 1995, Offerman *averaged* 31 errors per season, and led the majors in that category three times. Gagne, meanwhile, committed only 30 errors for Kansas City in the 1994–95 seasons combined. Three weeks following the Gagne signing, the Dodgers dealt Offerman to Kansas City.

Candiotti had allowed a major league-leading 19 unearned runs in 1995, and with a better defensive shortstop in 1996 there was every reason for him to believe his luck would change. Unfortunately, in his first regular-season start, on April 5, Candiotti was hurt by two Gagne errors at shortstop, which led to four unearned runs in a loss in Chicago. The Dodger offense, meanwhile, couldn't solve Cubs righthander Jim Bullinger, who tossed eight shutout innings in his 1996 debut after going 2–6 with a 6.97 ERA over the final two months in 1995. Amazingly, Bullinger would then go 0–3 with a 10.52 ERA in his next six starts, allowing at least six runs four times, before being demoted to the bullpen. He'd go on to compile a 6.54 ERA in 1996, but Los Angeles couldn't touch him.

The Dodgers, in fact, struggled early in the season, owning a mediocre 29–26 record entering June. An eight-game losing streak by NL West-leading San Diego in the first two weeks of the month, though, allowed them to stay close. On June 16, Candiotti pitched LA to a 3–2 victory in Atlanta, allowing only four hits and one walk over seven innings. His pitching—along with Mike Piazza's two homers off rookie Jason Schmidt—allowed the Dodgers to improve to 37–32 and move into a first-place tie with the Padres, the first time since Opening Day that they were atop the division. "He's one of those guys who frustrates you more than anyone in the league," Braves third baseman Chipper Jones said of the Dodger knuckleballer. "Anytime you go up there, you think you can kill the ball and all of a sudden you're 0–2 [in the count]."[12] Added Atlanta manager Bobby Cox, "Candiotti's one of the toughest guys to hit."[13]

Still, the season was otherwise a frustrating one for Candiotti. Earlier in the series, LA had pounded Braves aces Tom Glavine and Steve Avery for six runs apiece in 6–3 and 6–2 victories. But against Schmidt—who had a 6.54 ERA going in—Candiotti was involved in a nailbiter, with the Atlanta fifth starter allowing only three hits over seven innings. After receiving the league's worst run support twice in the past three seasons, Candiotti was seeing more of the same in '96 as the Dodgers scored three runs or fewer in 10 of his first 14 starts.

Through June 16, Candiotti was just 5–5 with a 3.46 ERA. Normally, he still found a way to keep the Dodgers in every game despite the poor support. On June 21, though, he finally had a rough outing when Houston pounded him for six runs over 2.1 innings. "That's the nature of that pitch," Candiotti says, acknowledging that his knuckler could be ineffective any given night. "When you pitch well, it looks like the easiest thing in the world. If you have a bad game, though, it looks real bad, and ugly. You have a game like that, and people say, 'That guy throws a knuckleball? I don't want him on my team.'"

However, Candiotti had been one of the most consistent pitchers in the NL. Prior to the meltdown against the Astros, he'd used his knuckleball to compile a 3.01 ERA in 37 starts (79 earned runs over 236.1 innings) dating back to May 25, 1995. (Take out a 10-run, four-inning outing in San Francisco in August 1995, and his ERA during that stretch would have been 2.67.) "You really cannot control the knuckleball," says Candiotti in trying to explain his consistency despite throwing what is universally recognized as an uncontrollable pitch. You aim for the catcher's mask and hope for the best. Normally, the ball will go to the left or to the right.

"But even at my age [38 in 1996], I wasn't a true knuckleball pitcher, because I still got ahead with my curveball and also threw my fastball. I simply relied on the knuckleball more, just like Bert Blyleven relied on his curveball more and Nolan Ryan relied on his fastball more. Again, for me, I visualized a triangle peaking at the catcher's mask, down to both of his knees. Then I aimed for the mask, and more often than not, it went for a strike. You just have to have the confidence to throw that pitch."

Still, many managers simply don't like the knuckleball, and in that Houston game, Candiotti showed why. "He just had a bad, bad, bad, bad day," Dodger skipper Tommy Lasorda said of Candiotti.[14] As it turned out, it was the last time Lasorda would manage a knuckleballer in the big leagues.

Three days later, the baseball world was stunned with the news that

Lasorda had been hospitalized with a heart attack. On June 24, the 68-year-old skipper drove himself to the hospital complaining of abdominal pains when in fact he was having a mild heart attack. He would not manage another major league game, officially retiring on July 29. Bench coach Bill Russell, who'd taken over as the acting manager during Lasorda's absence, was named the permanent manager for the rest of the season.

Russell, who'd long been thought of as the heir apparent to Lasorda's job, had been in the Dodger organization since 1966, when he was drafted as an outfielder. He eventually moved to the infield as he was converted to a second baseman in his third season in 1971 before becoming the everyday shortstop in '72. He played 18 seasons, all with Los Angeles, and after his retirement in 1987, became a coach on Lasorda's staff. Prior to his taking over for Lasorda, Russell's only professional managerial experience came in 1992–93 when he guided Albuquerque—the Dodgers' Triple-A club—to a 136–150 record before rejoining the Dodger coaching staff in '94. In any event, he'd been in the organization for the last 30 years, and was viewed as the right man to succeed Lasorda.

But he and Candiotti didn't get off on the right foot, with the veteran pitcher not convinced Russell knew how to manage a knuckleballer. The Dodgers, who were still in first place, trailed the Chicago Cubs, 4–3, in the fourth inning on June 26. With two on and two outs, Candiotti was due to bat but Russell instead sent up Dave Hansen to pinch-hit, not wanting to waste a run-scoring opportunity. An incensed Candiotti couldn't believe he had been pulled in only the fourth inning, and could only watch from the dugout as Hansen popped out to end the threat. "You don't know how to manage a knuckleball pitcher!" Candiotti screamed at Russell afterward. Los Angeles lost, 6–4, not getting its fourth run until the ninth inning.

Immediately following that loss to Chicago, the Dodgers dropped three of four in Denver against the Rockies. Colorado pounded Pedro Astacio and Ramon Martinez in the first two contests, winning, 13–1 and 13–4. The Dodgers then won, 13–10, before losing the finale, 16–15. That final game dropped the Dodgers to second place for the first time since Candiotti put them atop the division on June 16, when he defeated Atlanta, 3–2. Over the last four games, the Dodger bullpen had worked 12.2 innings and allowed 25 runs. Every reliever except Joey Eischen and Mark Guthrie had pitched three times over the past four days. Now the Dodgers, trailing the first-place Padres by one game, were headed to San Diego and had Candiotti on the mound in the opening contest on July 1.

In Bill Russell's first managerial experience with a knuckleballer, he had removed Candiotti after only four innings. But in San Diego, things were different. "You're our starter and reliever tonight," Russell told Candiotti before the game. The knuckleballer agreed, as both men knew they had to treat it like an American League game, where Candiotti would be out there for as long as he could no matter how many runs he gave up, given the fact the bullpen had been taxed. Candiotti delivered as he came within four outs of a complete game (with Guthrie finishing up), and the Dodgers won, 10–2, to move into a tie with San Diego atop the NL West.

Candiotti's performance allowed the bullpen to receive a much-needed night off, and the Dodgers benefited from it as they won six of their next eight contests to stay ahead of the Padres. Unfortunately for Candiotti, he wouldn't be able to contribute to the team's hot streak for the rest of July. He landed on the disabled list for three weeks after being hit on the right elbow by a pitch by Rockies pitcher Mark Thompson on July 6.

After Candiotti returned to action in mid–August, he pitched well for the rest of the month. By then, San Diego had taken over first place, with Los Angeles remaining within striking distance. On August 13, Candiotti allowed two runs over six innings to beat St. Louis, 8–4, helping the Dodgers creep to within one game of the Padres, the closest they'd been to San Diego in a week. On August 24, he gave up two runs on five hits over seven innings with eight strikeouts to beat the Mets, 7–5, and allow the Dodgers to stay a game behind San Diego. One day before his 39th birthday, on August 30, Candiotti allowed just four hits in Philadelphia, leaving in the sixth with a 6–2 lead. Though the bullpen allowed the tying runs, LA eventually won, 7–6.

September. The Dodgers were tied for first place in the NL West and were finishing their nine-game Eastern road trip. They'd gone 6–2 on the trip heading into the finale, and were poised to sweep the Mets at Shea Stadium. In the first two games, they'd won, 8–5 and 7–6. In the finale on September 4, Candiotti allowed one earned run through six innings, but the Dodgers lost, 3–2, in 12 innings. Entering play on September 10, the Dodgers and Padres were again tied atop the division. Candiotti defeated Cincinnati, 5–4, with a four-hitter over eight innings—fanning Curtis Goodwin in the eighth for his 1,500th strikeout—to help the Dodgers remain in first place. Los Angeles, though, collapsed on the final weekend of the season, losing three straight games at home to San Diego, allowing the Padres to win the division while the Dodgers earned the wild card.

Candiotti finished 9–11 with a 4.49 ERA—his worst season since a 7–18, 4.78 ERA mark in 1987—but as he says years later, there were extenuating circumstances. "It wasn't a good year, health-wise," the knuckleballer explains. "That spring, I pulled a calf muscle, and then I did it again early in the season. I injured my knee warming up before a game [against Chicago], and that required cortisone injections. Just before the All-Star break, I was hit by a pitch on the elbow while I was batting and had to go on the disabled list. Everything seemed to be working against me that year."

In the 1996 NL Division Series against Atlanta, the Dodgers opted to go with a starting rotation of Ramon Martinez, Ismael Valdez, Hideo Nomo, and Pedro Astacio. Candiotti still saw relief action in Game Three, however, after the Braves jumped out to a 5–0 lead off Nomo. Candiotti entered the game to start the fifth and tossed two hitless innings before leaving for a pinch-hitter in the seventh. Atlanta won, 5–2, completing the three-game sweep. It also proved to be the final post-season game of Candiotti's career.

Entering the 1997 campaign, Candiotti had a 3.53 ERA in 359 appearances—and a 2-to-1 strikeout-to-walk ratio (1,507 to 750)—through 13 major league seasons. But with the emergence of 23-year-old Chan Ho Park, Candiotti was now the odd man out on a Dodger rotation that already included Martinez, Nomo, Valdez, and Astacio. The Dodgers tried to unload Candiotti during the offseason but found no takers, so the knuckleballer began the year in the bullpen. When Martinez went down with a torn rotator cuff in June, Candiotti moved back into the rotation and immediately solidified the staff, allowing three earned runs or fewer in 13 of his 18 starts. The Dodgers kept Candiotti in the rotation when Martinez returned, and instead traded Astacio to Colorado for infielder Eric Young.

San Francisco, after two seasons of mediocrity, battled LA for the NL West title in 1997. Ironically, when the two teams met on September 18 with the Dodgers one game ahead, it was the veteran knuckleballer—who wasn't even part of the team's plans when the season began—who started against the Giants. Alas, Candiotti's Dodgers lost, 6–5, in 12 innings. The following night, Astacio—who was traded just a month earlier to the Rockies—celebrated his return to Dodger Stadium by beating Nomo, 6–4, improving to 5–0 in six starts with Colorado. More importantly, Astacio's victory knocked LA out of first place for good. On September 21, Colorado pounded Martinez and won, 10–5, finishing a three-game sweep and pushing the Dodgers two games behind San Francisco with only six to play. LA never recovered, and missed out on the postseason.

But back to the beginning. In 1996, Park went 3–3 with a 3.26 ERA in 10 starts while appearing in 48 games overall for the Dodgers. By spring training in 1997, the Dodgers believed the South Korean righthander—with his 95-mph fastball—was ready to become their fifth starter. Other than Park, the club had other quality arms on the pitching staff. Darren Dreifort, a hard-throwing 24-year-old righty who could also start, ended up being used as a set-up man. In the bullpen were such solid pitchers as Todd Worrell, Antonio

Osuna, and veteran lefties Scott Radinsky and Mark Guthrie. In fact, the Dodgers were so deep that one-time Toronto closer Darren Hall began the year in the minors. So, how many innings was Candiotti going to see for the Dodgers?

It was difficult for Candiotti to accept his new bullpen role. With the Dodgers in 1992–96, he had done everything the club had asked of him. He had pitched on two days' rest. He had entered games in relief on short notice because of injuries to other starters. Over those five seasons, Candiotti had led the Dodgers in innings (913), starts (141), and complete games (15). From 1992 to 1996, Candiotti's 3.57 ERA was fourth-best among NL pitchers with at least 900 innings pitched—behind only Greg Maddux (2.13), Tom Glavine (3.16), and John Smoltz (3.27)—and 11th-best in the majors overall, on par with former ERA champions like Kevin Brown (3.35), Dennis Martinez (3.37), and Roger Clemens (3.43).

Regardless, Candiotti was going to pitch out of the Dodger bullpen in 1997.

# 15

# *Who Says He Couldn't Start Anymore?*

It was off to the bullpen to begin the 1997 season for Tom Candiotti. Though he wasn't happy with his new role, Candiotti showed flashes of his old self. In his first 22 outings, all in relief, he had a 2.03 ERA in 26.2 innings, walking only five batters. He gave up 21 hits and had 18 strikeouts. "It was weird," he admits, recalling how his routine was messed up on Opening Day when the Dodgers took on Philadelphia. "I showed up to the ballpark early, got dressed, participated in the outfield practice, and then.... I had no idea what to do. I had no experience starting a season pitching out of the bullpen before. It was hard. I really had no idea what to do."

Candiotti knew what to do when he got on the mound after trotting in from the bullpen, though. He tossed a scoreless ninth inning on Opening Day, throwing 78-mph fastballs after the Phillies had seen 95-mph heaters for the first eight innings. When he mixed his fastball in with his knuckleballs, the hitters became frustrated. After Candiotti worked three scoreless innings over two appearances against Pittsburgh on April 4–5, Pirates pitching coach Pete Vuckovich told him, "Candy, our hitters are saying they don't want to face your knuckleball. They just don't know how to hit you. You've still got it working."

Candiotti even picked up a couple of victories early on. On April 4, he relieved Pedro Astacio in the sixth inning against Pittsburgh with the score 2–2, and tossed two hitless frames. Pinch-hitter Billy Ashley delivered a go-ahead RBI double in the seventh, and Candiotti received credit for the 5–3 Dodger win. Five nights later against the Mets, Candiotti came in with the score 2–2 in the 14th. He retired all three batters he faced while throwing only eight pitches (six for strikes), and watched as the Dodgers plated the game-winner in the bottom half, giving him another victory.

In the Dodgers' first nine games, Candiotti pitched five times, allowed only one hit and one walk in six scoreless innings with five strikeouts, and had a 2–0 record. "With all of the good pitchers on our staff, I didn't even think I was going to be pitching at all," he recalls. Indeed. At one point during the spring, Candiotti was 0–2 with an 8.24 ERA, walking 17 batters in 19.2 innings.[1]

Meanwhile, Chan Ho Park was happy to be a starting pitcher, but he felt bad for taking the spot of Candiotti, a man he considered his friend. That spring, Park recalled an incident from 1996 when his Dodger teammates, as a prank, took a pair of scissors and cut his favorite suit to shreds. Park—who didn't understand the joke because it would have been regarded as sign of disrespect in his native South Korea—was outraged, screaming obscenities and throwing things in the locker room. Candiotti was one of the first players— along with Mike Piazza and Todd Worrell, and manager Tommy Lasorda—to talk to him to try and calm him down. "He said it was a misunderstanding and not to worry about it," Park said. "I'd like to [be teammates] one more season with Candiotti because he's been nice to me. He talks to me a lot. That's big to me."[2] Park also admitted he was appreciative of the fact the knuckleballer often invited him out to shop and eat pasta, "but I feel a little sorry for Candiotti. I don't want to steal his job because he's been so nice to me. He's given me a lot of confidence. I'll always be thankful."[3]

"Even though Chan Ho took my job, I still wanted him to do well," explains Candiotti. "You want your team to do well. Even though you might not be happy with your own personal situation on the team, you still want the team to do well and win. So I was trying to help Chan Ho in his orientation, so to speak, into the United States. I'd take him to restaurants and order for him, teach him about things, and things like that. The cool thing was I was getting lots of email messages from [fans in] Korea, thanking me for being friends with Chan Ho and for taking care of him, not just in baseball, but in life too."

Though it normally took Candiotti a few innings to get a feel for his knuckleball, he threw strikes whenever he was summoned from the Dodger bullpen in 1997. On April 20, Candiotti gave up a two-run homer to Craig Biggio in the eighth inning as Los Angeles lost, 3–1, to Houston. Even in the loss, Candiotti wasn't wild. Of the nine pitches he threw, seven were strikes. Candiotti was such a strike-throwing machine that manager Bill Russell didn't shy away from him even in extra-inning games. Take May 2, for instance, in an 8–7 victory over the Cubs when Russell handed him the ball to start the top of the 10th. Candiotti responded by tossing a perfect inning on nine pitches—eight of which were for strikes—and recording two strikeouts. LA then plated the game-winner in the bottom half of the inning, giving Candiotti his third victory.

Sometimes Candiotti was lucky even if he couldn't throw strikes. On May 4 in a 5–2 victory over Chicago, he recorded an out without throwing a single strike when called upon with two outs in the seventh. With Brian McRae in scoring position and Jose Hernandez at the plate, Candiotti came on in relief of Chan Ho Park. "I throw three straight balls and the count's 3-and–0," says Candiotti. "McRae's on third base with two outs, and he then tries to steal home, but I throw a down-and-in fastball to the plate and Piazza catches it to tag him out. So I'd just thrown ball four—walking the guy—but still got the third out! How about that?"

Meanwhile, the trade rumors about Candiotti continued in May, with AL Central-leading Cleveland mentioned as a possible destination. The Indians would in 1997 rank third in the AL in batting (.286) and runs (868), and second in home runs (220). But they were lacking a fifth starter. Jack McDowell, the number three starter behind Orel Hershiser and Charles Nagy, was placed on the disabled list for the second time in two years. This time he was expected to undergo elbow surgery and miss at least a month.[4] Cleveland replaced McDowell with unproven Albie Lopez, leaving the fifth spot open.

As the *Cleveland Plain Dealer*'s Dennis Manoloff put it, Candiotti would have been the perfect solution. "The fifth-starter spot has been available since the season began, with no candidate staking a claim to it beyond one or two credible outings," he wrote. "What [Indians manager Mike] Hargrove cannot wait to employ is an innings-eater who keeps his team in the game. Victories are a bonus. Candiotti, according to the numbers, fits.... From 1986 to 1996, Candiotti averaged 30 starts and more than 200 innings. His career ERAs after last season were 3.51 in the National League and 3.57 in the American League."[5] (During the season, Cleveland would go on to acquire Jason Jacome, Jeff Juden, and John Smiley, who combine for four wins and a 5.27 ERA in 15 starts.)

Other AL teams were also looking for that elusive fifth starter. The three contenders in the AL West, for instance—Seattle, Texas, and Anaheim—were all reportedly interested in the veteran knuckleballer's services.[6] Though Candiotti looked like he could help one of those teams—through June 10 he had appeared in 22 games and was unscored upon 18 times while logging a 2.03 ERA with five walks over 26.2 innings—the price was ultimately too high. Nobody was willing to trade for a 39-year-old knuckleballer making $3 million.

Candiotti, who was used to making 30 starts a year while logging 200 innings, knew he could still pitch at least seven innings every fifth day. But now, on average he was out there for only 20 pitches per outing while facing five or so batters. Since NL pitchers had to bat, Candiotti would get pinch-hit for after working an inning or two. He did not go more than two innings in any outing until June 14 in Seattle in an interleague game where the designated hitter was used. That afternoon, Ramon Martinez struggled—allowing five runs and five walks in four innings—as the Mariners jumped out to a 5–0 lead. When Candiotti came in, he was just as ineffective as he hit a batter, threw a wild pitch, and allowed three runs over 2.2 innings in a game the Dodgers ultimately lost, 9–8.

General manager Fred Claire remembers Candiotti was the ultimate pro that 1997 season. No, the knuckleballer was not pleased about his situation, but through it all remained a positive influence in the Dodger clubhouse and always conducted himself in a professional manner. "We did use Tom in the bullpen and I know he wasn't happy with that," Claire adds, "but he understood the decision wasn't in his hands." Though Candiotti understood, it didn't make the situation any easier to accept. He wasn't good enough to start, but he was too good to trade. For the first two-and-a-half months in 1997, he was frustrated. He just never knew when he would be pitching.

Who knew then that the disaster in Seattle would be Candiotti's final relief appearance that season?

Charlie Hough threw his final big league pitch in 1994 but still remained in the game as a pitching coach in the Dodger minor league organization. Whenever he saw other knuckleballers, he always tried to work with them and give them advice. He once said in the late 1990s, "I tell them, 'Hey, nobody really wants you.' I felt that way my whole career. But the goal is to be the last man standing. When the other guys get hurt or don't pitch well, be there when they need someone."[7]

That philosophy applied to Candiotti's situation in 1997. Nobody really wanted him, not enough to make a trade with the Dodgers, who also really didn't want him. He was there when the club needed someone to replace guys who weren't pitching well, to suck up some innings. Take his outing in Seattle on June 14, for instance. Ramon Martinez had thrown 100 pitches over four ineffective innings, and Candiotti was brought in to save the bullpen. Though Candiotti allowed three runs and three extra-base hits—and was battling a stiff back—he was kept out there for 2.2 innings.

The other part of Hough's equation—be there when the other guys get hurt—rang true for Candiotti the night before Martinez's next scheduled start in San Francisco on June 21, when the Dodgers had to scratch their ace righthander when he complained about a tender right shoulder (which later was revealed to be a torn rotator cuff). With Martinez unavailable, manager

Bill Russell turned to Candiotti. "We need you to start against the Giants tomorrow afternoon," Russell told him. "Ramon has a sore shoulder."

"When I found out I was going to start, all of a sudden it just brought back all of the night-before jitters," Candiotti recalls. "When you're a reliever, you're ready to pitch every day so things are kind of normal. But as a starter, you go through your routine, your pre-game, looking at the lineup you're going to face, everything. I went through a lot of emotions trying to get ready for that start. Of course, it was in San Francisco, which is always a big game. And at the time, we were chasing the Giants in the standings, so we really couldn't afford to lose that game."

It was a big game for Candiotti, as he didn't know when he was going to pitch again after that. Reliever Darren Dreifort had just come off the disabled list that same week, and would be gobbling up some innings. The Dodgers activated Dreifort but chose not to demote another pitcher, instead deciding to have a 12-man staff and designating outfielder Eric Anthony for assignment.[8] Besides, at the time, Martinez was expected to return soon enough. "Hopefully it's nothing more than missing one start," Fred Claire said then.[9] The Dodgers had no idea that their ace had any arm trouble; they knew that he had been struggling but attributed it to problems with mechanics and throwing too many pitches per game.

Candiotti's start on June 21 was certainly a huge game for both Los Angeles and San Francisco. The Dodgers had beaten the Giants the night before but had to burn through five relievers because starter Ismael Valdez was ineffective despite being staked to an early 7–0 lead (giving up three homers in his 5.1 innings of work). LA needed to win again to close to within five games of the surprising Giants, who were expected to finish last after trading slugger Matt Williams to Cleveland in the offseason. The Giants, meanwhile, would improve to 42–30 with a victory and own a commanding seven-game lead over the underachieving Dodgers.

As it turned out, Los Angeles had no problems with the Giants' pitching in an 11–0 Dodger victory with Raul Mondesi and Tripp Cromer each driving in three runs. The story, though, was Candiotti, who allowed only four hits and one walk with six strikeouts over seven innings. He baffled the Giants with his knuckleballs, slow curveballs, and fastballs. "Candiotti had a great knuckleball today and he threw it for strikes," Giants third baseman Mark Lewis said.[10] Added Giants second baseman Jeff Kent, "I've never seen his ball move as much as it did today. With the wind behind him, it's awful tough."[11]

While Candiotti got through the Giants with ease, he had a tougher time at the start of the game because of the change in routine. "It was a strange feeling for me during the pre-game warm-ups," Candiotti recalls. "I'd been used to coming into games in relief, where you had to warm up quickly and be ready. But that afternoon, I finished my warm-up pitches and had to wait around for 10 minutes before the game started. I go, 'Geez, what do I do now?' So I told myself, 'You're not starting today. You're just waiting out a rain delay, coming into the game to take over for Ramon.'"

Candiotti was expected to pitch five innings and then turn things over to Darren Dreifort while the rest of the bullpen would have the day off. But he far exceeded everyone's expectations. "We had used the whole bullpen the last couple of nights and Candy went seven strong innings, which really picked us up," said reliever Darren Hall. "He's a true professional. Despite all the stuff he's put up with, he went out and pitched his heart out. It was remarkable."[12] Bill Russell was blown away by Candiotti's performance considering the pitcher had just gotten over a stiff back that same week. "Seven shutout innings," the Dodger skipper said while calling the knuckleballer a staff saver. "I don't think anyone expected that. I couldn't believe it."[13] No doubt Candiotti never would have believed he would start for the Dodgers again. But as it turned out, he was back in the rotation; it was announced two days later that Ramon Martinez was going on the disabled list.

Candiotti's effort came at a time when it was desperately needed, with starters Pedro Astacio (3–6) and Ismael Valdez (3–8) combining to go 6–14. Up to that point, Astacio was 0–2 with a 6.35 ERA in four starts in June, with LA losing three of them. Valdez was also 0–2 in four June starts—compiling a 5.91 ERA with 14 walks and 13 strikeouts in 21.1 innings—with the team losing three of his four outings. And as if the losses weren't enough, both pitchers were also upset about being pulled early. On June 5, Valdez confronted Russell in the dugout after being pinch-hit for in the fifth inning of a 5–4 loss to San Francisco. Three days later, in a 9–3 defeat to St. Louis, it was Astacio's turn to get in the manager's face, after he was pulled in the fourth. Both incidents were shown in full view of television cameras. Valdez would encounter more problems several weeks later on July 5 when he pulled his left hamstring in a start against San Diego and was placed on the disabled list.[14]

Then there was Hideo Nomo, 1–2 with a 4.05 ERA in June and only 6–6 with a 3.71 ERA on the year. Ramon Martinez, of course, struggled in Seattle and the immediate concern was how long he would be out of action with his sore shoulder. Ironically, the only pitcher thriving in June was the man who replaced Candiotti in the rotation. Chan Ho Park, the fifth starter, was 2–1 with a 3.25 ERA and 23 strikeouts in 27.2 innings that month. And since June 7, only Martinez, Park, and now Candiotti had pitched seven full innings. No Dodger starter had gone more than seven innings in that span, meaning the bullpen was overworked. That was why Russell called Candiotti "a staff saver."[15]

Before the season, the Dodgers had tried to trade him. Suddenly, with Martinez's injury, there was no way the knuckleballer would be dealt.

Los Angeles went 20–7 in July and tied San Francisco atop the NL West entering the month of August. Incredibly, the Dodgers had made up eight games in the standings since June 30, and Candiotti certainly contributed during the hot streak. He filled in for the injured Martinez and pitched as well as anybody not named Chan Ho Park (who went 5–0 with a 1.96 ERA). Candiotti was 3–1 with a 3.35 ERA in six July starts, and almost as importantly, stayed healthy and gave the club a lot of innings.

On July 1, Candiotti gave up three solo homers against Texas, but the Dodgers still won, 6–3, to begin a six-game winning streak. Five days later, he took a two-hit shutout into the eighth inning in San Diego as LA won, 5–2, to complete a three-game sweep of the Padres. On July 12, Candiotti pitched six-plus solid innings to outduel San Francisco's Mark Gardner, handing a 2–1 lead to the bullpen. Alas, the Giants struck for seven ninth-inning runs—six off closer Todd Worrell—to stun the Dodgers. On July 22, Candiotti allowed three solo home runs but only five hits overall in seven innings to defeat the Mets, 8–3. He closed out the month by beating Philadelphia, 7–1, on July 27, pitching 7.1 innings of seven-hit, five-strikeout ball.

The Dodgers were winning in July despite having several key injuries, including Martinez (torn rotator cuff) and Valdez (strained hamstring) being on the disabled list. There was also concern after Nomo was hit in his pitching elbow by a line drive off the bat of Philadelphia's Scott Rolen on July 26.[16] But there were Candiotti, Dreifort, and rookie Dennys Reyes to help out. Catcher Mike Piazza was out of the lineup with a pulled hamstring, but Tom Prince (a career backup with a .195 batting average in 512 at-bats entering the season) was there to homer in back-to-back games while batting .333 with six RBIs in 13 contests in July. Infielders Greg Gagne and Wilton Guerrero were ailing, but utility man Tripp Cromer (a career .217 hitter with five homers and 18 RBIs in 368 major league at-bats) was there to fill the void and bat .291 with four homers and 20 RBIs in 28 games.

"You look back in history at all the good teams," Candiotti said one night that July. "It takes the little people to come through usually to make a difference."[17] By "little people," he included himself "taking the ball for a couple of starts." As far as some were concerned, though, it was clear which "little" person had the biggest impact. Candiotti's contribution to the Dodgers' surge "is the biggest. It's gotta be," said Darren Hall. "It's amazing he can go out there and throw seven or eight innings at a time. He was in the bullpen and then, 'Hey, we need you to start.'"[18]

With Martinez still sidelined at the end of July, Candiotti remained in the rotation when August began. Through 11 starts in Martinez's absence, Candiotti was 6–2 with a 3.62 ERA, and the Dodgers won seven of those games. His best outing came in the 11th start on August 13, when he allowed only three hits over seven innings to beat Montreal, 3–1. Against the Expos, the veteran knuckleballer recorded seven strikeouts with only one walk (intentional) and did not give up a hit until the fifth inning.

With Martinez scheduled to return on August 20, the Dodgers suddenly had six capable starting pitchers. Candiotti had pitched well enough as a starter, and the Dodgers decided to keep him in the rotation. That meant it was fourth starter Pedro Astacio who was on his way out. Though Astacio had begun the season 3–0 with a 2.00 ERA, the righthander then went 0–7 with a 6.08 ERA over his next nine starts, from May 13 to June 24. On August 15 against Cincinnati, he was given a 3–0 cushion, but for the second straight start lasted only four innings, coughing that lead up by allowing a three-run double to pitcher Mike Remlinger in a 5–3 loss. For the season, the struggling Astacio was 7–9 with a 4.10 ERA, including 0–2 and 10.12 in his last two starts.

On August 18, the Dodgers traded Astacio to Colorado for second baseman Eric Young. It was an amazing fall for the righthander, who had been a standout in 1996 when the other starters were struggling. "I think he's been in the last month our best pitcher," Todd Worrell had said of Astacio the previous July. "Start for start, Pedro's been the man for us on the mound."[19] One year later, though, Astacio was banished to the worst pitchers' park in baseball, Coors Field.

On the day of the trade, meanwhile, Fred Claire explained the importance of Young in the Dodgers' new-look lineup. "Between him and Otis Nixon [acquired from Toronto a week earlier], we've added about 80 stolen bases, added experience, added good guys, good chemistry," said the Dodger general manager. "Now we just roll out the bats and balls and see how we fare."[20] With Nixon and Young batting atop the lineup and their knack for getting on and stealing bases, LA was supposed to be a much more potent club with Piazza, Karros, and Mondesi trying to drive them in. And Claire wasn't done. One day later, he signed aging slugger Eddie Murray, who had been released by Anaheim earlier in the week after batting .219 in 46 games, to be a pinch-hitter. On August 27, Claire acquired speedy outfielder Darren Lewis from the White Sox.

While everything looked great for LA to push for a post-season run, it didn't turn out that way. Murray would get two hits in his first two Dodger at-bats but would fail to come through in clutch situations down the stretch. Twice the slow-footed Murray came up in bases-loaded, one-out situations in the late innings and hit into double plays both times. LA wound up losing each game by one run. Meanwhile, Claire's comment about "chemistry" was a dubious one. Observers pointed out that while the team had plenty of talent, they lacked camaraderie. "The Dodgers have many strengths as a ball club, but camaraderie isn't one of them," noted *Sports Illustrated*'s Gerry Callahan.[21] One Dodger player would be anonymously quoted in the September 29 issue of *SI* as saying: "Our chemistry stinks. It never got any better. We just started winning."[22]

Candiotti remained in the starting rotation down the stretch following Astacio's departure but suffered from poor run support in the season's final weeks. The offense averaged just three runs per game for the knuckleballer, resulting in a 1–3 record over his final seven starts. In the latter half of August, Candiotti's ERA was 1.80 in his three starts and yet LA lost each contest by scores of 3–1, 4–3, and 3–1.

The Dodgers split a doubleheader on August 21 at Shea Stadium, with Candiotti losing, 3–1, and Chan Ho Park winning, 4–3. In the first game, Candiotti allowed six hits and two walks over six innings, but Los Angeles couldn't solve Mets rookie reliever Joe Crawford, who in his first major league start gave up just three hits in his six-plus innings. Manager Bill Russell was stunned his club couldn't get to the 27-year-old lefty, who came in with a 3.96 ERA in 12 career relief appearances. "We have to hit more and score more off a guy like that," Russell said, referring to Crawford, who would be released by the Mets five months later, never to pitch in the majors again. "We didn't help Candiotti out at all."[23] Naturally, LA then scored four runs off 10-game winner Rick Reed (2.86 ERA going in) in the nightcap.

The Dodgers left New York two games behind the Giants in the NL West, and the division lead would change hands within the next few days. Four straight wins—including a sweep in Philadelphia—vaulted LA past San Francisco in the standings, as the Giants lost three straight in Pittsburgh. The Dodgers then went into Pittsburgh for a four-game series, beginning with a doubleheader on August 25. In the first game, the Dodgers pounded Jason Schmidt for eight runs in his 4.1 innings, giving Ramon Martinez (two runs, five innings) an 8–2 victory. Incredibly, the Dodger bats were silenced in the nightcap by 25-year-old lefthander Chris Peters, with Candiotti pitching. Peters, normally a reliever, had a 5.96 ERA and was making his first start of 1997. His numbers in his last four outings included five innings, four homers allowed, and a 16.20 ERA.

But against the Dodgers, Peters yielded just three runs (none earned) on six hits and one walk over seven innings. Candiotti, meanwhile, allowed only one run on three hits and one walk over six innings before leaving for a pinch-hitter. The lone run off him was unearned, courtesy of a first-inning error as the Pirates scored without a hit, getting the runner home on a groundout and sacrifice fly. With LA leading, 3–1, in the bottom of the ninth, though, Dodger closer Todd Worrell walked Eddie Williams before Joe Randa smacked a 2–1 pitch into the seats in center field. Mark Smith then drilled Worrell's next offering to deep left, ending the game.

The Dodgers would take three of four in Pittsburgh, winning the final two games, 6–4 and 9–5. They followed that up by sweeping Oakland, 7–1 and 5–4, at Dodger Stadium. Then on August 30, LA roughed up Bob Wolcott and Seattle, 11–2, with Ramon Martinez (one run on three hits over six innings) getting the victory. The following day on August 31, Candiotti faced those same Mariners on his 40th birthday and allowed only four hits—a first-inning homer to Ken Griffey, Jr. and three singles—with two walks and five strikeouts over eight innings. In the fourth, Seattle loaded the bases with none out before Candiotti struck out Alex Rodriguez swinging and got Jay Buhner to ground into a double play. But the Dodgers, who were held hitless by Mariners starter Jamie Moyer until the seventh and did not get on the scoreboard until the ninth, lost, 3–1, in 10 innings.[24]

On September 7, Candiotti tossed a two-hitter through six innings to defeat NL wild card-leading Florida, 9–5, allowing Los Angeles to stay two games ahead of San Francisco in the NL West. The outing was Candiotti's 397th major league game, tying him with Dodger Hall of Famer Sandy Koufax, who appeared in the same number of games over a 12-year career that also included 314 starts. "For me, that record, to get into as many games as Sandy did, was special because I grew up idolizing him," says Candiotti. "It just means I was able to pitch effectively for many years to get a chance to pitch that long and get into that many games."

More importantly, Candiotti's victory meant the Dodgers did not lose any ground in the division standings. Fast forward to the morning of September 17, when they held that same two-game lead over the Giants with only 11 games remaining. It was evident that even with the wild card spot available, only one team from the West would make the postseason, given the fact that the Eastern Division's Florida Marlins—with their 87–62 record—had a four-game lead in the wild card race over the Dodgers, who were 84–67, and a six-game advantage over the Giants.

But when the Dodgers arrived in San Francisco on September 17 for a crucial two-game series, they reverted to the team that had underachieved for much of the first half. The Giants won both games to move into a first-place tie, beating Chan Ho Park, 2–1, in the opening contest and winning the second game, 6–5, on Brian Johnson's 12th-inning homer off Mark Guthrie. The Giants also pounded Candiotti in the second contest, battering the knuckleballer for five runs on 10 hits—including two home runs—over his 4.1 innings of work. From there, San Francisco was in control the rest of the way, winning six of its final nine games. Los Angeles, meanwhile, was swept at home by Colorado in a three-game series and lost five of its last nine, losing the NL West title to the Giants by two games and missing the postseason.

In the Colorado series, it was ex–Dodger Pedro Astacio's 6–4 victory over Hideo Nomo in the opening game on September 19 that knocked LA out of first place for good. The Dodgers had traded Astacio in mid–August, choosing to keep Candiotti in the starting rotation. Though that decision looked like it ultimately backfired—with Candiotti going 1–2 with a 6.43 ERA in September—at the time it made sense. In his first 11 starts from June 21 to August 13, the knuckleballer went 6–2 with a 3.62 ERA and the Dodgers went from six games back of first-place San Francisco to only one-and-a-half games out. During that period, Astacio went 4–4 with a 4.73 ERA, and was the obvious choice to be sent packing when Ramon Martinez returned from the disabled list. But the win over Nomo on September 19 improved Astacio's statistics to 5–0 with a 3.05 ERA in his first six Colorado starts.

The rest of the Dodger pitching staff faltered down the stretch, with both the starting rotation and the bullpen posted earned run averages over 5.00 in September. Nomo, 13–10 when September began, was 1–2 with a 5.64 ERA in five starts. Park had a 5.11 ERA in four starts, going 1–2 and lasting fewer than five innings twice. Ismael Valdez had a 2.60 ERA, but thanks to the Dodgers' lethargic offense, he was only 1–1 while the team lost three of his five outings. Martinez's September ERA was 5.14 as he went 2–2, including stinkers at Dodger Stadium against both Atlanta (seven runs) and Colorado (six runs). Astacio, meanwhile, was 4–0 with a 2.10 ERA in his first four September starts for Colorado, before giving up eight runs in his final outing of the season on September 25.

The numbers for the relievers were also discouraging. Lefthander Mark Guthrie, who never threw another pitch in 1997 after surrendering the Brian Johnson homer, had a 23.14 ERA in 4.2 innings in September. In his final five appearances, Guthrie either gave up a run or blew a late-inning lead, or both, and finished the year with a team-high 5.32 ERA. Todd Worrell, who recorded 35 saves, logged a 4.91 ERA in the season's final month after posting a 7.15 ERA in August. Set-up man Darren Dreifort, who had a stellar 2.04 ERA when August ended, compiled a 7.20 earned run average in September.

But the Dodgers' collapse wasn't that simple, according to some observers. The division-winning Giants simply had more heart than did the more-talented Dodgers, who evidently lacked any. "If you wanted to sum up what happened here on Wednesday night in the Dodgers' most revealing performance of this long, excruciating season," noted the *Orange County Register* after Candiotti's 4–1 loss to San Diego on September 24, "you could do it this way: One run, five hits, no passion. In the end, that's what really killed Bill Russell's club, not only in this game, but throughout a languid 1997. There was never any fire or intensity.... There was no chemistry, no camaraderie.... These were a bunch of guys who rarely showed any heart.... And there were Mike Piazza and Eric Karros, the two big guns, finishing the game and the home schedule by both passively taking called third strikes in their final at-bats."[25]

Despite his subpar September, Candiotti still had a solid season in 1997, pitching to a 2.76 ERA as a reliever and 3.83 as a starter. From 1982 to the present day, the Dodger knuckleballer is one of only five pitchers to have tossed at least 15 complete games in one year (which he accomplished in 1986) and then go on to make 15 or more relief appearances in another season later in his career.

| | Year | Complete Games | Year | Relief Appearances |
|---|---|---|---|---|
| Rick Langford | 1982 | 15 | 1985 | 20 |
| Dave Stieb | 1982 | 19 | 1998 | 16 |
| Mike Boddicker | 1984 | 16 | 1992 | 21 |
| **Tom Candiotti** | **1986** | **17** | **1997** | **23** |
| Curt Schilling | 1998 | 15 | 2005 | 21 |

All five pitchers also spent time in the starting rotation in those seasons in which they made those relief appearances. Only the Dodger knuckleballer had an ERA under 4.00 in both roles.

| | ERA in relief | ERA as a starter |
|---|---|---|
| Langford (1985) | 2.47 | 7.71 |
| Boddicker (1992) | 3.59 | 6.69 |
| **Candiotti (1997)** | **2.76** | **3.83** |
| Stieb (1998) | 3.63 | 7.47 |
| Schilling (2005) | 5.18 | 5.87 |

Though the Dodgers wanted to re-sign Candiotti after the 1997 season, they were only able to offer him a spot in the bullpen. Candiotti, who at that point was contemplating retirement, opted not to return to Los Angeles, ending his six-year Dodger career with a 3.57 ERA over 1,048 innings pitched.

# 16

## *200 Innings on a Bad Knee*

When he became a free agent following the 1997 season, Candiotti could have retired. In fact, his doctor suggested he strongly consider it. Candiotti had been pitching in pain for a couple of seasons, hindered by a nagging injury to his left knee. "The last two years of my career, really three years, were hampered by my knee," says Candiotti. "After the 1997 season, I saw a knee specialist in California. He gave me a micro-fracture surgery, which was radical. That was like, 'Oh, boy, it might not work.' We really weren't sure. When the doctor examined my knee, it wasn't an injury. It was bone on bone.... The cartilage had been pretty much gone. The micro-fracture surgery was pretty experimental, so we didn't know how it was going to [turn out]."

Candiotti wasn't sure if he would be able to land or push on his knee, so there was no telling if he was even physically able to pitch. Had Candiotti retired, he would have finished with a 136–142, 3.54 ERA mark, and 1,596 strikeouts in 2,452.2 innings, in 400 games (364 starts). "But I had to do the surgery because it was so painful anyway," Candiotti recalls. "The doctor performed the surgery and I wasn't even sure if I was going to play again. He did the surgery and then the A's called and offered me a contract. It was like, 'Shoot, I'll take it.' The doctor wasn't really happy with me, because I was probably going to destroy his surgery, which I did. That year in 1998, after my surgery, it was so painful. But I ended up pitching over 200 innings for a really bad team."

Oakland, which had a major league-worst 65–97 record in 1997, desperately wanted to sign Candiotti. The Athletics needed veteran arms to lead a young pitching staff, and knew the knuckleballer could be counted on to throw 200 innings and anchor their weak rotation. Though the A's slugged 197 homers—third-best in the AL—their starting pitching recorded the majors' worst team ERA at 5.48. Thirteen different pitchers started for Oakland; all had bad stats:

| | | |
|---|---|---|
| Ariel Prieto | 6–8 | 5.04 |
| Mike Oquist | 4–5 | 4.81 |
| Dave Telgheder | 4–6 | 6.24 |
| Andrew Lorraine | 3–1 | 7.30 |
| Jimmy Haynes | 3–6 | 4.42 |
| Steve Karsay | 3–12 | 5.77 |
| Willie Adams | 2–5 | 8.32 |
| Don Wengert | 2–6 | 7.13 |
| Eric Ludwick | 1–4 | 8.34 |
| Brad Rigby | 1–7 | 4.87 |
| Steve Wojciechowski | 0–2 | 7.84 |
| Carlos Reyes | 0–4 | 8.34 |
| Mike Mohler | 0–7 | 6.83 |

It was the second straight season in which no A's pitcher had 10 wins, and the starters accounted for only 29 of Oakland's 65 victories. The group that made up the five-man rotation to begin the season—Prieto, Adams, Karsay, Mohler, and Telgheder—went a combined 15–38 with a 6.06 ERA in 87 starts. Knowing Candiotti could be counted on to eat up innings and provide a veteran presence for their rookie-laden rotation, the A's made signing him a priority.

Meanwhile, at least five other teams were interested, including the Dodgers (for a spot in the bullpen), Tampa Bay, Minnesota, San Francisco, and Cleveland.[1] Joe Klein, for one, wasn't surprised several teams wanted Candiotti. "People continued to ask me about Tom's makeup over the years," says Klein, the former Indians general manager who signed him in 1985. "People wondered because he'd had a bad year or two and hadn't sustained what he'd had with us in Cleveland. I'd say, 'Hey, this guy's going to bounce back somewhere. He's going to bounce back for somebody. And if you can get him at the right price, get him.'"

In the winter of 1997, the price was right for the A's, who had also traded for Yankees lefthander Kenny Rogers in November. Candiotti inked a two-year, $6.35-million guaranteed contract in December to become one of the A's top two starters, along with Rogers. For Oakland, the decision to sign the knuckleballer was simple. With him in the fold, along with the acquisitions of Rogers and reliever Mike Fetters, the club had vastly improved its pitching. "We needed a significant upgrade in our pitching staff, and I think we've done that," said general manager Billy Beane the day he signed Candiotti.[2]

Candiotti decided to sign with Oakland after both Beane and manager Art Howe told him how much they wanted him. "Billy Beane was determined to make Tom his first free agent choice and he was true to his word," confirmed Candiotti's agent, Jeff Moorad, the day the Athletics signed him. "He wouldn't give up."[3] Recalls Candiotti: "Art phoned me and asked me to sign with them. He goes, 'We had a bad year in 1997, but we still scored more runs than the Dodgers.' It was great, getting a personal call from Art and being offered a contract. Even Billy phoned me to ask me to sign with them. Both of those guys expressed how well I would fit with the organization not only on the field, but also off the field as well. They made me feel wanted. When you hear words like that expressed by both the manager and general manager of a club, it certainly goes a long way."

In fact, Howe and Candiotti go a long way back, with their friendship dating to the 1980s. "I had Tom the first time he really started using the knuckleball, and that was in winter baseball," Howe recalls. "He was pitching for me down in Puerto Rico and he asked me at that point if he could just predominantly throw knuckleballs. I said, 'Go for it.' That was when he really started to go with the knuckleball. He pitched for me and he did a really great job for me there."

Now in the winter of 1997, Howe knew that Candiotti, even at age 40, could still pitch effectively. "We were looking for veteran leadership on the club in Oakland, with a veteran starting pitcher," Howe says. "Kenny Rogers was the only other veteran starting pitcher we had on the staff. I felt like Tom was really in the prime of his career. He could come in there and, first of all, give us quality innings and, secondly, give us a lot of innings to help our bullpen out. We didn't have any starters—other than Rogers—that could go 200 innings. Our bullpen was really taking a lot of beating."

That last statement was especially true on Opening Day. For each of the previous five seasons (1993–97), no A's starter had lasted more than five innings in the season opener, with those starters averaging 3.2 innings and pitching to a 10.31 ERA. In the previous two years, no Oakland pitcher had even cracked the 165-inning mark (and only one accomplished that feat in the last four seasons). Knowing Candiotti had averaged nearly 200 innings per year over the past 12 seasons, it was a no-brainer for Howe in 1998. Candiotti was going to become the A's sixth different Opening Day pitcher in six years, following Bob Welch (1993), Bobby Witt ('94), Dave Stewart ('95), Carlos Reyes ('96), and Ariel Prieto ('97). "Tom was exactly the type of guy we needed for the young pitchers to be around," recalls Howe. "We knew he'd give us 200 innings and stabilize the staff, and he did a terrific job for us."

On Opening Day, on April 1 in Oakland, Candiotti tossed seven innings of seven-hit ball with three strikeouts and no walks, only to lose, 2–0, to Boston. The nonexistent offense, as well as the lackluster A's defense, cost Can-

diotti the game. In the fifth inning, second baseman Scott Spiezio committed
a two-base throwing error, which led to an unearned run that came home on
a sacrifice fly. In the seventh, Candiotti loaded the bases with none out, but
got Nomar Garciaparra to ground to third. Dave Magadan threw home for a
forceout, but catcher A.J. Hinch's throw to first base for a double play attempt
pulled Jason Giambi off the bag, leaving the bases loaded with one out. A flyball to center by John Valentin became a sacrifice fly instead of the third out.[4]

Candiotti's defense again betrayed him on April 6 in a 6–5 loss against
Cleveland. With Travis Fryman aboard and two outs in the top of the second,
Candiotti struck out Jeff Manto swinging but Hinch dropped the third-strike
knuckleball, which prolonged the inning and eventually led to two unearned
runs. Two innings later, with Manto aboard with two outs, Pat Borders hit a
grounder to the left side of the infield. Alas, Magadan got a late jump and lunged
too late to stop the ball from rolling into left field. Kenny Lofton followed
with a single to center, but centerfielder Jason McDonald slipped on the grass
before hurrying a throw to third base. The ball skipped away and both runners
scored, giving the Indians a 4–2 lead en route to the one-run victory.

It was more of the same on April 11, when Candiotti lost, 3–1, at Yankee
Stadium and dropped to 0–3 with a 2.84 ERA. The Yankees in 1998 would
go on to capture their second World Series title in three years, setting a major
league record by winning 125 games against only 50 defeats, including the
postseason. It would have been a tall order for any pitcher to try to stop them,
especially on the afternoon following their 17–13 victory on April 10. In that
particular game, Oakland gave Jimmy Haynes a 5–0 lead, but New York chased
him after 2.1 innings and opened a 12–5 cushion through four. The A's then
knocked out David Cone in the fifth, an inning in which they plated eight
runs to go up 13–12. But who knew that one day after scoring 13 runs—including nine in just 4.1 innings off Cone—Oakland would get just one run on six
hits off Andy Pettitte?

Candiotti went the distance, allowing Art Howe to rest his bullpen, which
was spent after four relievers worked 5.2 innings in the 17–13 contest. But the
Yankees won the game in the third inning, when they scored twice after shortstop Rafael Bournigal couldn't turn a double play. With a runner on first, Candiotti got Derek Jeter to hit a one-hopper to the mound. The knuckleballer
threw to second base to start what could have been a 1–6–3 double play, but
Bournigal was slow to make the turn and Jeter beat the throw.[5] Instead of having two outs and none on, the Yankees scored two runs in that inning on Tino
Martinez's two-out single for the winning tallies.

After five starts, Candiotti improved to 1–3 with a 2.83 ERA. His solid
pitching—he'd thrown five good games in April alone—was something that

fans had not seen in Oakland for years. Early on, the newspaper scribes understood the losing record wasn't his fault. "With any support at all," observed
Jim Van Vliet of the *Sacramento Bee* after Candiotti's fifth start, "the knuckleballer could easily be 5–0 at this point. In the four starts he has not won
[three losses and a no-decision], Candiotti has allowed a total of seven [earned]
runs."[6] Van Vliet also pointed to the failures of his teammates, noting the fact
Candiotti had been receiving "shaky defense and poor offensive production."
The *Press Democrat*'s Jeff Fletcher agreed, noting the veteran knuckleballer
"could be 5–0 if he had a little defense behind him.... In his five starts, the A's
have allowed seven unearned runs while he's been on the mound."[7]

Candiotti closed the month of April with a 2–3 mark. Despite the losing
record, he was exactly what Art Howe wanted out of his number one starter.
In 1997, Howe had watched a slew of starters not make it past the fifth inning.
But fast forward to 1998, and it was a different story with Candiotti. In five
of his six April starts, he lasted at least seven innings (with the lone exception
coming in the Cleveland game that was interrupted twice by rain), taking pressure off the young starters as well as the A's bullpen. Three times in that first
month, Candiotti did not allow
any walks while working at least
seven innings. Howe was most
impressed Candiotti kept battling without complaining about

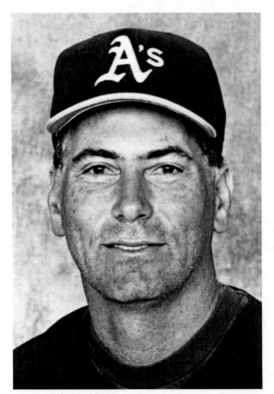

Though Candiotti suffered a losing
record with the last-place Athletics
in 1998, the season was not a total
write-off for the 40-year-old knuckleballer. He made his A's debut on
April 1 against the Boston Red Sox,
becoming the oldest pitcher in Oakland history to start on Opening Day.
With 11 victories, Candiotti also became just the second pitcher to post
a 10-win season at age 40 or older for
Oakland, joining Don Sutton, who
went 13–8 in 1985 at age 40. In addition, Candiotti was the recipient of
the 1998 Dave Stewart Community
Service Award, given annually to an
A's player in recognition of charitable
contributions throughout Northern
California and across the nation
(National Baseball Hall of Fame
Library, Cooperstown, New York).

the rotten support. "A young pitcher might have fallen apart. He certainly didn't," Howe said in recognizing his pitcher's bad luck while acknowledging his value was more than simply wins and losses. "We've gotten into the seventh inning [with the starting pitcher] more this first month than we did all last season."[8]

While Candiotti's 1998 numbers weren't pretty, he still exhibited good control with his knuckleball. In nine of his 33 starts, Candiotti did not walk a single batter. (It wasn't as though the knuckleballer was knocked out of those games early after surrendering a bunch of hits; he averaged 7.1 innings in those nine starts.) On five other occasions, Candiotti walked only one hitter. Nine other times he walked just two. That's a total of 23 starts out of 33 where he allowed two or fewer walks. "What happens is I usually struggled early with the command of my knuckler, but after a couple of innings after I got the feel for the pitch, I got locked in," Candiotti says in explaining his low walk rate. If he was able to get through the first two innings unscathed, he was going to have a good night. "If the ball moved well, the hitters usually got themselves out."

Unfortunately, Candiotti had a record of 2–9 in those games where he walked one batter or none, as Oakland was shut out in five of those contests. The month of June best exemplifies his hard luck, when Candiotti was 0–5 while receiving little help or getting few breaks. For instance:

June 7—Against Arizona, Candiotti was charged with the loss despite not allowing a hit. He pitched a perfect first inning before walking Matt Williams to lead off the second, and was then forced to leave the game because of back spasms. His replacement, Jay Witasick, served up a home run to his first batter, David Dellucci, and the Diamondbacks led, 2–0. In Oakland's 12–4 loss, Witasick allowed three homers and six runs. However, since Candiotti was charged with the first run and Arizona never trailed, he was tagged with the loss.

June 12—Against Seattle, Candiotti lost, 5–0, as Oakland recorded more errors (four) than hits (three). Lefthander Jamie Moyer, the opposing pitcher, had given up seven runs in each of his previous two starts while compiling a 12.19 ERA in only 10.1 innings, allowing five home runs. It was only the fifth major league shutout for Moyer, whose big league career had begun a dozen years earlier, in 1986. In September, he tossed another complete-game shutout against Candiotti. Incredibly, Moyer had four career complete-game shutouts in 242 major league starts entering this 5–0 game, but then two in three months against Candiotti.

June 18—In the scorching heat on a windy afternoon in Texas, Candiotti featured what the *San Francisco Chronicle*'s Steve Kettmann called a "nasty" knuckleball, saying "he had the ball dancing" all game long.[9] But the result was a 3–2 loss, as Oakland loaded the bases in four separate innings but couldn't get the tying and winning runs across. The decisive runs for the Rangers came in the third, when they loaded the bases with one out. Candiotti struck Will Clark out swinging on a knuckler that bounced in the dirt—but the ball eluded catcher A.J. Hinch for a wild pitch. Tom Goodwin and Rusty Greer both scored, as the Rangers plated two runs on that strikeout. "It was probably his best knuckleball of the day," Hinch said afterward.[10]

June 23—Against San Francisco, Candiotti retired the first 12 batters and allowed three runs on five hits with no walks in eight innings, but still lost, 4–2. Giants righthander Mark Gardner, who worked seven innings, improved to 6–3 with his 5.42 ERA. Candiotti? 4–10 with a 5.11 ERA. Their stats, following this game:

|           | IP   | H   | BB | SO | HR | ERA  |
|-----------|------|-----|----|----|----|------|
| Gardner   | 94.2 | 106 | 37 | 63 | 17 | 5.42 |
| Candiotti | 98.2 | 114 | 34 | 44 | 15 | 5.11 |

June 28—In Colorado's Coors Field, Candiotti allowed four hits and three earned runs with five strikeouts over six innings, only to see the bullpen cough up his three-run lead. Three A's relievers allowed five runs in the seventh, and Oakland lost, 11–10. "It was one of those games where you say, 'We should have won 12–4,'" Candiotti lamented. "I think most of the time if you can pitch here and kill six or seven innings and give up three earned runs or less, you should have a pretty good chance to win the ball game."[11]

Candiotti was 4–10 with a 5.07 ERA entering July, tied with three other pitchers for the AL lead in losses. However, others were having better success despite having high ERAs. Athletics teammate Mike Oquist had an AL-worst 5.87 ERA (over 95 innings), but a respectable 4–5 record. Bobby Witt of Texas was 5–4 with a 7.90 ERA. Boston's Bret Saberhagen and Tim Wakefield were sailing along at 9–5 and 9–3, despite ERAs of 5.10 and 4.40, respectively. Yankees righthander David Cone, with a 4.39 ERA, was 11–2.

Then there was Indians righthander Charles Nagy, who was 7–4 even with a 5.48 ERA. "Those pitchers in Cleveland had great records because of the hitting," Candiotti says matter-of-factly. "Look at those earned run averages. They weren't dominant pitchers. Nagy benefited from those great offenses of those Indians teams also. Anyone would've won all those games pitching for them in the 1990s. By the same token, you can't put a guy like Nagy on a lousy team of that era. It's when you pitch and who you pitch for."

On a bad Athletics team, Candiotti continued to pitch valiantly as the 1998 season progressed, but often without any results. On July 10, he battled Texas to a scoreless tie through eight innings—allowing seven hits with no walks against a mighty Rangers lineup that included Will Clark, Juan Gonzalez, and Ivan Rodriguez—and came away with a no-decision as the A's bullpen allowed the only run of the contest in the ninth. On July 15, Candiotti allowed three runs with no walks over seven innings, but lost, 5–1, to Kansas City's Jose Rosado. The game was decided in the fifth, when a misplay by shortstop Miguel Tejada led to two runs, breaking a 1–1 tie.[12] On July 26, Candiotti gave up three runs over seven innings in Tampa Bay but lost, 3–1, to Wilson Alvarez, who walked five over seven innings.

Though Candiotti threw a knuckleball as a main pitch, it did not mean that he wasn't laboring in those low-scoring contests. As he explains, when every game was tight, even a knuckleball pitcher like him got tired. "You get mentally drained," Candiotti says. "You go out there knowing every batter you face can cost you the game. You know if you give up a run, you may lose. So if you don't get any run support, the key inning of the game could come early. You know, there's a guy on third base in the first inning, and you really have to bear down because if that runner scores, that could be it. It's mentally draining to go through that every start. Sure, there's less strain on a knuckleball pitcher's arm, but the mental aspect of it is the same. When you're pitching in a low-scoring game, it takes a lot out of you, both physically and mentally. You really find yourself in a lot of clutch situations throughout the evening and those pitches take a lot out of you."

Entering August, Candiotti's record was 5–13. Catcher A.J. Hinch, though, knew that his knuckleball was still effective. "It's masterful the way he makes hitters look and even feel," Hinch said one evening in Oakland. "I know how they feel because I hear their remarks. They're frustrated. They're not happy or comfortable the way he adds and subtracts miles per hour. It's craftsmanship."[13]

Candiotti's fortunes would change in the second half. Though Oakland's overall record was only 19–17 from July 31 to September 6, Candiotti won six of his eight starts with a 3.30 ERA in that span. For ex–Indians general manager Joe Klein, the knuckleballer's late-season resurgence was hardly a surprise. "Every time Candiotti looked like he was done," Klein says, "he always seemed to find a way to bounce back."

Candiotti's best outing during that stretch came on August 5 against the Yankees, who would win an AL-record 114 games in 1998. New York, 80–28 at the time, finished among the league leaders in several offensive categories: first in runs (965) and walks (653), second in batting (.288) and steals (153), and fourth in homers (207). The Yankees had also defeated the Athletics seven straight times while outscoring them 70–36. In this four-game series in Oakland, they'd won the first three by scores of 14–1, 10–4, and 10–5—including the night before when they tallied nine ninth-inning runs to stun the Athletics.

A's general manager Billy Beane would, like many baseball observers, call the 1998 Yankees "one of the greatest teams in the history of the game."[14] Years later, he stated that "to win one game against them was a big deal" while recalling that Oakland literally ran out of pitching in this particular August series. "They wore you out. They pounded you. The impact they would have on your pitching staff when you were done playing them would carry over for another week," Beane added.[15] In the series finale, though, Candiotti made sure Oakland's shell-shocked bullpen had a night off, allowing only four hits in a complete-game 3–1 victory. He struck out six Yankees, including Darryl Strawberry to end the contest. "Darryl didn't look comfortable the whole night against my knuckler, and I threw him nothing but slow knuckleballs," says Candiotti of that final at-bat. "I just tried to see how slow I could throw it. I threw that last pitch 48 mph."

The victory also made Candiotti the oldest pitcher in franchise history to toss a complete-game win since June 23, 1958, when 41-year-old Murry Dickson of the Kansas City Athletics defeated the Washington Senators. Candiotti was 40 years and 339 days old at the time he beat the Yankees, making him the oldest pitcher in the history of Oakland baseball with a complete-game win. "Candy picked the whole team up, put us on his shoulders, and just carried us that night," manager Art Howe says years later. Said Strawberry following the game: "Those were some of the slowest pitches I've ever seen. I didn't expect that. I almost hurt my arm hanging on to the bat after swinging at the first pitch. I nearly came out of my shoes on the last pitch. He can make the ball dance."[16]

On August 27 in Boston, Candiotti also slowed down the playoff-bound Red Sox; so much so that even Boston slugger Mo Vaughn was grinning. In Oakland's 6–3 victory, Candiotti threw such slow pitches in the first inning— first a slow knuckler and then a slow fastball—that Vaughn couldn't help but laugh during the entire at-bat. "He knows his fastball is around 60 or 65 miles an hour," Vaughn said. "You have to laugh. It's a crazy thing.... Sometimes he throws it up there around 40 or 45 miles an hour."[17] While Vaughn was laughing then, knuckleballers normally do the opposite to hitters. "Usually we're up there looking at pitchers throwing the ball 88 to 92 mph," Vaughn would say one night in Anaheim a year later. "Then all [of a] sudden a knuckleballer is throwing 66. You think you're going to cream the ball, then you miss it. It ticks you off."[18]

Candiotti surpassed 200 innings for the season on September 17, becoming only the 23rd pitcher since 1980 with that many innings in a season in his

40s. He had also reached the goal that management had expected when he was signed in the offseason by giving the team as many innings as possible. In 1997, Don Wengert's 134 innings led the A's staff, meaning the bullpen was overworked. But thanks to Candiotti and left-hander Kenny Rogers, who also surpassed 200 innings on August 30, there was less pressure on the relievers in 1998. The team had not had two 200-inning pitchers in the same season since 1992. "If you look back over the course of the season, it means you had a chance to compete farther into games," Billy Beane said. "I didn't say I wanted wins. I said innings were the key. Candy has given us that. He's been everything I wanted and more. We wanted the innings, and we wanted the leadership."[19]

With a 4.84 ERA for the last-place A's, Candiotti finished

Candiotti surpassed the 200-inning mark nine times in his 16-year major league career, including 201 innings at the age of 40 in 1998 with the Athletics. Candiotti, shown here a few years after his playing career had ended, had a streak of eight consecutive seasons with 200 or more innings pitched from 1986 to 1993. He pitched 2,725 innings in the major leagues and recorded a 3.73 earned run average with 1,735 strikeouts in 451 appearances (author's collection).

11–16. However, if baseball writer William Darby's method for measuring a starting pitcher's effectiveness was used (awarding a victory to the pitcher in starts in which he allows fewer runs than what his team averages offensively), Candiotti would have won 15 games.[20] He simply needed more help from his teammates. For instance, there were 10 outings in which Candiotti didn't earn the win despite recording quality starts, pitching to a 2.85 ERA and going 0–6 with four no-decisions. In five of those contests, Oakland scored one run or none. In his 16 losses, he received 18 runs when he was in the game.

Art Howe knows Candiotti gave Oakland everything despite pitching with a bad left knee, and offers some perspective. "Tom came in and gave us 200 innings that first year and pitched well for us," Howe says. "Unfortunately, we couldn't give him a lot of run support. He could've won a lot more games. We just didn't give him a whole lot of support at times. Sometimes you give too much credence or emphasis on wins and losses, [but] you look at his ERA and innings pitched ... those were the important things for us."

Though Howe would argue that Candiotti pitched well in 1998, the same couldn't be said the following year. The 1999 season was a painful one for the veteran knuckleballer as he battled two bad knees, and he posted a 4–6, 7.32 ERA mark and wound up getting released by two teams. Both of Candiotti's knees were so bad that season that he was constantly receiving injections in between starts.

Still, there were some memorable moments along the way. On April 16, Candiotti pitched three-hit ball over 6.2 innings in his 400th career start and defeated Texas, 8–2, becoming the 98th pitcher in major league history with 400 or more starts. "I was still throwing about 70 percent knuckleballs and using my other pitches," Candiotti recalls, proud of the fact he wasn't throwing knuckleballs exclusively, even at age 41. "I was throwing strikes and changing speeds with my knuckleball and curveball. That night against Texas, it showed just how effective that repertoire was against big league hitters."

On April 22, Candiotti helped Oakland snap a three-game losing streak by defeating Cleveland, 4–1, in front of the 300th consecutive sellout at Jacobs Field. He allowed three hits over seven innings, retiring 13 of 14 batters in one stretch. And while the Indians had reached an impressive consecutive-game sellout streak, Candiotti was also nearing a milestone of his own. After that win, he was one victory shy of 150. "Tom certainly exceeded everything I thought he'd do," says Joe Klein. "I thought he'd be a quality pitcher in the major leagues for a long time. I wish he'd been 18 and not 28 when we signed him in Cleveland. He would've won a lot more games if he started earlier. Still, Candy had a nice run in the big leagues as a pitcher, that's for sure."

Candiotti would fail in his first five attempts at win number 150. His second try came on May 2, with Boston knuckleballer Tim Wakefield opposing him. Neither starter got a decision as Oakland won, 7–5. But talk about the difference in luck between the two knuckleballing veterans. Wakefield, a mainstay in the Red Sox's rotation despite a mediocre 4.26 ERA from 1995 to 1998, had a record of 59–44 during that period, averaging 30 starts a year. In 1996, Wakefield had a 5.14 ERA but somehow went 14–13. The following season, he was 3–10 with a 4.76 ERA in mid–July but still remained in the Boston rotation before rebounding to finish 12–15 by season's end. In 1998, Wakefield received 6.82 runs of support and was 17–8 with a 4.58 ERA for the playoff-bound Red Sox. "The East Coast is a great place for him to pitch," Candiotti, 37–48 with a 4.14 ERA from 1995–98, would say matter-of-factly of Wakefield. "He's on a team that scores a lot of runs in a league that doesn't steal a lot."[21]

In the contest against Wakefield, Candiotti had some hard luck, at least in the eyes of manager Art Howe. "Actually, I thought Tommy was pitching well," Howe noted. "One swing and the three-run homer changed the game."[22] That swing, John Valentin's fifth-inning three-run blast off Candiotti, gave Boston a 5–4 lead. Oakland, though, bailed him out, scoring seven runs off Red Sox pitching, including four on six hits and five walks in three-plus innings off Wakefield, whose ERA rose to 8.02.

Candiotti struggled in his next three starts, going 0–2 with an 8.10 ERA, as win number 150 again eluded him. By then, his season ERA was 6.90 and there were whispers that Tim Hudson would be called up from Triple-A Vancouver to take his spot if he continued to struggle. What a difference a year made. "If you look at the track record of quality starters over the years, you'll see guys go through stretches like this," pitching coach Rick Peterson said in 1998 when Candiotti had gone through a similar bad stretch. "He showed flashes of being dominating early in the season. And obviously, warm weather is his weather."[23] But a year later, Oakland's patience was running out.

Candiotti wasn't the only Athletics starter who'd been scuffling. Staff ace Kenny Rogers was only 1–2 with a 4.58 ERA. He had to leave a start in the second inning on May 11 due to back spasms, and subsequently missed one start. Number three starter Jimmy Haynes was 2–5 with a 6.14 ERA. He would log a 5.30 ERA with three teams from 1999 to 2004, going 0–3 with a 9.60 ERA with Cincinnati in his final major league season in 2004. Journeyman Gil Heredia, the A's fourth starter, allowed seven runs on May 18 (and would allow eight runs in his next outing on May 23). He compiled a 5.68 ERA in June, with Oakland losing all five of his starts. In fact, the A's would lose 12 of Heredia's 16 starts to begin the year. His final big league season came in 2001, when he posted a 5.58 ERA for Oakland.

While Candiotti's failures in his last five starts were magnified, what perhaps wasn't as apparent to the A's was the team's lack of offensive production. The Athletics went 0–6 during a six-game road trip in Kansas City and Minnesota from May 18 to 23, recording only seven multiple-hit innings in the six losses. Against the Twins, they scored just five runs in 34 innings over three games despite facing starters with bad stats, such as LaTroy Hawkins (9.00 ERA) and Eric Milton (7.14 ERA), and relievers like Bob Wells (5.40 ERA), Joe Mays (5.97), and Eddie Guardado (5.52). In fact, Oakland was last in the majors in hitting with a .239 batting average—35 points below the AL average. The team was also hitting just .217 with men in scoring position, and didn't play small ball either with a major league-worst 15 stolen bases.

The A's offensive struggles weren't surprising. Their payroll entering the season was the league's third-lowest at just over $20 million, and realistically they wouldn't match up against the other three AL West teams that had rosters stacked with high-priced All-Stars. Seattle, with a $44-million payroll, had superstars Ken Griffey, Jr., Edgar Martinez, and Alex Rodriguez. Anaheim, at $49 million, was led by sluggers Mo Vaughn and Tim Salmon and lefthander Chuck Finley. Texas, the biggest spender in the division at $81 million, was an offensive juggernaut with two-time AL MVP Juan Gonzalez, Ivan Rodriguez, Rusty Greer, and Rafael Palmeiro leading the way.

Oakland's lineup, meanwhile, had quite a few rookies or second-year players. More than half of its Opening Day lineup—centerfielder Jason McDonald, leftfielder Ben Grieve, catcher A.J. Hinch, shortstop Miguel Tejada, and rookie third baseman Eric Chavez—had barely a year's worth of big league experience. The youngsters—other than Grieve, the '98 AL Rookie of the Year—didn't do much in 1998, as Hinch (.231), Tejada (.233), McDonald (.251), and Ryan Christenson (.257) all struggled at the plate. The A's, who finished last in four of those six seasons, were clearly in a rebuilding phase with their young players. And with some of baseball's oldest players on the roster—Candiotti (41 years old), relievers Doug Jones (42) and Billy Taylor (37), and outfielders Tony Phillips (40) and Tim Raines (39)—Oakland wasn't expected to compete in 1999.

But with the A's only two-and-a-half games behind first-place Texas on May 27, management figured they might as well make a run for it. And despite the offensive woes, it seemed Oakland was content to fix its problems by tweaking its pitching staff, with rumors surfacing that Candiotti's days were numbered because of his slow start and the emergence of Triple-A righthander Tim Hudson.[24] Candiotti downplayed the rumors then, saying he fully expected his season—and his knuckleball—would turn around once the warmer weather rolled around. "I've always pitched great in June, July, and August," he said, referring to his 3.30 ERA in those months from 1983 to 1998. "And this year I got hardly any spring training because of my knee problem. So I knew I'd get off to a slow start."[25]

When Candiotti faced Baltimore on May 28 in Oakland, all signs pointed to an Orioles win, especially with ace Mike Mussina (114–54 with a 3.54 ERA from 1992 to 1998) pitching and with Baltimore's offense seemingly always coming through for him. In 1995, Mussina had a 4.45 ERA going into August but a 12–5 record (while teammate Kevin Brown was only 5–6 even with a 3.65 ERA). In 1993, Mussina went 14–6 despite a 4.46 ERA. In 1996, he had a 4.81 ERA but finished 19–11. Entering this matchup against Candiotti in 1999, Mussina had a 4.45 ERA while allowing 81 hits over 64.2 innings but had received 8.6 runs per start, resulting in a 7–1 record.

On this night, though, Candiotti stymied the Orioles to lead Oakland to a 2–1 victory. "I remember I threw the ball really well in the bullpen [during the pre-game warm-ups]," Candiotti recalls. "Of course, the bullpen mound and the mound on the field face the exact opposite direction. Plus, it was a windy night in Oakland, so you didn't know how the knuckleball would move during the game with the wind blowing in the opposite direction."

Still, Candiotti began the game with four perfect innings. Over his 6.1 innings in the cool weather at the Coliseum—where the chilly conditions weren't ideal for his knuckler—he held the Orioles to four hits and no walks. There were signs of trouble in the fifth when Baltimore had runners on second and third with just one out. Candiotti, though, got ahead of Cal Ripken 0–and–2 before getting the future Hall of Famer to hit a comebacker to the mound. Charles Johnson then struck out on three pitches, flailing at a slow knuckler for strike three.

Baltimore went down, 2–1, allowing Candiotti to become the 175th pitcher in big league history with 150 victories. "It was a great milestone for him," manager Art Howe recalls, "so I was really happy that he was able to get it. He got started at an older age than most pitchers do. For him to get to 150 after what he started [at], age-wise—I think he was in his late 20s when he actually got opportunities to pitch on a regular basis—it's a real credit to him to be able to get that many wins."

Candiotti, though, wasn't always sure if Howe knew he had 15 seasons under his belt by then, with a perfect example coming on June 2 against Tampa Bay. Candiotti had given up three straight singles to start the third inning and load the bases but bounced back and struck out both Dave Martinez and Jose Canseco swinging. Unfortunately, catcher A.J. Hinch dropped the third-strike knuckleball to Canseco, allowing the runner from third to score. With runners on second and third, Candiotti was ready to face Fred McGriff. Pitching coach Rick Peterson, however, walked out of the dugout toward the mound for a little conference. "I know you don't want me out here," said Peterson. "But Art sent me here to tell you there's a base open."

Candiotti looked at Peterson in disbelief. The veteran knuckleballer was stunned Howe wanted to remind him there was a base open, something a manager might tell a rookie pitcher. Regardless, Candiotti struck out McGriff swinging to escape the jam, his third strikeout of the inning. When he returned to the dugout, he told lefthander Kenny Rogers what Peterson had said on the mound. Rogers replied, "You've gotta be kidding me!" And both pitchers laughed.

But neither pitcher was laughing five days later. On the morning of June 7, with Oakland only four-and-a-half games behind first-place Texas, the club called up rookie Tim Hudson from Triple-A and designated Candiotti for assignment. The knuckleballer was released nine days later. "It's never easy when you have to inform a quality person like Tom was," Howe recalls. "Tom was very understanding. It's a shame sometimes when an injury takes place, it ends up curtailing someone's career. He was bone-on-bone on his landing knee. The pain was just getting too great for him to go out there and compete. All careers come to an end at some point, and unfortunately, as a manager, you sometimes have to be the one to end someone's career. I guess that's what they pay you to do sometimes."

For Candiotti, the news was devastating. "I'm flabbergasted because the past two weeks I've been feeling great," he told reporters. "I feel I can still pitch effectively and at times better than that. I pitched pretty good games against Cleveland and Texas and they're both in first place."[26] Candiotti, who had a 6.35 ERA at the time, wasn't the only pitcher with bad numbers; it was a problem on nearly every staff in baseball. With offenses dominating in the majors—both Mark McGwire (70 HRs) and Sammy Sosa (66 HRs) broke Roger Maris's single-season record of 61 homers in 1998, and were threatening to do it again in '99—even elite pitchers were struggling.

Four-time Cy Young winner Greg Maddux was 5–3 with a pedestrian 4.65 ERA after posting a major league-best 2.22 ERA the year before and a 2.15 earned-run average from 1992 to 1998. The Atlanta righthander had allowed 111 hits over 79.1 innings, and batters were hitting him at a .330 clip. Lefthander Tom Glavine, meanwhile, was 3–7 with a 5.00 ERA, with Atlanta losing eight of his 12 starts. Glavine, a four-time 20-game winner, had gone 140–64 with a 2.96 ERA from 1991 to 1998 before the slow start in '99. Yankee southpaw Andy Pettitte, a former 20-game winner and World Series star, was 3–3 with a 5.58 ERA. He slumped so badly that owner George Steinbrenner, according to Joe Torre's *The Yankee Years* memoir, "considered Pettitte a drag on the staff and wanted him gone" before the trade deadline.[27] Steinbrenner apparently had a deal in place to ship him to Philadelphia but eventually decided not to consummate the trade.[28] Mets ace Al Leiter, third in the majors with a 2.47 ERA in '98, had slumped to 3–5 with a 5.87 ERA.

As the *San Francisco Chronicle*'s Mark Camps noted that June, "major league pitching is putting on its worst performance in more than 60 years. It's gotten so bad that a pitcher with an ERA under 5.00 is considered the ace of most staffs."[29] By that definition, the Yankees' Roger Clemens, a five-time Cy Young Award winner, wasn't the ace in New York with his 5.18 earned run average. It wasn't just the elite pitchers who were having a hard time; other high-profile veterans were finding it hard to keep up with the increase in home runs and offense around baseball.

Tim Belcher, 3–5 with a 7.23 ERA, was still in the Angels' rotation as Anaheim was battling for second place in the AL West. Mike Morgan, 6–4 despite a 6.26 ERA, still had a role with first-place Texas. The Rangers' top two starters, Rick Helling and Aaron Sele (a combined 39–18 in 1998), were 5–6 with a 4.81 ERA and 5–4 with a 5.58 ERA, respectively. Jeff Fassero, the Mariners' Opening Day starter, was 3–6 with a 6.90 ERA and had allowed a major league-worst 19 homers. Jamie Moyer, Seattle's number two starter, was 6–4 with a 5.22 ERA. Arizona's Andy Benes, despite a 4–5 record and a 5.40 ERA, would remain a starter all year, as would San Francisco's Shawn Estes, 2–4 and 5.75. Scott Erickson was struggling with a 1–8, 7.11 ERA mark—with Baltimore going 2–10 in his 12 starts—but also managed to keep his job.

At the time of Candiotti's banishment from Oakland, he hadn't pitched a lot of innings (56.2 innings), but his numbers were comparable to other veterans like Hershiser (4–5, 5.77 ERA, 53.0 innings), Clemens (5–1, 5.18 ERA, 48.2 innings), and Red Sox knuckleballer Tim Wakefield (3–5, 5.86 ERA, 55.1 innings). Boston, though, never gave up on Wakefield, who earlier in the season had a stretch of four starts where he couldn't make it out of the fourth inning three times, logging a 10.80 ERA with 12 walks and 25 hits in 15 innings. In 12 starts since August 30, 1998, Wakefield was 3–7 with a 7.00 ERA, with six of those outings lasting four innings or fewer, including a post-season loss to Cleveland. Manager Jimy Williams, however, still gave him a vote of confidence. "Just keep pitching him," Williams said. "He's going to start. He's going to turn this thing around."[30] No such opportunity for Candiotti in Oakland.

"What ended his stay in Oakland was his knee," Art Howe says, referring to the three different tears in Candiotti's left knee and the loose particles that had built up in his right knee. "He was getting injections into his knee and that really curtailed his career with us in Oakland. He had to keep getting shots in one of his knees to be able to go out there and throw. His arm was fine. It was his knee that was bothering him. It's really unfortunate that an injury curtails a ballplayer's career, as it did in Tom's case."

# 17

# *Final Goodbye in Cleveland*

After Oakland released Tom Candiotti in mid–June of 1999, several teams contacted the veteran knuckleballer wondering if he would be interested in signing. However, he was holding out hope to rejoin Cleveland, the team he had pitched for from 1986 to 1991.

Candiotti's patience paid off when Indians general manager John Hart phoned him on June 25. "When the A's released me, there wasn't a big need in Cleveland," Candiotti says. "Then the Indians had a doubleheader [the following week] and they needed an extra pitcher. So John called me to work out the details. Obviously, it didn't take much to convince me to sign with them. I think, as an athlete, when your career's nearing the end, it's always a thrill to be able to return to where you started. My career didn't start in Cleveland, but that was where I threw the knuckleball and really learned how to pitch."

Indians manager Mike Hargrove, who was a coach with Cleveland in the early 1990s when Candiotti was the Tribe's best pitcher, knew all about the knuckleballer. Nearly a decade later, Hargrove believed Candiotti could still do it—bad knees and all—well aware that he could definitely mess up a hitter's swing and rhythm. "We brought Candiotti in here because we think he's an effective major league pitcher," Hargrove noted. "We think he has some gas left in his tank."[1]

The 1999 Indians, who had an 11-and-a-half-game lead in the AL Central by June 25, were a pitcher's dream. They were an offensive machine that would set a franchise record with 1,009 runs, becoming the first major league team since the 1950 Red Sox to reach quadruple digits. Cleveland would also lead the AL in batting average, hits, and walks.

Candiotti witnessed the offensive fireworks firsthand on July 3 with Kansas City in town for a day-night doubleheader at Jacobs Field. In the first game, the Royals came out hitting in the first two innings, battering Charles Nagy for eight runs and an 8–0 lead. With Nagy struggling, Hargrove had Candiotti begin warming up in the bullpen in the second inning. Cleveland scored three runs in the bottom of the second, and Candiotti started the third inning with the score 8–3.

Candiotti retired his first nine batters, throwing curveballs and fastballs in his first two innings—as he was trying to get the feel for the knuckler early on—before throwing more knuckleballs as the game progressed. The game rolled into the sixth, when Carlos Febles opened the inning with a bunt single and moved to third base on a passed ball and sacrifice bunt. With Febles on third, Candiotti struck out both Carlos Beltran and Joe Randa swinging, keeping the score 8–3. Cleveland scored five runs in the bottom of the sixth—highlighted by Travis Fryman's two-run triple—and suddenly the game was tied.

In the seventh, Candiotti retired the Royals' third, fourth and fifth hitters—Johnny Damon, Mike Sweeney, and Jermaine Dye—in order on nine pitches, before David Justice homered in the bottom of the inning to give the Indians the lead. Cleveland won, 9–8, with Candiotti receiving credit for the victory. The knuckleballer retired 17 of his 19 batters and tossed 5.2 innings with no walks and five strikeouts, giving up only two hits. "He was really tough," noted Febles. "He threw a soft one and a hard one and they were really moving."[2]

Thanks to Candiotti's long relief stint, Cleveland was able to rest its bullpen for the second game of the doubleheader. It was something that Indians rooters had come to love about Candiotti, saving the bullpen and giving Cleveland a chance to win. Just like the old days. "I came in after Charles Nagy was just getting hit really hard in the first couple innings," Candiotti recalls. "They brought me in from the bullpen and I pitched great. After every inning, I'd get a standing ovation from the crowd every time I got back to the dugout. They gave me four loud ovations when I was out there. I mean, it was really spectacular for me.

"It goes to show that the people in Cleveland really respected me. I never wanted to leave in 1991. I made it perfectly clear I didn't want to leave Cleveland. They were a bad team but I really wanted to be there when things turned around. Most players at that time, they couldn't wait to get out of Cleveland. When you had a player who wanted to stay, the people loved that. They respected that. They remembered that. It was like, I was in one last go-around, and all the fans were acknowledging me for all those years in the 1980s when I had to suffer. It really brought a tear to my eye, seeing how the fans were appreciative of all the years I'd given them."

The *Akron Beacon Journal's* Sheldon Ocker was even suggesting that Candiotti should probably be given a long-term contract. "If standing ovations were the currency of the realm," wrote Ocker, "Candiotti would right now be signing a multi-year, multi-million-dollar deal. And that might eventually happen."[3] And based on the Jacobs Field crowd's reaction toward him, Ocker had every reason to believe Candiotti was headed to the starting rotation. "If the fans could call the shots, Tom Candiotti would be the Indians' newest starter," the veteran sportswriter stated.[4] Ocker, who covered Candiotti's career in Cleveland for years, thought he still could be a factor in 1999. "Installing Tom Candiotti in the rotation could be a monumental move," he wrote a week later. "Theoretically, there is no reason why Candiotti and his maddening (to the hitters) knuckleball can't dominate an opposing lineup. At 41, he's a youngster, as knuckleball specialists go. Don't be surprised if Candiotti suddenly shoots to the head of the class."[5]

But things weren't right with Candiotti because of the persistent pain in both of his knees, in particular his left knee. "After I pitched that one game, my left knee swelled up probably twice the size as normal," Candiotti recalls. "And I'm trying to nurse it, get swelling out of it." The pain had gotten so bad that he hoped to stay in the bullpen. But Dwight Gooden, 2–3 with a 6.01 ERA in 15 starts, had been so awful as Cleveland's fifth starter that the Indians had no choice but to bump him from the rotation. Gooden wasn't even averaging five innings per start, and had gone winless in his last eight with an 0–3, 7.14 ERA mark.

When the fifth starter's spot came up on July 10, Candiotti was given a shot against Cincinnati. The Reds jumped on Candiotti for seven runs, knocking him out in the third. They increased their lead to 9–4, as Gooden walked six and allowed two more runs in relief. The Indians, though, rallied to win, 11–10, getting Candiotti off the hook. "The Indians were a potent team," Candiotti recalls. "Every pitcher would've loved to be on that team. If you look at the earned run averages of those pitchers, you can see they benefited from the great Indians' offense. If you were a pitcher on that 1999 Indians team and you pitched five innings every time out, you were going to win a lot of games."

All season long, Cleveland's pitching staff had been brutal, with the starters posting a 5.31 ERA with just one complete game. But with the offense coming through on most nights, the Indians still owned a major league-best 56–30 record, 13 games ahead of second-place Chicago in the AL Central. Cleveland had both Gooden and Candiotti in the bullpen for the next week— while Mark Langston was given a shot as the fifth starter—with the knuckleballer doing well. Candiotti pitched three hitless innings with five strikeouts in a pair of outings in Pittsburgh and Houston (while Gooden had a 4.32 ERA and seven walks in 8.1 innings over four appearances).

"The Indians didn't really have a fifth starter that year," Candiotti says. "Langston was being used more as a left-handed specialist out of the bullpen. Gooden was kind of like a five-inning pitcher at the time. He couldn't give you a whole lot. And my knees were messed up. They tried me in there a couple of times, but I was pitching well in relief, going an inning or two and getting the job done." After five games with Cleveland, Candiotti had 10 strikeouts in 12.1 innings. In his four relief appearances, he'd allowed just two hits over 9.2 innings with a 0.93 ERA.

|  | IP | H | R | ER | BB | SO | HR |  |
|---|---|---|---|---|---|---|---|---|
| 7/3 vs KC (W 9–8) | 5.2 | 2 | 0 | 0 | 0 | 5 | 0 | (W) |
| 7/10 vs CIN (W 11–10) | 2.2 | 7 | 7 | 7 | 2 | 0 | 1 |  |
| 7/17 @ PIT (L 10–13) | 1.0 | 0 | 0 | 0 | 1 | 3 | 0 |  |
| 7/18 @ HOU (L 0–2) | 2.0 | 0 | 0 | 0 | 0 | 2 | 0 |  |
| 7/19 @ HOU (L 2–3) | 1.0 | 0 | 1 | 1 | 1 | 0 | 0 | (L) |

The swelling on Candiotti's knees, though, was simply too much. He pitched on back-to-back nights in Pittsburgh and Houston on July 17–18, and then had to pitch a third straight day. By then, Candiotti thought he was ready to go on the disabled list. But manager Mike Hargrove had other ideas. With a three-game series coming up at Yankee Stadium on July 23–25, the Indians needed that fifth starter, especially with righthander Jaret Wright on the DL. All the newspaper stories early on were indicating they would start Gooden in the opener on July 23 against David Cone in a matchup of former Mets aces in the Yankees' 15,001st regular-season game in franchise history.[6] Hargrove, however, changed his mind, thinking Gooden wasn't the best option. That decision would prove to be disastrous for the Indians. And for Candiotti.

The Indians arrived in New York owning a 58–37 record and a 12-game lead in the AL Central over Chicago—as well as a half-game lead over the AL East-leading Yankees (57–37) for the majors' best record. They were, however, slumping with 11 losses in their last 19, including six of their last seven. Their starting rotation was struggling with a 5.25 ERA. Starter Jaret Wright was on the disabled list, as was their best reliever, Steve Karsay. Cleveland was also without catcher Sandy Alomar, third baseman Travis Fryman, and outfielder Wil Cordero.

In the matchup between the two teams with the best records in baseball, it initially seemed Cleveland was catching New York at the right time as the Yankee bullpen was slumping. Yankee set-up man Mike Stanton, with his 4.45 ERA, had struggled in his last outing against lowly Tampa Bay. Allen Watson—recently acquired following his release by Seattle a month earlier—had a 4.64 ERA. Closer Mariano Rivera had blown three saves in his last eight chances and had pitched in three straight games, meaning he would be unavailable in this series. Jeff Nelson, who had a 5.75 ERA, was on the DL for the second time on the season. Despite the bullpen issues, though, the Yankees turned it up a notch against Cleveland, pulling off a three-game sweep of the Indians.

Though Mike Hargrove originally wanted to start Gooden in the opener on July 23, he ultimately gave the assignment to Candiotti. At that point, however, Candiotti didn't think he could handle the start because of his knees. "Oh, I don't know if my knees can take seven innings of going out there," Candiotti told Hargrove when informed of the starting assignment the night before the game. "I might be able to go a couple of innings here, an inning there, pitch out of the bullpen. I'm pretty comfortable I can give you a couple of innings in relief. But I'm not sure what I can give you as a starter."

But the manager figured he would get more out of Candiotti as a starter than he would from Gooden. As Hargrove explained that weekend, he thought Candiotti "just gives us a better chance to win" in the opener against Yankees righthander David Cone.[7] The fact that Candiotti was starting was noteworthy only because he had deprived every New Yorker of the dream Gooden-Cone matchup. Gooden and Cone, two ex–Met superstar righthanders pitching against each other, would have been perfect. Instead, as the *New York Daily News* called it, it was "Cone against just another guy."[8]

With the score 2–2 in the second inning, the Yankees went ahead, 4–2, on RBI singles by Scott Brosius and Chuck Knoblauch. Candiotti, pitching through the pain in his left knee, retired Joe Girardi and Derek Jeter before Hargrove pulled the knuckleballer with the left-handed Paul O'Neill due up. Candiotti's night was done after throwing just 37 pitches. "This," the *Daily News* remarked sarcastically the following day, "is who's jumped ahead of Gooden" in the Indians' rotation.[9] Though the Indians reached Cone for six runs to take a 6–5 lead in the fourth, they still went on to lose, 8–7, in 10 innings. Their pitching staff was in bad shape after the contest, as they had to use six relievers over the final eight innings. To make things worse, Gooden was supposed to be a long reliever the following night but came up with a migraine headache and wasn't available.

Mark Langston started that second game—a 21–1 Yankee victory—and was ripped for nine runs in 4.1 innings, with Hargrove admitting the lefthander would have been pulled much earlier had Gooden been available. "I guess if you're going to get [a migraine]," Gooden, who spent most of the game passed out in the visitors' clubhouse, said later, "this was a good day to get it."[10] In the fourth inning, pitching coach Phil Regan asked Candiotti if he could pitch at all. Candiotti responded he could in an emergency, but also asked where Gooden was, only to learn about the migraine.

According to the *Cleveland Plain Dealer*'s Paul Hoynes, some players were privately wondering if Gooden's condition was legit. Wrote Hoynes: "The timing of Gooden's migraine was questioned by members of the bullpen. 'I wonder if that headache came around the fifth or sixth inning,' said one reliever."[11] Some, meanwhile, wondered why Doc was on the roster when he wasn't even used in a game when Cleveland needed somebody to stop the bleeding. "Gooden has only two victories in his last 17 starts dating back to last season," wrote one newspaper scribe. "The Indians can't trade him. They are afraid to pitch him. He doesn't even warm up in a game where the Indians give up 21 runs? What's going on here?"[12]

With the score 15–0 in the sixth and with Cleveland out of pitching options, Hargrove gave Candiotti the ball to try and save the depleted bullpen. Unfortunately, Candiotti's arm simply had nothing, even though he threw only 37 pitches the night before. "They informed me Thursday night I was starting on Friday," he recalls. "I hadn't pitched in a game for three days, so that night I threw a bullpen session to get ready for the start. I started on Friday, and then went into the game Saturday in relief. To throw a bullpen session, start the day after, and then relieve the day after that, it wasn't normal. So I really didn't have any arm strength [by Saturday]."

Plus there were those two bad knees. "I remember so distinctly how bad my leg felt, how torn it was," Candiotti says. "I had the brace on. I had to go out and pitch [on Friday] and it was swelling. Then I went out there again the next day because of Dwight's migraine and he couldn't pitch. It was bad." Candiotti allowed five runs while recording only two outs before Hargrove pulled him. "After that, I had to have my knee surgery," Candiotti recalls. "[The left knee] just got so bad I had to get the surgery after that game. If they'd just left me in the bullpen, I could've gotten through it and had my operation after the season was over. But my left knee couldn't take it when I had to keep going out there. My knee was twice the size as normal. It was just a disaster."

The entire series was a disaster. The Indians lost, 2–1, in the finale, their ninth defeat in their last 10 games. Though Cleveland still owned an 11-game division lead, the three-game sweep in New York proved to the baseball world that the Gooden-Langston-Candiotti experiment was a failure. Over Langston's last 250 innings—a span which began on June 5, 1996—his ERA was 5.65. In six of Gooden's 15 starts in 1999, he allowed at least five runs. After Gooden's latest start on July 2 bumped his ERA to 6.01, he was finally demoted to the bullpen. Candiotti? An 11.05 ERA with Cleveland.

With Steve Karsay returning from the DL on July 26, the Indians designated Candiotti for assignment to open a roster spot for him. While his ERA made it seem like he was the obvious choice, some newspaper scribes thought the knuckleballer probably deserved another shot. As Bill Madden of the *New York Daily News* noted before Candiotti's release, Cleveland likely would have said goodbye to Gooden if not for money. "If he wasn't owed another $1.7 million in salary and buyout, it probably would be Dwight Gooden. Gooden still gets it up in the mid–90s, but no longer challenges hitters and has battled with his control all season. Still, he probably will be kept around a while longer and the Indians will take the cheaper route by releasing either Mark Langston or Tom Candiotti."[13]

The *Akron Beacon Journal's* Sheldon Ocker thought there were extenuating circumstances for Candiotti's failure. Without a true role—he was flip-flopping back and forth from relieving to starting—it was hard for him to maintain any consistency. In addition, his knee problems from spring training had continued to hamper him. "Candiotti never had much chance to succeed" given the circumstances, Ocker wrote, while noting the knuckleballer was "impressive" as a reliever and "was ill-equipped" to pitch in the 21–1 debacle especially after he had started the night before.[14]

Though Candiotti's second stint with Cleveland lasted only three weeks, he was still grateful he had the chance to return. "My first game back in Cleveland was just a great feeling, when I won the game in relief and the fans gave me several standing ovations," Candiotti reflects. "It was like getting a final curtain call. As far as I was concerned, it was a great three weeks back. Even though my left knee hurt every time I went out there to pitch, it was great to be back in Cleveland."

A week following his release, Candiotti underwent season-ending arthroscopic surgery on his left knee. If not for that knee, Candiotti would have still been pitching. "A knuckleball's a knuckleball," he says, referring to the fact he could still throw one now, even more than a decade after his retirement. "If it's good, nobody's going to hit it. Unfortunately, it was my knees. The knees affect everything when you throw, when you don't have your lower body strength. In my case, it wasn't the arm. It wasn't the knuckleball. It had to do with my knees."

By January of 2000, Candiotti's knees felt strong enough and he wanted to attempt a comeback. He signed a minor league contract with the Anaheim Angels, and received an invitation to spring training. Though Candiotti's ERA through nine spring appearances was 6.85 in 22.1 innings, Angels manager Mike Scioscia still thought he had pitched decent enough in relief and was willing to tab him as the long reliever out of the bullpen.[15]

But as Candiotti realized during the spring, his left knee was too painful for him to continue. "The pain was just killing me," Candiotti recalls. "Twice during that spring I wanted to retire but Scioscia talked me out of it." At the end of the spring, the Angels decided they simply couldn't afford to have a 41-year-old with recurring knee problems taking up a roster spot.[16] Anaheim released Candiotti on April 1, and the knuckleballer's major league career was officially over.

Though Candiotti had retired, he could still throw the knuckleball, as film director and life-long Yankee fan Billy Crystal found out. During the 2000 season, Crystal got in contact with Candiotti because he needed a knuckleball pitcher for a movie. Crystal was directing a baseball film called *61\**, which was about the Mickey Mantle–Roger Maris home run chase in 1961, and wanted Candiotti to portray Baltimore Orioles knuckleballer Hoyt Wilhelm in the movie.

Candiotti's scene was filmed in the LA Coliseum, which was made to look like Baltimore's Memorial Stadium. Candiotti, playing Wilhelm, was to enter the game to retire Barry Pepper, the actor playing Maris, on a grounder in his last at-bat of the 154th game of the 1961 season. The significance of the scene was that Maris would remain stuck at 59 homers after that contest, one round-tripper short of Babe Ruth's single-season record set in 1927 in a 154-game schedule. Baseball commissioner Ford Frick had said if Maris didn't tie or break the Babe's mark within 154 games, there would be an asterisk next to Maris's home run total in the record book if he hit number 60 in the remaining games.

With Crystal being a stickler for details, he instructed Candiotti to throw his best knuckleballs during the filming so that the scene would look as realistic as possible. As Crystal discovered, Candiotti still had his knuckleball working—too well. He threw one knuckler. And another. And another. And another. Unfortunately, Pepper couldn't hit any of them. Pepper swung and missed 17 straight times before a frustrated Crystal called timeout. "You're doing great," Crystal told Candiotti. "But we're having a film problem here. Either you need to hit his bat, or you're going to have to slow it down so he can hit it!"

On his 18th pitch, Candiotti threw his slowest knuckler. One more problem. It hit Pepper in the chest and he fell to the ground. "He fell down like he'd been shot with a gun," recalls Candiotti. "You look at his face and you see he was acting like he was in a lot of pain. I go, 'Hey, get up. That was only 55 miles an hour! You've gotta get back up after something like that!'"

Interestingly, *61\** isn't Candiotti's favorite sports movie. He still smiles every time *Major League*—a 1989 movie about how the hapless Cleveland Indians came together in spite of their evil owner—is brought up. His most memorable moment about *Major League* wasn't the movie itself, but rather what happened at the ballpark. Candiotti recalls when the Indians had a fireworks night on July 1, 1988, so they could fill Cleveland Stadium to get over-head shots for the movie. "I remember they were doing a shot and—if you watch during the show, [you see] a helicopter shot showing the field with the light and people—they had a Marathon gas night at the old Cleveland Sta-dium. So there were [about 50,000] people. Afterwards, they were going to have fireworks, and they also wanted to have a shot where the helicopter could come and take a picture of that stadium for the movie. So, we were all in the dugout. Our friends and family could come down, and I had my son Brett—who was probably about three years old at the time—with me."

But not for long. Unbeknownst to his father, Brett Candiotti snuck out of the dugout and ran out onto the field, making it all the way to second base! "We were sitting in the dugout after the game waiting for the fireworks to start, and I thought it'd be a good idea to grab Cory Snyder's glove and run the bases," says Brett Candiotti, now in his 20s. "When I started, the crowd started to cheer a bit."

As the aerial shot was being taken, the crowd suddenly began roaring. Soon enough, Tom Candiotti understood why. The fans were laughing and clapping because young Brett was standing out there with a glove. "The PR director down there yelled out, 'Candy! Go get your kid off the field!' So now, I'm running out on the field to get my son," continues Tom Candiotti. "He's stand-ing out at second base and he sees me running out to get him. And he starts running away. I was trying to catch him and all these people were clapping."

"When I was out there, the crowd started to cheer a bit," Brett Candiotti continues, "and when my dad started chasing me, they cheered louder! When he finally caught me, he threw me over his shoulder and the entire stadium started to boo him. It's ironic because he [usually got cheered by the crowd] and now he was getting booed by all his home fans."

It's a moment father and son will always remember. They both have sev-eral black-and-white pictures taken by a photographer, of Tom chasing Brett and later carrying him. They talk about it whenever *Major League* is on. "Every time my son and I watch that movie," says the knuckleballer, "I go, 'That was you out at second base. Can't see it there but I got you out of there.'"

In 2001, Candiotti worked in the Indians' front office for seven months before moving into the broadcast booth with ESPN. He then became a color commentator for the Blue Jays before landing the same gig with the Diamond-backs. Though he didn't stay long in the Cleveland front office, the organiza-tion appreciated having him around. "We brought Candy back," says Indians president Mark Shapiro, "because he's one of those guys that represents a com-bination of a high level of intellect and great, great playing experience with good awareness while he played the game. We thought he'd offer us a tremen-

dous perspective and he did. Candy's one of those rare guys with the person-
ality, intelligence, and playing experience all added up, and would be an asset
to any organization. Certainly, if you look at the career path he took, for a
short period of time, he was back in the organization and made a positive
impact on everybody he was around."

Candiotti admits once a pro athlete's career is over, he still has that com-
petitiveness. Even today, Candiotti looks to other sports for his competition
fix. "I was trying to be a professional golfer," he says. "So I was on those celebrity
players' tours. I got myself to be like a one handicap in golfing. One day, I'm
watching bowling on TV. I saw guys throw a curveball for strikes, and I thought,
'Oh, I can do that.' So I went down and practiced for months, every single day,
for three or four hours, and I got myself good enough where I entered some
PBA tournaments."

Candiotti made his debut in the PBA Tour in Tucson in February 2004,
and was immediately thrown into a group of bowling superstars in his first
tournament. There was Danny Wiseman, a 10-time tour winner, and Walter
Ray Williams, Jr., a six-time PBA Player of the Year and winner of 39 titles,
second on the all-time list. "I actually beat Walter Ray Williams in one game,"
Candiotti laughs. "There I was, just trying it for fun, and I beat the number
one player in the world. How
about that?" Candiotti didn't
advance past the first round in
that tournament, but he kept at
it and competed in several PBA
national and regional events over
the next few years. Candiotti's
efforts paid off in 2007, when he
became the second celebrity to
be inducted into the Interna-

Even at the age of 51, Candiotti's
knuckleball was still working.
Candiotti, shown here in his 50s,
threw batting practice against the
Diamondbacks' hitters in 2008
prior to a game at Boston's Fenway
Park. According to Candiotti, everybody had trouble with his knuckleball, including Arizona slugger
Mark Reynolds, who "swung and
missed seven times" (author's collection.

tional Bowling Museum and Hall of Fame, joining former Pittsburgh Steelers running back Jerome Bettis.

And at age 51, Candiotti also made the Diamondbacks' hitters look silly. On June 25, 2008, Boston knuckleballer Tim Wakefield defeated Arizona, 5–0, at Fenway Park, but the pitching highlight was the Diamondbacks color analyst's stint on the mound during batting practice. "Bob Melvin, the Diamondbacks' manager, asked me to come out early to throw knuckleballs for extra hitting," Candiotti recalls. "I said, 'Bob, I don't think it's a good idea. If you want me to throw knuckleballs, they might not hit mine. So, it's not going to give them a good feeling going into the game.' You can't learn how to hit a knuckleball in one day. You can't have a guy out there throwing batting practice and expect them to learn how to hit it. It just gets hitters in a bad mood."

Melvin, though, insisted the former knuckleballer throw batting practice so that his players could get ready for Wakefield. Candiotti gave in and indeed threw his knuckleball to the Diamondback hitters. The results? "Mark Reynolds swung and missed seven times," Candiotti laughs. "Next thing you know, they can't hit balls out of the [batting] cage. And I wasn't even throwing a good knuckleball!"

Tom Candiotti will be known first and foremost as a knuckleball pitcher. That knuckler, a pitch that he always seemed to have good command of by simply aiming for the catcher's mask and trusting the ball to somehow break into the strike zone consistently, allowed him to prolong his career until knee problems forced him to retire after 16 seasons. But that knuckleball still works even to this day, as Billy Crystal, Barry Pepper, and Mark Reynolds found out. Candiotti, who turns 57 in August of 2014, isn't about to make a comeback on the mound, though. But who knows? With Arizona owning baseball's worst bullpen in 2010, then-manager A.J. Hinch made a comment in jest to the former knuckleballer.

"We're on the team's charter plane one night after another loss," recalls Candiotti. "A.J. sees me and goes, 'How long will it take for you to get your arm ready?'"

# Appendix: Statistics

## Thomas Caesar Candiotti

Born in Walnut Creek, California, August 31, 1957; throws right; bats right; 6'3"; 205 lbs.

### Minor League Baseball Statistics

| Year | Team | W–L | ERA | G | GS | CG | SHO | IP | H | BB | SO | HR |
|------|------|-----|-----|---|----|----|-----|----|----|----|----|----|
| 1979 | Victoria (A-) | 5– 1 | 2.44 | 12 | 9 | 3 | 0 | 70.0 | 63 | 16 | 66 | 1 |
| 1980 | Jacksonville (AA) | 7– 8 | 2.77 | 17 | 17 | 8 | 2 | 117.0 | 98 | 40 | 93 | 6 |
| 1980 | Fort Myers (A) | 3– 2 | 2.25 | 7 | 5 | 3 | 0 | 44.0 | 32 | 9 | 31 | 0 |
| 1981 | El Paso (AA) | 7– 6 | 2.80 | 21 | 14 | 6 | 1 | 119.0 | 137 | 27 | 68 | 8 |
| 1982 | Vancouver (AAA) | | | | Did Not Pitch—Injured | | | | | | | |
| 1983 | El Paso (AA) | 1– 0 | 2.92 | 7 | 0 | 0 | 0 | 24.2 | 23 | 7 | 18 | 1 |
| 1983 | Vancouver (AAA) | 6– 4 | 2.81 | 15 | 14 | 5 | 2 | 99.1 | 87 | 16 | 61 | 6 |
| 1984 | Beloit (A) | 0– 1 | 2.70 | 2 | 2 | 0 | 0 | 10.0 | 12 | 5 | 12 | 1 |
| 1984 | Vancouver (AAA) | 8– 4 | 2.89 | 15 | 15 | 4 | 0 | 96.2 | 96 | 22 | 53 | 4 |
| 1985 | El Paso (AA) | 1– 0 | 2.76 | 4 | 4 | 1 | 1 | 29.1 | 29 | 7 | 16 | 2 |
| 1985 | Vancouver (AAA) | 9–13 | 3.94 | 24 | 24 | 5 | 1 | 150.2 | 178 | 36 | 97 | 14 |
| 1996 | San Bernardino (A+) | 0– 1 | 5.00 | 2 | 2 | 0 | 0 | 9.0 | 11 | 4 | 10 | 0 |

| | W–L | ERA | G | GS | CG | SHO | IP | H | BB | SO | HR |
|------|-----|-----|---|----|----|-----|----|----|----|----|----|
| Career | 47–40 | 2.99 | 126 | 106 | 35 | 7 | 769.2 | 766 | 189 | 525 | 43 |

### Major League Baseball Statistics

REGULAR SEASON

| Year | Team | W–L | ERA | G | GS | CG | SHO | IP | H | BB | SO | HR |
|------|------|-----|-----|---|----|----|-----|----|----|----|----|----|
| 1983 | MIL | 4– 4 | 3.23 | 10 | 8 | 2 | 1 | 55.2 | 62 | 16 | 21 | 4 |
| 1984 | MIL | 2– 2 | 5.29 | 8 | 6 | 0 | 0 | 32.1 | 38 | 10 | 23 | 5 |
| 1986 | CLE | 16–12 | 3.57 | 36 | 34 | 17 | 3 | 252.1 | 234 | 106 | 167 | 18 |
| 1987 | CLE | 7–18 | 4.78 | 32 | 32 | 7 | 2 | 201.2 | 193 | 93 | 111 | 28 |

| Year | Team | W–L | ERA | G | GS | CG | SHO | IP | H | BB | SO | HR |
|------|------|-----|-----|---|----|----|----|----|----|----|----|-----|
| 1988 | CLE | 14– 8 | 3.28 | 31 | 31 | 11 | 1 | 216.2 | 225 | 53 | 137 | 15 |
| 1989 | CLE | 13–10 | 3.10 | 31 | 31 | 4 | 0 | 206.0 | 188 | 55 | 124 | 10 |
| 1990 | CLE | 15–11 | 3.65 | 31 | 29 | 3 | 1 | 202.0 | 207 | 55 | 128 | 23 |
| 1991 | CLE | 7– 6 | 2.24 | 15 | 15 | 3 | 0 | 108.1 | 88 | 28 | 86 | 6 |
| 1991 | TOR | 6– 7 | 2.98 | 19 | 19 | 3 | 0 | 129.2 | 114 | 45 | 81 | 6 |
| 1991 | Total | 13–13 | 2.65 | 34 | 34 | 6 | 0 | 238.0 | 202 | 73 | 167 | 12 |
| 1992 | LA | 11–15 | 3.00 | 32 | 30 | 6 | 2 | 203.2 | 177 | 63 | 152 | 13 |
| 1993 | LA | 8–10 | 3.12 | 33 | 32 | 2 | 0 | 213.2 | 192 | 71 | 155 | 12 |
| 1994 | LA | 7– 7 | 4.12 | 23 | 22 | 5 | 0 | 153.0 | 149 | 54 | 102 | 9 |
| 1995 | LA | 7–14 | 3.50 | 30 | 30 | 1 | 1 | 190.1 | 187 | 58 | 141 | 18 |
| 1996 | LA | 9–11 | 4.49 | 28 | 27 | 1 | 0 | 152.1 | 172 | 43 | 79 | 18 |
| 1997 | LA | 10– 7 | 3.60 | 41 | 18 | 0 | 0 | 135.0 | 128 | 40 | 89 | 21 |
| 1998 | OAK | 11–16 | 4.84 | 33 | 33 | 3 | 0 | 201.0 | 222 | 63 | 98 | 30 |
| 1999 | OAK | 3– 5 | 6.35 | 11 | 11 | 0 | 0 | 56.2 | 67 | 23 | 30 | 11 |
| 1999 | CLE | 1– 1 | 11.05 | 7 | 2 | 0 | 0 | 14.2 | 19 | 7 | 11 | 3 |
| 1999 | Total | 4– 6 | 7.32 | 18 | 13 | 0 | 0 | 71.1 | 86 | 30 | 41 | 14 |

| | W–L | ERA | G | GS | CG | SHO | IP | H | BB | SO | HR |
|---|-----|-----|---|----|----|----|----|----|----|----|-----|
| Career | 151–164 | 3.73 | 451 | 410 | 68 | 11 | 2725.0 | 2662 | 883 | 1735 | 250 |

**POSTSEASON**

| Year | Team | Series | W–L | ERA | G | GS | CG | SHO | IP | H | BB | SO | HR |
|------|------|--------|-----|-----|---|----|----|----|----|----|----|----|-----|
| 1991 | TOR | ALCS | 0–1 | 8.22 | 2 | 2 | 0 | 0 | 7.2 | 17 | 2 | 5 | 1 |
| 1995 | LA | NLDS | | | | | Did Not Pitch | | | | | | |
| 1996 | LA | NLDS | 0–0 | 0.00 | 1 | 0 | 0 | 0 | 2.0 | 0 | 0 | 1 | 0 |
| Career | | | 0–1 | 6.52 | 3 | 2 | 0 | 0 | 9.2 | 17 | 2 | 6 | 1 |

# Chapter Notes

## Preface

1. Honorable mention: Gene Bearden, 1948 Cleveland Indians. Ryan somehow didn't consider the three-month dominance of the Indians' rookie knuckleballer, whose efforts deprived New Englanders of an all–Boston World Series. From July 8 onwards, including the World Series, Bearden's 27 appearances (19 starts) included 12 complete games, five shutouts, 159.1 innings, a 15–4 record, two saves, and a 2.03 ERA. In his final eight starts, he was 8–0 with seven complete games, including a win over the Red Sox in a one-game playoff at Fenway for the AL pennant (while pitching on only one day of rest) and a World Series shutout over the Boston Braves. Over a 10-day period, Bearden also pitched four complete-game victories. In Cleveland's six-game World Series triumph over the Braves, Bearden also saved the final contest. Since he also did go 20–7 *and* win the league ERA title (2.43) as a rookie, Bearden's 1948 performance, it can be argued, easily trumps Wakefield's 1995 season.

2. Bob Ryan, "Wakefield Has A Leg to Stand On," *Boston Globe*, February 24, 1997.

3. Bill Plaschke, "Dodgers Should Bring Back Pedro Martinez," *Los Angeles Times*, March 12, 2009.

## Introduction

1. Anthony Giacalone, "Len Barker's Perfect Game," baseballthinkfactory.org, May 15, 2006.

2. Steve Aschburner, "Brewers Settle for Split," *Milwaukee Journal*, August 9, 1983.

3. "Candiotti Shows Brewers," *Milwaukee Journal*, May 22, 1986.

4. Neil MacCarl, "Chilly Stadium No Prob-

lem for Indians' Knuckleball Ace," *Toronto Star*, April 5, 1987.

## Chapter 1

1. Jonah Keri, "Interview with Dr. Frank Jobe," ESPN.com, September 13, 2007.

2. Ibid.

3. Lindsay Berra, "Force of Habit," *ESPN The Magazine*, April 2, 2012.

4. Dan Schlossberg, *The 300 Club: Have We Seen the Last of Baseball's 300-Game Winners?* (Overland Park, KS: Ascend Books, 2010), p. 266.

5. Jayson Stark, "Tommy John Surgery: Cutting Edge to Commonplace," ESPN.com, August 13, 2003.

6. Schlossberg, *The 300 Club*, p. 266.

7. Jayson Stark, "Tommy John Surgery: Cutting Edge to Commonplace," ESPN.com, August 13, 2003.

8. Rogers Sportsnet telecast, Tigers vs. Blue Jays, August 28, 2010.

9. Ibid.

10. Jonah Keri, "Interview with Dr. Frank Jobe," ESPN.com, September 13, 2007.

11. Even as of 2013, Candiotti's name still shows up on the team's official website as having nine walks in that Detroit contest to tie the single-game record. Candiotti, in fact, never came close to nine walks in any game with the Blue Jays. I contacted the organization by email in 2010 to notify them of the error, but to this day Candiotti's name still appears on the blue-jays.com website. Also, in the team's media guide, his combined one-hitter with Tom Henke from August 28, 1991, was not included on the list of one-hitters, even though other combined one-hit efforts in club history were listed.

12. Adam Kilgore, "Stephen Strasburg 'Probably' Needs Tommy John Surgery, Will Miss 12 to 18 Months," *Washington Post*, August 27, 2010.

13. Wikipedia entry of Stephen Strasburg, http://en.wikipedia.org/wiki/Stephen_Strasburg.

## Chapter 2

1. Peter Pascarelli, "Another Phenom— Phils Will Get a Look at Pirates' DeLeon," *Philadelphia Inquirer*, August 10, 1983.

2. Thomas Boswell, "Mighty Brewers Have Gone From Muscle to Hustle Team," *Washington Post*, August 22, 1983.

3. Ibid.

4. Ibid.

5. "Candiotti Pitches Brewers to Sweep," Associated Press/*Bangor Daily News*, August 19, 1983.

6. Bill Brophy, "Brewers Reclaim East Lead," *Wisconsin State Journal*, August 18, 1983.

7. Ibid.

8. Tom Flaherty, "Candiotti Beats Idol in the Bionic Battle," *Milwaukee Journal*, August 26, 1983.

9. "Candiotti Act Leaves Vuke Awaiting Turn," *Milwaukee Sentinel*, August 26, 1983.

10. Tom Flaherty, "Brewer Notes," *Milwaukee Journal*, August 26, 1983.

11. Tom Flaherty, "Candiotti Beats Idol in the Bionic Battle," *Milwaukee Journal*, August 26, 1983.

12. Thomas Boswell, "Mighty Brewers Have Gone From Muscle to Hustle Team," *Washington Post*, August 22, 1983.

13. Jim Cohen, "Sports Et Cetera," *Milwaukee Journal*, August 26, 1983.

14. Dan Hafner, "Candiotti Makes Slow Work of the Yankees, 3–1," *Los Angeles Times*, September 6, 1983.

15. Ibid.

16. "Brewers' Brouhard on Target with Guess," *The Day-New London*, September 6, 1983.

17. Ibid.

18. Bill Brophy, "Brewers Move Back to Second," *Wisconsin State Journal*, September 6, 1983.

19. Tom Flaherty, "Baseball," *Milwaukee Journal*, February 12, 1984.

## Chapter 3

1. Ian Browne, "Knuckleballers' Paths as Tricky as the Pitch," MLB.com, August 20, 2010.

2. Jack Etkin, "Aging Pitchers Knuckle Down for Long Haul," *Rocky Mountain News*, August 8, 1993.

3. Ibid.

4. Woody Paige, "Hurlers Coming to Grips with Awkward Pitch," *Denver Post*, May 31, 1993.

5. Matt Trowbridge, "Baseball's Unique Pitch," *Illinois Rockford Register Star*, May 12, 2006.

6. Ibid.

7. Mark Emmons, "Knuckling Under," *Orange County Register*, August 11, 1999.

8. Tom Verducci, "Radar Love," *Sports Illustrated*, April 4, 2011.

9. "West Coast Conference Announces WCC/Rawlings 40th Anniversary Baseball Team," WCCSports.com, January 3, 2007.

10. "Baseball Mourns the Loss of Miles McAfee," smcgaels.com, March 12, 2009.

11. Ibid.

12. "Mariners Shut Down Hernandez For Final Weekend," Yahoo! Sports/Associated Press, September 30, 2010.

13. Stephen Hawkins, "Mariners Undecided on Hernandez Pitching Again," Yahoo! Sports/Associated Press, September 29, 2010.

14. Mark Zwolinski, "Jays' Reyes Can Find Inspiration in Fellow-Streaker Matt Keough," *Toronto Star*, May 29, 2011.

15. Dan Hafner, "Candiotti Makes Slow Work of the Yankees, 3–1," *Los Angeles Times*, September 6, 1983.

16. Gordon Verrell, "Trench Warfare: Baseball Strike Appears Certain," *Long Beach Press-Telegram*, June 19, 1994.

17. "West Coast Conference Announces WCC/Rawlings 40th Anniversary Baseball Team," WCCSports.com, January 3, 2007.

18. According to Baseball-Reference.com, the 1980 Montgomery Rebels did not have a player by the name of Cochrane on their roster. However, they had a left-handed hitter named Jeff Kenaga, whose name at least sounded similar. Other left-handed hitters who played on that Rebels club were Gary Armstrong, Ted Dasen, Todd Ervin, Les Filkins, Steven Michael, and Michael Schoeller.

19. Bob Finnigan, "Candiotti Becoming Diamond Dinosaur," *Seattle Times*, June 28, 1991.

## Chapter 4

1. Tom Flaherty, "Porter Makes His Pitch to Join Brewers' Starting Rotation," *Milwaukee Journal*, April 6, 1984.

2. Bob Wolf, "...and Candiotti is Forgotten Man," *Milwaukee Journal*, March 25, 1984.

3. Bob Wolf, "Candiotti Considers His Future," *Milwaukee Journal*, March 25, 1984.

4. Ibid.

5. Tom Flaherty, "What's Brewing?" *Milwaukee Journal*, January 20, 1985.

6. Peter Morris, *A Game of Inches: The Stories Behind the Innovations That Shaped Base-*

*ball: The Game on the Field (Volume 1)* (Chicago: Ivan R. Dee, 2006), pp. 156–160.

7. Fox 5 telecast, Indians vs. Yankees, July 23, 1999.

8. Tom McCollister, "Trick Pitch Not A Treat For Batters," *Atlanta Journal*, October 9, 1992.

9. Jeff Lenihan, "Foes Still Knuckle Under to Candiotti and Hough," *Minneapolis Star Tribune*, August 11, 1991.

10. Maryann Hudson, "Hanging On By His Fingertips," *Los Angeles Times*, July 31, 1994.

11. Kevin Maney, "Skill in Throwing Knuckleball Deserves More Respect," *USA Today/Baseball Digest*, October 1998.

12. George Will, *Men at Work: The Craft of Baseball* (New York: Harper, 1990), p. 86.

13. Rich Westcott, *Winningest Pitchers: Baseball's 300-Game Winners* (Philadelphia: Temple University Press, 2002), p. 157.

14. Tom Haudricourt, "Orioles Flatten Brewers Early," *Milwaukee Sentinel*, September 27, 1985.

15. Dan O'Neill, "Knuckle Down," *St. Louis Post-Dispatch*, June 13, 1993.

16. Jason Beck, "Knuckleballer to Knuckleballer," MLB.com, March 11, 2003.

17. Jerome Holtzman, "How Teams Shape Up for '87 Division Races," *Baseball Digest*, April 1987, p. 25.

## Chapter 5

1. CBS telecast, Twins vs. Blue Jays, October 13, 1991.

2. Gerry Monigan, "Rangers Stop Royals," United Press International, March 20, 1986.

3. Tracy Ringolsby, "This And That," *Dallas Morning News/Orlando Sentinel*, March 23, 1986.

4. Sheldon Ocker, "Tribe's Candiotti Does Well, But..." *Akron Beacon Journal*, April 11, 1986.

5. "Candiotti Has Orioles Sold on His New Pitch," *Eugene-Oregon Register-Guard*/Associated Press, April 22, 1986.

6. "Candiotti Shows Brewers," *Milwaukee Journal*, May 22, 1986.

7. Jeff Mayers, "Candiotti Doesn't Get Mad, He Just Gets Even," Associated Press/*The Vindicator*, May 22, 1986.

8. Tom Haudricourt, "Candiotti Shuts Off Brewers," *Milwaukee Sentinel*, May 22, 1986.

9. Terry Pluto, "Knucksie II? Idol Niekro is Inspiration for Candiotti," *Akron Beacon Journal*, August 5, 1986.

10. Murray Chass, "Demise and Pall of the Indians," *New York Times*, July 2, 1991.

11. James A. Toman, *Cleveland Stadium: The Last Chapter* (Cleveland: Cleveland Landmarks Press, 1997), p. 87.

12. Sheldon Ocker, "Tribe, Yankees Split Before 65,394," *Akron Beacon Journal*, August 2, 1986.

13. Candiotti also became only the fifth major league pitcher since 1916 with 12 or more strikeouts and no walks against the Minnesota Twins/Washington Senators franchise. For the decade of the 1980s, Candiotti was one of only 11 Indians pitchers to register at least 10 strikeouts in a game, against any opponent. Barker led the way with nine such games in the 1980s, followed by Blyleven with six and Candiotti was third with five.

14. In 1988, Blyleven apparently would do something fairly similar to help Twins left-hander Allan Anderson win the league ERA title, according to *Milwaukee Sentinel* journalist Tom Haudricourt in an October 3, 1998, piece titled "Higuera Isn't Upset by Losing ERA Title." Blyleven was the person who, on the season's penultimate night, informed manager Tom Kelly that Anderson would win the championship by simply sitting out his scheduled start in the season finale. By not pitching, he finished with a 2.4465 ERA, ahead of Milwaukee's Teddy Higuera, despite the fact that Anderson had not led the ERA race all season! Higuera, whose ERA was 2.41 entering the penultimate day, finished at 2.4545 after allowing three earned runs in 6.2 innings that night. Kelly gave Anderson a choice, and the lefty decided not to pitch, winning the ERA championship.

## Chapter 6

1. Sheldon Ocker, "Candiotti Overcomes Tribe, Foe," *Akron Beacon Journal*, August 25, 1988.

2. Pete Dougherty, "Baseball: Game Story," *Green Bay Press-Gazette/USA Today*, August 2, 1989.

3. Ibid.

4. Andy Baggot, "Brewers Thrown a Curve," *Wisconsin State Journal*, August 3, 1989.

5. Ibid.

6. Jerome Holtzman, "Here's the Pitch on AL East Jam," *Chicago Tribune*, August 3, 1989.

7. "Vote: What Are the Top National League blunders?" ESPN SportsNation, http://espn.go.com/sportsnation/poll/_/id/2185, May 24, 2006.

8. Dan O'Neill, "Knuckle Down," *St. Louis Post-Dispatch*, June 13, 1993.

9. "Rookies Keep Brewers, Pirates in Thick of Title Races," United Press International/*Iowa Telegraph-Herald*, August 26, 1983.

10. "Angels Blanked Again," United Press International/*Valley Independent*, August 26, 1983.

11. Bill Brophy, "Brewers Move Back to Second," *Wisconsin State Journal*, September 6, 1983.

12. Ibid.

13. "It's 'Time for Indians' to Live Up to Billing, Open in Toronto Today," *The Vindicator*/Associated Press, April 6, 1987.

14. "Baseball," *Chicago Tribune*, March 16, 1987.

15. Sheldon Ocker, "No Dazzle, No Flutter, No Strikes," *Akron Beacon Journal*, April 7, 1987; Sheldon Ocker, "Indians' Candiotti Displays Top Form in Shutout of A's," *Akron Beacon Journal*, March 28, 1987.

16. Neil MacCarl, "Chilly Stadium No Problem for Indians' Knuckleball Ace," *Toronto Star*, April 5, 1987.

17. Bud Geracie, "Jackson Blames Distractions for His Troubles at the Plate," *San Jose Mercury News*, March 28, 1987.

18. Alex Semchuck, "Addie Joss," SABR Baseball Biography Project, http://sabr.org/bioproj/person/5e51b2e7; Baseball-Reference.com.

19. Michael Martinez, "Indians Blank Yankees on Candiotti's One-Hitter," Associated Press/*New York Times*, August 4, 1987.

## Chapter 7

1. Bill Livingston, "ALCS is 'Odd' in Year of Ex-Indians," *Cleveland Plain Dealer*, October 8, 1991.

2. Tracy Ringolsby, "Pitching Could Make Indians' Summer Long," *Dallas Morning News*, March 27, 1988.

3. Ben Brown, "Mounds of Improvement," *USA Today*, April 28, 1988.

4. Russell Schneider and Rich Schneider, *Tales from the Tribe Dugout: A Collection of the Greatest Cleveland Indians Stories Ever Told* (Champaign, IL: Sports Publishing, 2002), p. 173.

5. Terry Pluto, "Knucksie II? Idol Niekro Is Inspiration for Candiotti," *Akron Beacon Journal*, August 5, 1986.

6. Bob Gibson and Reggie Jackson, *Sixty Feet, Six Inches: A Hall of Fame Pitcher and a Hall of Fame Hitter Talk About How the Game is Played* (New York: Doubleday, 2009), p. 88.

7. "Candiotti Selected AL Player of Week," United Press International/*South Florida Sun Sentinel*, August 11, 1987.

8. "American League Roundup: Candiotti One-Hits Yankees," *Los Angeles Times*, August 4, 1987.

9. Wikipedia entry of Silver King, http:// en.wikipedia.org/wiki/Silver_King_(baseball); Wikipedia entry of No-hitter, http://en.wikipedia.org/wiki/No-hitter.

10. Tom Gage, "Baseball: Game Story," *USA Today*, September 3, 1987.

11. Dick Fenlon, "Indians' Candiotti Adjusts Repertoire," *Columbus Dispatch*, March 9, 1988.

12. Bill James, *Bill James Baseball Abstract, 1988* (New York: Ballantine Books, 1988).

13. Sheldon Ocker, "Tribe Can Keep Candiotti, for a Few Million," *Akron Beacon Journal*, December 20, 1990.

## Chapter 8

1. "Mariners Continue Rush," Associated Press/*Spokesman-Review*, March 31, 1988.

2. "Candiotti Too Much for Twins," Associated Press/*Toledo Blade*, April 15, 1988.

3. Alan Solomon, "After Great Start, Sox Are Finished," *Chicago Tribune*, April 22, 1990.

4. Sean McAdam, "Red Sox Journal: Pal or Not, Tribe's Candiotti 'Cleans' Sox' Clark," *Providence Journal*, April 15, 1991.

5. Fox 5 telecast, Indians vs. Yankees, July 23, 1999.

6. Tim McCarver and Danny Peary, *Tim McCarver's Baseball for Brain Surgeons and Other Fans* (New York: Villard, 1999), p. 56.

7. Richard Justice, "Orioles Get Three Hits, Make Four Errors and Lose, 7–0," *Washington Post*, April 22, 1986.

8. Roberto Dias, "Indians Win Again," United Press International/*The Bryan Times*, July 12, 1986.

9. "Candiotti Shuts Out Minnesota," Associated Press/*Toledo Blade*, September 16, 1986.

10. "Indians Sweep Away Red Sox," Associated Press/*The Day-New London, Conn.*, August 30, 1987.

11. Pete Dougherty, "Baseball: Game Story," *Green Bay Press-Gazette*/*USA Today*, August 2, 1989.

12. Earl Bloom, "Candiotti, Indians Shut Down Angels," *Orange County Register*, May 31, 1990.

13. Sean McAdam, "Candiotti Puts Brakes on Sox' Express," *Providence Journal*, June 11, 1990.

14. Mel Antonen, "Catchers to Knuckle Down with Candiotti on Jays' Staff," *USA Today*, June 28, 1991.

15. Carrie Muskat, "Morris Pitches for Heroes," United Press International/*The Bryan Times*, October 8, 1991.

16. Terry Johnson, "Take It From AL: Candiotti Tough," *Torrance Daily Breeze*, March 13, 1992.

17. Kevin Kernan, "Padres Lose in Home

Opener," *San Diego Union-Tribune*, April 10, 1992.

18. "Dodgers, Candiotti Work Over Giants," *Lewiston Morning Tribune*/Associated Press, June 22, 1997.

19. Ross Newhan, "Belated Indian Uprising," *Los Angeles Times*, May 3, 1988.

20. Jake Curtis, "Knuckleball Seems To Be Losing Grip in Majors," *San Francisco Chronicle*, July 7, 1991.

21. "Game 80: Crush Your Enemies," http://www.battersbox.ca, July 2, 2005.

22. Tony Cooper, "Candiotti's Knuckleballs Baffle Giants," *San Francisco Chronicle*, July 29, 1993.

23. Susan Slusser, "Giants Knuckle Under: Candiotti, Dodgers Frustrate SF—Again," *Sacramento Bee*, July 29, 1993.

24. Sean McAdam, "Red Sox Journal: Pal or Not, Tribe's Candiotti 'Cleans' Sox' Clark," *Providence Journal*, April 15, 1991.

25. "Tribe's Belle Lets Bat Do the Talking Again," Associated Press/*Ohio Chronicle Telegram*, May 2, 1991.

26. Ken Rosenthal, "They're All Still 'Crankees' After All These Years," *Baltimore Sun*, August 12, 1989.

## Chapter 9

1. Richard Hoffer, "Every Game Is A Home Game," *Sports Illustrated*, April 16, 1990.

2. Russell Schneider, "Players Guarded on Trade," *Cleveland Plain Dealer*, June 28, 1991.

3. "Candiotti Back With the Indians," Associated Press, June 29, 1999.

4. Bob Sherwin, "Long-Term Shortstop Solution?" *Seattle Times*, July 22, 1990.

5. "New York Sluggers Spoil Indian Bid for 1-hit Win," Associated Press/*Kentucky New Era*, August 4, 1990.

6. "Hitters Say No-No to No-Hitter History Friday Night," *Salina Journal*/Associated Press, August 5, 1990.

7. As of 2013, no Indians pitcher has registered five straight 200-inning seasons since Candiotti accomplished the feat from 1986 to 1990. In fact, as of 2013, only seven Tribe pitchers have even recorded consecutive 200-inning seasons: Greg Swindell (1990–91), Charles Nagy (1991–92, 1996–99), Dave Burba (1998–99), Bartolo Colon (1998–99), Jake Westbrook (2004–06), Cliff Lee (2005–06), and Justin Masterson (2011–12).

8. Steve Love, "Indians Can Pay Candiotti Now... Or Lose Him Later," *Akron Beacon Journal*, January 30, 1991.

9. Murray Chass, "Baseball: Rijo Is Given a 3-Year Contract for $9 Million by Reds," *New York Times*, February 20, 1991.

10. Bob Hertzel, "Drabek Comes in With a High, Hard One," *Pittsburgh Press*, February 15, 1991; "Putting Salaries in Perspective," *Chicago Tribune*, March 10, 1991.

11. "Notes," *Chicago Tribune*, October 20, 1991.

12. "Yankees Sign Witt for 3 Years, $8 Million," *St. Petersburg Times*, January 3, 1991.

13. "Notes," *Chicago Tribune*, October 20, 1991.

14. Paul Hoynes, "Return to Tribe Unlikely," *Cleveland Plain Dealer*, November 14, 1991.

15. "Feller Not Impressed by Today's Pitchers," Associated Press/*Seattle Times*, March 17, 1991.

16. Allan Ryan, "Indians Looking and Jays Have What They Need," *Toronto Star*, June 11, 1991.

17. Peter Gammons, "Sooner or Later, a Good Deal," *Boston Globe*, June 30, 1991.

18. "Where Will Bo Go for Chisox Debut? / Stieb Still Ailing," Associated Press/*Gainesville Sun*, August 21, 1991.

19. "Carter Has Last Laugh," *Toledo Blade*, June 13, 1991.

20. Paul Hoynes, "Tribe's Win Streak Ends at One with 1–0 Loss," *Cleveland Plain Dealer*, June 13, 1991.

## Chapter 10

1. Barry Rozner, "Cubs Talking About Candiotti," *Chicago Daily Herald*, June 7, 1991.

2. Peter Gammons, "Clubs Making Futile Pitches," *Boston Globe*, June 16, 1991.

3. "Where Will Bo Go for Chisox Debut? / Stieb Still Ailing," Associated Press/*Gainesville Sun*, August 21, 1991.

4. "6-Player Deal Sends Candiotti to Jays," *New York Times*/Associated Press, June 28, 1991.

5. "Ripken, Fielder Light up SkyDome in HR Derby," *Seattle Times*, July 9, 1991.

6. Ibid.

7. Bill Madden, "Gentlemen, Start Your Pennant Races," *New York Daily News*/*Austin American-Statesman*, July 11, 1991.

8. "Jays Gave Away Too Much in Trade," *Kitchener-Waterloo Record*, June 28, 1991.

9. Rosie DiManno, *Glory Jays: Canada's World Series Champions* (Champaign, IL: Sagamore, 1993), p. 84.

10. Mel Antonen, "Catchers to Knuckle Down with Candiotti on Jays' Staff," *USA Today*, June 28, 1991.

11. Ibid.

12. Ibid.

13. Ed Giuliotti, "Indians Get Three of a Kind, But Jays Get Ace They Need," *South Florida Sun-Sentinel*, June 30, 1991.

14. Paul Hoynes, "Red Sox Wanted Candiotti," *Cleveland Plain Dealer*, July 3, 1991.

15. Bill Madden, "Busy Gillick Keeping Jays Potent With Trades," *New York Daily News/ Austin American-Statesman*, July 1, 1991.

16. Ibid.

17. Ross Newhan, "All-Star Voters Must Be Watching Different Games," *Los Angeles Times*, June 30, 1991.

18. Ed Giuliotti, "Indians Get Three of a Kind, But Jays Get Ace They Need," *South Florida Sun-Sentinel*, June 30, 1991.

19. In the 2–0 victory over Texas, Candiotti struck out 10 with no walks over eight innings, and entered the Blue Jays' record books with the performance. He became the first pitcher ever in SkyDome history to pitch scoreless baseball while fanning at least 10 batters without issuing any walks. As of the 2013 season, only Candiotti, Roger Clemens (1997, 1998), Chris Carpenter (2001), and Roy Halladay (2005) have accomplished that feat at the ballpark now known as Rogers Centre.

20. *Four Million Memories: The 1991 Toronto Blue Jays* Highlight Video.

21. The Sports Network, *TSN 25 Years: 25 Years of Hits and Highlights, Top Tens and Turning Points, Through the Lens of Canada's Sports Network* (Hoboken, NJ: Wiley, 2009), p. 44.

22. http://www.ballparksofbaseball.com.

23. Tim Kawakami, "Moving Beyond," *Los Angeles Times*, March 23, 1994.

24. Wikipedia entry of Cleveland Stadium, http://en.wikipedia.org/wiki/Cleveland_Stadium.

25. Murray Chass, "Demise and Pall of the Indians," *New York Times*, July 2, 1991.

26. Ibid.

27. Allan Ryan, "Last-Inning Blues Hit Candiotti Again," *Toronto Star*, July 24, 1991.

28. Tracy Ringolsby, "Candiotti Fills Bill for Blue Jays," *Dallas Morning News*, October 8, 1991.

29. Peter Gammons, "Sooner or Later, a Good Deal," *Boston Globe*, June 30, 1991.

30. Hank Hersch, "Flying High," *Sports Illustrated*, August 26, 1991.

31. "Jays Earn 2-Game Lead," *Associated Press/Kitchener-Waterloo Record*, August 29, 1991.

32. Allan Ryan, "TERRIFIC! Candy Man Hurls One-Hitter," *Toronto Star*, August 29, 1991.

33. "American League: Red Sox Bobble Chance," *Associated Press/Milwaukee Journal*, September 15, 1991.

## Chapter 11

1. "Baseball: 8th-Inning Burst by Bonds Helps Pirates Hold off Reds," *Associated Press/*

*New York Times*, July 12, 1991; 1991 Toronto Blue Jays split stats on Baseball-Reference.com.

2. Bill Livingston, "ALCS Is 'Odd' in Year of Ex-Indians," *Cleveland Plain Dealer*, October 8, 1991.

3. Ibid.

4. Tracy Ringolsby, "Candiotti Fills Bill for Blue Jays," *Dallas Morning News*, October 8, 1991.

5. Jennifer Frey, "From Worst to First: Candiotti Gets the Call Tonight to Cap Escape From Cleveland," *Philadelphia Daily News*, October 8, 1991.

6. Bill Livingston, "ALCS Is 'Odd' in Year of Ex-Indians," *Cleveland Plain Dealer*, October 8, 1991.

7. Paul Hoynes, "Candiotti Opens ALCS for Toronto," *Cleveland Plain Dealer*, October 8, 1991.

8. "Toronto Out to 'Steal' AL Title," *Associated Press/Lodi News-Sentinel*, October 8, 1991.

9. Jim Proudfoot, "Jays Could Go All The Way If Gruber Saves The Day," *Toronto Star*, October 10, 1991.

10. Bill Madden, "Busy Gillick Keeping Jays Potent With Trades," *New York Daily News/ Austin American-Statesman*, July 1, 1991.

11. Ross Newhan, "Once Again Toronto Comes up Short," *Los Angeles Times*, October 14, 1991.

12. Larry Grossman, *A Baseball Addict's Diary: The Blue Jays' 1991 Rollercoaster* (Toronto: Penguin Group, 1991), p. 205.

13. Ibid.

14. Allan Ryan, "Candiotti in Opener; Key Draws Game 3," *Toronto Star*, October 5, 1991.

15. Grossman, *A Baseball Addict's Diary*, p. 205.

16. Allan Ryan, "Gaston's Hiding the Key to Jays' Playoff Pitching," *Toronto Star*, October 4, 1991.

17. John Kernaghan, "Candy's Showing Puts Plans out the Window," *Hamilton Spectator*, October 9, 1991.

18. Dave Perkins, "Settled Rotation Gives the Twins Big Advantage," *Toronto Star*, October 7, 1991.

19. Ibid.

20. Allan Ryan, "Candiotti in Opener; Key Draws Game 3," *Toronto Star*, October 5, 1991.

21. Ibid.

22. Dave Perkins, "Settled Rotation Gives the Twins Big Advantage," *Toronto Star*, October 7, 1991.

23. "Twins 9–5 Favorites over the Blue Jays," *Canadian Press/Kitchener-Waterloo Record*, October 4, 1991.

24. Ken McKee, "Bookies off Base, Underdog Jays Say," *Toronto Star*, October 4, 1991.

25. Whitey Herzog and Jonathan Pitts, *You're Missin' a Great Game: From Casey to Ozzie, the Magic of Baseball and How to Get it Back* (New York: Simon & Schuster, 2007), p. 233.

26. Stephen Brunt, *Diamond Dreams: 20 Years of Blue Jays Baseball* (Toronto: Penguin Books Canada, 1997), p. 225.

27. Bob Ryan, "Preparation and Execution an Unbeatable Combination for Twins," *Boston Globe*, October 9, 1991.

28. Kelly Gruber and Kevin Boland, *Kelly: At Home on Third*, (Toronto: Penguin Books Canada, 1992), p. 134.

29. Dick Polman, "Blue Jays Looking to 1992," *Philadelphia Inquirer*, October 12, 1991.

30. Sid Hartman, "Davis Says Twins Didn't Knuckle Under," *Minneapolis Star Tribune*, October 9, 1991.

31. Mike Augustin, "Candiotti Knuckles Under to Twins Hitters," *St. Paul Pioneer Press*, October 9, 1991.

32. Brunt, *Diamond Dreams*, p. 227.

33. Michael Gee, "Blue Jays' Way Off Beaten Path," *Boston Herald*, October 9, 1991.

34. Brunt, *Diamond Dreams*, p. 227.

35. Dave Perkins, "Myers Brought Out Best in Candiotti," *Toronto Star*, November 29, 1991.

36. Ibid.

37. Bob Smizik, "NL Knuckles Under to Candiotti's Style," *Pittsburgh Press*, April 27, 1992.

38. Ibid.

39. Peter Gammons, "Sooner or Later, a Good Deal," *Boston Globe*, June 30, 1991.

40. Fox 5 telecast, Indians vs. Yankees, July 23, 1999.

41. Fan 590, Bob McCown's Prime Time Sports, May 31, 2010; Fan 590, Bob McCown's Prime Time Sports, September 7, 2010.

42. David Wells and Chris Kreski, *Perfect I'm Not: Boomer on Beer, Brawls, Backaches, and Baseball* (New York: Perennial Currents, 2004), p. 358.

43. Wells, *Perfect I'm Not*, p. 350.

44. Ibid., p. 355.

45. Rosie DiManno, "They're Out," *Toronto Star*, October 14, 1991.

46. Ibid.

47. Jim Proudfoot, "Blue Jays Winning East Flag Nothing to Get Excited About," *Toronto Star*, October 1, 1991.

48. Steve Fainaru, "New Jays Got Old Results," *Boston Globe*, October 15, 1991.

49. Sportsnet telecast, Tigers vs. Blue Jays, August 28, 2010.

# Chapter 12

1. Grossman, *A Baseball Addict's Diary*, p. 229.

2. "Stieb Takes Step on Comeback Trail," *Toronto Star*, October 13, 1991.

3. CBS telecast, Twins vs. Blue Jays, October 13, 1991.

4. Ibid.

5. Ibid.

6. Grossman, *A Baseball Addict's Diary*, p. 229.

7. "M's Knuckle Down to Win," Associated Press/*Spokesman-Review*, June 29, 1991.

8. Ray Sons, "No Lunacy: Twins Stars Eclipse Jays," *Chicago Sun-Times*, October 15, 1991.

9. CBS telecast, Twins vs. Blue Jays, October 13, 1991.

10. Bill Livingston, "Carter, Candiotti Find New Place to Suffer," *Cleveland Plain Dealer*, October 14, 1991.

11. "Once Again Toronto Comes Up Short," *USA Today*, October 14, 1991.

12. "Blue Jays Earn Shot at a Breakthrough," Associated Press/*Los Angeles Times*, October 4, 1992.

13. Dave Perkins, "Will Gaston Pay the Ultimate Price?" *Toronto Star*, October 14, 1991.

14. Steve Milton, "Jays Still Searching for Answers," *Hamilton Spectator*, October 15, 1991.

15. Steve Fainaru, "New Jays Got Old Results," *Boston Globe*, October 15, 1991.

16. Bill Livingston, "Carter, Candiotti Find New Place to Suffer," *Cleveland Plain Dealer*, October 14, 1991.

17. Sheldon Ocker, "Candiotti Not Expecting a Tribe Offer," *Akron Beacon Journal*, November 9, 1991.

18. Neil MacCarl, "Jays, Candiotti Won't Budge on Contract," *Toronto Star*, November 23, 1991.

19. Peter Schmuck, "Mets Sign Coleman to Four-Year Pact," *Baltimore Sun*, December 6, 1990.

20. "Reds Lose Pitcher Jackson to Cubs, But Keep Browning," Associated Press/*Pittsburgh Post-Gazette*, November 22, 1990.

21. Neil MacCarl, "Jays, Candiotti Won't Budge on Contract," *Toronto Star*, November 23, 1991.

22. Dave Perkins, "What If Candiotti Gave In, For Once?" *Toronto Star*, November 26, 1991.

23. Michael Salfino, "Is Greinke the Unluckiest Pitcher Ever?" *Wall Street Journal Sports/Online.wsj.com*, May 5, 2010.

24. "Dodgers Appear Ready to Make Run at Braves," Associated Press/*The Victoria Advocate*, December 5, 1991.

25. "Eric the Red Turns Dodger Blue, Davis Acquired for Belcher; Murray Signs with Mets," *Daily News of Los Angeles*, November 28, 1991.

26. *Baseball Digest*, April 1992, p. 41.

27. Ibid.

28. Steve Delsohn, *True Blue: The Dramatic History of the Los Angeles Dodgers, Told by the Men Who Lived It* (New York: Perennial, 2002), p. 219.

29. Mal Florence, "Strange But True: Dodgers Did Merge With the Yanks," *Los Angeles Times*, December 12, 1991.

30. Brunt, *Diamond Dreams*, p. 230.

31. Dave Perkins, "Will Jays Miss Candiotti? No!" *Toronto Star*, December 5, 1991.

32. Dave Perkins, "The Glory Years," *Toronto Star*, April 8, 2001.

33. Scott Radley, "The Good, the So-So and the Ugly," *The Hamilton Spectator*, August 2, 2006.

34. Brunt, *Diamond Dreams*, p. 227.

35. Ron Kroichick, "Mariners Take A Turn for the Worse," *Sacramento Bee*, May 17, 1992.

36. Maryann Hudson, "Hanging On By His Fingertips," *Los Angeles Times*, July 31, 1994.

37. The 1985 National League West-leading squad, for instance, led the majors in errors but still won 95 games, the most for a Dodger team in the decade. Also, the 1988 World Series champions and 1983 West champs were among the worst four teams defensively both years.

38. Neither player would have any impact for the Dodgers beyond 1992. Davis was traded to the Detroit Tigers in August of 1993 for pitcher John DeSilva, who would appear in only six major league games (three with Los Angeles). Strawberry, meanwhile, would check into a rehab center for substance abuse on the eve of the 1994 season opener before being released on May 25 without appearing in a single game for the Dodgers that year. He batted only .140 with five homers and 12 RBIs in 100 at-bats in 1993.

39. Alan Solomon, "Cubs' Morgan Remains Steady," *Chicago Tribune*, March 7, 1993.

40. "'BucFeevah' New Hysteria Hitting Most Pittsburghers," United Press International/*Wisconsin State Journal*, August 25, 1966.

41. Some sources state that the Houston pitcher was Dave Giusti. However, according to newspapers from 1966, Prince first noticed the Green Weenie during a game on July 23. The only Astros pitcher to issue a walk that day was Bruce. Giusti, meanwhile, didn't pitch at all during that series. He faced the Pirates four times, winning on May 28 in Houston, and losing June 28 and August 30 in Pittsburgh, and falling again on September 13 back in Houston. The only time he walked any Pirates was in the June 28 start, when he lost, 4–3, and the freebies didn't come during the game-winning rally.

42. Leonard Koppett, "Green Weenie Lucky for Bucs," *New York Times*/*Arizona Republic*, August 2, 1966.

43. Shannon George, "Let's Talk About:

Green Weenies," *Pittsburgh Post-Gazette*/http://www.post-gazette.com, August 13, 2009.

## Chapter 13

1. "Around the League," *Austin American-Statesman*, August 10, 1992.

2. Bill Plaschke, "Baseball/Daily Report," *Los Angeles Times*, August 21, 1992.

3. "Pirate Rookie Wakefield Wins Knuckleball Clash," Associated Press/*Oxnard Press-Courier*, August 27, 1992.

4. Ken Daley, "Candiotti's Gem Is Tarnished," *Daily News of Los Angeles*, September 1, 1992.

5. Brunt, *Diamond Dreams*, p. 243.

6. Murray Chass, "Blue Jays Are True to Their Tradition of Late-Season Deals," *New York Times*, August 28, 1992.

7. Doug Haller, "Few Knuckleballers Remain in Game," *Arizona Republic*, July 20, 2006.

8. Tom Glavine with Brian Tarcy, *Baseball for Everybody: Tom Glavine's Guide to America's Game* (Worcester, MA: Chandler House Press, 1999), p. 41.

9. Jason Beck, "Knuckleballer to Knuckleballer," MLB.com, March 11, 2003.

10. "Baseball: Dodgers Lose Exhibition in Taiwan 1–0," *Daily News of Los Angeles*, October 31, 1993.

11. Ross Newhan, "Braves Sweep Reeling Giants," *Los Angeles Times*, August 26, 1993.

12. "Valenzuela Has Good Outing," *The Daily Gazette*/Associated Press, March 28, 1993.

13. Chris Dufresne, "Candiotti, Dodgers Cruise Past Angels," *Los Angeles Times*, April 3, 1993.

14. Ibid.

15. Maryann Hudson, "Dodgers: Worrell Wasn't There for Lasorda," *Los Angeles Times*, July 10, 1993.

16. Tim Kawakami, "Candiotti Laughs Last in Victory," *Los Angeles Times*, June 1, 1993.

17. Maryann Hudson, "Spoil Sports: Dodgers Beat Braves in Ninth," *Los Angeles Times*, September 7, 1993.

18. Ross Newhan, "Braves Sweep Reeling Giants," *Los Angeles Times*, August 26, 1993.

19. Ken Daley, "Dodgers Notes," *Daily News of Los Angeles*, September 18, 1993.

20. Ken Peters, "Giants Beat LA to Pull Even," Associated Press/*South Carolina Item*, October 1, 1993.

21. Gordon Verrell, "Gross Says Dodger Pitching As Good As Atlanta," *Long Beach Press-Telegram*, March 8, 1993.

22. Ken Daley, "Dodgers' Gift to Giants: A Tie," *Los Angeles Daily News*, October 1, 1993.

23. Kevin Gross, the winning pitcher that afternoon, held the trio of Will Clark, Matt

Williams, and Barry Bonds to two hits in 11 at-bats—a feat that Candiotti had accomplished three nights earlier. In fact, Candiotti (8 IP, 7 H, 2 BB, 6 SO) pitched just as well as Gross (9 IP, 6 H, 1 BB, 5 SO) but suffered the 3–1 loss in the opening game of the series.

24. Bill James, *Whatever Happened to the Hall of Fame? Baseball, Cooperstown, and the Politics of Glory* (New York: Free Press, 1995), p. 81.
25. Tom Withers, "Atlanta Remains Unbeaten; Expos Defeat Chicago," Associated Press/ *Daily Courier (North Carolina)*, April 11, 1994.
26. Gordon Edes, "Dodger Blueprint," *South Florida Sun-Sentinel*, June 7, 1994.
27. Lyle Spencer, "Dodgers Still Can't Find Way to Spell Relief," *Riverside Press-Enterprise*, July 28, 1994.
28. Allen Barra, "Baseball's Costliest Walk," *Wall Street Journal/Online.wsj.com*, October 28, 2009.

## Chapter 14

1. Bob Ryan, "This One Was Put to Bed Early," *Boston Globe*, May 24, 2004.
2. Bob Ryan, "Wakefield Has A Leg to Stand On," *Boston Globe*, February 24, 1997.
3. "Dodgers vs. Giants," Associated Press/ Nando.net, May 1, 1995.
4. Chris Baker, "Ingram Learns as He Loses," *Los Angeles Times*, May 15, 1995.
5. Bob Nightengale, "Dodger Desire is Questioned After 5–0 Loss," *Los Angeles Times*, May 31, 1995.
6. "Dodgers vs. Cubs," Associated Press/ Nando.net, June 16, 1995.
7. Simon C. Gonzalez, "Jays Taking Choosy Stance," *Fort Worth Star-Telegram*, July 16, 1995.
8. Gordon Edes, "Hammond Keeps Dodgers Off Base," *South Florida Sun-Sentinel*, July 15, 1995.
9. "Dodgers vs. Marlins," Associated Press/ Nando.net, July 14, 1995.
10. Stephen Cannella, "Jonesin' For Some Run Support," Sports Illustrated/CNNSI.com, June 1, 2001.
11. Lew Price, "Dodgers Support Candiotti," *Riverside Press-Enterprise*, July 19, 1993.
12. "Dodgers vs. Braves," usatoday.com, June 17, 1996.
13. Ibid.
14. Chris Baker, "Candiotti's Knucklers Get Rapped," *Los Angeles Times*, June 22, 1996.

## Chapter 15

1. Bob Nightengale, "Fifth Starter Park Right on Schedule," *Los Angeles Times*, March 24, 1997.
2. Kevin Acee, "Dodgers Spring Training Notebook: Fonville Fights for Roster Spot," *Los Angeles Daily News*, March 18, 1997.
3. Bob Nightengale, "Fifth Starter Park Right on Schedule," *Los Angeles Times*, March 24, 1997.
4. Paul Hoynes, "McDowell Placed on Disabled List," *Cleveland Plain Dealer*, May 19, 1997.
5. Dennis Manoloff, "Candiotti Bides Time," *Cleveland Plain Dealer*, May 31, 1997.
6. "Candiotti May Have Future in AL," *Torrance Daily Breeze*, May 25, 1997.
7. Mark Emmons, "Knuckling Under," *Orange County Register*, August 11, 1999.
8. Bill Shaikin, "Angels an Attractive Choice for Candiotti," *Orange County Register*, June 18, 1997.
9. Kevin Acee, "Dodgers Notebook: Martinez Will Miss Start, Candiotti In," *Los Angeles Daily News*, June 21, 1997.
10. Henry Schulman, "Giants Hit by Knuckle Sandwich," *San Francisco Examiner*, June 22, 1997.
11. "Dodgers vs. Giants," usatoday.com, June 22, 1997.
12. Chris Baker, "Candiotti Puts His Spin on the Giants," *Los Angeles Times*, June 22, 1997.
13. Kevin Acee, "Candiotti Does His Job Again," *Los Angeles Daily News*, June 22, 1997.
14. Chris Baker, "Candiotti Volunteers for Duty," *Los Angeles Times*, July 7, 1997.
15. Kevin Acee, "Candiotti Does His Job Again," *Los Angeles Daily News*, June 22, 1997.
16. Eric Noland, "Hit But Not Beaten; Line Drive KO's Nomo; Dodgers Win," *Los Angeles Daily News*, July 27, 1997.
17. Kevin Acee, "Dodgers Sprint to Break; Candiotti Comes Through, Securing Sixth Straight Win," *Los Angeles Daily News*, July 7, 1997.
18. Kevin Acee, "No Cheap Sweep; Dodgers Now Within 1-1/2 of First," *Los Angeles Daily News*, July 28, 1997.
19. Tim Brown, "Astacio, Dodgers Pitchers Are Shouldering the Load," *Los Angeles Daily News*, July 26, 1996.
20. Kevin Acee, "Astacio Traded," *Los Angeles Daily News*, August 19, 1997.
21. Gerry Callahan, "A Fall Classic," *Sports Illustrated*, September 29, 1997.
22. Ibid.
23. "Dodgers vs. Mets," usatoday.com, August 21, 1997.
24. Moyer would post a 1–4, 6.37 ERA mark in eight career starts at Dodger Stadium, with his teams going 2–6. In 1986, he was chased in

the first inning in the Cubs' 11–4 loss at Chavez Ravine. In 2007, Moyer allowed 10 earned runs in Philadelphia's 10–3 defeat at Dodger Stadium. Meanwhile, Candiotti started a game on his birthday (August 31) twice in his career, in 1992 and 1997. He allowed one earned run total in those two birthday outings, but received zero runs of support in those 16 innings pitched. When pitching between one to three days before his birthday, though, Candiotti had better luck, as he was 5–1 in eight starts with a 2.02 ERA, including 4–0 on the road.

25. Steve Bisheff, "Dodgers Lack Key Ingredient: Big Heart," *Orange County Register/Daily News*, September 25, 1997.

## Chapter 16

1. Jeff Fletcher, "A's Signing Candiotti Today to 2-Year, $6.35-Million Deal," *Santa Rosa Press Democrat*, December 9, 1997.

2. Edvins Beitiks, "Candiotti Comes Back to the Bay," *San Francisco Examiner*, December 9, 1997.

3. Edvins Beitiks, "Finally, A's Like Pitching," *San Francisco Examiner*, December 10, 1997.

4. Tike Narry, "A's Shut Down by Martinez," *Union Democrat*, April 2, 1998.

5. Howard Bryant, "Yankees' Ace Trumps A's, Candiotti 3–1," *San Jose Mercury News*, April 12, 1998.

6. Jim Van Vliet, "Candiotti Weathers Storm in Oakland," *Sacramento Bee*, April 23, 1998.

7. Jeff Fletcher, "A's Win in 12th for Two-Game Win Streak," *Santa Rosa Press Democrat*, April 22, 1998.

8. Steve Kettmann, "A's Slap Together Winning Rally," *San Francisco Chronicle*, April 22, 1998.

9. Steve Kettmann, "Rangers Trade A 'K' for 'W,'" *San Francisco Chronicle*, June 19, 1998.

10. Ibid.

11. Frank Blackman, "Candiotti Knuckles Under Again," *San Francisco Examiner*, June 29, 1998.

12. Steve Kettmann, "A's Youth Shows in Loss to Royals," *San Francisco Chronicle*, July 16, 1998.

13. Lowell Cohn, "Candiotti's Timing Crucial," *Santa Rosa Press Democrat*, May 29, 1999.

14. Joe Torre and Tom Verducci, *The Yankee Years*, (New York: Doubleday, 2009), p. 51.

15. Ibid.

16. Jack O'Connell, "Irabu Second Best," *Hartford Courant*, August 6, 1998.

17. Steve Kettmann, "A's Notebook: Candiotti Proving It's OK to Be Slow," *San Francisco Chronicle*, August 28, 1998.

18. Mark Emmons, "Knuckling Under," *Orange County Register*, August 11, 1999.

19. Steve Kettmann, "Durable Candiotti Helps Lead Rout of Tampa Bay," *San Francisco Chronicle*, September 7, 1998.

20. William Darby, *Deconstructing Major League Baseball, 1994–2004: How Statistics Illuminate Individual and Team Performances* (Jefferson, NC: McFarland, 2006), p. 8.

21. Paul White, "Wakefield Takes Baseball's Wildest Pitch to All-Star Game," *USA Today*, July 11, 2009.

22. "Baseball Report," *Seattle Times*, May 3, 1999.

23. Frank Blackman, "A's, Giants See Glasses Half Full," *San Francisco Examiner*, July 9, 1998.

24. Susan Slusser, "Analysis," *San Francisco Chronicle*, May 25, 1999.

25. Susan Slusser, "A's Drop Candiotti," *San Francisco Chronicle*, June 8, 1999.

26. Ibid.

27. Torre, *The Yankee Years*, p. 75.

28. Ibid., p. 75–76.

29. Mark Camps, "Good ERAs in an Era of Hitting," *San Francisco Chronicle*, June 11, 1999.

30. Gordon Edes, "White-knuckle Time for Sox," *Boston Globe*, May 3, 1999.

## Chapter 17

1. Roger Negin, "Candiotti Back but Role Left up in Air," *Ohio Chronicle Telegram*, June 30, 1999.

2. "Thome Homer: 511 Feet," *Toledo Blade*, July 4, 1999.

3. Sheldon Ocker, "Candy Man Is Sweet in Debut," *Akron Beacon Journal*, July 4, 1999.

4. Ibid.

5. Sheldon Ocker, "'99 Indians Holding the Line, But...," *Akron Beacon Journal*, July 11, 1999.

6. Dom Amore, "Facing Indians Will Be Cone's Reality Check," *Hartford Courant*, July 23, 1999.

7. Vic Ziegel, "Switch to the Bullpen Not What Doc Ordered," *New York Daily News*, July 24, 1999.

8. Ibid.

9. Ibid.

10. Lisa Olson, "Chili Turns Up the Burner on Indians," *New York Daily News*, July 25, 1999.

11. Paul Hoynes, "A Walk Along the Razor's Edge," *Cleveland Plain Dealer*, October 28, 1999.

12. Terry Pluto, "Armed and Dangerous? Well, Sort Of," *Akron Beacon Journal*, July 25, 1999.

13. Bill Madden, "Major Leagues Drop Ball for Baseball Greats," *New York Daily News*, July 14, 1999.

14. Sheldon Ocker, "Indians Believe Candiotti Can't," *Akron Beacon Journal*, July 27, 1999.

15. Mike DiGiovanna, "Candiotti Shrugs Off Poor Outing," *Los Angeles Times*, March 19, 2000.

16. Billy Witz, "Veteran Pitcher is Out at 42, Candiotti Too Old for Angels," *Los Angeles Daily News*, April 2, 2000.

# Bibliography

## Books

Brunt, Stephen. *Diamond Dreams: 20 Years of Blue Jays Baseball*. Toronto: Penguin Books Canada, 1997.

Darby, William. *Deconstructing Major League Baseball, 1994–2004: How Statistics Illuminate Individual and Team Performances*. Jefferson, NC: McFarland, 2006.

Delsohn, Steve. *True Blue: The Dramatic History of the Los Angeles Dodgers, Told by the Men Who Lived It*. New York: Perennial, 2002.

DiManno, Roise. *Glory Jays: Canada's World Series Champions*. Champaign, IL: Sagamore, 1993.

Gibson, Bob, and Reggie Jackson. *Sixty Feet, Six Inches: A Hall of Fame Pitcher and a Hall of Fame Hitter Talk About How the Game Is Played*. New York: Doubleday, 2009.

Glavine, Tom, with Brian Tarcy. *Baseball for Everybody: Tom Glavine's Guide to America's Game*. Worcester, MA: Chandler House Press, 1999.

Grossman, Larry. *A Baseball Addict's Diary: The Blue Jays' 1991 Rollercoaster*. Toronto: Penguin Group, 1991.

Gruber, Kelly, and Kevin Boland. *Kelly: At Home on Third*. Toronto: Penguin Books Canada, 1992.

Herzog, Whitey, and Jonathan Pitts. *You're Missin' a Great Game: From Casey to Ozzie, the Magic of Baseball and How to Get it Back*. New York: Simon & Schuster, 2007.

James, Bill. *Bill James Baseball Abstract*. New York: Ballantine Books, 1988.

____. *Whatever Happened to the Hall of Fame? Baseball, Cooperstown, and the Politics of Glory*. New York: Free Press, 1995.

McCarver, Tim, and Danny Peary. *Tim McCarver's Baseball for Brain Surgeons and Other Fans*. New York: Villard, 1999.

Morris, Peter. *A Game of Inches*: The Stories Behind the Innovations That Shaped Baseball: The Game on the Field (Volume 1). Chicago: Ivan R. Dee, 2006.

Schlossberg, Dan. *The 300 Club: Have We Seen the Last of Baseball's 300-Game Winners?* Overland Park, KS: Ascend Books, 2010.

Schneider, Russell, and Rich Schneider. *Tales from the Tribe Dugout: A Collection of the Greatest Cleveland Indians Stories Ever Told*. Champaign, IL: Sports Publishing, 2002.

The Sports Network. *TSN 25 Years: 25 Years of Hits and Highlights, Top Tens and Turning Points, Through the Lens of Canada's Sports Network*. Hoboken, NJ: Wiley, 2009.

Toman, James A. *Cleveland Stadium: The Last Chapter*. Cleveland: Cleveland Landmarks Press, 1997.

Torre, Joe, and Tom Verducci. *The Yankee Years*. New York: Doubleday, 2009.

Wells, David, and Chris Kreski. *Perfect I'm Not: Boomer on Beer, Brawls, Backaches, and Baseball*. New York: Perennial Currents, 2004.

Westcott, Rich. *Winningest Pitchers: Baseball's 300-Game Winners*. Philadelphia: Temple University Press, 2002.

Will, George. *Men at Work: The Craft of Baseball*. New York: Harper, 1990.

## Newspapers and Magazines

Akron Beacon Journal
Arizona Republic
Atlanta Journal
Austin American-Statesman
Baltimore Sun
Bangor Daily News
Baseball Digest
Boston Globe
Boston Herald
The Bryan Times
Chicago Daily Herald
Chicago Sun-Times
Chicago Tribune
Cleveland Plain Dealer
Columbus Dispatch
The Daily Courier (North Carolina)
The Daily Gazette (New York)
Daily News of Los Angeles
Dallas Morning News
The Day-New London, Conn.
Denver Post
ESPN The Magazine
Eugene-Oregon Register-Guard
Fort Worth Star-Telegram
Gainesville Sun
Green Bay Press-Gazette
Hamilton Spectator
Hartford Courant
Illinois Rockford Register Star
Iowa Telegraph-Herald
Kentucky New Era
Kitchener-Waterloo Record
Lewiston Morning Tribune
Lodi News-Sentinel (Lodi, California)
Long Beach Press-Telegram
Los Angeles Times
Milwaukee Journal
Milwaukee Sentinel
Minneapolis Star Tribune
New York Daily News
New York Times
Ohio Chronicle Telegram
Orange County Register
Orlando Sentinel
Oxnard Press-Courier
Philadelphia Daily News
Philadelphia Inquirer
Pittsburgh Post-Gazette
Pittsburgh Press
Providence Journal
Riverside Press-Enterprise
Rocky Mountain News
Sacramento Bee
St. Louis Post-Dispatch
St. Paul Pioneer Press
St. Petersburg Times
Salina Journal
San Diego Union-Tribune
San Francisco Chronicle
San Francisco Examiner
San Jose Mercury News
Santa Rosa Press Democrat
Seattle Times
South Carolina Item
South Florida Sun-Sentinel
Spokesman-Review
Sports Illustrated
Toledo Blade
Toronto Star
Torrance Daily Breeze
Union Democrat
USA Today
Valley Independent (Monessen, Pennsylvania)
The Victoria Advocate
The Vindicator (Youngstown, Ohio)
Washington Post
Wisconsin State Journal

## Video and Audio

CBS telecast, Twins vs. Blue Jays, October 13, 1991.
Fan 590, Bob McCown's Prime Time Sports.
Four Million Memories: The 1991 Toronto Blue Jays Highlight Video.
FOX 5 (New York) telecast, Indians vs. Yankees, July 23, 1999.
Rogers Sportsnet telecast, Tigers vs. Blue Jays, August 28, 2010.

## Websites

ballparksofbaseball.com
baseball-almanac.com
baseball-reference.com
baseballthinkfactory.org
battersbox.ca
books.google.com
CNNSI.com
en.wikipedia.org
espn.com
MLB.com
nando.net
news.google.com
newspaperarchive.com
online.wsj.com
pqasb.pqarchiver.com
retrosheet.org
sabr.org
smcgaels.com
sports.yahoo.com
usatoday.com
WCCSports.com

# *Index*

Numbers in **bold italics** indicate pages with photographs.

251